TRAVELS IN ASIA AND AFRICA 1325 TO 1354

TRAVELS IN ASIA AND AFRICA 1325 TO 1354

IBN BATTUTA

TRANSLATED AND SELECTED
BY
H. A. R. GIBB

GYAN

Published by

Gyan Publishing House
5, Ansari Road
Daryaganj, New Delhi-110002
Phone: 011-47034999, 9811692060
E-mail: books@gyanbooks.com

Distribution Network
gyanbooks.com
India, USA, Canada, UK, Australia, France

ISBN : 978-81-212-4141-0 (PB)
First Published, London, 1929

2nd Impression 2020

Printed at: Gyan Press, Delhi.

Travels in Asia and Africa
From
1325 to 1354
Author: IBN Battuta

IBN BATTUTA

TRAVELS IN ASIA AND AFRICA

1325 TO 1354

TRANSLATED AND SELECTED
BY
H. A. R. GIBB

WITH AN INTRODUCTION AND NOTES

ASIAN EDUCATIONAL SERVICES
NEW DELHI ♦ CHENNAI ♦ 2011

ASIAN EDUCATIONAL SERVICES

* 6A SHAHPUR JAT, NEW DELHI - 110 049
Tel. : +91-11- 26491586, 26494059 Fax : 011- 26494946
email : aes@aes.ind.in

* 2/15, 2nd FLOOR, ANSARI ROAD,
DARYAGANJ, NEW DELHI - 1100 02
Tel : +91- 11- 23262044
email : aesdg@aes.ind.in

* 19, (NEW NO. 40), BALAJI NAGAR FIRST STREET,
ROYAPETTAH, CHENNAI - 600 014
Tel. : +91- 44 - 28133040 / 28131391 Fax : 044 - 28131391
email : asianeds@md3.vsnl.net.in

www.aes.ind.in

Printed and Hand-Bound in India

First Published : London, 1929.
First AES Reprint : New Delhi, 1992.
Fourth AES Reprint : New Delhi, 2011.

ISBN : 8120608097
EAN : 9788120608092

Published by Gautam Jetley
For ASIAN EDUCATIONAL SERVICES,
6A, Shahpur Jat, New Delhi - 110 049.
Processed by AES Publications Pvt. Ltd., New Delhi-110049.
Printed at Chaudhry Offset Process, Delhi - 110 051.

INDIAN HAREM SCENE

THE BROADWAY TRAVELLERS

EDITED BY SIR E. DENISON ROSS
AND EILEEN POWER

IBN BATTÚTA

TRAVELS IN ASIA AND AFRICA

1325–1354

Translated and selected by

H. A. R. GIBB
Lecturer in Arabic, School of Oriental Studies, University of London

With an Introduction and Notes

Published by

GEORGE ROUTLEDGE & SONS, LTD.
BROADWAY HOUSE, CARTER LANE, LONDON

CONTENTS

LIST OF MAPS AND ILLUSTRATIONS

Selections from the Travels of Ibn Battúta

INTRODUCTION

§ I. IBN BATTÚTA AND HIS WORK

To the world of today the men of medieval Christendom already seem remote and unfamiliar. Their names and deeds are recorded in our history-books, their monuments still adorn our cities, but our kinship with them is a thing unreal, which costs an effort of the imagination. How much more must this apply to the great Islamic civilization, that stood over against medieval Europe, menacing its existence and yet linked to it by a hundred ties that even war and fear could not sever. Its monuments too abide, for those who may have the fortune to visit them, but its men and manners are to most of us utterly unknown, or dimly conceived in the romantic image of the *Arabian Nights*. Even for the specialist it is difficult to reconstruct their lives and see them as they were. Histories and biographies there are in quantity, but the historians, for all their picturesque details, seldom show the ability to select the essential and to give their figures that touch of the intimate which makes them live again for the reader. It is in this faculty that Ibn Battúta excels. Of the multitudes that crowd upon the stage in the pageant of medieval Islam there is no figure more instinct with life than his. In his book he not only lays before us a faithful portrait of himself, with all his virtues and his failings, but evokes a whole age as it were from the dead. These travels have been ransacked by historians and geographers, but no estimate of his work is even faintly satisfactory which does not bear in mind that it is first and foremost a human diary, in which the tale of facts is subordinated to the interests and preoccupations of the diarist and his audience. It is impossible not to feel a liking for the character it reveals to us, generous to excess, humane in an age when life was its at cheapest, bold (did ever medieval traveller fear the sea less ?), fond of pleasure and uxorious to a degree, but controlled withal by a deep vein of piety and devotion, a man with all the makings of a sinner, and something of a saint.

Of the external events of Ibn Battúta's life we know little beyond what he himself tells us. The editor of the travels, Ibn Juzayy, notes that he was born at Tangier on 24th February, 1304, and from a brief reference in a later book of biographies we know that after his return to Morocco he was appointed qádí or judge in one of the Moroccan towns, and died there in 1368 or 1369. His own name was Muhammad son of Abdalláh, Ibn Battúta being the family name, still to be found in Morocco. His family had apparently been settled in Tangier for some generations and belonged to the Berber tribe of the Luwáta, which first appears in history as a nomadic tribe in Cyrenaica and on the borders of Egypt. For the rest he divulges incidentally in a passage relating to his appointment as qádí in Delhi, that he came of a house which had produced a succession of qádís, and later on he mentions a cousin who was qádí of Rondah in Spain. He belonged, in consequence, to the religious upper-class, if the term may be used, of the Muhammadan community, and must have received the usual literary and scholastic education of the theologians. On one occasion he quotes a poem of his own composition, but the other verses quoted here and there obviously bear a more popular character than the elaborate productions of the best Arabic poetic schools. His professional interest in men and matters religious may be seen on nearly every page of his work. It is evident from the list of qádís and other theologians whom he saw in every town on his travels (sometimes to the exclusion of all other details), but above all from his eagerness to visit famous shaykhs and saints wherever he went, and the enthusiasm with which he relates instances of their miraculous gifts.

But to rate him, as some European scholars have done, for his "rigmaroles about Muhammadan saints and spiritualists" and for his "stupidity" in paying more attention to theologians than to details of the places he visited, is singularly out of place. Such religious details were matters in which he and his audience were most closely interested, and are by no means devoid of interest and value even to us. Out of them, moreover, spring some of the most lively passages of his narrative, such as his escape at Koel (the modern Aligarh), and his account of the Sharíf Abú Ghurra. But it is of far greater importance to remember that it was because he was a theologian and because of his interest in theologians that he undertook his travels at all and survived to complete them. When as a young man of twenty-one he set out from his native town with a light heart, and not much heavier purse, it was with no other aim than that of making the pilgrimage to Mecca and the holy places of his faith. The duty laid upon every Muslim of visiting Mecca at least once in his lifetime, so long as it lies within his power to do so, has been in all ages a stimulus to travel, far greater in degree than the stimulus of Christian pilgrimage in the Middle Ages. At the same time, it created the organization necessary to enable Muslims of every class from every country to carry out this obligation. The pilgrim on his journey travelled in a caravan whose numbers swelled at every stage. He found all arrangements made for his marches and his halts, and if the road lay through dangerous country, his caravan was protected by an escort of soldiers. In all large centres as well as many intermediate stations were rest houses and hospices where he was hospitably welcomed and entertained out of endowments created by generations of benefactors. When such was the lot of every pilgrim, the theologian received still greater consideration. His brethren in every town received him as one of themselves, furnished his wants, and recommended him to those at the next station. Under these circumstances the brotherhood of Islám, which knows no difference of race or birth, showed at its best, and provided an incentive to travel unknown in any other age or community.

Nor was the Pilgrimage the only institution which smoothed the traveller's path. Throughout the Middle Ages the trade routes of Africa and Asia and the sea-borne trade of the Indian Ocean were almost exclusively in the hands of the Muslim merchants. The travels of Ibn Battúta are but one of many sources which reveal how widespread were their activities. Though their caravans were exposed to greater dangers in times of lawlessness and disorganization than were the pilgrim caravans, they offered at least a measure of security to the casual traveller. It is evident from our narratives that in the great majority of cases they were animated by the same spirit of kindliness and generosity that has always marked the mutual relations of Muslims, and readily shared their resources with their fellow-travellers in case of need. Later on Ibn Battúta had more than once occasion to appreciate their services, but at the outset he had no thought of what the future held for him.

On his arrival in Egypt, with his mind still wholly set on Mecca, he received the first premonitions of his future from two of the *illuminati*, or saints who had attained a high rank in the hierarchy of the Muslim orders. From this point we see his vague desires gradually crystallize into a definite ambition, though he still hesitates from time to time, especially when his contacts with persons of saintly life awaken all his instincts of devotion. Foiled in his first intention of taking the direct route to Mecca through Upper Egypt (the usual route of the pilgrim caravans from the West), he determined to join instead the pilgrim caravan from Damascus, and on his way thither tasted for the first time the joys of travel for its own sake. As time was not pressing, he wandered at leisure through the whole of Syria as far as the borders of Asia Minor, before returning to Damascus to join the caravan as it set out for the Holy Cities.

Hardly was this first Pilgrimage over than he set out again to visit 'Iráq, but turned back sharply before reaching Baghdád, and made a long detour through Khuzistán. By now, he tells us, he had taken the resolve never to cover the same ground twice, as far as possible. His mind was still set on the Pilgrimage, however, and he planned his journey to cover the interval before returning to Mecca at the end of the year. This time he renounced further travelling for a space of three years and gave himself up to study and devotion at Mecca. For the theologian the Pilgrimage meant not only the performance of one of the principal obligations of the Faith, but an opportunity of putting himself in touch with the activities of the religious centre of Islam. Mecca was the ideal centre of religious study, in the company of many of the most eminent doctors of the day. All this, no doubt, was in Ibn Battúta's mind. But we may, I think, discern a further purpose. He had already made up his mind to seek his fortune in India, to which the boundless munificence of the reigning Sultan of Delhi was then attracting large numbers of scholars and theologians from other countries. The years spent at Mecca would confer on him a better status, and render him eligible for a higher post than he could otherwise hope for.

On completing his years of study he made a tour with a retinue of followers to the trading stations on the east coast of Africa, returning as before to Mecca, then turned his back on the Holy City and set out for India. But the journey was to be longer and more adventurous than he anticipated. At Jedda there was no ship to be had bound for India, whereupon moved by some obscure impulse he turned northwards instead and began his great tour. As we follow him through the cities of Asia Minor, where he received an enthusiastic welcome from the local religious brotherhoods, across the Black Sea to the territories of the Mongol Khán of the Golden Horde, and after taking advantage of an opportunity to visit Constantinople, striking across the steppes to Central Asia and Khurásán, we find him becoming an increasingly important personage, attended by a swelling throng of followers, and becoming possessed of such means that he "dare not mention the number of his horses in case some sceptic should accuse him of lying."

So at last he entered India by the north-western gateway, being received with honour and escorted to Delhi, where, though he obtained a full share of the Sultan's bounty and was appointed to a rich sinecure as Málikite qádí of Delhi, he was but one figure, and in no way specially remarkable among many. For seven years or so Ibn Battúta remained in this position, sometimes accompanying the Sultan on his expeditions, sometimes engaged in his occupations at Delhi, storing up in his memory all the while those acute observations which he afterwards wove into one of the most remarkable descriptions we possess of any medieval Muslim court. Little did Sultan or courtiers think that six centuries afterwards their reputations would depend on the notes and reminiscences of the obscure and spendthrift qádí from the West. At last the inevitable rupture occurred, whose consequences were usually swift and fatal to the victim of the royal displeasure. Ibn Battúta took refuge in his last resort, the adoption of the ascetic life, resigning all his offices and giving away all his possessions. It was a genuine act of world-renuncaition, such as always lay near to the heart of the medieval theologian, and seems to have convinced Sultan Muhammad of the traveller's real integrity and devotion. At all events, when he required shortly afterwards a trustworthy person to send as his envoy to China, it was Ibn Battúta whom he summoned. Ibn Battúta, for his part, it would seem, was reluctant to doff his hermit's garments and "become entangled in the world again." But the bribe was too great, and in 1342 he set off in semi-regal state at the head of the mission to the most powerful ruler in the world of his time, the Mongol Emperor of China.

Scarcely had he left the walls of Delhi when his adventures began. For eight days he was a hunted fugitive, and though he escaped to rejoin his embassy in its progress through India, it was only to be left with nothing but the clothes he stood up in and his prayer-mat on the shore at Calicut. To go on with his mission in the circumstances was impossible; to return to Dehli was to incur the wrath of Sultan Muhammad. He chose instead to indulge his love of adventure with the independent rulers of the Malabar coast, and eventually found himself at the Maldive Islands, once again a qádí and a personage of importance. Here too after eighteen months of lotos-eating his reforming zeal made of him an object of suspicion and dislike, and he found it expedient to leave the islands. The devotee in him again asserted itself, and his first object was to make a pilgrimage to the "Foot of Adam" on the highest peak of Ceylon. This done he returned to the Coromandel and Malabar coasts, paid another brief visit to the Maldive Islands and prepared in earnest for his journey to China. Some months had still to elapse before the sailing season, however, and he chose to spend them in a voyage to Bengal, for no other reason, apparently, than to visit a famous shaykh living in Assam. He then intercepted the "Chinese" vessels—really vessels owned by Muhammadan merchants, with Chinese and Malay crews—at Sumatra and went by a route that has taxed the ingenuity of his commentators to the "Shanghai" of China in the thirteenth and fourteenth centuries, the port of Ts'wan-chow-fu, or Zaytún, as it was known to the foreign merchants. For this journey Ibn Battúta reassumed his role of ambassador, though it may strike us as curious that no one seemed to entertain any suspicions of an ambassador who travelled without embassy or credentials. It was, however, his only device for making his way through China, though his theological reputation stood him in good stead amongst his fellow-Muslims in the trading ports. In every city on his progress to and from Peking he was received with full honours, but at Peking itself he was disappointed of seeing the Emperor, owing to his absence from the capital.

Returning to Zaytún, he took ship again for Sumatra, and thence for Malabar, but decided not to expose himself a second time to the treacherous splendours of Delhi, and made westwards instead. He was in Syria at the outbreak of the first "Black Death" in 1348, and in a few terse sentences reveals its frightful ravages. At this time he seems to have had no definite plans for the future, and was aiming only at completing yet another Pilgrimage, his seventh, to Mecca. What eventually led him to return to his native land is not clear. His own narrative places more weight on the rapid access of strength and prosperity which Morocco enjoyed under Sultan Abu'l-Hasan and his son Abú 'Inán, than on those ties of family and kindred which appear to us so much more natural a reason. Possibly allowances should be made for the part of exaggeration and flattery, but the brevity of his stay in Tangier, and the unemotional, almost brusque, manner in which he mentions it, scarcely witness to an overmastering homesickness, which, in any case, was hardly to be expected in a society so cosmopolitan as that of medieval Islam.

The journey from Alexandria to the Barbary coast was not without its alarms. Twice Ibn Battúta narrowly escaped capture by Christian corsairs, and in addition his party was threatened by a robber band almost within sight of Fez. Even yet his ambition was not appeased. There were still two Muslim countries which he had not visited—Andalusia and the Negrolands on the Niger. Once again he took up the staff of travel, not to lay it down again until some three years later he could claim with justice the title of "The Traveller of Islam." He was in fact the only medieval traveller who is known to have visited the lands of every Muhammadan ruler of his time, quite apart from such infidel countries as Constantinople, Ceylon, and China, which were embraced in his journeys. The mere extent of his wanderings is estimated by Yule at not less than 75,000 miles, without allowing for deviations, a figure which is not likely to have been surpassed before the age of steam.

Unfortunately no account of Ibn Battúta has come down to us (so far as is known) from anyone who saw him on his journeys. There appear to be only two known references to him in the writings of contemporaries, and both are concerned chiefly with the credibility of his stories, which was hotly disputed. What they thought of him personally we are not told, but are able to infer occasionally from his own candid statements. Twice we find him, after receiving a cordial welcome, becoming an object of dislike or suspicion, at Delhi and again in the Maldive Islands. In the first case the cause was his extravagance, in the second it was fear of his growing influence and resentment at his haughty independence. There can be no question that he expected of princes and ministers a lavish exercise of the virtue of generosity, which was indeed in his eyes—as in those of his age and community generally—their principal claim to respect. It may be taken as a general rule that when Ibn Battúta says of this or the other prince that he is "a good sultan" or "one of the best of rulers," he means only that he is scrupulous in the performance of his religious duties and openhanded in his dealings, especially with theologians. We can well understand that this attitude was apt to pall on his patrons and lead at length to unpleasant incidents, or at least mutual dislike. Apart from these rare cases, however, he appears to have been liked and respected wherever he went.

In attempting to estimate the value of Ibn Battúta's work, some description must be given of the book itself. Ibn Battúta *may* have taken notes of the places that he visited, but the evidence is rather against it. Only once does he refer to notes, when he says that at Bukhárá he copied a number of epitaphs from the tombs of famous scholars, but afterwards lost them when the Indian pirates stripped him of all that he had. These epitaphs were of special interest to men of letters and theologians because they contained lists of the writings of the deceased. Ibn

Battúta was not himself a man of letters who was likely to regard his experiences as material for a book; on the contrary, he seems to have entertained no idea of writing them down.

On his return to Fez he had related his adventures to the sultan and the court, where they were received with general incredulity, as we know from a passage in the works of his great contemporary, the historian Ibn Khaldún. He found, however, a powerful supporter in the wazír, at whose instigation possibly the sultan gave instructions to one of the principal secretaries, Muhammad ibn Juzayy, to commit them to writing. Ibn Juzayy accordingly compiled the work which we possess at the dictation of Ibn Battúta. The result is a book of somewhat composite character. The writer was not always content to take down Ibn Battúta's narratives as they were delivered. He shows commendable care in registering the exact pronunciation of every foreign name (a matter of some importance in view of the nature of the Arabic script), but in some other respects his editing is open to criticism. By his own statement the work is an abridgment, which possibly accounts for the brevity of one or two of the later sections. The bulk of the narrative has been left with but little touching-up in the simple, straightforward style of the narrator, but at points Ibn Juzayy has embellished it in the taste of the age, with passages of rhetorical prose and extracts from poems, which seldom add much of interest. His interpolation of incidents from his own experience may be excused, but another of his proceedings is more questionable. He had before him the narrative of the travels of Ibn Jubayr, an Andalusian scholar who visited Egypt, the Hijáz, and Syria in the twelfth century, and wrote an account of his experiences which enjoyed a great reputation in the West. Where Ibn Battúta covers the same ground, Ibn Juzayy has often substituted (possibly at Ibn Battúta's desire or with his permission) an abridgment of Ibn Jubayr's work, notably in the account of the ceremonies observed at Mecca during the Pilgrimage and at other seasons of the year. We have consequently to bear in mind that the book is not entirely Ibn Battúta's work; there are indeed indications (for example, in the transcriptions and translations of Persian phrases) that the reputed author did not himself read the book at all, or if he did, read it negligently.

Taking the work, then, as a whole, we must regard it as primarily intended to present a descriptive account of Muhammadan society in the second quarter of the fourteenth century. Ibn Battúta's interest in places was, as we have seen, subordinate to his interest in persons. He is the supreme example of *le géographe malgré lui*, whose geographical knowledge was gained entirely from personal experience and the information of chance acquaintances. For his details he relied exclusively on his memory, a memory, it is true, which had been highly cultivated by the ordinary system of theological education, involving the memorizing of large numbers of works, but still liable to slips and confusions, more or less great. In his itineraries he sometimes misplaces the order of towns, and twice at least leaves himself in the air, as it were, with a gap of hundreds of miles. He gives wrong names at several points, especially when he is dealing with non-Muslim countries, where his knowledge of Arabic and Persian was of little service to him. In his historical narratives, which are generally trustworthy, similar mistakes are found. It is indeed remarkable that the errors are comparatively few, considering the enormous number of persons and places he mentions. The most serious difficulty is offered by the chronology of the travels, which is utterly impossible as it stands. Many of the dates give the impression of having been inserted more or less at haphazard, possibly at the editor's request, but the examination and correction of them offers a task so great that it has not been attempted in this selection.

There is finally the question of his veracity. There can be no doubt that in his narratives of the Muslim countries, notwithstanding errors of exaggeration and misunderstanding, Ibn Battúta faithfully relates what he believes to be true. Some critics have, however, regarded his claim to have visited Constantinople and China with considerable dubiety. The principal difficulties as regards the visit to Constantinople are the vagueness of his route and his claim to have met the ex-Emperor, when by his own chronology the ex-Emperor had been dead for over a year. The first can be explained by the difficulties of an Arabic-speaking traveller in such unfamiliar surroundings, the second by an error in dating. The account of the city itself is so full and accurate that it cannot be other than the narrative of an eye-witness, who enjoyed exceptional facilities such as Ibn Battúta had, and his interview with the ex-Emperor in particular bears the unmistakable stamp of truth.

The difficulties contained in the narrative of the journeys to and in China are generally of the same order, and will be more fully considered in their place. It need only be said here that to deny them raises even greater difficulties, and that by exactly the same kind of reasoning it can be "proved" that though Ibn Battúta undoubtedly was *in* India he never went there! Ibn Battúta is always unsatisfactory when he relies on second-hand information, and it is most unlikely that he could have put together so personal a narrative had the statements of others not been supplemented by his own observations. There are also some material arguments in favour of his claim to have visited China. He had, in his capacity as envoy from the Sultan of Delhi, very good reason for going there, and facilities for travel in China which were denied to the ordinary merchant. In the second place one obscure passage in the narrative of his doings at Khansa (Hang-chow) is cleared up by an earlier passage relating to his visit to Shaykh Jalál ad-Dín in Assam, with which the journey to China is closely connected. Thirdly, if his claim were false, he stood a reasonable chance of being exposed. He relates with some emphasis that in his journey through Northern China he met a merchant from Ceuta, the brother of a man living in Sijilmása, in Morocco, whom he subsequently met also. That this merchant should have had some communication with Morocco, even in those days, is not impossible, since Ibn Battúta himself had once transmitted a sum of money from India to Mequinez. On the whole, therefore, the narrative dealing with China seems to me to be genuine, though it is certainly related with greater brevity than usual, either because Ibn Battúta could not recall the Chinese names, if he learned them, with the same ease as the more familiar Arabic and Persian names, or because it was more drastically abridged by the editor. I can in fact see no alternative, except to suppose that he was hypnotized into the belief that he had gone there by one of the miracle-working saints whom he met in India.

Ibn Battúta was first brought into prominence by the translation of an abridged text by Dr. Samuel Lee in 1829. The complete text of the Travels, which was found in Algeria a few years later, was published with a French translation and critical apparatus by Defrémery and Sanguinetti in the middle of the century from a number of manuscripts, one of which, containing the second half of the work, is the autograph of the original editor, Ibn Juzayy. The French translation, though on the whole remarkably accurate, suffers from the absence of explanatory notes. Various sections of the book (chiefly from the French text) have been annotated by scholars familiar with the countries themselves, but a large amount still remains to be worked over. In the present selections, which have been translated afresh from the Arabic text, Ibn Battúta is treated as a traveller, and not as a writer of geography. Sufficient indications have, it is hoped, been added in the text and the notes to enable the course of his journeys to be followed in detail on any large-scale atlas, but many problems of geography have been passed over in silence. The easy colloquialism of his style has been retained in translation as far as possible, in preference to a stilted Elizabethan language. It has not been easy to make a selection from the wealth of narrative and anecdote contained in the work, and many interesting sections have necessarily been omitted or abridged. But until the appearance of a complete version (such as the writer is now preparing for the Hakluyt Society) it is hoped that this extract may be of service in introducing to a wider circle of English readers one of the most remarkable travellers of his own or any age.

§ 2. THE HISTORICAL BACKGROUND OF IBN BATTÚTA'S TRAVELS

The Islamic world in the fourteenth century differed, in extent and outward splendour, but little from the magnificent empire ruled by the Caliphs of Damascus and Baghdád in the eighth. If in the West it had been shorn of its outposts in Spain and Sicily, it could justly claim to have more than balanced the loss by its extension in India and Malaysia. It had recently wiped out the last traces of the humiliation inflicted upon it by the crusading Franks, and was on the point of exacting a signal vengeance by the sword of the Ottomans in Europe. Yet it was true, notwithstanding all these apparent signs of progress, that the political fabric of Islám was stricken with mortal disease. The centuries had taken a heavy toll of vitality from that huge frame, and had left it still formidable, it may be, but wounded at the heart.

The last Crusader had indeed been driven from the shores of Syria, but at what a cost! Two centuries of struggle and intrigue had been necessary to repel attacks that the warriors of the early generations had regarded as the minor incidents of outpost warfare. The sceptre had passed from the hands of the supple Arab and the cultured Persian to those of the violent and illiberal Turk. For more than two centuries after the year 1000 the ambitions of Turkish generals and chieftains had torn and retorn the body of Islám, devastating its lands by their misgovernment and continual warfare more effectively than any foreign foe. Convulsion succeeded to convulsion, until at length the heathen Mongols from Central Asia made hares of the Turkish lions, and in 1258 formed the derelict eastern lands of Islam into a province of their immense empire.

This event, the shock of which seemed to the Muslim peoples like the Last Judgment of the Wrath of God, proved in the end a blessing in disguise. Once again the eastern provinces enjoyed a period of firm and relatively undisturbed government, under which commerce and agriculture took heart and began to re-create a prosperity that seemed to have vanished for ever. Simultaneously Egypt and Syria, which had withstood the Mongol onset, enjoyed under a succession of capable rulers a rare period of peace and prosperity. The Turkish captains who had hitherto quarrelled over the mangled fragments of the central provinces, were relegated to the frontiers, where they indulged their taste for warfare at the expense of the infidel and the heathen, winning for themselves a goodly portion of the riches of this world, and the reputation of "Warriors for the Faith" to ensure their portion in the world to come. The Mongol conquests thus effectually contributed to the successes gained by the arms of Islam in India, and a few years later also in Thrace and the Balkan Peninsula, successes which were supplemented by the missionary labours of saints and darwísh orders.

When in 1325 Ibn Battúta set out on his journeys, the political conditions in the Islamic lands were, in consequence, relatively stable and unusually favourable for travel. From Aswán to the frontier of Cilicia the word of the Sultan of Egypt was undisputed; the Crusaders were but a bitter memory, and relations with the Mongols, though not cordial, had not led to warfare since the last great victory of the youthful Násir at Damascus in 1303. 'Iráq and Persia still acknowledged the rule of the Mongol Il-kháns, now good Muslims, but destined soon to disappear. To the north and north-east the other Mongol khanates of the Golden Horde and of Jaghatáy were on friendly terms. Finally in India the ferocious but energetic Sultan of Delhi, Muhammad ibn Tughlaq, was imposing his overlordship on the greater part of the sub-continent. On the fringes of the great kingdoms, and in such outlying parts as Anatolia, Afghanistan, and the shores of the Indian Ocean, there existed a host of petty sultans and amírs, who acknowledged no master and maintained a precarious throne on the proceeds of trade or freebooting, but these could hardly inflict serious damage, even had they been so minded, on the Islamic community in general. Commerce proceeded freely both within and without the frontiers of Islam, in spite of heavy dues and occasional vexations; and if the indigenous industries had declined, in some cases to the point of extinction, the revival of the

European market brought unwonted prosperity to the carrying trade, which had not yet to face the formidable competition of the European merchants in the Eastern Seas.

The essential weakness of the later Muslim civilization stands revealed most clearly in the cultural inequality of its several divisions, an inequality due mainly to the failure of the old empire to withstand the forces making for disintegration and decay. While in the tenth century the Islamic culture, then at its height, was distributed almost uniformly throughout the whole length and breadth of the settled lands from the Atlantic to the mountains of Central Asia, we shall find, as we follow Ibn Battúta's progress eastwards, how poor was the soil, how shallow the roots, which nourished the social life and supported the magnificent courts of many of the kingdoms in the fourteenth.

North-west Africa, called by the Arabs the *Maghrib* or West, which, together with Muslim Spain, had been united under the empires of the Almoravids and the Almohads in the twelfth century, was partitioned in the thirteenth between three dynasties: the Marínids in the Farthest West, or Morocco; the Ziyánids in the Central West, with their capital at Tlemsen; and the Hafsids of Tunis, whose province of Ifríqíya extended from Algiers to Tripoli. The dangers arising from this dismemberment were accentuated by the jealousies of the reigning houses, as they dissipated in internal feuds and barren mutual struggles the resources urgently required to protect the cultivated lands from the ceaseless encroachments of the nomadic Arabs and Berbers, and the growing threat of the maritime Christian states. Even the most prosperous of the three dynasties, the Hafsids of Tunis, constantly found their authority flouted by the governors of the outlying provinces, and, though they had successfully repulsed the Crusade of St. Louis in 1270, lost Jerba to the

Sicilians less than twenty years later, and only recovered it in 1334 with Neapolitan and Genoese help. Their empire extended in fact only over the coastal strip, with some few fortified towns in the interior. The prosperity of Tunis was due solely to its advantageous position at the debouchment of the main trade routes from the interior, which made it the premier commercial city of the Maghrib and second only to Alexandria among the Muslim Mediterranean ports, while its culture, like that of the Maghrib generally, was mainly sustained by refugees from the reconquered provinces of Spain.

The Marínid dynasty of Morocco, masters of a richer territory, were in still worse case. Their history is a monotonous record of blood and strife; few rulers were able to withstand the revolts and intrigues of their ambitious relatives, and these few used what respite they gained in military expeditions against their neighbours, or, more worthily, against the Christians in Spain. The dynasty reached its zenith under Abu'l-Hasan (1331-48) and his son Abú 'Inán (1348-58), whose names frequently recur in the latter part of Ibn Battúta's narrative. Abu'l-Hasan succeeded in capturing Sijilmása and Tlemsen, and, in spite of a sanguinary defeat by the Spaniards at Tarifa in 1340, was able to add Tunis to his dominions in 1347, only to lose it immediately and simultaneously lose his throne to his rebel son Abú 'Inán. The latter in turn, having recaptured Tlemsen and re-entered Tunis in 1357, was deserted by his army and strangled on his return to Fez, leaving the kingdom a prey to indescribable anarchy. Nevertheless Morocco itself enjoyed during these two reigns a period of relative prosperity, and its great cities were beautified by many public buildings, which in their day can have been little inferior to the magnificent monuments of Egypt and India. There is, in consequence, some justification for the exuberant praise which Ibn Battúta bestows upon Abú 'Inán's beneficent administration, especially if it is remembered how chaotic were the conditions which, as will be seen, he had just left behind in the East.

It is a pity that Ibn Battúta did not put on record the first impressions left on his mind when, as a young man fresh from the narrow provincial life of Tangier, he traversed the highly cultivated Delta of Egypt and set foot in its opulent and teeming capital, then the metropolis of Islam. Alone of all the Islamic lands outside Arabia, Egypt had preserved the heritage of Muslim culture, while the Mongols in the East and the nomadic Arabs and Berbers in the West carried devastation up to its very gates. Though the dynasty founded by the great Saladin had given place to the military oligarchy known as the Mamlúks, or White Slaves, a form of government than which in theory none could be worse, Egypt from 1260 to 1341 enjoyed, with short intervals of turmoil, not only widespread power and prestige, but also a high degree of prosperity. This was due mainly to three things. The Mamlúk Sultans Baybars I (1260-77), Qalá'ún (1279-90), and al-Malik an-Násir (1299-1341), whatever their personal faults (and they were many), were exceedingly capable and far-sighted rulers. In the second place the bureaucratic administration which Egypt had inherited from its Byzantine and Fátimid governors was in all probability the most efficient instrument of government which existed in the Middle Ages. Thirdly Egypt enjoyed almost a monopoly of the Indian trade, the most profitable of all medieval commerce, and drew from it the vast revenues which were needed for the upkeep of its elaborate organization, as well as for the construction of the unsurpassed series of architectural monuments which are the peculiar glory of Cairo. Under these circumstances the Mamlúk sultans were able not only to maintain their authority against the Mongols in Syria and the Hijáz, but also to extend it into Nubia and Anatolia, and even westwards to Tripoli for a time.

The measure of Egypt's fortune may be gauged from the state of the rival kingdom of 'Iráq and Persia. Of its former imperial cities some, like Balkh, were now mere names clinging to mounds of rubbish, and those which had escaped their fate were either, like Baghdád and Basra, withered and shrunken, or else the prey of contending factions, and though new cities, such as Tabríz and Sultáníya, had risen into prominence, their prosperity was evanescent. Already wasted by the successive nomadic invasions and civil struggles of the two preceding centuries, the ruin of 'Iráq and Northern Persia seemed to have been consummated by the Mongol invasions between 1218 and 1260. Under the first heathen rulers of the Mongol dynasty, moreover, the Muslims were persecuted, but with the official conversion to Islám of Ghazán-Khán in 1295 a brighter era seemed to dawn. Though disorders continued to some extent under his successors Úljáytú (1305-16) and Abú Sa'íd (1317-35), 'Iráq, at least, recovered some of its former prosperity. The rich province of Fárs, on the other hand, seems to have been little affected by the disasters which befell the rest of Persia; though subject to the Mongols, it remained, as it had always been, somewhat apart from its neighbours, with its own peculiar culture and traditions. To the north-east of Persia, across the Oxus, were the territories of another Mongol dynasty, the Jaghatáy-Kháns. During the early centuries of Islám Transoxania had been one of the most flourishing provinces of the Caliphate. Bukhárá and Samarqand had a reputation inferior to none of the great cities of the East, and even during the troublous times of Turkish overlordship in the eleventh and twelfth centuries something of their prosperity still lingered. But it was on Transoxania that the first fury of the Mongol onset fell in 1219 and 1220, and under the Jaghatáy-Kháns, the most turbulent and barbarian of all the great Mongol dynasties, the shattered cities and wasted countryside had little hope of recovering more than a shadow of their former prosperity.

The Muslim states in India have a totally different history. Sind had, indeed, formed a province of the Caliphate, but the beginnings of an Indian Muslim empire go no farther back than the twelfth century. It was a great misfortune for India that the lateness of this conquest delivered her into the hands of merciless and turbulent Turkish generals, whose aim was solely to establish themselves as independent princes and to extort as much as possible from its almost inexhaustible resources for their interminable wars. The sultans of Delhi, the line of which begins with Qutb ad-Dín Aybak (1206-11), claimed a suzerainty over the other states, which they were able to enforce only sporadically and at appalling cost in blood and treasure. Unrestrained by the cultural traditions and bureaucratic organization of the old Islámic lands, which their fellow-countrymen, the Saljúqs and the Mamlúks, had been compelled to respect, they gave free rein to their impulses. In consequence "the bloodstained annals of the Sultanate of Delhi," as Vincent Smith, the historian of India, remarks, "are not pleasant reading." Of all the successors of Qutb ad-Dín down to the establishment of the Timúrid dynasty (the "Grand Moguls") in 1526, there is scarcely one who was not intolerant, tyrannical, and cruel, and the same may be said, with few exceptions, of the minor dynasties. Among the early sultans the most notable were Altamsh or Íltutmish (1211-36), who completed Qutb ad-Dín's buildings at Delhi, and 'Alá ad-Dín of the Khiljí dynasty (1296-1315), who repelled a series of Mongol invasions and added many monuments to the architecture of Delhi in addition to building the new town of Sírí.

In 1321 the throne was occupied by Ghiyáth ad-Dín Tughlaq, under whom some sort of order was restored and the authority of Delhi extended again into Bengal and the Deccan. His son Júná, the Sultan Muhammad of Ibn Battúta's time, had his father murdered in 1325, and ascending the throne without opposition "occupied it for twenty-six years of human tyranny as atrocious as any on record in the sad annals of human devilry and then died in his bed." Yet the ambition of the sultans of Delhi to create a vast Indian empire was more nearly achieved by him than by any other sultan prior to the Moguls. His success might have been still greater had it not been for the strange contradictions in his character so impartially exposed by Ibn Battúta (see Chapter VI.) and confirmed by all other available evidence. It would take us too far afield to discuss here in detail the activities of this extraordinary ruler, and the reader may be referred to the penetrating analysis contained in Vincent Smith's *Oxford History of India*, pages 236 to 246.

Such were the conditions which Ibn Battúta found on his eastward journey. When we follow him as he retraced his steps, less than twenty years later, it is impossible not to stand amazed at the anarchy which within so short a period had spread over all the central lands of Islám. In India itself, Sultan Muhammad's grandiose designs had proved impossible to realize. Without an organized administration and a system of government both flexible and consistent, neither the central nor the outlying provinces could be ruled from Delhi or anywhere else. Even before the sultan's death, Bengal, the Deccan, and Malabar had begun to break away, and in spite of the talents of his cousin and successor, Fírúz Sháh (1351-88), the prestige of

Delhi rapidly decayed, and the dismemberment of India for the profit of petty princes continued unchecked.

The malady from which India was suffering had broken out again with redoubled violence in 'Iráq and Persia on the extinction of the Mongol Ílkhánate in 1336. The hopes that their conversion had raised, the promise of a government able and willing to give commerce and agriculture a chance of recovery, were savagely betrayed. It would have mattered little to the people who or which of the amírs seized the sovereignty, but the division of the empire between a dozen quarrelling amírs spelled ruin and disaster. Here and there, no doubt, were islands of prosperity; Ibn Battúta speaks of one such on the Euphrates above Anbár. But the most serious feature was that the population under these repeated bludgeonings had lost heart, and a few years of anarchy now resulted in more depopulation than a century of anarchy had formerly caused.

Nor was Egypt exempt from the general decline. The death of Násir in 1341 opened the door to a prolonged series of dynastic disputes. No fewer than eight of his sons were thrust upon the throne between 1341 and 1351, and though the struggles over the succession involved only the Mamlúk soldiery and not the people as a whole, yet at a time of repeated changes of government the wretched subjects naturally suffered more severely than from the calculated extortions of a settled régime, and the disordered state of the kingdom is sufficiently indicated by the diminution of the revenues.

Even yet the cup of misery was not full. In 1348 the Muslim lands were swept by the first outbreak of the devouring pestilence known as the "Black Death." The extent of its ravages there will never be fully known, but, from the figures given by Ibn Battúta (see Chapter XII.) and in other sources, the loss of life during the visitation itself and in the famine which accompanied it was certainly appalling. In a young and vigorous society the effects of such a disaster soon disappear; but where the social order is already reeling, many decades are required before equilibrium can be regained. This respite was not granted to the Islámic world. A generation later, in 1381, the visitation was repeated, with as terrible effect, and before the horror of it passed from men's minds the whirlwind from Central Asia swept once more over all the Muslim lands from Delhi to Damascus and Smyrna, when Tímúr, who called himself a fellow-Muslim, reduced to waste and ashes what two invasions of the heathen Mongols and two visitations of the Plague had spared.

There is one other aspect of the history of this period which deserves a short reference. It may cause surprise that Ibn Battúta, though he regularly calls the Christians infidels or heathens, rarely betrays any animosity towards them, and even travels on Genoese and Catalan vessels. The inconsistency is explained by the several relations in which the Muslims stood to the Christians. The Sacred Law of Islám places all Christians in one of two categories: native Christian communities, living peacefully in Muslim lands with their own social organization, but definitely inferior in status; and unsubdued Christian states with which the Muslim state is theoretically at war. In general, therefore, its attitude, and that of the Muslims, to Christians was either hostile or frigidly aloof. But Muslim and Christian met on a third footing, which the Canon Law had not envisaged and which the religious authorities on either side vainly tried to oppose. When the Normans had wrested the command of the Mediterranean from the Arabs in the eleventh century, the commercial expansion of the Italian republics and of Roussillon led to the conclusion of trading agreements with the Muslim states and the foundation of trading stations in their ports. Though for mutual safety and convenience the Christian traders were subject to certain restrictions, such as the Muslims themselves were subject to in China, all these economic negotiations were transacted on the basis of complete equality and mutual respect. This friendliness, in spite of the frequency of piracy on both sides, was maintained on the whole until the sixteenth century, and is reflected in Ibn Battúta's relations with the Christian traders and during his visit to Constantinople.

§ 3. THE RELIGIOUS BACKGROUND OF IBN BATTÚTA'S TRAVELS

To the Muslim world in general, however, political events, though not devoid of interest, were matters of minor import. The medieval Muslim society was above all a religious society. To religion it owed its existence, for the religion of Islám was its sole bond of union. To religion it owed its common language of intercourse, for Islám intervened to prevent the dissolution of Arabic into local dialects, and imposed a knowledge of Arabic on Persians and Turks. To religion it owed its heritage of literature, for religion had supplied the incentive to those studies out of which Arabic literature (poetry alone excepted) arose. To religion it owed its social organization and its laws, for Islám had built up a new legal system, obliterating, at least in all the civilized lands, the old social organizations and social inequalities. To religion it owed its corporate feeling, for Islám gave to every believer the sense of common fellowship in its universal Brotherhood. Religion, in fine, not only created the cultural background and psychological orientation of Muslim society, but supplied for its members a philosophy of living and ordained even the least activities of their daily life.

The whole of Arabic literature reflects these social circumstances by an insistence on religious values and an interest in matters of religion, which is apt to make heavy demands on the patience and knowledge of modern readers. This naturally applies with special force to Ibn Battúta's book, no version of which can possibly exclude all allusions to religious subjects. For this reason it may lighten the English reader's way to give here some account of the religious institutions of Islám and the organizations which sprang up on Islámic soil.

The general beliefs of Islám require little explanation. The central dogma is that there is but One God, Creator of heaven and earth, Who alone is to be worshipped, the absolute Master of all His creatures, whose lives He has, in His inscrutable Love and Wisdom, foreordained, and whom He shall judge on the last awful Day. For their guidance He has raised up a succession of Prophets, the line of which, beginning with Adam, and continued through Noah, Abraham, Moses, David, Solomon, and Jesus, together with an unnumbered host of minor Prophets, culminated in Muhammad. The doctrine preached by all these Prophets is essentially one and the same, with slight modifications for time and place, namely *Islám*, or self-surrender to the Will of God. It is set forth in a series of verbally inspired books given by Divine Revelation to several of the Prophets, notably the Torah (Pentateuch) to Moses, the Psalms to David, the Evangel (which is not exactly the Gospels of the New Testament) to Jesus, and the Koran—the final and perfect repository of the Divine Word—to Muhammad. Such revelations were made not directly to the Prophet, but transmitted through the Archangel Gabriel. In addition to men and angels, there is a third class of created beings, namely the Jinn, who being made of fire have bodies more subtle than those of men, and possess superhuman powers, but, like men, shall be called to account on the Day of Judgment.

But Islám is much more than the mere affirmation of certain beliefs. No one has fully earned the name of Muslim who does not also carry out with regularity the religious duties imposed upon him. The main "Pillars of the Faith" are four: (1) The five daily prayer-rituals, each made up of a fixed number of repetitions of a uniform series of bodily postures and recitations, with the face towards the *qibla*, *i.e.* Mecca. The prayers are to be performed either congregationally or in private at stated hours: just before sunrise, just after noon, in mid-afternoon, just after sunset, and two or three hours after nightfall. Congregational prayers are performed in a mosque and are led by one (it is immaterial which one) of the worshippers. In the mosque there are no images, no paintings, nothing to distract the mind of the austere monotheist from concentration on the act of devotion. At most the walls may be decorated with a tracery of geometrical designs, whose endless interlacings may perhaps serve to weary the outward vision and give fuller play to the inner spiritual perceptions. The principal congregational service of the week, which is held only in "cathedral" mosques, is the noon prayer on Friday, when, in addition to the ordinary ritual prayers, the official Preacher of the mosque delivers from the pulpit a formal *Khutba* or allocution, containing *inter alia* prayers for the reigning ruler, followed usually by a sermon or exhortation (*maw'iza*). Similar services are held on the two great festival days, thc lesser festival at the close of the fasting month of Ramadán, and the greater festival on the tenth day of the month of Pilgrimage. Before beginning to pray the worshipper must in every case be in a state of ritual purity, which is ensured by the formal ablution of face, arms, and feet at the fountain provided in every mosque. (2) The payment of a fixed alms-tax on all property, averaging two and a half per cent. annually. (3) The observance of the annual fast during the month of Ramadán, *i.e.* complete abstinence from all food and drink (including nowadays smoking) between the hours of sunrise and sunset for the period of one lunar month. (4) For those who are of age and have the means to carry it out, the obligation to make the Pilgrimage to Mecca at least once in a lifetime.

Besides its dogmatics and its religious practices, Islám includes a complete legal and social system, based on the Koran and the *Hadíth*—the sayings and actions attributed to the Prophet. This Islámic Law was expounded by four schools of jurists in the second and third centuries of the Muslim era. The schools differ only in minor points of interpretation, and all are regarded as equally orthodox. The Law was administered by the *qádí*, and in the capital cities of the East there was usually a supreme qádí for each rite. In practice criminal actions were often decided by the Sultan or his officers and sometimes legalized by the formal assent of a qádí. The point at which the social system of Islam diverges most radically from European systems is found in the sphere of marriage and divorce. It is commonly known that a Muslim may possess up to four wives at one time in addition to slave concubines, and that he is at liberty, subject to certain none too rigorous legal safeguards, to divorce the former at will, and to dispose of the latter unless they have borne him male children. Such provisions were admirably suited to a roving life, and Ibn Battúta took full advantage of them. Details that no European—far less any Christian clergyman—

would communicate are set down by him quite simply and naturally, since they stand in a measure outside the moral field, in a category not unlike that of eating and drinking. One should not, however, draw overhasty conclusions from the casual manner in which Ibn Battúta speaks of his wives. It is not good manners for a Muslim to refer to his womenfolk in ordinary social intercourse, and when, on rare occasions, Ibn Battúta breaks through the convention, it is generally no more than a brief explanatory reference made in connection with some other circumstance.

In regard to a second feature of the Muslim social system, the practice of slavery, it is important to bear in mind that the slave was generally the body-servant or retainer of his master, and that slavery was in no sense the economic basis of Muslim society. Master and slave thus stood in a more humane relationship than did the slave cultivator to the Roman landed proprietor or the American planter. There was consequently less stigma attaching to slavery, and in no other society has there been anything resembling the system by which, as has been shown in the preceding section, the white slaves came to furnish the privileged cadres whence the high officers of state, commanders, governors, and at length even sultans, were almost exclusively drawn.

The following story, told by a theologian of the third century, represents without serious distortion the relations, which, as numerous parallels in Arabic literature indicate, often existed between master, wife, and slave.

I saw a slave-boy being auctioned for thirty dínárs, and as he was worth three hundred I bought him. I was building a house at the time, and I gave him twenty dínárs to lay out on the workmen. He spent ten on them and bought a garment for himself with the other ten. I said to him " What's this ?" to which he replied "Don't be hasty; no gentleman scolds his slaves." I said to myself "Here have I bought the Caliph's tutor without knowing it." Later on I wanted to marry a woman unknown to my cousin (*i.e.* my first wife), so I swore him to secrecy and gave him a dínár to buy some things, including some of the fish called ḥázibá. But he bought something else, and when I was wroth with him he said "I find that Hippocrates disapproves of ḥázibá." I said to him "You worthless fool, I was not aware that I had bought a Galen," and gave him ten blows with the whip. But he seized me and gave me seven back saying, "Sir, three blows is enough as a punishment, and the seven I gave you are my rightful retaliation." So I made at him and gave him a cut on the head, whereupon he went off to my cousin, and said to her "Sincerity is a religious duty, and whoever deceives us is not one of us. My master has married and he swore me to silence, and when I said to him that my lady must be told of it he broke my head." So my cousin would neither let me into the house nor let me have anything out of it, until at last I had to divorce the other woman. After that she used to call the boy "The honest lad," and I could not say a word to him, so I said to myself "I shall set him free, and then I shall have peace."

The most original features of the Islámic system are to be found in its religious organizations, of which there were two, to some extent rivals of one another. The official religious system of Islám excludes the conception of a clergy, and consequently of a hierarchy. There are no sacraments. All believers stand on an equal footing in matters of religion, and none is entitled to claim any spiritual functions which are not shared by every member of the community. In actual practice, however, it was impossible to maintain the theory of equality. Where a society is bound up with a religious system, the cleric, the expounder of doctrine, the arbiter on points of law, inevitably establishes a moral predominance over his more ignorant fellows, that is none the less real or even tyrannical because it has no outward legal support. The mere maintenance of the religious system thus called into being a religious aristocracy, as we have already termed the body of theologians, differing, however, from the Christian hierarchy in that the elaborate gradations of the latter were unknown, that it had no spiritual prerogatives, and was open to all without seeking any man's leave or taking any vows. For the rest, the system had much the same merits and defects as a priesthood, though the theologians of Islám generally held more aloof from the civil administration than did the Christian hierarchy, and adopted an attitude which in the long run produced disastrous effects on both church and civil government. In the political field their influence was mainly negative. Since it devolved upon the community as a whole to ensure the observance of the Faith, the theologians soon found that they could use their influence to mould public opinion and create of it a weapon with which to intimidate law-breakers and keep in check local autocrats and tyrants. It was rarely that even the most despotic ruler ventured to brave the public disapproval, as may be seen from some of the stories related by Ibn Battúta. On the other hand the example of Sultan Muhammad of Delhi is sufficient to show that when the ruler was astute enough to humour the theologians with his left hand, there were few who dared enquire too closely into what he did with his right.

On the community as a whole was laid yet another duty, which could not be delegated to the professional theologians, the duty of defending by the sword the territorial and religious heritage of Islám. The *Jihád*, which was reckoned by some jurists as an obligation of the same degree as prayer and fasting, and in the early days had indeed been the constant occupation of every Muslim, in a form more offensive than defensive, was revived by the Crusades and the Christian reconquest in Spain. No longer, however, was it regarded as the personal duty of every Muslim to take up arms for the defence of Islám, and for the most part the Syrians and Andalusians were left to defend their territories by themselves. Nevertheless, the inducement of Paradise, held out as the reward of the martyr who dies fighting for the Faith, was strong enough to maintain a steady movement of volunteers to the theatres of war against the Christian or heathen. These volunteers lived on the frontier in forts or fortified lines called by the name of *ribát* (which means literally "pickets"), and were known as *Gházís* or *Murábits*, the nearest English equivalent for which is "mounted frontiersmen." By the fourteenth century it was probably only in Andalusia that the institution preserved its primitive character. Elsewhere it had developed along two very different lines. On the one hand the fighting life attracted all the most turbulent elements in the Muslim empire, and the Gházís rapidly degenerated into bands of condottieri and brigands, a source of much greater vexation to Muslim rulers than to the infidels.

On the other hand it was associated with the rise of the ascetic and mystical movement within Islám. Early Muslim asceticism was dominated by fear of Hell. Since death on Jihád was the only sure passport to Paradise, it came about that in the early days ascetics had generally taken a prominent part in the frontier warfare. Later on Jihád was interpreted to apply to the inward and spiritual struggle against the temptations of the world, and the *Súfís* (as the mystics were now called) withdrew from secular warfare, but retained the old terminology. The *ribát* was now the ascetic's hermitage or the convent or hospice where the devotees congregated to live the religious life. In course of time the loose primitive associations became linked up in an organization which tended to grow more elaborate and hierarchical, with ascending grades of spiritual perception and power. We may here, however, omit the details of this mystical hierarchy, and pass at once to examine the working of the *súfí* or *darwísh* orders in the fourteenth century, and their relations with the theologians.

In general the followers of the mystic's path were by this time grouped in congregations, called after some eminent shaykh, who was regarded as the founder of the *taríqa* or rule, including the ritual litany, which, as will be explained shortly, was one of the distinguishing marks of each congregation. Round the convent of the founder rose a girdle of daughter houses, as disciples of the order spread throughout the Muslim world, and in most cases all the members looked up to the descendants or successors of the founder (for in Islám asceticism does not imply celibacy) as their head. The older individualist asceticism was not yet extinct, however, and everywhere, but especially in North-west Africa and in Mt. Lebanon, were to be found recluses who were completely independent of the darwísh orders, though they also often claimed spiritual affiliation with and descent from the great Súfí leaders of the early centuries. Still more freely, outside the walls of convent or cell, roamed numbers of darwíshes or *faqírs*, affiliated and non-affiliated, distinguished by the patched robe, wallet, and staff, who scorned to earn so much as a mite by their own labours, trusting to the Providence of God and the charity of the Faithful, and who at times displayed an importunity and effrontery more easily associated with professional mendicants than pious "almsmen."

The fundamental aim of the Súfí life, however or

wherever lived, was to pierce the veils of human sense which shut man off from the Divine and so attain to communion with and absorption into God. Their days and nights were spent in prayer and contemplation, in fasting and ascetic exercises. At frequent intervals all the inhabitants of the convent, or the local members of the *taríqa*, met to celebrate the ritual litany, the *dhikr*, according to their peculiar rites. The *dhikr* was intended to produce a hypnotic effect on the participants and so allow them to taste momentarily the joys of reunion with the Divine. With that extravagance which accompanies all expression of rising emotion in Eastern life and thought, the litany in most cases passed into a fantastic exhibition of marvellous or thaumaturgical feats, such as Ibn Battúta describes on several occasions. Some would whirl and pirouette for hours at a time, others would chew serpents or glass, walk in fire, or thrust knives through their limbs, without any worse effects than at most a temporary nervous exhaustion.

The faculty of self-torture without inflicting visible injury, which is amply vouched for by modern travellers who have witnessed the lamentations of the Shi'ites for the death of Husayn, or, like the late Lord Curzon, have attended the séances of the 'Isawíya darwíshes in North-west Africa, leads up to a related and difficult question. All European commentators of Ibn Battúta have referred to his credulity, his fondness for the miraculous and uncritical acceptance of reported miracles worked by the famous shaykhs and saints whom he met. His powers of belief are not, however, entirely unlimited, as may be seen from the doubts which he expresses on more than one occasion in regard to extravagant claims. The stories of miracles which he relates at secondhand do him no discredit; the power of saints to perform miracles was and still is believed by the mass of Muslims, and such tales interested both narrator and audience. It is when he tells of miraculous events directly associated with himself that the problem of their truth must be definitely faced. In some cases it may be possible to explain them by hypnotism (if that in fact "explains" them), as the Muslim theologian explained the Chinese magician's tricks at Hang-chow; in others, we may suspect the arts of the conjurer; but there is a residue, including, for example, the account of his escape after his capture at Koel in India, where we must either accept the miraculous element or give the lie direct to the traveller. To the naturalistic and mechanistic mind of the nineteenth century the choice was simple, as it is still to those who charge Ibn Battúta with wholesale invention in regard to his travels. But the twentieth-century reader has greater faith in the powers of God and man, and while he may remain critical he will not reject *a priori* any narrative that involves the "miraculous." There can be no doubt that in certain orders, at least, the severe bodily and mental training undergone by a darwísh as he advances to the higher grades of initiation is accompanied by an expansion of mental powers, beginning with simple telepathy. The doubting reader may be referred to an illuminating account by Professor D. B. Macdonald (*Aspects of Islam*, p. 170) of an ex-darwísh converted to Christianity who still retained his telepathic gifts. The only prudent course, it would seem, is to suspend judgment, and in the meantime give Ibn Battúta the credit for relating what he at least believed to be the truth.

It is a little surprising, however, to find him so deeply interested in and so sympathetic in general towards the darwíshes and Súfís. The average theologian regarded them with suspicion, if not with aversion, for various reasons, religious and secular, while the mystic in turn frequently despised the theologian for his formalism and cult of the letter. The first point of issue between them dealt with the nature of religious knowledge. To the theologians, there was but one road to the apprehension of truth, *'ilm* or *savoir*, the science of theology, with all its scholastic appurtenances involved in the study of the Koran and the Traditions of the Prophet. The darwísh, on the other hand, sought *ma'rifa* or *connaissance*, that direct knowledge of God, which in his view was often actually hindered by the study of theology. Sufism showed an antinomian tendency which could not but excite the disapprobation of the legalist, who sought and found satisfaction for his religious instincts in the ritual duties prescribed by the Faith. Moreover the reverence accorded by the disciple to his shaykh when alive, and the elevation of former shaykhs to the rank of saints, to whom invocations were addressed, seemed to the theologian to destroy the non-sacerdotal principle, and even to trespass into polytheism, the one mortal sin in Islám. At first the breach between theologian and Súfí had been much wider, but in course of time the popular influence enjoyed by the Súfís forced the theologians, however unwillingly, to terms in the matter of saint-worship. The success of the Súfís in legitimating their practices was possibly not a little due to pressure exerted outside the purely religious field. They formed, as has been seen, a rival religious organization, and it is evident that some of the hostility felt by the theologians was due to competition for popular favour and support. As the balance of popularity turned in favour of the Súfís, especially with the influx of the Turkish element into the social and political life of Islám, the theologians found it necessary to admit much that they had formerly resisted and perhaps continued to chafe at. By the fourteenth century their capitulation was complete, when the last outstanding opponent of the Súfí heresies, that Ibn Taymíya whom Ibn Battúta saw in Damascus, and whom he speaks of as " having a bee in his bonnet," was silenced. But the hostility remained, now more, now less openly shown. In North-west Africa it seems to have been much weaker than elsewhere, possibly because of the strong inherited attachment of the Berbers, which they still show, to the principle of local sanctuaries and " holy men," islamized under the name of *murábits* (" marabouts "). This may serve to explain why Ibn Battúta, trained theologian as he was, still had all a Berber's interest in the holy men whom he met on his travels.

The antagonism between legist and follower of the Inner Light was, however, unimportant by comparison with the hatred engendered by the Great Schism of Islam, the division between *Sunní* and *Shí'ite*. The Shí'ite movement began in the first century of Islám as political propaganda against the Umayyad dynasty of Caliphs in favour of the house of 'Alí, the son-in-law and cousin of the Prophet. It was then hand in glove with the orthodox, and succeeded both in impressing its historical point of view on orthodox sentiment and in overthrowing the hated dynasty, only to be cheated of its political hopes by the establishment of the rival 'Abbásid line, and to fall instead under a more methodical persecution than hitherto. Shí'ism now took to the catacombs, and soon became a separate heretical sect, distinguished by the doctrine of allegiance to a divinely appointed, sinless, and infallible spiritual leader, the Imám, instead of an elective lay head or Caliph. The Imámate they held to be hereditary in the house of 'Alí, but the various sub-groups differed on the point at which the succession of Imáms was interrupted. The belief of the principal group, or " Twelvers," to which the Shí'ites of Persia and 'Iráq still belong, was that the twelfth Imám of the line disappeared about the year 873 into a cave at

Hilla, but that he continues, through the heads of the religious organization, to provide spiritual and temporal guidance for his people, and will reappear as the promised Mahdí to bring the long reign of tyranny to an end. This strange doctrine of a "Hidden Imám" or "Expected Imám," often referred to as the "Master of the Age," is recalled by the ceremony at Hilla, of which Ibn Battúta gives a graphic description.

Shi'ism has always shown a much stronger sectarian tendency than orthodox Islám, and was distinguished from its earliest days by the number and variety of its offshoots. The general tendency of the sects was to adopt, under the influence of various syncretist philosophies, still more extreme views on the person of 'Alí and his descendants, even to the extent of defying them. Such *Ghulát* or "Extremists" seem to have found special favour in Syria where, indeed, two of the largest of these communities are still to be found, the Druse and the Nusayrís (now called 'Alawís), alongside the majority Shi'ites of the Twelvers sect, locally known as Mutawális. From the same cause arises its intolerance. The Shi'ite hates, where the Sunní merely despises. His hatred is by no means reserved for non-Muslims, but is freely bestowed upon the other Islámic sects, especially upon the Súfís, whose views admit of no reconciliation with the pontifical system of Shi'ism. With such feelings on the one side reciprocated on the other, it is not surprising to find a constant feud raging in Syria, in spite of the efforts of the Mamlúk governors. Over and over in Ibn Battúta's work the reader will note traces of the enmity that divided Sunní from Shi'ite, not least in the writer's personal animosity, which shows in the substitution of the opprobrious *Ráfidhí* or "Refuser," for Shi'ite or 'Alawí. The explanation of this term is to be found in a practice adopted by the Shi'ites, as a logical consequence of their Imámate theory. Holding that 'Alí alone had the right to succeed his cousin Muhammad, they regard the three Caliphs who reigned before him as usurpers and traitors, and substitute a curse for the blessing which the pious Sunní Muslim pronounces after the names of these the closest companions of the Prophet—a deliberate insult which naturally arouses the indignation of the Sunnís in a far greater degree than their more theoretical dogmatic heresies.

IN THE NAME OF GOD THE MERCIFUL THE COMPASSIONATE

Praise be to God, Who hath subdued the earth to His servants that they may tread thereon spacious ways, Who hath made therefrom and thereunto the three moments of growth, return, and recall, and hath perfected His Bounty toward His creatures in subjecting to them the beasts of the field and vessels towering like mountains, that they may bestride the ridge of the wilderness and the deeps of the ocean. May the blessing of God rest upon our chief and master Muhammad who made plain a way for mankind and caused the light of His guidance to shine forth in radiance, and upon all who are honoured by relationship with him.

Amongst those who presented themselves at the illustrious gates of our lord the Caliph and Commander of the Faithful Abú 'Inán Fáris was the learned and most veracious traveller Abú 'Abdalláh Muhammad of Tangier known as *Ibn Battúta* and in the eastern lands as Shams ad-Dín, who having journeyed round the world and visited its cities observantly and attentively, having investigated the diversities of nations and experienced the customs of Arabs and non-Arabs, laid down the staff of travel in this noble metropolis. A gracious command prescribed that he should dictate an account of the cities which he had seen on his journeys, of the interesting events which he retained in his memory and of the rulers of countries, learned men and pious saints whom he had met, and that the humble servant Muhammad ibn Juzayy should unite the morsels of his dictation into a book which should include all their merits and preserve them in a clear and elegant style. I have therefore rendered the sense of the Shaykh Abú 'Abdalláh's narrative in language adequate to his purposes, often reproducing without alteration his own words, and I have reported all his stories and narratives of events without investigating their truthfulness since he himself has authenticated them with the strongest proofs.

Here begins the narrative of the Shaykh Abú 'Abdalláh [Ibn Battúta].

BOOK I

CHAPTER I

I LEFT Tangier, my birthplace, on Thursday, 2nd Rajab, 725 [14th June, 1325], being at that time twenty-two [lunar] years of age,[1] with the intention of making the Pilgrimage to the Holy House [at Mecca] and the Tomb of the Prophet [at Madína]. I set out alone, finding no companion to cheer the way with friendly intercourse, and no party of travellers with whom to associate myself. Swayed by an overmastering impulse within me, and a long-cherished desire to visit those glorious sanctuaries, I resolved to quit all my friends and tear myself away from my home. As my parents were still alive, it weighed grievously upon me to part from them, and both they and I were afflicted with sorrow.

On reaching the city of Tilimsán [Tlemsen], whose sultan at that time was Abú Táshifín,[2] I found there two ambassadors of the Sultan of Tunis, who left the city on the same day that I arrived. One of the brethren having advised me to accompany them, I consulted the will of God in this matter,[3] and after a stay of three days in the city to procure all that I needed, I rode after them with all speed. I overtook them at the town of Miliána, where we stayed ten days, as both ambassadors fell sick on account of the summer heats. When we set out again, one of them grew worse, and died after we had stopped for three nights by a stream four miles from Miliána. I left their party there and pursued my journey, with a company of merchants from Tunis. On reaching al-Jazá'ir [Algiers] we halted outside the town for a few days, until the former party rejoined us, when we went on together through the Mitíja[4] to the mountain of Oaks [Jurjúra] and so reached Bijáya [Bougie].[5] The commander of Bijáya at this time was the chamberlain Ibn Sayyid an-Nás. Now one of the Tunisian merchants of our party had died leaving three thousand dinars of gold, which he had entrusted to a certain man of Algiers to deliver to his heirs at Tunis. Ibn Sayyid an-Nás came to hear of this and forcibly seized the money. This was the first instance I witnessed of the tyranny of the agents of the Tunisian government. At Bijáya I fell ill of a fever, and one of my friends advised me to stay there till I recovered. But I refused, saying, "If God decrees my death, it shall be on the road with my face set toward Mecca." "If that is your resolve," he replied, "sell your ass and your heavy baggage, and I shall lend you what you require. In this way you will travel light, for we must make haste on our journey, for fear of meeting roving Arabs on the way."[6] I followed his advice and he did as he had promised—may God reward him! On reaching Qusantínah [Constantine] we camped outside the town, but a heavy rain forced us to leave our tents during the night and take refuge in some houses there. Next day the governor of the city came to meet us. Seeing my clothes all soiled by the rain he gave orders that they should be washed at his house, and in place of my old worn headcloth sent me a headcloth of fine Syrian cloth, in one of the ends of which he had tied two gold dinars. This was the first alms I received on my journey. From Qusantínah we reached Bona where, after staying in the town for several days, we left the merchants of our party on account of the dangers of the road, while we pursued our journey with the utmost speed. I was again attacked by fever, so I tied myself in the saddle with a turban-cloth in case I should fall by reason of my weakness. So great was my fear that I could not dismount until we arrived at Tunis. The population of the city came out to meet the members of our party, and on all sides greetings and questions were exchanged, but not a soul greeted me as no one there was known to me. I was so affected by my loneliness that I could not restrain my tears and wept bitterly, until one of the pilgrims realized the cause of my distress and coming up to me greeted me kindly and continued to entertain me with friendly talk until I entered the city.

The Sultan of Tunis at that time was Abú Yahyá, the son of Abú Zakaríya II., and there were a number of notable scholars in the town.[7] During my stay the festival of the Breaking of the Fast fell due, and I joined the company at the Praying-ground.[8] The inhabitants assembled in large numbers to celebrate the festival, making a brave show and wearing their richest apparel. The Sultan Abú Yahyá arrived on horseback, accompanied by all his relatives, courtiers, and officers of state walking on foot in a stately procession. After the recital of the prayer and the conclusion of the Allocution the people returned to their homes.

Some time later the pilgrim caravan for the Hijáz was formed, and they nominated me as their qádí (judge). We left Tunis early in November, following the coast road through Súsa, Sfax, and Qábis,[9] where we stayed for ten days on account of incessant rains. Thence we set out for Tripoli, accompanied for several stages by a hundred or more horsemen as well as a detachment of archers, out of respect for whom the Arabs kept their distance. I had made a contract of marriage at Sfax with the daughter of one of the syndics at Tunis, and at Tripoli she was conducted to me, but after leaving Tripoli I became involved in a dispute with her father, which necessitated my separation from her. I then married the daughter of a student from Fez, and when she was conducted to me I detained the caravan for a day by entertaining them all at a wedding party.

At length on April 5th (1326) we reached Alexandria. It is a beautiful city, well-built and fortified with four gates[10] and a magnificent port. Among all the ports in the world I have seen none to equal it except Kawlam [Quilon] and Cálicút in India, the port of the infidels [Genoese] at Súdáq in the land of the Turks, and the port of Zaytún in China, all of which will be described later. I went to see the lighthouse on this occasion and found one of its faces in ruins. It is a very high square building, and its door is above the level of the earth. Opposite the door, and of the same height, is a building from which there is a plank bridge to the door; if this is removed there is no means of entrance. Inside the door is a place for the lighthouse-keeper, and within the lighthouse there are many chambers. The breadth of the passage inside is nine spans and that of the wall ten spans; each of the four sides of the lighthouse is 140 spans in breadth. It is situated on a high mound and lies three miles from the city on a long tongue of land which juts out into the sea from close by the city wall, so that the lighthouse cannot be reached by land except from the city. On my return to the West in the year 750 [1349] I visited the lighthouse again, and found that it had fallen into so ruinous a condition that it was not possible to enter it or climb up to the door.[11] Al-Malik an-Násir had started to build a similar lighthouse alongside it but was prevented by death from completing the work. Another of the marvellous things in this city is the awe-inspiring marble column in its outskirts which they call the "Pillar of Columns." It is a single block, skilfully carved, erected on a plinth of square stones like enormous platforms, and no one knows how it was erected there nor for certain who erected it.[12]

One of the learned men of Alexandria was the qádí, a master of eloquence, who used to wear a turban of extraordinary size. Never either in the eastern or the western lands have I seen a more voluminous headgear. Another of them was the pious ascetic Burhán ad-Dín, whom I met during my stay and whose hospitality I enjoyed for three days. One day as I entered his room he said to me "I see that you are fond of travelling through foreign lands." I replied "Yes, I am" (though I had as yet no thought of going to such distant lands as India or China). Then he said "You must certainly visit my brother[13] Faríd ad-Dín in India, and my brother Rukn ad-Dín in Sind, and my brother Burhán ad-Dín in China, and when you find them give them greeting from me." I was amazed at his prediction, and the idea of going to these countries having been cast into my mind, my journeys never ceased until I had met these three that he named and conveyed his greeting to them.

During my stay at Alexandria I had heard of the pious Shaykh al-Murshidí, who bestowed gifts miraculously created at his desire. He lived in solitary retreat in a cell in the country where he was visited by princes and ministers. Parties of men in all ranks of life used to come to him every day and he would supply them all with food. Each one of them would desire to eat some flesh or fruit or sweetmeat at his cell, and to each he would give what he had suggested, though it was frequently out of season. His fame was carried from mouth to mouth far and wide, and the Sultan too had visited him several times in his retreat. I set out from Alexandria to seek this shaykh and passing through Damanhúr came to Fawwá [Fua], a beautiful township, close by which, separated from it by a canal, lies the shaykh's cell. I reached this cell about mid-afternoon, and on saluting the shaykh I found that he had with him one of the sultan's aides-de-camp, who had encamped with his troops just outside. The shaykh rose and embraced me, and calling for food invited me to eat. When the hour of the afternoon prayer arrived he set me in front as prayer-leader, and did the same on every occasion when we were together at the times of prayer during my stay. When I wished to sleep he said to me " Go up to the roof of the cell and sleep there " (this was during the summer heats). I said to the officer " In the name of God,"[14] but he replied [quoting from the Koran] " There is none of us but has an appointed place." So I mounted to the roof and found there a straw mattress and a leather mat, a water vessel for ritual ablutions, a jar of water and a drinking-cup, and I lay down there to sleep.

That night, while I was sleeping on the roof of the cell, I dreamed that I was on the wing of a great bird which was flying with me towards Mecca, then to Yemen, then eastwards, and thereafter going towards the south, then flying far eastwards, and finally landing in a dark and green country, where it left me. I was astonished at this dream and said to myself " If the shaykh can interpret my dream for me, he is all that they say he is." Next morning, after all the other visitors had gone, he called me and when I had related my dream interpreted it to me saying: " You will make the pilgrimage [to Mecca] and visit [the Tomb of] the Prophet, and you will travel through Yemen, 'Iráq, the country of the Turks, and India. You will stay there for a long time and meet there my brother Dilshád the Indian, who will rescue you from a danger into which you will fall." Then he gave me a travelling-provision of small cakes and money, and I bade him farewell and departed. Never

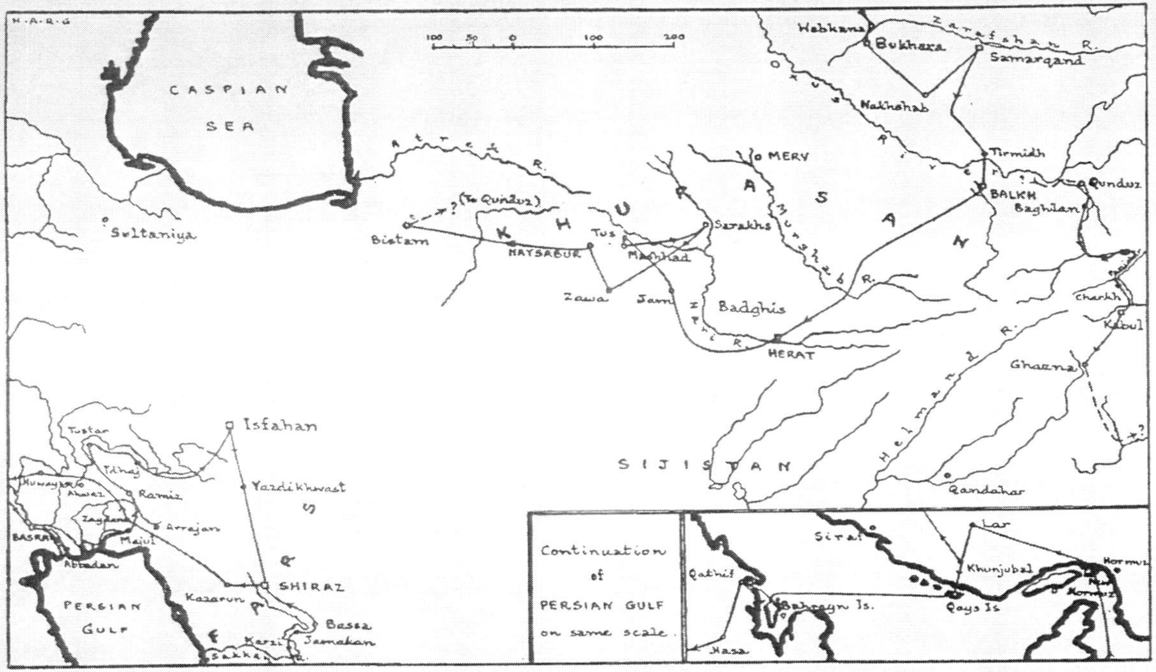

SKETCH MAP OF PERSIA TO ILLUSTRATE IBN BATTŪTA'S TRAVELS

[face p. 84

since parting from him have I met on my journeys aught but good fortune, and his blessings have stood me in good stead.

We rode from here to Damietta through a number of towns, in each of which we visited the principal men of religion. Damietta lies on the bank of the Nile, and the people in the houses next to the river draw water from it in buckets. Many of the houses have steps leading down to the river. Their sheep and goats are allowed to pasture at liberty day and night; for this reason the saying goes of Damietta "Its walls are sweetmeats and its dogs are sheep." Anyone who enters the city may not afterwards leave it except by the governor's seal. Persons of repute have a seal stamped on a piece of paper so that they may show it to the gatekeepers; other persons have the seal stamped on their forearms. In this city there are many seabirds with extremely greasy flesh, and the milk of its buffaloes is unequalled for sweetness and pleasant taste. The fish called búrí[15] is exported thence to Syria, Anatolia, and Cairo. The present town is of recent construction; the old city was that destroyed by the Franks in the time of al-Malik as-Sálih.[16]

From Damietta I travelled to Fáriskúr, which is a town on the bank of the Nile, and halted outside it. Here I was overtaken by a horseman who had been sent after me by the governor of Damietta. He handed me a number of coins, saying to me "The Governor asked for you, and on being informed about you, he sent you this gift"—may God reward him! Thence I travelled to Ashmún, a large and ancient town on a canal derived from the Nile. It possesses a wooden bridge at which all vessels anchor, and in the afternoon the baulks are lifted and the vessels pass up and down. From here I went to Samannúd, whence I journeyed upstream to Cairo, between a continuous succession of towns and villages. The traveller on the Nile need take no provision with him, because whenever he desires to descend on the bank he may do so, for ablutions, prayers, provisioning, or any other purpose. There is an uninterrupted chain of bazaars from Alexandria to Cairo, and from Cairo to Assuan in Upper Egypt.

I arrived at length at Cairo, mother of cities and seat of Pharaoh the tyrant, mistress of broad regions and fruitful lands, boundless in multitude of buildings, peerless in beauty and splendour, the meeting-place of comer and goer, the halting-place of feeble and mighty, whose throngs surge as the waves of the sea, and can scarce be contained in her for all her size and capacity.[17] It is said that in Cairo there are twelve thousand water-carriers who transport water on camels, and thirty thousand hirers of mules and donkeys, and that on the Nile there are thirty-six thousand boats belonging to the Sultan and his subjects, which sail upstream to Upper Egypt and downstream to Alexandria and Damietta, laden with goods and profitable merchandise of all kinds. On the bank of the Nile opposite Old Cairo is the place known as *The Garden*,[18] which is a pleasure park and promenade, containing many beautiful gardens, for the people of Cairo are given to pleasure and amusements. I witnessed a fête once in Cairo for the sultan's recovery from a fractured hand; all the merchants decorated their bazaars and had rich stuffs, ornaments and silken fabrics hanging in their shops for several days. The mosque of 'Amr is highly venerated and widely celebrated. The Friday service is held in it, and the road runs through it from east to west. The madrasas [college mosques] of Cairo cannot be counted for multitude. As for the Máristán [hospital], which lies "between the two castles" near the mausoleum of Sultan Qalá'ún, no description is adequate to its beauties. It contains an innumerable quantity of appliances and medicaments, and its daily revenue is put as high as a thousand dinars.[19]

There are a large number of religious establishments [" convents "], which they call *khánqahs*, and the nobles vie with one another in building them. Each of these is set apart for a separate school of darwíshes, mostly Persians, who are men of good education and adepts in the mystical doctrines. Each has a superior and a doorkeeper and their affairs are admirably organized. They have many special customs, one of which has to do with their food. The steward of the house comes in the morning to the darwíshes, each of whom indicates what food he desires, and when they assemble for meals, each person is given his bread and soup in a separate dish, none sharing with another. They eat twice a day. They are each given winter clothes and summer clothes, and a monthly allowance of from twenty to thirty dirhams. Every Thursday night they receive sugar cakes, soap to wash their clothes, the price of a bath, and oil for their lamps. These men are celibate; the married men have separate convents.

At Cairo too is the great cemetery of al-Qaráfa, which is a place of peculiar sanctity, and contains the graves of innumerable scholars and pious believers. In the Qaráfa the people build beautiful pavilions surrounded by walls, so that they look like houses.[20] They also build chambers and hire Koran-readers, who recite night and day in agreeable voices. Some of them build religious houses and madrasas beside the mausoleums and on Thursday nights they go out to spend the night there with their children and womenfolk, and make a circuit of the famous tombs. They go out to spend the night there also on the " Night of mid-Sha'bán," and the market-people take out all kinds of eatables.[21] Among the many celebrated sanctuaries [in the city] is the holy shrine where there reposes the head of al-Husayn.[22] Beside it is a vast monastery of striking construction, on the doors of which there are silver rings and plates of the same metal.

The Egyptian Nile[23] surpasses all rivers of the earth in sweetness of taste, length of course, and utility. No other river in the world can show such a continuous series of towns and villages along its banks, or a basin so intensely cultivated. Its course is from south to north, contrary to all the other [great] rivers. One extraordinary thing about it is that it begins to rise in the extreme hot weather, at the time when rivers generally diminish and dry up, and begins to subside just when rivers begin to increase and overflow. The river Indus resembles it in this feature. The Nile is one of the five great rivers of the world, which are the Nile, Euphrates, Tigris, Syr Darya and Amu Darya; five other rivers resemble these, the Indus, which is called Panj Áb [*i.e.* Five Rivers], the river of India which is called Gang [Ganges]—it is to it that the Hindus go on pilgrimage, and when they burn their dead they throw the ashes into it, and they say that it comes from Paradise—the river Jún [Jumna, or perhaps Brahmaputra] in India, the river Itil [Volga] in the Qipchaq steppes, on the banks of which is the city of Sará, and the river Sarú [Hoang-Ho] in the land of Cathay. All these will be mentioned in their proper places, if God will. Some distance below Cairo the Nile divides into three streams,[24] none of which can be crossed except by boat, winter or summer. The inhabitants of every township have canals led off the Nile; these are filled when the river is in flood and carry the water over the fields.

From Cairo I travelled into Upper Egypt, with the intention of crossing to the Hijáz. On the first night I stayed at the monastery of Dayr at-Tín, which was built to house certain illustrious relics—a fragment of the Prophet's wooden basin and the pencil with which he used to apply kohl, the awl he used for sewing his sandals, and the Koran belonging to the Caliph 'Ali written in his own hand. These were bought, it is said, for a hundred thousand dirhams by the builder of the monastery, who also established funds to supply food to all comers and to maintain the guardians of the sacred relics. Thence my way lay through a number of towns and villages to Munyat Ibn Khasíb [Minia], a large town which is built on the bank of the Nile, and most emphatically excels all the other towns of Upper Egypt. I went on through Manfalút, Asyút, Ikhmím, where there is a *berba*[25] with sculptures and inscriptions which no one can now read—another of these *berbas* there was pulled down and its stones used to build a madrasa—Qiná, Qús, where the governor of Upper Egypt resides, Luxor, a pretty little town containing the tomb of the pious ascetic Abu'l-Hajjáj,[26] Esná, and thence a day and a night's journey through desert country to Edfú. Here we crossed the Nile and, hiring camels, journeyed with a party of Arabs through a desert, totally devoid of settlements but quite safe for travelling. One of our halts was at Humaythira, a place infested with hyenas. All night long we kept driving them away, and indeed one got at my baggage, tore open one of the sacks, pulled out a bag of dates, and made off with it. We found the bag next morning, torn to pieces and with most of the contents eaten.

After fifteen days' travelling we reached the town of Aydháb,[27] a large town, well supplied with milk and fish; dates and grain are imported from Upper Egypt. Its inhabitants are Bejás. These people are black-skinned; they wrap themselves in yellow blankets and tie headbands about a fingerbreadth wide round their heads. They do not give their daughters any share in their inheritance. They live on camels' milk and they ride on Mehárís [dromedaries]. One-third of the city belongs to the Sultan of Egypt and two-thirds to the King of the Bejás, who is called al-Hudrubí.[28] On reaching Aydháb we found that al-Hudrubí was engaged in warfare with the Turks [*i.e.* the troops of the Sultan of Egypt], that he had sunk the ships and that the Turks had fled before him. It was impossible for us to attempt the sea-crossing, so we sold the provisions that we had made ready for it, and returned to Qús with the Arabs from whom we had hired the camels. We sailed thence down the Nile (it was at the flood time) and after an eight days' journey reached Cairo, where I stayed only one night, and immediately set out for Syria. This was in the middle of July, 1326.

My route lay through Bilbays and as-Sálihíya, after which we entered the sands and halted at a number of stations. At each of these there was a hostelry, which they call a *khán*,[29] where travellers alight with their beasts. Each khán has a water wheel supplying a fountain and a shop at which the traveller buys what he requires for himself and his beast. At the station of Qatyá[30] customs-dues are collected from the merchants, and their goods and baggage are thoroughly examined and searched. There are offices here, with officers, clerks, and notaries, and the daily revenue is a thousand gold dinars. No one is allowed to pass into Syria without a passport from Egypt, nor into Egypt without a passport from Syria, for the protection of the property of the subjects and as a measure of precaution against spies from 'Iráq. The responsibility of guarding this road has been entrusted to the Badawin. At nightfall they smooth down the sand so that no track is left on it, then in the morning the governor comes and looks at the sand. If he finds any track on it he commands the Arabs to bring the person who made it, and they set out in pursuit and never fail to catch him. He is then brought to the governor, who punishes him as he sees fit. The governor at the time of my passage treated me as a guest and showed me great kindness, and allowed all those who were with me to pass. From here we went on to Gaza, which is the first city of Syria on the side next the Egyptian frontier.

From Gaza I travelled to the city of Abraham [Hebron], the mosque of which is of elegant, but substantial, construction, imposing and lofty, and built of squared stones. At one angle of it there is a stone, one of whose faces measures twenty-seven spans. It is said that Solomon commanded the *jinn*[31] to build it. Inside it is the sacred cave containing the graves of Abraham, Isaac, and Jacob, opposite which are three graves, which are those of their wives. I questioned the imám, a man of great piety and learning, on the authenticity of these graves, and he replied: "All the scholars whom I have met hold these graves to be the very graves of Abraham, Isaac, Jacob and their wives. No one questions this except introducers of false doctrines; it is a tradition which has passed from father to son for generations and admits of no doubt." This mosque contains also the grave of Joseph, and somewhat to the east of it lies the tomb of Lot,[32] which is surmounted by an elegant building. In the neighbourhood is Lot's lake [the Dead Sea], which is brackish and is said to cover the site of the settlements of Lot's people. On the way from Hebron to Jerusalem, I visited Bethlehem, the birthplace of Jesus. The site is covered by a large building; the Christians regard it with intense veneration and hospitably entertain all who alight at it.

We then reached Jerusalem (may God ennoble her!), third in excellence after the two holy shrines of Mecca and Madína, and the place whence the

Prophet was caught up into heaven.[33] Its walls were destroyed by the illustrious King Saladin and his successors,[34] for fear lest the Christians should seize it and fortify themselves in it. The sacred mosque is a most beautiful building, and is said to be the largest mosque in the world. Its length from east to west is put at 752 "royal" cubits[35] and its breadth at 435. On three sides it has many entrances, but on the south side I know of one only, which is that by which the imám enters. The entire mosque is an open court and unroofed, except the mosque al-Aqsá, which has a roof of most excellent workmanship, embellished with gold and brilliant colours. Some other parts of the mosque are roofed as well. The Dome of the Rock is a building of extraordinary beauty, solidity, elegance, and singularity of shape. It stands on an elevation in the centre of the mosque and is reached by a flight of marble steps. It has four doors. The space round it is also paved with marble, excellently done, and the interior likewise. Both outside and inside the decoration is so magnificent and the workmanship so surpassing as to defy description. The greater part is covered with gold so that the eyes of one who gazes on its beauties are dazzled by its brilliance, now glowing like a mass of light, now flashing like lightning. In the centre of the Dome is the blessed rock from which the Prophet ascended to heaven, a great rock projecting about a man's height, and underneath it there is a cave the size of a small room, also of a man's height, with steps leading down to it. Encircling the rock are two railings of excellent workmanship, the one nearer the rock being artistically constructed in iron,[36] and the other of wood.

Among the grace-bestowing sanctuaries of Jerusalem is a building, situated on the farther side of the valley called the valley of Jahannam [Gehenna] to the east of the town, on a high hill. This building is said to mark the place whence Jesus ascended to heaven.[37] In the bottom of the same valley is a church venerated by the Christians, who say that it contains the grave of Mary. In the same place there is another church which the Christians venerate and to which they come on pilgrimage. This is the church of which they are falsely persuaded to believe that it contains the grave of Jesus. All who come on pilgrimage to visit it pay a stipulated tax to the Muslims, and suffer very unwillingly various humiliations. Thereabouts also is the place of the cradle of Jesus,[38] which is visited in order to obtain blessing.

I journeyed thereafter from Jerusalem to the fortress of Askalon, which is a total ruin. Of the great mosque, known as the mosque of 'Omar, nothing remains but its walls and some marble columns of matchless beauty, partly standing and partly fallen. Amongst them is a wonderful red column, of which the people tell that the Christians carried it off to their country but afterwards lost it, when it was found in its place at Askalon. Thence I went on to the city of ar-Ramlah, which is also called Filastín [Palestine], in the *qibla* of those mosque they say three hundred of the prophets are buried. From ar-Ramlah I went to the town of Nábulus [Shechem], a city with an abundance of trees and perennial streams, and one of the richest in Syria for olives, the oil of which is exported thence to Cairo and Damascus. It is at Nábulus that the carob-sweet is manufactured and exported to Damascus and elsewhere. It is made in this way: the carobs are cooked and then pressed, the juice that runs out is gathered and the sweet is manufactured from it. The juice itself too is exported to Cairo and Damascus. Nábulus has also a species of melon which is called by its name, a good and delicious fruit. Thence I went to Ajalún[39] making in the direction of Ládhiqíya, and passing through the Ghawr, followed the coast to

'Akká [Acre], which is in ruins. Acre was formerly the capital and port of the country of the Franks in Syria, and rivalled Constantinople itself.

I went on from here to Súr [Tyre], which is a ruin, though there is outside it an inhabited village, most of whose population belong to the sect called "Refusers." It is this city of Tyre which has become proverbial for impregnability, because the sea surrounds it on three sides and it has two gates, one on the landward side and one to the sea. That on the landward side is protected by four outer walls each with breastworks, while the sea gate stands between two great towers. There is no more marvellous or more remarkable piece of masonry in the world than this, for the sea surrounds it on three sides and on the fourth there is a wall under which the ships pass and come to anchor. In former times an iron chain was stretched between the two towers to form a barrier, so that there was no way in or out until it was lowered. It was placed under the charge of guards and trustworthy agents, and none might enter or leave without their knowledge. Acre also had a harbour resembling it, but it admitted only small ships. From Tyre I went on to Saydá [Sidon], a pleasant town on the coast, and rich in fruit; it exports figs, raisins, and olive oil to Cairo.

Next I went on to the town of Tabaríya [Tiberias].[40] It was formerly a large and important city, of which nothing now remains but vestiges witnessing to its former greatness. It possesses wonderful baths with separate establishments for men and women, the water of which is very hot. At Tiberias is the famous lake [the Sea of Galilee], about eighteen miles long and more than nine in breadth. The town has a mosque known as the "Mosque of the Prophets," containing the graves of Shu'ayb [Jethro] and his daughter, the wife of Moses, as well as those of Solomon, Judah, and Reuben. From Tiberias we went to visit the well into which Joseph was cast, a large and deep well, in the courtyard of a small mosque, and drank some water from it. It was rain water, but the guardian told us that there is a spring in it as well. We went on from there to Bayrút, a small town with fine markets and a beautiful mosque. Fruit and iron are exported from it to Egypt.

We set out from here to visit the tomb of Abú Ya'qúb Yúsuf, who, they say, was a king in North-west Africa. The tomb is at a place called Karak Núh,[41] and beside it is a religious house at which all travellers are entertained. Some say that it was the Sultan Saladin who endowed it, others that it was the Sultan Núr ad-Dín. The story goes that Abú Ya'qúb, after staying some time at Damascus with the Sultan, who had been warned in a dream that Abú Ya'qúb would bring him some advantage, left the town in solitary flight during a season of great coldness, and came to a village in its neighbourhood. In this village there was a man of humble station who invited him to stay in his house, and on his consenting, made him soup and killed a chicken and brought it to him with barley bread. After his meal Abú Ya'qúb prayed for a blessing on his host. Now this man had several children, one of them being a girl who was shortly to be conducted to her husband. It is a custom in that country that a girl's father gives her an outfit, the greater part of which consists in copper utensils. These are regarded by them with great pride and are made the subject of special stipulations in the marriage contract. Abú Ya'qúb therefore said to the man, "Have you any copper utensils?" "Yes" he replied, "I have just bought some for my daughter's outfit." Abú Ya'qúb told him to bring them and when he had brought them said "Now borrow all that you can from your neighbours." So he did so and laid them all before him. He then lit fires round them, and taking out a purse which he had containing an elixir, threw some of it over the brass, and the whole array was changed into gold. Leaving these in a locked chamber, Abú Ya'qúb wrote to Núr ad-Dín at Damascus, telling him about them, and exhorting him to build and endow a hospital for sick strangers and to construct religious houses on the highways. He bade him also satisfy the owners of the copper vessels and provide for the maintenance of the owner of the house. The latter took the letter to the king, who came to the village and removed the gold, after satisfying the owners of the vessels and the man himself. He searched for Abú Ya'qúb, but failing to find any trace or news of him, returned to Damascus, where he built the hospital which is known by his name and is the finest in the world.

I came next to the city of Atrábulus [Tripoli], one of the principal towns in Syria. It lies two miles inland, and has only recently been built. The old town was right on the shore; the Christians held it for a time, and when it was recovered by Sultan Baybars[42] it was pulled down and this new town built. There are some fine bath-houses in it, one of which is called after Sindamúr, who was a former governor of the city. Many stories are told of his severity to evildoers. Here is one of them. A woman complained to him that one of the mamlúks of his personal staff had seized some milk that she was selling and had drunk it. She had no evidence, but Sindamúr sent for the man. He was cut in two, and the milk came out of his entrails. Similar stories are told of al-Atrís at the time when he was governor of Aydháb under Sultan Qalá'ún, and of Kebek, the Sultan of Turkestan.[43]

From Tripoli I went by way of Hisn al-Akrád [*Krak des Chevaliers*, now Qal'at al-Hisn] and Hims to Hamáh, another of the metropolitan cities of Syria. It is surrounded by orchards and gardens, in the midst of which there are waterwheels like revolving globes. Thence to Ma'arra, which lies in a district inhabited by some sort of Shi'ites, abominable people who hate the Ten Companions and every person whose name is 'Omar.[44] We went on from there to Sarmín, where brick soap is manufactured and exported to Cairo and Damascus. Besides this they manufacture perfumed soap, for washing hands, and colour it red and yellow. These people too are revilers, who hate the Ten, and—an extraordinary thing—never mention the word *ten*. When their brokers are selling by auction in the markets and come to ten, they say "nine and one." One day a Turk happened to be there, and hearing a broker call "nine and one," he laid his club about his head saying "Say 'ten,'" whereupon quoth he "Ten with the club." We journeyed thence to Halab [Aleppo],[45] which is the seat of the *Malik al-Umará*, who is the principal commander under the sultan of Egypt. He is a jurist and has a reputation for fair-dealing, but he is stingy.

I went on from there to Antákíya [Antioch], by way of Tízín, a new town founded by the Turkmens.[46] Antioch was protected formerly by a wall of unrivalled solidity among the cities of Syria, but al-Malik az-Záhir [Baybars] pulled it down when he captured the town.[47] It is very densely populated and possesses beautiful buildings, with abundant trees and water. Thence I visited the fortress of Baghrás,[48] at the entrance to the land of Sís [Little Armenia], that is, the land of the Armenian infidels, and many other castles and fortresses, several of which belong to a sect called Isma'ilites or Fidáwís[49] and may be entered by none but members of the sect. They are the arrows of the sultan; by means of them he strikes those of his enemies who escape into 'Iráq and other lands. They receive fixed salaries, and when the sultan desires to send one of them to assassinate one of his enemies, he pays him his blood-money. If after carrying out his allotted task he escapes with his life, the money is his, but if he is killed it goes to his sons. They carry poisoned daggers, with which they strike their victim, but sometimes their plans miscarry and they themselves are killed.

From the castles of the Fidáwis I went on to the town of Jabala, which lies on the coast, about a mile inland. It contains the grave of the famous saint Ibráhím ibn Adham, he who renounced a kingdom and consecrated himself to God.[50] All visitors to this grave give a candle to the keeper, with the result that many hundredweights of them are collected. The majority of the people of this coastal district belong to the sect of the Nusayris, who believe that 'Alí[51] is a God. They do not pray, nor do they purify themselves, nor fast. Al-Malik az-Záhir [Baybars] compelled them to build mosques in their villages, so in every village they put up a mosque far away from their houses, and they neither enter them nor keep them in repair. Often they are used for refuges for their cattle and asses. Often too a stranger comes to their country and he stops at the mosque and recites the call to prayer and then they call out "Stop braying; your fodder is coming to you." There are a great many of these people.

They tell a story that an unknown person arrived in the country of this sect and gave himself out as the Mahdí. They flocked round him, and he promised them the possession of the land and divided Syria up between them. He used to nominate them each to a town and tell them to go there, giving them olive-leaves and saying "Take these as tokens of success, for they are as warrants of your appointment." When any one of them came to a town, the governor sent for him, and the man would say " The Imám al-Mahdí has given me this town." The governor would reply " Where is your warrant ?" and he would produce the olive-leaves, and be punished and put in prison. Later on he ordered them to make ready to fight with the Muslims and to begin with the town of Jabala. He told them to take myrtle rods instead of swords and promised them that these would become swords in their hands at the moment of the battle. They made a surprise attack on Jabala while the inhabitants were attending a Friday service in the mosque, and entered the houses and dishonoured the women. The Muslims came rushing out of their mosque, seized weapons, and killed them as they pleased. When the news was brought to Ládhiqíya the governor moved out with his troops, and the news having been sent by carrier-pigeons to Tripoli, the chief commandant joined him with his troops. The Nusayris were pursued until about twenty thousand of them had been killed. The remainder fortified themselves in the hills and sent a message to the chief commandant, undertaking to pay him one dinar per head if he would spare them. The news had been sent by pigeons to the Sultan, who replied ordering them to be put to the sword. The chief commandant, however, represented to him that these people were tillers of the soil for the Muslims and that if they were killed the Muslims would suffer in consequence, so their lives were spared.

I went next to the town of Ládhiqíya [Latakia]. In the outskirts is a Christian monastery known as Dayr al-Fárús, which is the largest monastery in Syria and Egypt. It is inhabited by monks, and Christians visit it from all quarters. All who stop there, Muslims or Christians, are entertained; their food is bread, cheese, olives, vinegar and capers. The harbour of Ládhiqíya is protected by a chain between two towers, so that no ship can either enter or leave it until the chain is lowered for it. It is one of the best harbours in Syria. From there I went to the fortress of al-Marqab [Belvedere], a great fortress resembling Karak. It is built on a high hill and outside it is a suburb where strangers stop. They are not allowed to enter the castle. It was captured from the Christians by al-Malik al-Mansúr Qalá'ún, and close by it was born his son al-Malik an-Násir [the reigning sultan of Egypt]. Thence I went to the mountain of al-Aqra', which is the highest mountain in Syria, and the first part of the country visible from the sea. The inhabitants of this mountain-range are Turkmens, and it contains springs and running streams. I went on from there to the mountains of Lubnán [Lebanon]. These are among the most fertile mountains on earth, with all sorts of fruits and springs of water and shady coverts. There are always large numbers of devotees and ascetics to be found in these mountains (the place is noted for this) and I saw a company of anchorites there.

We came next to the town of Ba'albek, an old town and one of the finest in Syria, rivalling Damascus in its innumerable amenities. No other district has such an abundance of cherries, and many kinds of sweetmeats are manufactured in it, as well as textiles, and wooden vessels and spoons that cannot be equalled elsewhere. They make a series of plates one within the other to as many as ten in all, yet anyone looking at it would take them to be one plate. They do the same with spoons, and put them in a leather case. A man can carry this in his belt, and on joining in a meal with his friends take out what looks like one spoon and distribute nine others from within it. Ba'albek is one day's journey from Damascus by hard going; caravans on leaving Ba'albek spend a night at a small village called az-Zabdání and go on to Damascus the following morning. I reached Ba'albek in the

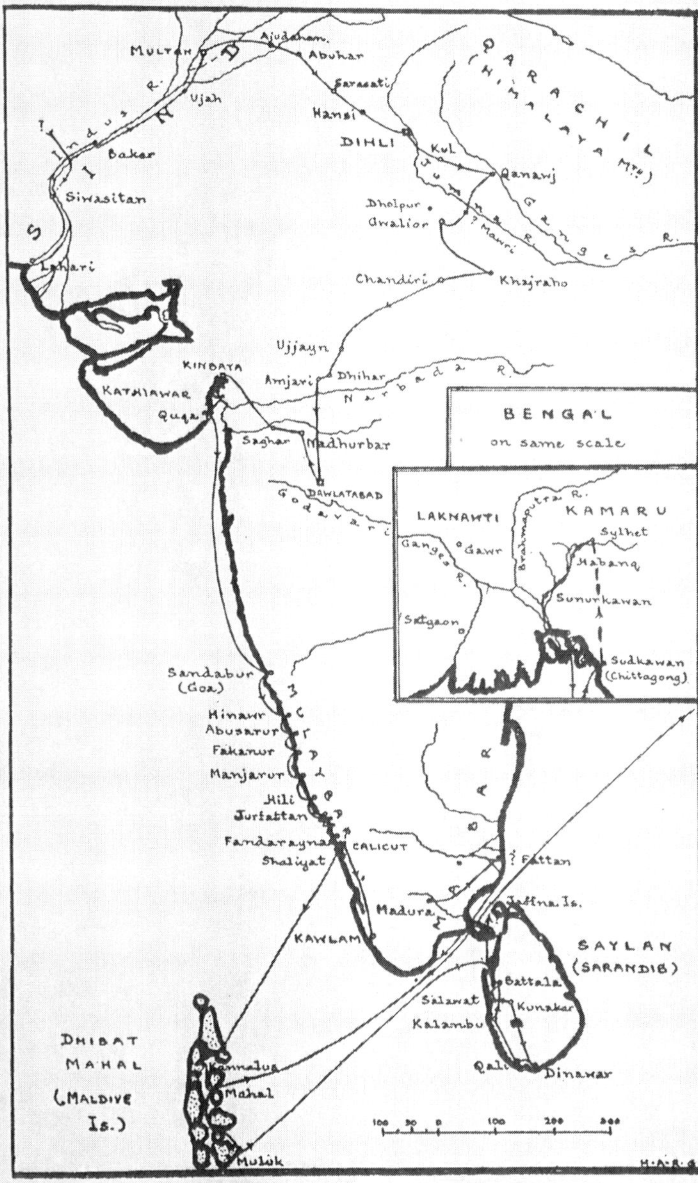

SKETCH MAP OF INDIA TO ILLUSTRATE IBN BATTŪTA'S TRAVELS

[*face p. 184*

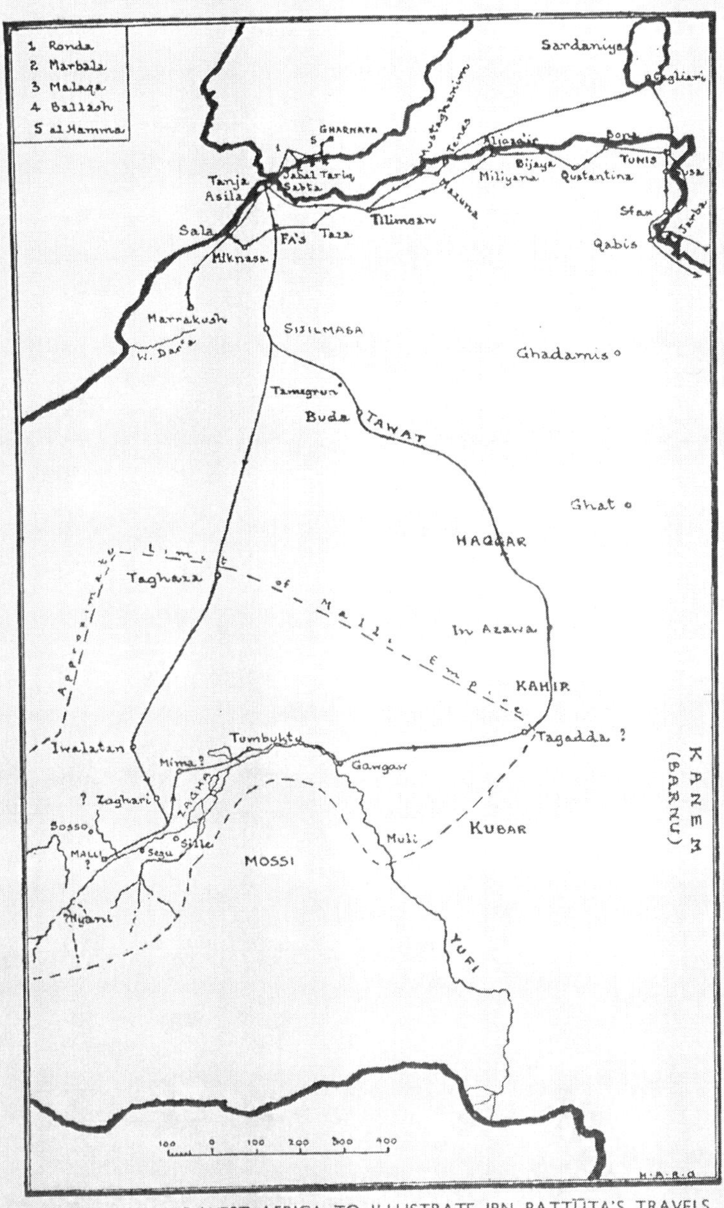

SKETCH MAP OF WEST AFRICA TO ILLUSTRATE IBN BATTŪTA'S TRAVELS

[face p. 310

evening and left it next morning because of my eagerness to get to Damascus.

I entered Damascus on Thursday 9th Ramadán 726 [9th August, 1326], and lodged at the Málikite college called ash-Sharábishíya. Damascus surpasses all other cities in beauty, and no description, however full, can do justice to its charms. Nothing, however, can better the words of Ibn Jubayr in describing it.[52] The Cathedral Mosque, known as the Umayyad Mosque, is the most magnificent mosque in the world, the finest in construction and noblest in beauty, grace and perfection; it is matchless and unequalled. The person who undertook its construction was the Caliph Walíd I. [705-715]. He applied to the Roman Emperor at Constantinople ordering him to send craftsmen to him, and the Emperor sent him twelve thousand of them. The site of the mosque was a church, and when the Muslims captured Damascus, one of their commanders entered from one side by the sword and reached as far as the middle of the church, while the other entered peaceably from the eastern side and reached the middle also. So the Muslims made the half of the church which they had entered by force into a mosque and the half which they had entered by peaceful agreement remained as a church. When Walíd decided to extend the mosque over the entire church he asked the Greeks to sell him their church for whatsoever equivalent they desired, but they refused, so he seized it. The Christians used to say that whoever destroyed the church would be stricken with madness and they told that to Walíd. But he replied "I shall be the first to be stricken by madness in the service of God," and seizing an axe, he set to work to knock it down with his own hands. The Muslims on seeing that followed his example, and God proved false the assertion of the Christians.[53]

This mosque has four doors. The southern door, called the "Door of Increase," is approached by a spacious passage where the dealers in second-hand goods and other commodities have their shops. Through it lies the way to the [former] Cavalry House, and on the left as one emerges from it is the coppersmiths' gallery, a large bazaar, one of the finest in Damascus, extending along the south wall of the mosque. This bazaar occupies the site of the palace of the Caliph Mu'áwiya I.,[54] which was called al-Khadrá [The Green Palace]; the 'Abbásids pulled it down and a bazaar took its place. The eastern door, called the Jayrún door, is the largest of the doors of the mosque. It also has a large passage, leading out to a large and extensive colonnade which is entered through a quintuple gateway between six tall columns. Along both sides of this passage are pillars, supporting circular galleries, where the cloth merchants amongst others have their shops; above these again are long galleries in which are the shops of the jewellers and booksellers and makers of admirable glass-ware. In the square adjoining the first door are the stalls of the principal notaries, in each of which there may be five or six witnesses in attendance and a person authorized by the qádí to perform marriage-ceremonies. The other notaries are scattered throughout the city. Near these stalls is the bazaar of the stationers, who sell paper, pens, and ink. In the middle of the passage there is a large round marble basin, surrounded by a pavilion supported on marble columns but lacking a roof. In the centre of the basin is a copper pipe which forces out water under pressure so that it rises into the air more than a man's height. They call it "The Waterspout," and it is a fine sight. To the right as one comes out of the Jayrún door, which is called also the "Door of the Hours," is an upper gallery shaped like a large arch, within which there are small open arches furnished with doors, to the number of the hours of the day. These doors are painted green on the inside and yellow on the outside, and as each hour of the day passes the green inner side of the door is turned to the outside, and vice versa. They say that inside the gallery there is a person in the room who is responsible for turning them by hand as the hours pass.[56] The western door is called the "Door of the Post"; the passage outside it contains the shops of the candlemakers and a gallery for the sale of fruit. The northern door is called the "Door of the Confectioners"; it too has a large passageway, and on the right as one leaves it is a *khánqáh*, which has a large basin of water in the centre and lavatories supplied with running water. At each of the four doors of the mosque is a building for ritual ablutions, containing about a hundred rooms abundantly supplied with running water.

One of the principal Hanbalite doctors at Damascus was Taqí ad-Dín Ibn Taymíya, a man of great ability and wide learning, but with some kink in his brain. The people of Damascus idolized him. He used to preach to them from the pulpit, and one day he made some statement that the other theologians disapproved; they carried the case to the sultan and in consequence Ibn Taymíya was imprisoned for some years. While he was in prison he wrote a commentary on the Koran, which he called "The Ocean," in about forty volumes. Later on his mother presented herself before the sultan and interceded for him, so he was set at liberty, until he did the same thing again. I was in Damascus at the time and attended the service which he was conducting one Friday, as he was addressing and admonishing the people from the pulpit. In the midst of his discourse he said "Verily God descends to the sky over our world [from Heaven] in the same bodily fashion that

I make this descent," and stepped down one step of the pulpit. A Málikite doctor present contradicted him and objected to his statement,[56] but the common people rose up against this doctor, and beat him with their hands and their shoes so severely that his turban fell off and disclosed a silken skull-cap on his head. Inveighing against him for wearing this,[57] they haled him before the qádí of the Hanbalites, who ordered him to be imprisoned and afterwards had him beaten. The other doctors objected to this treatment and carried the matter before the principal amír, who wrote to the sultan about the matter and at the same time drew up a legal attestation against Ibn Taymíya for various heretical pronouncements. This deed was sent on to the sultan, who gave orders that Ibn Taymíya should be imprisoned in the citadel, and there he remained until his death.[58]

One of the celebrated sanctuaries at Damascus is the Mosque of the Footprints (al-Aqdám), which lies two miles south of the city, alongside the main highway which leads to the Hijáz, Jerusalem, and Egypt. It is a large mosque, very blessed, richly endowed, and very highly venerated by the Damascenes. The footprints from which it derives its name are certain footprints impressed upon a rock there, which are said to be the mark of Moses' foot. In this mosque there is a small chamber containing a stone with the following inscription "A certain pious man saw in his sleep the Chosen One [Muhammad], who said to him 'Here is the grave of my brother Moses.'" I saw a remarkable instance of the veneration in which the Damascenes hold this mosque during the great pestilence, on my return journey through Damascus in the latter part of July 1348. The viceroy Arghún Sháh ordered a crier to proclaim through Damascus that all the people should fast for three days and that no one should cook anything eatable in the market during the daytime.[59] For most of the people there eat no food but what has been prepared in the market.[60] So the people fasted for three successive days, the last of which was a Thursday, then they assembled in the Great Mosque, amírs, sharífs, qádís, theologians, and all the other classes of the people, until the place was filled to overflowing, and there they spent the Thursday night in prayers and litanies. After the dawn prayer next morning they all went out together on foot, holding Korans in their hands, and the amírs barefooted. The procession was joined by the entire population of the town, men and women, small and large; the Jews came with their Book of the Law and the Christians with their Gospel, all of them with their women and children. The whole concourse, weeping and supplicating and seeking the favour of God through His Books and His Prophets, made their way to the Mosque of the Footprints, and there they remained in supplication and invocation until near midday. They then returned to the city and held the Friday service, and God lightened their affliction; for the number of deaths in a single day at Damascus did not attain two thousand, while in Cairo and Old Cairo it reached the figure of twenty-four thousand a day.

The variety and expenditure of the religious endowments at Damascus are beyond computation. There are endowments in aid of persons who cannot undertake the pilgrimage to Mecca, out of which are paid the expenses of those who go in their stead. There are other endowments for supplying wedding outfits to girls whose families are unable to provide them, and others for the freeing of prisoners. There are endowments for travellers, out of the revenues of which they are given food, clothing, and the expenses of conveyance to their countries. Then there are endowments for the improvement and paving of the streets, because all the lanes in Damascus have pavements on either side, on which the foot passengers walk, while those who ride use the roadway in the centre. Besides these there are endowments for other charitable purposes. One day as I went along a lane in Damascus I saw a small slave who had dropped a Chinese porcelain dish, which was broken to bits. A number of people collected round him and one of them said to him, "Gather up the pieces and take them to the custodian of the endowments for utensils." He did so, and the man went with him to the custodian, where the slave showed the broken pieces and received a sum sufficient to buy a similar dish. This is an excellent institution, for the master of the slave would undoubtedly have beaten him, or at least scolded him, for breaking the dish, and the slave would have been heartbroken and upset at the accident. This benefaction is indeed a mender of hearts—may God richly reward him whose zeal for good works rose to such heights!

The people of Damascus vie with one another in building mosques, religious houses, colleges and mausoleums. They have a high opinion of the North Africans, and freely entrust them with the care of their moneys, wives, and children. All strangers amongst them are handsomely treated, and care is taken that they are not forced to any action that might injure their self-respect. When I came to Damascus a firm friendship sprang up between the Málikite professor Núr ad-Dín Sakháwí and me, and he besought me to breakfast at his house during the nights of Ramadán. After I had visited him for four nights I had a stroke of fever and absented myself. He sent in search of me, and although I pleaded my illness in excuse he refused to accept it. I went back to his house and spent the night there, and when I desired to take my leave the next morning he would not hear of it, but said to me "Consider my house as your own or as your father's or brother's." He then had a doctor sent for, and gave orders that all the medicines and dishes that the doctor prescribed were to be made for me in his house. I stayed thus with him until the Fast-breaking, when I went to the festival prayers and God healed me of what had befallen me. Meanwhile all the money I had for my expenses was exhausted. Núr ad-Dín, learning this, hired camels for me and gave me travelling and other provisions, and money in addition, saying "It will come in for any serious matter that may land you in difficulties"—may God reward him!

The Damascenes observe an admirable order in funeral processions. They walk in front of the bier, while reciters intone the Koran in beautiful and affecting voices, and pray over it in the Cathedral mosque. When the reading is completed the muezzins rise and say "Reflect on your prayer for so-and-so, the pious and learned," describing him with good epithets, and having prayed over him they take him to his grave. The Indians have a funeral ceremony even more admirable than this. On the morning of the third day after the burial they assemble in the burial-place of the deceased, which is spread with fine cloths, the grave being covered with magnificent hangings and surrounded by sweet-scented flowers, roses, eglantine, and jasmine, for these flowers are perennial with them. They bring lemon and citrus trees as well, tying on their fruits if they have none, and put up an awning to shade the mourning party. The qádís, amírs and other persons of rank come and take their seats, and after recitation of the Koran, the qádí rises and delivers a set oration, speaking of the deceased, and mourning his death in an elegiac ode, then comforting his relatives, and praying for the sultan. When the sultan's name is mentioned the audience rise and bow their heads towards the quarter in which the sultan is. The qádí then resumes his seat, and rose-water is brought in and sprinkled on all the people, beginning with the qádí. After this syrup is brought in and served to everyone, beginning with the qádí. Finally the betel is brought. This they hold in high esteem, and give to their guests as a mark of respect; a gift of betel from the sultan is a greater honour than a gift of money or robes of honour. When a man dies his family eat no betel until the day of this ceremony, when the qádí takes some leaves of it and gives them to the heir of the deceased, who eats them, after which the party disperses.

When the new moon of the month Shawwál appeared in the same year [1st September 1326], the Hijáz caravan left Damascus and I set off along with it.[61] At Bosra the caravans usually halt for four days so that any who have been detained at Damascus by business affairs may make up on them. Thence they go to the Pool of Zíza, where they stop for a day, and then through al-Lajjún to the Castle of Karak. Karak, which is also called " The Castle of the Raven," is one of the most marvellous, impregnable, and celebrated of fortresses. It is surrounded on all sides by the river-bed, and has but one gate, the entrance to which is hewn in the living rock, as also is the approach to its vestibule. This fortress is used by kings as a place of refuge in times of calamity, as the sultan an-Násir did when his mamlúk Salár seized the supreme authority. The caravan stopped for four days at a place called ath-Thaníya outside Karak, where preparations were made for entering the desert. Thence we journeyed to Ma'án, which is the last town in Syria, and from 'Aqabat as-Sawán entered the desert, of which the saying goes: " He who enters it is lost, and he who leaves it is born." After a march of two days we halted at Dhát Hajj, where there are subterranean waterbeds but no habitations, and then went on to Wádí Baldah (in which there is no water)[62] and to Tabúk, which is the place to which the Prophet led an expedition. The Syrian pilgrims have a custom that, on reaching the camp at Tabúk, they take their weapons, unsheathe their swords, and charge upon the camp, striking the palms with their swords and saying "Thus did the Prophet of God enter it." The great caravan halts at Tabúk for four days to rest and to water the camels and lay in water for the terrible desert between Tabúk and al-'Ulá. The custom of the water-carriers is to camp beside the spring, and they have tanks made of buffalo hides, like great cisterns, from which they water the camels and fill the waterskins. Each amír or person of rank has a special tank for the needs of his own camels and personnel; the other people make private agreements with the watercarriers to water their camels and fill their waterskins for a fixed sum of money.

From Tabúk the caravan travels with great speed night and day, for fear of this desert. Halfway through is the valley of al-Ukhaydir, which might well be the valley of Hell (may God preserve us from it).[63] One year the pilgrims suffered terribly here from the samoom-wind; the water-supplies dried up and the price of a single drink rose to a thousand dinars, but both seller and buyer perished. Their story is written on a rock in the valley. Five days after leaving Tabúk they reach the well of al-Hijr, which has an abundance of water, but not a soul draws water there, however violent his thirst, following the example of the Prophet, who passed it on his expedition to Tabúk and drove on his camel, giving orders that none should drink of its waters. Here, in some hills of red rock, are the dwellings of Thamúd. They are cut in the rock and have carved thresholds. Anyone seeing them would take them to be of recent construction. Their decayed bones are to be seen inside these houses.[64] Al-'Ulá, a large and pleasant village with palm-gardens and water-springs, lies half a day's journey or less from al-Hijr.[65] The pilgrims halt there four days to provision themselves and wash their clothes. They leave behind them here any surplus of provisions they may have, taking with them nothing but what is strictly necessary. The people of the village are very trustworthy. The Christian merchants of Syria may come as far as this and no further, and they trade in provisions and other goods with the pilgrims here. On the third day after leaving al-'Ulá the caravan halts in the outskirts of the holy city of Madína.

That same evening we entered the holy sanctuary and reached the illustrious mosque, halting in salutation at the Gate of Peace; then we prayed in the illustrious "garden" between the tomb of the Prophet and the noble pulpit, and reverently touched the fragment that remains of the palm-trunk against which the Prophet stood when he preached. Having paid our meed of salutation to the lord of men from first to last, the intercessor for sinners, the Prophet of Mecca, Muhammad, as well as to his two companions who share his grave, Abú Bakr and 'Omar, we returned to our camp, rejoicing at this great favour bestowed upon us, praising God for our having reached the former abodes and the magnificent sanctuaries of His holy Prophet, and praying Him to grant that this visit should not be our last, and that we might be of those whose pilgrimage is accepted. On this journey our stay at Madína lasted four days. We used to spend every night in the illustrious mosque, where the people, after forming circles in the courtyard and lighting large numbers of candles, would pass the time either in reciting the Koran from volumes set on rests in front of them, or in intoning litanies, or in visiting the sanctuaries of the holy tomb.

We then set out from Madína towards Mecca, and halted near the mosque of Dhu'l-Hulayfa, five miles away. It was at this point that the Prophet assumed the pilgrim garb and obligations, and here too I divested myself of my tailored clothes, bathed, and putting on the pilgrim's garment I prayed and dedicated myself to the pilgrimage. Our fourth halt from here was at Badr, where God aided His Prophet and performed His promise.[66] It is a village containing a series of palm-gardens and a bubbling spring with a stream flowing from it. Our way lay thence through a frightful desert called the Vale of Bazwá for three days to the valley of Rábigh, where the rainwater forms pools which lie stagnant for a long time. From this point (which is just before Juhfa) the pilgrims from Egypt and Northwest Africa put on the pilgrim garment. Three days after leaving Rábigh we reached the pool of Khulays, which lies in a plain and has many palm-gardens. The Badawin of that neighbourhood hold a market there, to which they bring sheep, fruits, and condiments. Thence we travelled through 'Usfán to the Bottom of Marr,[67] a fertile valley with numerous palms and a spring supplying a stream from which the district is irrigated. From this valley fruit and vegetables are transported to Mecca. We set out at night from this blessed valley, with hearts full of joy at reaching the goal of our hopes, and in the morning arrived at the City of Surety, Mecca (may God ennoble her!), where we immediately entered the holy sanctuary and began the rites of pilgrimage.[68]

The inhabitants of Mecca are distinguished by many excellent and noble activities and qualities, by their beneficence to the humble and weak, and by their kindness to strangers. When any of them makes a feast, he begins by giving food to the religious devotees who are poor and without resources, inviting them first with kindness and delicacy. The majority of these unfortunates are to be found by the public bake-houses, and when anyone has his bread baked and takes it away to his house, they follow him and he gives each one of them some share of it, sending away none disappointed. Even if he has but a single loaf, he gives away a third or a half of it, cheerfully and without any grudgingness. Another good habit of theirs is this. The orphan children sit in the bazaar, each with two baskets, one large and one small. When one of the townspeople comes to the bazaar and buys cereals, meat and vegetables, he hands them to one of these boys, who puts the cereals in one basket and the meat and vegetables in the other and takes them to the man's house, so that his meal may be prepared. Meanwhile the man goes about his devotions and his business. There is no instance of any of the boys having ever abused their trust in this matter, and they are given a fixed fee of a few coppers. The Meccans are very elegant and clean in their dress, and most of them wear white garments, which you always see fresh and snowy. They use a great deal of perfume and kohl and make free use of toothpicks of green arák-wood. The Meccan women are extraordinarily beautiful and very pious and modest. They too make great use of perfumes to such a degree that they will spend the night hungry in order to buy perfumes with the price of their food. They visit the mosque every Thursday night, wearing their finest apparel; and the whole sanctuary is saturated with the smell of their perfume. When one of these women goes away the odour of the perfume clings to the place after she has gone.

Among the personages who were living in religious retirement at Mecca was a pious and ascetic doctor who had a long-standing friendship with my father, and used to stay with us when he came to our town of

Tangier. In the daytime he taught at the Muzaffaríya college, but at night he retired to his dwelling in the convent of Rabí'. This convent is one of the finest in Mecca; it has in its precincts a well of sweet water which has no equal in Mecca, and its inhabitants are all men of great piety. It is highly venerated by the people of the Hijáz, who bring votive offerings to it, and the people of Tá'if supply it with fruit. Their custom is that all those who possess a palm garden, or orchard of vines, peaches or figs, give the alms-tithe from its produce to this convent, and fetch it on their own camels. It is two days' journey from Tá'if to Mecca. If any person fails to do this, his crop is diminished and dearth-stricken in the following year. One day the retainers of the governor of Mecca came to this convent, led in the governor's horses, and watered them at the well mentioned above. After the horses had been taken back to their stables, they were seized with colic and threw themselves to the ground, beating it with their heads and legs. On hearing of this the governor went in person to the gate of the convent and after apologizing to the poor recluses there, took one of them back with him. This man rubbed the beasts' bellies with his hand, when they expelled all the water that they had drunk, and were cured. After that the retainers never presented themselves at the convent except for good purposes.

CHAPTER II

On the 17th of November I left Mecca with the commander of the 'Iráq caravan, who hired for me at his own expense the half of a camel-litter as far as Baghdád, and took me under his protection. After the farewell ceremony of circumambulation [of the Ka'ba] we moved out to the Bottom of Marr with an innumerable host of pilgrims from 'Iráq, Khurásán, Fárs and other eastern lands, so many that the earth surged with them like the sea and their march resembled the movement of a high-piled cloud. Any person who left the caravan for a moment and had no mark to guide him to his place could not find it again because of the multitude of people. With this caravan there were many draught-camels for supplying the poorer pilgrims with water, and other camels to carry the provisions issued as alms and the medicines, potions, and sugar required for any who fell ill. Whenever the caravan halted food was cooked in great brass cauldrons, and from these the needs of the poorer pilgrims and those who had no provisions were supplied. A number of spare camels accompanied it to carry those who were unable to walk. All those measures were due to the benefactions and generosity of the sultan [of 'Iráq] Abú Sa'íd. Besides this the caravan included busy bazaars and many commodities and all sorts of food and fruit. They used to march during the night and light torches in front of the files of camels and litters, so that you saw the country gleaming with light and the darkness turned into day.

We returned through Khulays and Badr to Madína, and were privileged to visit once more the [tomb of the] Prophet. We stayed in Madína for six days, and having provided ourselves there with water for a three-nights' journey, set out and halted on the third night at Wádi'l-'Arús, where we drew supplies of water from underground water-beds. They dig down into the ground for them and procure sweet running water. On leaving Wádi'l-'Arús we entered the land of Najd, which is a level stretch of country extending as far as eye can see, and we inhaled its fine scented air. After four marches we halted at a waterpoint called al-'Usayla, then resumed our march and halted at a waterpoint called an-Naqira, where there are the remains of watertanks like vast reservoirs. Thence we journeyed to a waterpoint known as al-Qárúra, which consists of tanks filled with rainwater. These are some of the tanks which were constructed by Zubayda, the daughter of Ja'far. Every tank, water-basin, and well on this road between Mecca and Baghdád is a noble monument to her memory—may God give her richest reward! This locality is in the centre of the district of Najd; it is spacious, with fine healthy air, excellent soil, and a temperate climate at all seasons of the year. We went on from al-Qárúra and halted at al-Hájir, where there are watertanks which often dry up, so that temporary wells must be dug in order to procure water. We journeyed on and halted at Samíra, which is a patch of low-lying country on a plain, where there is a kind of fortified enceinte which is inhabited. It has plenty of water in wells, but brackish. The Badawin of that district come there with sheep, melted butter, and milk, which they sell to the pilgrims for pieces of coarse cotton cloth. That is the only thing they will take in exchange. We set out again and halted at the "Hill with the Hole." This hill lies in a tract of desert land, and has at the top of it a hole through which the wind whistles. We went on from there to Wádi'l-Kurúsh, which has no water, and after a night march came in the morning to the castle of Fayd.[1]

Fayd is a large walled and fortified enceinte on a level plain, with a suburb inhabited by Arabs, who make a living by trading with the pilgrims. On their journey to Mecca the pilgrims leave a portion of their provisions here, and pick them up again on their return journey.[2] Fayd lies halfway between Mecca and Baghdád and is twelve days' journey from Kúfa, by an easy road furnished with supplies of water in tanks. The pilgrims are accustomed to enter this place armed and in warlike array, in order to frighten the Arabs who collect there and to cut short their greedy designs on the caravan. We met there the two amírs of the Arabs, Fayyádh and Hiyár, sons of the amír Muhanná b. 'Ísá, accompanied by an innumerable troop of Arab horsemen and foot-soldiers. They showed great zeal for the safety of the pilgrims and their encampments. The Arabs brought camels and sheep, and the pilgrims bought from them what they could.

We resumed our journey through al-Ajfur, Zarúd, and other halting-places to the defile known as "Devil's Pass." We encamped below it [for the night] and traversed it the next day. This is the only rough and difficult stretch on the whole road, and even it is neither difficult nor long. Our next halt was at a place called Wáqisa, where there is a large castle and watertanks. It is inhabited by Arabs, and is the last watering point on this road; from there on to Kúfa there is no other watering place of any note except streams deriving from the Euphrates. Many of the people of Kúfa come out to Wáqisa to meet the pilgrims, bringing flour, bread, dates and fruit, and everybody exchanges greetings with everybody else. Our next halts were at a place called Lawza, where there is a large tank of water; then a place called al-Masájid [The Mosques], where there are three tanks; and after that at a place called Manárat al-qurún [The Minaret of the Horns], which is a tower standing in a desert locality, conspicuous for its height, and decorated at the top with horns of gazelles, but there are no dwellings near it. We halted again in a fertile valley called al-'Udhayb, and afterwards at al-Qádisíya, where the famous battle was fought against the Persians, in which God manifested the triumph of the Religion of Islam. There are palm-gardens and a watercourse from the Euphrates there.[3]

We went on from there and alighted in the town of Mash-had 'Alí at Najaf. It is a fine town, situated in a wide rocky plain—one of the finest, most populous, and most substantially built cities in 'Iráq. It has beautiful clean bazaars. We entered by the [outer] Báb al-Hadra, and found ourselves first in the market of the greengrocers, cooks, and butchers, then in the fruit market, then the tailors' bazaar and the *Qaysaríya*, then the perfumers' bazaar, after which we came to the [inner] Báb al-Hadra, where there is the tomb, which they say is the tomb of 'Alí.[4] One goes through the Báb al-Hadra into a vast hospice, by which one gains access to the gateway of the shrine, where there are chamberlains, keepers of registers and eunuchs. As a visitor to the tomb approaches, one or all of them rise to meet him according to his rank, and they halt with him at the threshold. They then ask permission for him to enter saying "By your leave, O Commander of the Faithful, this feeble creature asks permission to enter the sublime resting-place," and command him to kiss the threshold, which is of silver, as also are the lintels. After this he enters the shrine, the floor of which is covered with carpets of silk and other materials. Inside it are candelabra of gold and silver, large and small. In the centre is a square platform about a man's height, covered with wood completely hidden under artistically carved plaques of gold fastened with silver nails. On this are three tombs, which they declare are the graves of Adam, Noah, and 'Alí. Between the tombs are dishes of silver and gold, containing rose-water, musk, and other perfumes; the visitor dips his hand in these and anoints his face with the perfume for a blessing. The shrine has another doorway, also with a silver threshold and hangings of coloured silk, which opens into a mosque. The inhabitants of the town are all Shi'ites, and at this mausoleum many miracles are performed, which they regard as substantiating its claim to be the tomb of 'Alí. One of these miracles is that on the eve of the 27th Rajab[6] cripples from the two 'Iráqs, Khurásán, Persia and Anatolia, numbering about thirty or forty in all, are brought here and placed on the holy tomb. Those present await their arising and pass the time in prayer, or reciting litanies, or reading the Koran or contemplating the tomb. When the night is half or two-thirds over or so, they all rise completely cured, saying "There is no God but God; Muhammad is the Prophet of God and 'Alí is the Friend of God." This fact is widely known among them, and I heard of it from trustworthy authorities, but I was not actually present on any such night. I saw however three cripples in the Guests' College and asked them about themselves, and they told me that they had missed the night and were waiting for it in a future year. This town pays no taxes or dues and has no governor, but is under the sole control of the Naqíb al-Ashráf [Keeper of the Register of the descendants of the Prophet]. Its people are traders of great enterprise, brave and generous and excellent company on a journey, but they are fanatical about 'Alí. If any of them suffers from illness in the head, hand, foot, or other part of the body, he makes a model of the member in gold or silver and brings it to the sanctuary. The treasury of the sanctuary is considerable and contains innumerable riches. The Naqíb al-Ashráf holds a high position at the court. When he travels he has the same retinue and status as the principal military officers, with banners and kettledrums. Military music is played at his gate every evening and morning. Before the present holder of the office it was held jointly by a number of persons, who took turns of duty as governor.

One of these personages was the Sharíf Abú Ghurra. In his youth he was given over to devotions and study, but after his appointment as Naqíb al-Ashráf he was overcome by the world, gave up his ascetic habits, and administered his finances corruptly. The matter was brought before the sultan, and Abú Ghurra, on hearing of this, went to Khurásán and thence made for India. After crossing the Indus, he had his drums beaten and his trumpets blown, and thereby terrified the villagers, who, imagining that the Tatars had come to raid their country, fled to the city of Ūja [Uch] and informed its governor of what they had heard. He rode out with his troops and prepared for battle, when the scouts whom he had sent out saw only about ten horsemen and a number of men on foot and merchants who had accompanied the Sharíf, carrying banners and kettledrums. They asked them what they were doing and received the reply that the Sharíf, the Naqíb of 'Iráq, had come on a mission to the king of India. The scouts returned with the news to the governor, who thought that the Sharíf must be a man of little sense to raise banners and beat drums outside his own country. The Sharíf stayed for some time at Ūja, and every morning and evening he had the drums beaten at the door of his house, for that used to give him much gratification. It is said that when the drums were beaten before him in 'Iráq, as the drummer finished beating he would say to him "One more roll, drummer," until these words stuck to him as a nickname. The governor of Ūja wrote to the king of India about the Sharíf and his drum-beating, both on his journey and before his house morning and evening, as well as flying banners. Now the custom in India is that no person is entitled to use banners and drums except by special privilege from the king, and even then only while travelling. At rest no drums are beaten except before the king's house alone. In Egypt, Syria and 'Iráq, on the other hand, drums are beaten before the houses of the military governors. The king was therefore displeased and annoyed at the Sharíf's action. Now it happened that as the Sharíf approached the capital, with his drums beating as usual, suddenly he met the sultan, with his cortege on his way to meet the amír of Sind. The Sharíf went forward to the sultan to greet him, and the sultan, after asking how he was and why he had come and hearing his answers, went on to meet the amír, and returned to the capital, without paying the slightest attention to the Sharíf or giving orders for his lodging or anything else. He was then on the point of setting out for Dawlat Ábád, and before going he sent the Sharíf 500 dinars (which equal 125 of our Moroccan dinars) and said to the messenger: "Tell him that if he wants to go back to his country, this is his travelling provision, and if he wants to come with us it is for his expenses on the journey, but if he prefers to stay in the capital it is for his expenses until we return." The Sharíf was vexed at this for he was desirous that the sultan should make as rich presents to him as he usually did to his equals. He chose to travel with the sultan and attached himself to the wazír, who came to regard him with affection, and so used his influence with the king that he formed a high opinion of him, and assigned him two villages in the district of Dawlat Ábád, with the order to reside in them. For eight years the Sharíf stayed there, collecting the revenue of these two villages, and amassed considerable wealth. Thereupon he wanted to leave the country but could not, since those who are in the king's service are not allowed to leave without his permission, and he is much attached to strangers and rarely gives any of them leave. The Sharíf tried to escape by the coast road, but was turned back; then he went to the capital and by the wazír's good offices received the sultan's permission to leave India, together with a gift of 10,000 Indian dinars. The money was given him in a sack, and he used to sleep on it, out of his love of money, and fear lest some of it should get to any of his companions. As a result of sleeping on it he developed a pain in his side as he was just about to start on his journey, and eventually he died twenty days after receiving the sack. He bequeathed the money to the Sharíf Hasan al-Jaráni, who distributed the whole amount in alms to the Shi'ites living in Delhi. The Indians do not sequestrate inheritances for the treasury, and do not interfere with the property of strangers nor even make enquiries about it, however much it may be. In the same way, the negroes never interfere with the property of a white man, but it is left in charge of the principal members of his company until the rightful heir comes to claim it.

After our visit to the tomb of the Caliph 'Alí, the caravan went on to Baghdád, but I set out for Basra, in the company of a large troop of the Arab inhabitants of that country. They are exceedingly brave and it is impossible to travel in those regions except in their company. Our way lay along the Euphrates by the place called al-'Idhár, which is a waterlogged jungle of reeds, inhabited by Arabs noted for their predatory habits. They are brigands and profess adhesion to the Shi'ite sect. They attacked a party of darwíshes behind us and stripped them of everything down to their shoes and wooden bowls. They have fortified positions in this jungle and defend themselves in these against all attacks. Three days' march through this district brought us to the town of Wásit. Its inhabitants are among the best people in 'Iráq—indeed, the very best of them without qualification. All the 'Iráqís who wish to learn how to recite the Koran come here, and our caravan contained a number of students who had come for that purpose. As the caravan stayed here three days, I had an opportunity of visiting the grave of ar-Rifá'í, which is at a village called Umm 'Ubayda, one day's journey from there. I reached the establishment at noon the next day and found it to be an enormous monastery, containing thousands of darwíshes.[6] After the mid-afternoon prayer drums and kettledrums were beaten and the darwíshes began to dance. After this they prayed the sunset prayer and brought in the meal, consisting of rice-bread, fish, milk and dates. After the night prayer they began to recite their litany. A number of loads of wood had been brought in and kindled into a flame, and they went into the fire dancing; some of them rolled in it and others ate it in their mouths until they had extinguished it entirely. This is the peculiar custom of the Ahmadí darwíshes. Some of them take large snakes and bite their heads with their teeth until they bite them clean through.

After visiting ar-Rifá'í's tomb I returned to Wásit, and found that the caravan had already started, but overtook them on the way, and accompanied them to Basra. As we approached the city I had remarked at a distance of some two miles from it a lofty building resembling a fortress. I asked about it and was told that it was the mosque of 'Alí. Basra was in former times a city so vast that this mosque stood in the centre of the town, whereas now it is two miles outside it. Two miles beyond it again is the old wall that encircled the town, so that it stands midway between the old wall and the present city.[7] Basra is one of the metropolitan cities of 'Iráq, and no place on earth excels it in quantity of palm-groves. The current price of dates in its market is fourteen pounds to an 'Iráqí dirham, which is one-third of a *nuqra*.[8] The qádí sent me a hamper of dates that a man could scarcely carry; I sold them and received nine dirhams, and three of those were taken by the porter for carrying the basket from the house to the market. The inhabitants of Basra possess many excellent qualities; they are affable to strangers and give them their due, so that no stranger ever feels lonely amongst them. They hold the Friday service in the mosque of 'Alí mentioned above, but for the rest of the week it is closed. I was present once at the Friday service in this mosque and when the preacher rose to deliver his discourse he committed many gross errors of grammar.[9] In astonishment at this I spoke of it to the qádí and this is what he said to me: "In this town there is not a man left who knows anything of the science of grammar." Here is a lesson for those who will reflect on it—Magnified be He who changes all things! This Basra, in whose people the mastery of grammar reached its height, from whose soil sprang its trunk and its branches, amongst whose inhabitants is numbered the leader whose primacy is undisputed—the preacher in this town cannot deliver a discourse without breaking its rules!

At Basra I embarked in a *sumbuq*, that is a small boat, for Ubulla,[10] which lies ten miles distant. One travels between a constant succession of orchards and palm-groves both to right and left, with merchants sitting in the shade of the trees selling bread, fish, dates, milk and fruit. Ubulla was formerly a large town, frequented by merchants from India and Fárs, but it fell into decay and is now a village. Here we embarked after sunset on a small ship belonging to a man from Ubulla and in the morning reached 'Abbádán, a large village on a salt plain with no cultivation. *I was told that there was at 'Abbádán a devotee of great merit, who lived in complete solitude.* He used to come down to the shore once a month and catch enough fish for his month's provisions and then disappear again. I made it my business to seek him out, and found him praying in a ruined mosque. When he had finished praying he took my hand and said "May God grant you your desire in this world and the next." I have indeed—praise be to God—attained my desire in this world, which was to travel through the earth, and I have attained therein what none other has attained to my knowledge. The world to come remains, but my hope is strong in the mercy and clemency of God. My companions afterwards went in search of this devotee, but they could get no news of him. That evening one of the darwíshes belonging to the religious house at which we had put up met him, and he gave him a fresh fish saying "Take this to the guest who came today." So the darwísh said to us as he came in "Which of you saw the Shaykh today?" I replied "I saw him," and he said "He says to you 'This is your hospitality gift.'" I thanked God for that, then the darwísh cooked the fish for us and we all ate of it. I have never tasted better fish. For a moment I entertained the idea of spending the rest of my life in the service of this Shaykh, but my spirit, tenacious of its purpose, dissuaded me.

We sailed thereafter for Májúl. I made it a habit on my journey never, so far as possible, to cover a second time any road that I had once travelled. I was aiming to reach Baghdád, and a man at Basra advised me to travel to the country of the Lúrs, thence to 'Iráq al-'Ajam and thence to 'Iráq al-'Arab, and I followed his counsel. Four days later we reached Májúl,[11] a small place on the Persian Gulf, and thence I hired a mount from some grain-merchants. After travelling for three nights across open country inhabited by nomadic Kurds we reached Rámiz [Rám-hurmuz], a fine city with fruit trees and rivers, where I stayed only one night before continuing our journey for three nights more across a plain inhabited by Kurds. At the end of each stage there was a hospice, at which every traveller was supplied with bread, meat, and sweetmeats. Thereafter I came to the city of Tustar [Shushtar] which is situated at the edge of the plain and the beginning of the mountains. I stayed there sixteen days at the madrasa of the Shaykh Sharaf ad-Dín Músá, one of the handsomest and most upright of men. He preaches every Friday after the midday service, and when I heard him, all the preachers whom I had heard previously in the Hijáz, Syria and Egypt sank in my estimation, nor have I ever met his equal. One day I was present with him at a gathering of notables, theologians and darwíshes in an orchard on the river-bank. After he had served them all with food, he delivered a discourse with solemnity and dignity. When he finished, bits of paper were thrown to him from all sides, for it is a custom of the Persians to jot down questions on scraps of paper and throw them to the preacher, who answers them. The shaykh collected them all and began to answer them one after the other in the most remarkable and elegant manner.

From Tustar we travelled three nights through lofty mountains, halting at a hospice at each station, and came to the town of Idhaj, also called Mál al-Amír, the capital of the sultan Atábeg (which is a title common to all the rulers of that country).[12] I wished to see the sultan, but that was not easily come by, as he goes out only on Fridays because of his addiction to wine. Some days later the sultan sent me an invitation to visit him. I went with the messenger to the gate called the Cypress Gate, and we mounted a long staircase, finally reaching a room, which was unfurnished because they were in mourning for the sultan's son. The sultan was sitting on a cushion, with two covered goblets in front of him, one of gold and the other of silver. A green rug was spread for me near him and I sat down on this. No one else was in the room but his chamberlain and one of his boon-companions. The sultan asked me about myself and my country, the sultan of Egypt, and the Hijáz, and I answered all his questions. At this juncture a noted doctor of the law came in, and as the sultan started praising him I began to see that he was intoxicated. Afterwards he said to me in Arabic, which he spoke well, "Speak." I said to him "If you will listen to me, I say to you 'You are a son of a sultan noted for piety and uprightness, and there is nothing to be brought against you as a ruler but this,'" and I pointed to the goblets. He was overcome with confusion at what I said, and sat silent. I wished to go, but he bade me sit down and said to me, "To meet with men like you is a mercy." Then I saw him reeling and on the point of falling asleep, so I withdrew. I could not find my sandals, but the doctor I have mentioned went up and found them in the room and brought them to me. His kindness ashamed me and I made my excuses, but thereupon he kissed my sandals and put them on his head saying "God bless you. What you said to the sultan none could say but you. I hope this will make an impression on him."

A few days later I left Ídhaj, and the sultan sent me a number of dinars [as a farewell gift] with a like sum for my companions. For ten days we continued to travel in the territories of this sultan amidst high mountains, halting every night at a madrasa, where each traveller was supplied with food for himself and forage for his beast. Some of the madrasas are in desolate localities, but all their requirements are transported to them. One-third of the revenues of the state is devoted to the maintenance of these hospices and madrasas. We travelled on across a well-watered plain belonging to the province of the city of Isfahán, passing through the towns of Ushturkán and Fírúzán. On reaching the latter place we found its inhabitants outside the town escorting a funeral. They had torches lit behind and in front of the bier, and they followed it up with fifes and singers, singing all sorts of merry songs. We were amazed at their conduct. The next day our way lay through orchards and streams and fine villages, with very many pigeon towers, and in the afternoon we reached Isfahán or Ispahán, in 'Iráq al-'Ajam. Isfahán is one of the largest and fairest of cities, but the greater part of it is now in ruins, as a result of the feud between Sunnís and Shi'ites, which is still raging there. It is rich in fruits, among its products being apricots of unequalled quality with sweet almonds in their kernels, quinces whose sweetness and size cannot be paralleled, splendid grapes, and wonderful melons. Its people are goodlooking, with clear white skins tinged with red, exceedingly brave, generous, and always trying to outdo one another in procuring luxurious viands. Many curious stories are told of this last trait in them. The members of each trade form corporations, as also do the leading men who are not engaged in trade, and the young unmarried men; these corporations then engage in mutual rivalry, inviting one another to banquets, in the preparations for which they display all their resources. I was told that one corporation invited another and cooked its viands with lighted candles, then the guests returned the invitation and cooked their viands with silk.

We then set out from Isfahán on purpose to visit the Shaykh Majd ad-Dín at Shíráz, which is ten days' journey from there. After six days' travelling we reached Yazdikhwást, outside of which there is a convent where travellers stay. It has an iron gate and is extremely well fortified; inside it are shops at which the travellers can buy all that they need. Here they make the cheese called Yazdikhwástí, which is unequalled for goodness; each cheese weighs from two to four ounces. Thence we travelled across a stretch of open country inhabited by Turks, and reached Shíráz, a densely populated town, well built and admirably planned. Each trade has its own bazaar. Its inhabitants are handsome and clean in their dress. In the whole East there is no city that approaches Damascus in beauty of bazaars, orchards and rivers, and in the handsome figures of its inhabitants, but Shíráz. It is on a plain surrounded by orchards on all sides and intersected by rivers, one of which is the river known as Rukn Ábád,[13] whose water is sweet, very cold in summer and warm in winter. The people of Shíráz are pious and upright, especially the women, who have a strange custom. Every Monday, Thursday, and Friday they meet in the principal mosque to listen to the preacher, one or two thousand of them, carrying fans with which they fan themselves on account of the great heat. I have never seen in any land so great an assembly of women.

On entering Shíráz I had but one desire, which was to seek out the illustrious Shaykh Majd ad-Dín Ismá'íl, the marvel of the age. As I reached his dwelling he was going out to the afternoon prayer; I saluted him and he embraced me and took my hand until he came to his prayer mat, when he signed me to pray beside him. After this, the notables of the town came forward to salute him, as is their custom morning and evening, then he asked me about my journey and the lands I had visited, and gave orders to lodge me in his madrasa. The Shaykh Majd ad-Dín is held in the highest esteem by the king of 'Iráq, for reasons which the following story will show. The [late] king of 'Iráq, Sultan Muhammad Khudábanda,[14] had as a companion, while he was yet an infidel, a Shi'ite theologian, and when the sultan embraced Islám together with the Tatars, he showed the greatest respect for this man, who persuaded him to establish the Shi'ite faith throughout his dominions. At Baghdád, Shíráz, and Isfahán the population prevented the execution of the order, whereupon the king ordered the qádís of these three towns to be brought. The first of them to be brought was the qádí Majd ad-Dín of Shíráz. The sultan was then at a place called Qarábágh,[15] which was his summer residence, and when the qádí arrived, he ordered him to be thrown to the dogs which he had there. These are enormous dogs with chains on their necks, trained to eat men. When anyone is brought to be delivered to the dogs, he is placed at liberty and without chains in a wide plain; the dogs are then loosed on him and he flees, but finds no refuge; they overtake him and tear him to pieces and eat his flesh. But when the dogs were loosed on the qádí Majd ad-Dín, they would not attack him but wagged their tails before him in the friendliest manner. The sultan, on hearing of this, showed the greatest reverence and respect to him, and renounced the doctrines of the Shi'ites. He made vast presents to the qádí, including a hundred of the villages of Jamkán, which is the best district in Shíráz. I met the qádí again on my return from India in 1347. He was then too weak to walk, but he recognized me and rose to embrace me. I visited him one day and found the sultan of Shíráz sitting in front of him, holding his own ear. This is the height of good manners amongst them, and all the people do so when they sit in the presence of the king.

The sultan of Shíráz at the time of my visit was Abú Isháq,[16] one of the best of sultans, handsome and well-conducted, of generous character, humble, but powerful and the ruler of a great kingdom. He has an army of more than fifty thousand men, Turks and Persians, but he does not trust the people of Shíráz. He will not take them into his service, and allows none of them to carry arms, because they are very brave and apt to rise against their rulers. He made himself master of Shíráz, as well as of Fárs and Isfahán, after the death of Sultan Abú Sa'íd [in 1335], when every amír seized what he possessed. At one time Sultan Abú Isháq desired to build a palace like the Aywán Kisrá,[17] and ordered the inhabitants of Shíráz to undertake the digging of its foundations. They set to work on this, each corporation of artisans rivalling the other, and carried their rivalry to such lengths that they made baskets of leather to carry the earth and covered them with embroidered silk. They did the same with the donkey panniers. Some of them made tools of silver, and lit numerous candles. When they went to dig they put on their best garments, with girdles of silk, and the sultan watched their work from a balcony. When the foundations were dug the inhabitants were freed from service, and paid artisans took their place. Several thousands of them were collected for this work, and I heard from the governor of the town that the greater part of its taxes were spent on it. Abú Isháq wished to be compared to the king of India for the magnificence of his gifts, but "How distant are the Pleiads from the clod!" The largest gift of Abú Isháq that I ever heard tell of was that he gave an ambassador from the king of Herát seventy thousand dinars, whereas the king of India never ceases to give many times more than that to an innumerable number of persons. One instance may be cited.

The amír Bakht one day felt indisposed at the capital of the king of India, who went to visit him. As the king entered he wished to rise, but the king swore that he must not come down from his bed. A divan was brought on which the sultan sat down. He then called for gold and a balance, and when these were brought he ordered the sick man to sit on one of the trays. The amír said, "O master of the world, had I known that you would do this, I should have put on many clothes." The sultan replied, "Put on now all the clothes that you have." So he put on the clothes that he wore in the cold weather, which were padded with cotton-wool, and sat on one of the trays of the balance. The other was filled with gold until it tipped down, when the king said "Take this, and give it in alms for your recovery," and left him.

Shíráz contains many sanctuaries which are visited and venerated by its inhabitants. Among them is the tomb of the imám 'Abdalláh ibn Khafíf, who is known there simply as "The Shaykh." He occupies a high place among the saints, and the following story is told of him. One day he went to the mountain of Sarandíb [Adam's Peak] in the island of Ceylon accompanied by about thirty darwíshes. They were overcome by hunger on the way, in an uninhabited locality, and lost their bearings. They asked the shaykh to allow them to seize one of the small elephants, of which there are a very large number in that place, and which are transported thence to the king of India. The shaykh forbade them, but their hunger got the better of them and they disobeyed him and, seizing a small elephant, killed and ate it. The shaykh however refused to eat it. That night, as they slept, the elephants gathered from all quarters and came upon them, smelling each one of them and killing him until they had made an end of them all. They smelled the shaykh too but offered no violence to him; one of them lifted him with its trunk, put him on its back, and brought him to the inhabited district. When the people of that part saw him, they marvelled at him and came to out meet him and hear his story. As it came near them, the elephant lifted him with its trunk and placed him on the ground in full view of them.

I visited this island of Ceylon. Its people still live in idolatry [Buddhism], yet they show respect for Muslim darwíshes, lodge them in their houses, and give them to eat, and they live in their houses amidst their wives and children. This is contrary to the usage of the other Indian idolators [Brahmans and Hindus], who never make friends with Muslims, and never give them to eat or to drink out of their vessels, although at the same time they neither act nor speak offensively to them. We were compelled to have some flesh cooked for us by some of them, and they would bring it in their pots and sit at a distance from us. They would also serve us with rice, which is their principal food, on banana leaves, and then go away, and what we left over was eaten by dogs and birds. If any small child, who had not reached the age of reason, ate any of it, they would beat him and make him eat cow dung, this being, as they say, the purification for that act.

Among the sanctuaries outside Shíráz is the grave of the pious shaykh known as as-Sa'dí,[18] who was the greatest poet of his time in the Persian language, and sometimes introduced Arabic verses into his compositions. There is a fine hospice which he built in this place having a beautiful garden within it, close by the source of the great river known as Rukn Ábád. The Shaykh [Sa'dí] had constructed some small cisterns in marble there to wash clothes in. The citizens of Shíráz go out to visit his tomb, and they eat from his table [*i.e.* eat food prepared at the convent] and wash their clothes in the river. I did the same thing there —may God have mercy upon him!

I left Shíráz to visit the tomb of the pious shaykh Abú Isháq al-Kázarúní at Kázarún, which lies two days' journey [west] from Shíráz. This shaykh is held in high honour by the inhabitants of India and China. Travellers on the Sea of China, when the wind turns against them and they fear pirates, usually make vows to Abú Isháq, each one setting down in writing what he has vowed. When they reach safety the officers of the convent go on board the ship, receive the list, and take from each person the amount of his vow. There is not a ship coming from India or China but has thousands of dinars in it [vowed to the saint]. Any mendicant who comes to beg alms of the shaykh is given an order, sealed with the shaykh's seal stamped in red wax, to this effect: "Let any person who has made a vow to the Shaykh Abú Isháq give thereof to so-and-so so much," specifying a thousand or a hundred, or more or less. When the mendicant finds anyone who has made a vow, he takes from him the sum named and writes a receipt for the amount on the back of the order.

From Kázarún we went by way of Zaydán to Huwayza, and thence by a five days' march through waterless desert to Kúfa.[19] Though it was once the abode of the Companions of the Prophet and of scholars and theologians, and the capital of 'Alí, the Commander of the Faithful, Kúfa has now fallen into ruins, as a result of the attacks which it has suffered from the nomad Arab brigands in the neighbourhood. The town is unwalled. Its principal mosque is a magnificent building with seven naves supported by great pillars of immense height, made of carved stones placed one on top of the other, the interstices being filled with molten lead. We resumed our journey and halted for the night at Bi'r Malláha [" Salt Well "], which is a pretty town lying amongst palm gardens. I encamped outside it, and would not enter the place, because the inhabitants are fanatical Shi'ites.

Next morning we went on and alighted at the city of Hilla, which is a large town lying along the western bank of the Euphrates, with fine markets where both natural products and manufactured goods may be had. At this place there is a great bridge fastened upon a continuous row of boats from bank to bank, the boats being held in place both fore and aft by iron chains attached on either bank to a huge wooden beam made fast ashore. The inhabitants of Hilla are all Shi'ites of the " Twelvers " sect, but they are divided into two factions, known as the " Kurds " and the " Party of the Two Mosques," between whom there is constant factional strife and fighting. Near the principal market in this town there is a mosque, the door of which is covered with a silk curtain. They call this the Sanctuary of the Master of the Age.[20] Every evening before sunset, a hundred of the townsmen, following their custom, go with arms and drawn swords to the governor of the city and receive from him a saddled and bridled horse or mule. With this they go in procession, with drums beating and trumpets and bugles blowing, fifty of them in front of it and fifty behind, while others walk to right and left, to the Sanctuary of the Master of the Age. They halt at the door and call out " In the Name of God, O Master of the Age, in the Name of God, come forth! Corruption is abroad and injustice is rife! This is the hour for thy advent, that by thee God may discover the true from the false." They continue to call out thus, sounding their drums and bugles and trumpets, until the hour of sunset prayer, for they hold that

Muhammad, the son of al-Hasan al-'Askarí, entered this mosque and disappeared from sight in it, and that he will emerge from it, for he, in their view, is the "Expected Imám."

We travelled thence to the town of Karbalá, the shrine of al-Husayn, the son of 'Alí.[21] The surroundings of the tomb and the ceremonies of visitation resemble those of the tomb of 'Alí at Najaf. In this town too the inhabitants form two factions between whom there is constant fighting, although they are all Shi'ites and descended from the same family, and as a result of their feuds the town is in ruins.

Thence we travelled to Baghdád, the Abode of Peace and Capital of Islám.[22] Here there are two bridges like that at Hilla, on which the people promenade night and day, both men and women. The town has eleven cathedral mosques, eight on the right bank and three on the left, together with very many other mosques and madrasas, only the latter are all in ruins. The baths at Baghdád are numerous and excellently constructed, most of them being painted with pitch, which has the appearance of black marble. This pitch is brought from a spring between Kúfa and Basra, from which it flows continually. It gathers at the sides of the spring like clay and is shovelled up and brought to Baghdád. Each establishment has a large number of private bathrooms, every one of which has also a wash-basin in the corner, with two taps supplying hot and cold water. Every bather is given three towels, one to wear round his waist when he goes in, another to wear round his waist when he comes out, and the third to dry himself with. In no town other than Baghdád have I seen all this elaborate arrangement, though some other towns approach it in this respect.[23] The western part of Baghdád was the earliest to be built, but it is now for the most part in ruins. In spite of that there remain in it still thirteen quarters, each like a city in itself and possessing two or three baths. The hospital (máristán) is a vast ruined edifice, of which only vestiges remain. The eastern part has an abundance of bazaars, the largest of which is called the Tuesday bazaar. On this side there are no fruit trees, but all the fruit is brought from the western side, where there are orchards and gardens.

My arrival at Baghdád coincided with a visit of the sultan of the two 'Iráqs and of Khurásán, the illustrious Abú Sa'íd Bahádur Khán,[24] son of Sultan Muhammad Khudábanda whose conversion we related above. He was an excellent and generous king. He was still a boy when he succeeded his father, and the power was seized by the principal amír, Júbán, who left him nothing of sovereignty but the name. This went on until one day his father's wives complained to him of the insolence of Júbán's son Dimashq Khwája, and the sultan had him arrested and put to death. Júbán was then in Khurásán with the army of the Tatars. They agreed to fight the sultan, and marched against him, but when the two forces met, the Tatars deserted to their sultan and Júbán was left without support. He fled to the desert of Sijistán [Sistan], and afterwards took refuge with the king of Herát, who betrayed him a few days later, killed him and his youngest son and sent their heads to the sultan. When Abú Sa'íd had become sole master, he desired to marry Júbán's daughter, who was called Baghdád Khátún, and was one of the most beautiful of women. She was married to Shaykh Hasan, the same who became master of the kingdom after the death of Abú Sa'íd, and who was his cousin by his father's sister. Shaykh Hasan divorced her on Abú Sa'íd's order, and she became his favourite wife. Among the Turks and the Tatars their wives hold a high position; when they issue an order they say in it "By order of the Sultan and the Khátúns." Each khátún possesses several towns and districts and vast revenues, and when they travel with the sultan they have a separate camp. After this had gone on for some time the king married a woman called Dilshád, of whom he was very fond.[25] He neglected Baghdád Khátún, who became jealous and poisoned him with a kerchief. On his death his line became extinct, and the amírs seized the provinces for themselves. When they learned that it was Baghdád Khátún who had poisoned him, they decided to put her to death. A Greek slave, called Khwája Lu'lu', who was one of the principal amírs, came to her while she was in her bath and beat her to death with his club. Her body lay there for some days, covered only with a piece of sacking.

I left Baghdád with the *mahalla*[26] of Sultan Abú Sa'íd, on purpose to see the way in which the king's marches are conducted, and travelled with it for ten days, thereafter accompanying one of the amírs to the town of Tabríz.[27] We reached the town after ten days' travelling, and encamped outside it in a place called ash-Shám. Here there is a fine hospice, where travellers are supplied with food, consisting of bread, meat, rice cooked in butter, and sweetmeats. The next morning I entered the town and we came to a great bazaar, called the Gházán bazaar, one of the finest bazaars I have seen the world over. Every trade is grouped separately in it. I passed through the jewellers' bazaar, and my eyes were dazzled by the varieties of precious stones that I beheld. They were displayed by beautiful slaves wearing rich garments with a waist-sash of silk, who stood in front of the merchants, exhibiting the jewels to the wives of the Turks, while the women were buying them in large quantities and trying to outdo one another. As a result of all this I witnessed a riot—may God preserve us from such! We went on into the ambergris and musk market, and witnessed another riot like it or worse.

We spent only one night at Tabríz. Next day the amír received an order from the sultan to rejoin him, so I returned along with him, without having seen any of the learned men there. On reaching the camp the amír told the sultan about me and introduced me into his presence. The sultan asked me about my country, and gave me a robe and a horse. The amír told him that I was intending to go to the Hijáz, whereupon he gave orders for me to be supplied with provisions and to travel with the cortege of the commander of the pilgrim caravan, and wrote instructions to that effect to the governor of Baghdád. I returned therefore to Baghdád and received in full what the sultan had ordered. As more than two months remained before the period when the pilgrim caravan was to set out, I thought it a good plan to make a journey to Mosul and Diyár Bakr to see those districts, and then return to Baghdád when the Hijáz caravan was due to start.

Leaving Baghdád we reached a station on the Dujayl canal, which is derived from the Tigris and waters a large tract of villages, and two days later stopped at a large village called Harba. From there we travelled to a place on the Tigris near a fort called al-Ma'shúq, opposite which on the eastern bank, is the town of Surra-man-rá'a or Sámarrá. This town is a total ruin and only a very small part of it remains. It has an equable climate and is exceedingly beautiful in spite of its disasters and the ruins of its noble buildings.[28] One day further on we reached Takrít, a large city with fine markets and many mosques, whose inhabitants are distinguished by their good qualities. Two marches from there brought us to a village called al-'Aqr, from which there is a continuous strip of villages and cultivation to Mosul. We came next to some black land in which there are wells of pitch, like the one already mentioned between Kúfa and Basra, and two stages on from these wells we reached al-Mawsil [Mosul].

Mosul is an ancient and prosperous city, whose fortress, known as al-Hadbá' [" The Humpback "], is famous for its strength. Next to it are the sultan's palaces. These are separated from the town by a long and broad street, running from the top to the bottom of the town. Round the town run two strong walls, with close-set towers. So thick is the wall that there are chambers inside it one next the other all the way round. I have never seen city walls like it except at Delhi. Outside the town is a large suburb, containing mosques, baths, hostelries and markets. It has a cathedral mosque on the bank of the Tigris, round which there are lattice windows of iron, and adjoining it are platforms overlooking the river, exceedingly beautiful and well constructed. In front of the mosque there is a hospital, and there are two other cathedral mosques inside the town. The Qaysaríya of Mosul is a fine building with iron gates.[29]

From Mosul we journeyed to Jazírat ibn 'Omar, a large town surrounded by the river, which is the reason why it is called Jazírah [island]. The greater part of it is in ruins. Its inhabitants are men of excellent character and very kind to strangers. The day that we stayed there we saw Mount Júdí, which is mentioned in the Book of God [the Koran] as that on which Noah's vessel came to rest. Two stages from Jazírat ibn 'Omar we reached the town of Nasíbín, an ancient town of moderate size, for the most part in ruins, lying in a wide and fertile plain. In this town rose-water is manufactured which is unequalled for perfume and sweetness. Round it there runs like a bracelet a river which flows from sources in a mountain close by. One branch enters the town, flows amidst its streets and dwellings, cuts through the court of the principal mosque, and empties into two basins. The town has a hospital and two madrasas.

Thereafter we travelled to the town of Sinjár,[30] which is built at the foot of a mountain. Its inhabitants are Kurds, and are brave and generous. We went on next to the town of Dárá, a large, ancient and glistening town, with an imposing fortress,[31] but now in ruins and totally uninhabited. Outside it there is an inhabited village in which we stopped. We journeyed on from there and reached the town of Máridín, a great city at the foot of a hill, one of the most beautiful, striking and substantially built cities in the lands of Islám. Here they manufacture the woollen fabrics known by its name. At Máridín there is a fortress of exceptional height, situated on the hilltop. The sultan of Máridín at the time of my stay was al-Malik as-Sálih.[32] There is no one in 'Iráq, Syria or Egypt who is more openhanded than he, and poets and darwíshes come to visit him and receive munificent gifts.

I then started to make my way back to Baghdád. On reaching Mosul I found its pilgrim caravan outside the city setting out for Baghdád and joined them. When we arrived at Baghdád I found the pilgrims preparing for the journey, so I went to visit the governor and asked him for the things which the sultan had ordered for me. He assigned me the half of a camel-litter and provisions and water for four persons, writing out an order to that effect, then sent for the leader of the caravan and commended me to him. I had already made the acquaintance of the latter, but our friendship was strengthened and I remained under his protection and favoured by his bounty, for he gave me even more than had been ordered for me. As we left Kúfa I fell ill of a diarrhœa and had to be dismounted from the camel many times a day. The commander of the caravan used to make enquiries for my condition and give instructions that I should be looked after. My illness continued until I reached Mecca, the Sanctuary of God (may He exalt her honour and greatness !). I made the circuit of the Sacred Edifice [the Ka'aba] on arrival, but I was so weak that I had to carry out the prescribed ceremonies seated, and I made the circuit and the ritual visitation of Safá and Marwa riding on the amír's horse.[33] When we camped at Miná I began to feel relief and to recover from my malady. At the end of the Pilgrimage I remained at Mecca all that year, giving myself up entirely to pious exercises and leading a most agreeable existence. After the next Pilgrimage [of 1328] I spent another year there, and yet another after that.

CHAPTER III

AFTER the Pilgrimage at the close of the year 1330 I set out from Mecca, making for Yemen. I arrived at Judda [Jedda], an ancient town on the sea-coast, which is said to have been built by the Persians. A strange thing happened to me here. A blind man, whom I did not know and who did not know me, called me by name, and taking my hand said "Where is the ring?" Now, as I left Mecca, a religious mendicant had met me and asked me for alms, and as I had nothing with me at the time, I had given him my ring. I told the blind man this, and he said "Go back and look for it, for there are names written on it which contain a great secret." I was greatly astonished at him and at his knowledge of this—God knows who he was. At the Friday service at Judda, the muezzin comes and counts the number of the inhabitants of the town present. If they amount to forty the preacher holds the Friday service, but if they are fewer he prays the midday prayer four times, taking no account of the strangers present, however many they may be.

We embarked here on a boat which they called a *jalba*. The Sharíf Mansúr embarked on another and desired me to accompany him, but I refused. He had a number of camels in his *jalba* and that frightened me, as I had never travelled on sea before. For two days we sailed with a favouring wind, then it changed and drove us out of our course. The waves came overboard into our midst and the passengers fell grievously sick. These terrors continued until we emerged at a roadstead called Ra's Dawá'ir[1] between Aydháb and Sawákin. We landed here and found on the shore a reed hut shaped like a mosque, inside which were ostrich egg-shells filled with water. We drank from these and cooked food. A party of Bejás came to us, so we hired camels from them and travelled with them through a country in which there are many gazelles. The Bejás do not eat them so they are tame and do not run away from men. After two days' travelling we reached the island of Sawákin [Suakin]. It is a large island lying about six miles off the coast, and has neither water nor cereal crops nor trees. Water is brought to it in boats, and it has large reservoirs for collecting rainwater. The flesh of ostriches, gazelles and wild asses is to be had in it, and it has many goats together with milk and butter, which is exported to Mecca. Their cereal is *jurjúr*, a kind of coarse grained millet, which is also exported to Mecca. The sultan of Sawákin when I was there was the Sharíf Zayd, the son of the amír of Mecca.

We took ship at Sawákin for Yemen. No sailing is done on this sea at night because of the number of rocks in it. At nightfall they land and embark again at sunrise. The captain of the ship stands constantly at the prow to warn the steersman of rocks. Six days after leaving Sawákin we reached the town of Hali,[2] a large and populous town inhabited by two Arab tribes. The sultan is a man of excellent character, a man of letters and a poet. I had accompanied him from Mecca to Judda, and when I reached his city he treated me generously and made me his guest for several days. I embarked in a ship of his and reached the township of Sarja, which is inhabited by Yemenite merchants.[3] They are generous and open-handed, supply food to travellers and assist pilgrims, transporting them in their ships and providing for them from their own funds. We stayed at Sarja only one night as their guests, then sailed on to the roadstead of al-Ahwáb and thence went up to Zabíd.[4]

Zabíd is a hundred and twenty miles from San'á, and is after San'á the largest and wealthiest town in Yemen. It lies amidst luxuriant gardens with many streams and fruits, such as bananas and the like. It is in the interior, not on the coast, and is one of the capital cities of the country. The town is large and populous, with palm-groves, orchards, and running streams—in fact, the pleasantest and most beautiful town in Yemen. Its inhabitants are charming in their manners, upright, and handsome, and the women especially are exceedingly beautiful. The people of this town hold the famous [junketings called] *subút an-nakhl* in this wise. They go out to the palm-groves every Saturday during the season of the colouring and ripening of the dates.[5] Not a soul remains in the town, whether of the townsfolk or of the visitors. The musicians go out [to entertain them], and the shopkeepers go out selling fruits and sweetmeats. The women go in litters on camels. For all we have said of their exceeding beauty they are virtuous and possessed of excellent qualities. They show a predilection for foreigners, and do not refuse to marry them, as the women in our country do. When a woman's husband wishes to travel she goes out with him and bids him farewell, and if they have a child, it is she who takes care of it and supplies its wants until the father returns. While he is absent she demands nothing from him for maintenance or clothes or anything else, and while he stays with her she is content with very little for upkeep and clothing. But the women never leave their own towns, and none of them would consent to do so, however much she were offered.

We went on from there to the town of Ta'izz, the capital of the king of Yemen, and one of the finest and largest towns in that country.[6] Its people are overbearing, insolent, and rude, as is generally the case in towns where kings reside. Ta'izz is made up of three quarters; the first is the residence of the king and his court, the second, called 'Udayna, is the military station, and the third, called al-Mahálib, is inhabited by the commonalty, and contains the principal market. The sultan of Yemen is Núr ad-Dín 'Alí of the house of Rasúl. He uses an elaborate ceremonial in his audiences and progresses. The fourth day after our arrival was a Thursday, on which day the king holds a public audience. The qádí presented me to him and I saluted him. The way in which one salutes is to touch the ground with the index-finger, then lift it to the head and say "May God prolong thy Majesty." I did as the qádí had done, and the king, having ordered me to sit in front of him, questioned me about my country and the other lands and princes I had seen. The wazír was present, and the king ordered him to treat me honourably and arrange for my lodging.[7] After staying there for some days as his guest, I set out for the town of San'á, which was the former capital, a populous town built of brick and plaster, with a temperate climate and good water. A strange thing about the rain in India, Yemen, and Abyssinia is that it falls only in the hot weather, and mostly every afternoon during that season, so travellers always make haste about noon to avoid being caught by the rain, and the townsfolk retire indoors, for their rains are heavy downpours. The whole town of San'á is paved, so that when the rain falls it washes and cleans all the streets.

I travelled thence to 'Aden, the port of Yemen, on the coast of the ocean. It is surrounded by mountains and can be approached from one side only; it has no crops, trees, or water, but has reservoirs in which rainwater is collected. The Arabs often cut off the inhabitants from their supply of drinking-water until they buy them off with money and pieces of cloth. It is an exceedingly hot place. It is the port of the Indians, and to it come large vessels from Kinbáyat [Cambay], Kawlam [Quilon], Cálicút, and many other Malabar ports. There are Indian merchants living there, as well as Egyptian merchants. Its inhabitants are all either merchants, porters, or fishermen. Some of the merchants are immensely rich, so rich that sometimes a single merchant is sole owner of a large ship with all it contains, and this is a subject of ostentation and rivalry amongst them. In spite of that they are pious, humble, upright, and generous in character, treat strangers well, give liberally to devotees, and pay in full the tithes due to God.

I took ship at 'Aden, and after four days at sea reached Zayla' [Zeila], the town of the Berberah, who are a negro people. Their land is a desert extending for two months' journey from Zayla' to Maqdashaw. Zayla' is a large city with a great bazaar, but it is the dirtiest, most abominable, and most stinking town in the world. The reason for the stench is the quantity of its fish and the blood of the camels that they slaughter in the streets. When we got there, we chose to spend the night at sea, in spite of its extreme roughness, rather than in the town, because of its filth.

On leaving Zayla' we sailed for fifteen days and came to Maqdashaw [Mogdishu], which is an enormous town. Its inhabitants are merchants and have many camels, of which they slaughter hundreds every day [for food]. When a vessel reaches the port, it is met by *sumbuqs*, which are small boats, in each of which are a number of young men, each carrying a covered dish containing food. He presents this to one of the merchants on the ship saying "This is my guest," and all the others do the same. Each merchant on disembarking goes only to the house of the young man who is his host, except those who have made frequent journeys to the town and know its people well; these live where they please. The host then sells his goods for him and buys for him, and if anyone buys anything from him at too low a price or sells to him in the absence of his host, the sale is regarded by them as invalid. This practice is of great advantage to them. When these young men came on board our vessel, one of them approached me. My companions said "This man is not a merchant, but a theologian," whereupon the young man called out to his friends "This is the qádí's guest." Amongst them was one of the qádí's men, who went to tell him of this, so he came down to the beach with a number of students, and sent one of them to me. When I disembarked with my party, I saluted him and his party, and he said "In the name of God, let us go and salute the Shaykh." Thereupon I said "And who is this Shaykh?" He answered "The sultan," for they call the sultan 'the Shaykh.' I said to him "When I have settled down I shall go to him," and he replied "It is the custom that whenever a theologian, or sharíf, or man of religion comes here, he must see the sultan before taking his lodging." So I went to him as they asked. The sultan, whose name is Abú Bakr, is of Berberah origin, and he talks in the Maqdishí language, though he knows Arabic. When we reached the palace and news of my arrival was sent in, a eunuch came out with a plate containing betel leaves and areca nuts. He gave me ten leaves and a few nuts, the same to the qádí, and the rest to my companions and the qádí's students, and then said "Our master commands that he be lodged in the students' house." Later on the same eunuch brought food from the 'Shaykh's' palace. With him came one of the wazírs, whose duty it was to look after the guests, and who said "Our master greets you and bids you welcome." We stayed there three days, food being brought to us three times a day, and on the fourth, a Friday, the qádí and one of the wazírs brought me a set of garments. We then went to the mosque and prayed behind the [sultan's] screen.[8] When the 'Shaykh' came out I greeted him and he bade me welcome. He put on his sandals, ordering the qádí and myself to do the same, and set out for his palace on foot. All the other people walked barefooted. Over his head were carried four canopies of coloured silk, each surmounted by a golden bird. After the palace ceremonies were over, all those present saluted and retired.

I embarked at Maqdashaw for the Sawáhil country, with the object of visiting the town of Kulwá [Kilwa, Quiloa] in the land of the Zanj.[9] We came to Mambasá [Mombasa], a large island two days' journey by sea from the Sawáhil country.[10] It possesses no territory on the mainland. They have fruit trees on the island, but no cereals, which have to be brought to them from the Sawáhil. Their food consists chiefly of bananas and fish. The inhabitants are pious, honourable, and upright, and they have well-built wooden mosques. We stayed one night in this island, and then pursued our journey to Kulwá, which is a large town on the coast. The majority of its inhabitants are Zanj, jet-black in colour, and with tattoo-marks on their faces. I was told by a merchant that the town of Sufála lies a fortnight's journey [south] from Kulwá, and that gold dust is brought to Sufála from Yúfí in the country of the Límís, which is a month's journey distant from it.[11] Kulwá is a very fine and substantially built town, and all its buildings are of wood. Its inhabitants are constantly engaged in military expeditions, for their country is contiguous to the heathen Zanj. The sultan at the time of my visit was Abu'l-Muzaffar Hasan, who was noted for his gifts and generosity. He used to devote the fifth part of the booty made on his expeditions to pious and charitable purposes, as is prescribed in the Koran,[12] and I have seen him give the clothes off his back to a mendicant who asked him for them. When this liberal and virtuous sultan died, he was succeeded by his brother Dáwúd, who was at the opposite pole from him in this respect. Whenever a petitioner came to him, he would say "He who gave is dead, and left nothing behind him to be given." Visitors would stay at his court for months on end, and finally he would make them some small gift, so that at last people gave up going to his gate.

From Kulwá we sailed to Dhafári [Dhofar], at the extremity of Yemen. Thoroughbred horses are exported from here to India, the passage taking a month with a favouring wind. Dhafári is a month's journey from 'Aden across the desert, and is situated in a desolate locality without villages or dependencies. Its market is one of the dirtiest in the world and the most pestered by flies because of the quantity of fruit and fish sold there. Most of the fish are of the kind called sardines, which are extremely fat in that country. A curious fact is that these sardines are the sole food of their beasts and flocks, a thing which I have seen nowhere else. Most of the sellers [in the market] are female slaves, who wear black garments. The inhabitants cultivate millet and irrigate it from very deep wells, the water from which is raised in a large bucket drawn up by a number of ropes attached to the waists of slaves. Their principal food is rice, imported from India. Its population consists of merchants who live entirely on trade. When a vessel arrives they take the master, captain and writer in procession to the sultan's palace and entertain the entire ship's company for three days in order to gain the goodwill of the shipmasters. Another curious thing is that its people closely resemble the people of Northwest Africa in their customs. In the neighbourhood of the town there are orchards with many banana-trees. The bananas are of immense size; one which was weighed in my presence scaled twelve ounces and was pleasant to the taste and very sweet. They grow also betel-trees and coco-palms, which are found only in India and the town of Dhafári.[13] Since we have mentioned these trees, we shall describe them and their properties here.

Betel-trees are grown like vines on cane trellises or else trained up coco-palms. They have no fruit and are grown only for their leaves. The Indians have a high opinion of betel, and if a man visits a friend and the latter gives him five leaves of it, you would think he had given him the world, especially if he is a prince or notable. A gift of betel is a far greater honour than a gift of gold and silver. It is used in this way. First one takes areca-nuts, which are like nutmegs, crushes them into small bits and chews them. Then the betel leaves are taken, a little chalk is put on them, and they are chewed with the areca-nuts. They sweeten the breath and aid digestion, prevent the disagreeable effects of drinking water on an empty stomach, and stimulate the faculties.

The coco-palm is one of the strangest of trees, and looks exactly like a date-palm. The nut resembles a man's head, for it has marks like eyes and a mouth, and the contents, when it is green, are like the brain. It has fibre like hair, out of which they make ropes, which they use instead of nails to bind their ships together and also as cables. Amongst its properties are that it strengthens the body, fattens, and adds redness to the face. If it is cut open when it is green it gives a liquid deliciously sweet and fresh. After drinking this one takes a piece of the rind as a spoon and scoops out the pulp inside the nut. This tastes like an egg that has been broiled but not quite cooked, and is nourishing. I lived on it for a year and a half when I was in the Maldive islands. One of its peculiarities is that oil, milk and honey are extracted from it. The honey is made in this fashion. They cut a stalk on which the fruit grows, leaving two fingers' length, and on this they tie a small bowl, into which the sap drips. If this has been done in the morning, a servant climbs up again in the evening with two bowls, one filled with water. He pours into the other the sap that has collected, then washes the stalk, cuts off a small piece, and ties on another bowl. The same thing is repeated next morning until a good deal of the sap has been collected, when it is cooked until it thickens. It then makes an excellent honey, and the merchants of India, Yemen, and China buy it and take it to their own countries, where they manufacture sweetmeats from it. The milk is made by steeping the contents of the nut in water, which takes on the colour and taste of milk and is used along with food. To make the oil, the ripe nuts are peeled and the contents dried in the sun, then cooked in cauldrons and the oil extracted. They use it for lighting and dip bread in it, and the women put it on their hair.

We left Dhafári for 'Omán in a small ship belonging to a man from Masíra. On the second day of our journey we disembarked at the roadstead of Hásik,[14] which is inhabited by Arab fishermen. Here they have a great quantity of frankincense trees. They have thin leaves out of which drips, when they are slashed, sap like milk. This turns into a gum, which is the frankincense. The people living in this port are dependent on fishing for their food, and the fish they catch is the *lukham*, which is like a dogfish. They slice these fish up, dry them in the sun and use them for food, and build their houses with the fish bones, using camel skins for roofs.

Six days later we reached the Island of Birds, which is uninhabited. We cast anchor and went on shore, and found it full of birds like blackbirds, only bigger. The sailors brought some of their eggs, cooked and ate them, then caught a number of the birds which they cooked without previously slitting their throats.[15] My food during the voyage consisted of dried dates and fish, for they used to fish every morning and evening. The fish they caught were cut up into pieces and broiled, and every person on board received a portion, no preference being shown to anyone, not even to the master. We celebrated the Pilgrimage Festival at sea, being stormtossed all that day from sunrise until sunrise the next day, and in danger of foundering. A ship in front of us was sunk, and only one man escaped by swimming after great efforts. We called next at the island of Masíra, a large island whose inhabitants live entirely on fish,[16] but we did not land as the roadstead is at some distance from the shore. Besides I had taken a dislike to these people after seeing them eat birds without slitting their throats.

We sailed for a day and a night from Masíra and reached the roadstead of a large village called Súr, from which we could see the town of Qalhát, situated on the slope of a hill apparently close at hand.[17] As we had anchored just after midday, I desired to walk to Qalhát and spend the night there, for I had taken a dislike to the company on the ship. On enquiry, I was told that I should get there in the mid-afternoon, so I hired one of the sailors as a guide. An Indian named Khidr, who had been one of my fellow-passengers, came with me, and the rest of my party were left on board with my goods to rejoin me the next day. I took with me some of my clothes, giving them to the guide to carry to spare myself fatigue and myself carried a lance. Now the guide wished to steal the clothes, so he led us to an inlet of the sea and set about crossing it with the clothes. I said to him "You cross over alone and leave the clothes; if we can cross we shall, and if not we shall look for a ford higher up." He drew back then, and afterwards we saw some men swimming across, so we were convinced that he had wanted to drown us and get away with the clothes. Though I made a show of vivacity I was on my guard and kept brandishing the lance, so that the guide became frightened of me. We then came on a waterless plain and suffered greatly from thirst, but God sent us a horseman with a company of men who gave us to drink, and we went on, thinking that the town was close at hand, while actually we were separated from it by nullahs in which we walked for miles. In the evening the guide wished to lead us towards the shore, where there is no road, for the coast is rocky, hoping that we should get stuck among the rocks and he would make away with the clothes, but I said that we should take no road but the one that we were on. When night fell, as I was afraid of being molested on the road and did not know exactly how far we still were from the town, I decided that we should go aside from the road and sleep. Although I was tired out I pretended to be full of vigour, and put the clothes under my garments and grasped my lance in my hand. My companion was worn out, and both he and the guide slept, but I stayed awake and every time the guide moved I spoke to him to show him that I was awake. In the morning I sent the guide to fetch us some water and my companion took the clothes. We had still some ravines and nullahs to cross, but the guide brought us water and eventually we reached Qalhát in a state of extreme fatigue. My feet were so swollen inside my shoes that the blood was almost starting from under the nails. Then, as a final touch to our misfortunes, the gatekeeper insisted on taking me to be interrogated by the governor of the town. The governor, however, was an excellent man and very kind, and he put me up. I stayed with him for six days, during which I was unable to walk because of the soreness of my feet. The town of Qalhát lies on the shore; it has fine bazaars and an exceedingly beautiful mosque, the walls of which are decorated with Qáshání tilework, and which occupies a lofty situation overlooking the town and the harbour. I ate fish there of a sort which I have found in no other country. I preferred it to any kind of flesh and used to eat nothing else. They broil it on the leaves of trees and serve it with rice, which is brought to them by sea from India. The inhabitants are traders and live [entirely] on what comes to them from the Indian Ocean. Whenever a vessel arrives at their town, they show the greatest joy.

We then set out for the country of 'Omán and arrived there after six days' travelling.[18] It is a fertile land, with streams, trees, orchards, palm gardens, and fruit trees of various kinds. Its capital, the town of Nazwa, lies at the foot of a mountain and has fine bazaars and splendid clean mosques. Its inhabitants make a habit of eating meals in the courts of the mosques, every person bringing what he has, and all sitting down to the meal together, and travellers join in with them. They are very warlike and brave, always fighting between themselves. The sultan of 'Omán is an Arab of the tribe of Azd, and is called Abú Muhammad, which is the title given to every sultan who governs 'Omán.[19] The towns on the coast are for the most part under the government of Hormuz.

I travelled next to the country of Hormuz. Hormuz is a town on the coast, called also Múghistán, and in the sea facing it and nine miles from shore is New Hormuz, which is an island.[20] The town on it is called Jarawn. It is a large and fine city, with busy markets, as it is the port from which the wares from India and Sind are despatched to the 'Iráqs, Fárs and Khurásán. The island is saline, and the inhabitants live on fish and dates exported to them from Basra. They say in their tongue *Khurmá wamáhí lúti pádishâhí*, which means "Dates and fish are a royal dish." Water is a valuable commodity in this island. They have wells and artificial reservoirs to collect rainwater at some distance from the town. The inhabitants go there with waterskins, which they fill and carry on their backs to the shore, load them on boats and bring them to the town. A strange thing I saw there was a fish's head at the gate of the cathedral mosque as large as a hillock and with eyes like doors, and you would see people entering by one eye and coming out by the other. The sultan of Hormuz is Qutb ad-Dín Tahamtan, a most generous and humble ruler, who makes a habit of visiting every theologian or pious man or sharíf who comes to his town and of paying to each his due. We found him engaged in a war with his nephews, who were in revolt. We stayed there sixteen days, and when we wished to leave I said to one of my companions "How can we go away without seeing this sultan?" So we went to the house of the wazír, who took me by the hand and went with me to the palace. I saw there an old man wearing skimpy and dirty garments with a turban on his head and a kerchief as a girdle. The wazír saluted him and I did the same, not knowing that he was the king, and then I began to converse with a person I knew who was standing beside him. When the wazír enlightened me I was covered with confusion and made my excuses. The king rose and went into the palace, followed by the generals and ministers and when I entered with the wazír we found him sitting on his throne with the same shabby clothes on. He asked me about myself and my journey and the kings I had seen, then, after food had been served, he rose and I said farewell to him and went away.

We set out from Hormuz to visit a saintly man in the town of Khunjubál, and after crossing the strait, hired mounts from the Turkmens who live in that country. No travelling can be done there except in their company, because of their bravery and knowledge of the roads. In these parts there is a desert four days' journey in extent, which is the haunt of Arab brigands, and in which the deadly samúm blows in June and July. All who are overtaken by it perish, and I was told that when a man has fallen a victim to this wind and his friends attempt to wash his body [for burial], all his limbs fall apart.[21] All along the road there are graves of persons who have succumbed there to this wind. We used to travel by night, and halt from sunrise until late afternoon in the shade of the trees. This desert was the scene of the exploits of the famous brigand Jamál al-Lúk, who had under him a band of Arab and Persian horsemen. He used to build hospices and entertain travellers with the money that he gained by robbery, and it is said that he used to claim that he never employed violence except against those who did not pay the tithes on their property. No king could do anything against him, but afterwards he repented and gave himself up to ascetic practices, and his grave is now a place of pilgrimage. After traversing these deserts we reached Kawrástán, a small town with running streams and orchards and extremely hot.[22] From there we marched through another desert like the former for three days and reached the town of Lár,[23] a large town with perennial streams and orchards and fine bazaars. We lodged in a convent inhabited by a group of darwíshes who have the following custom. They assemble in the convent every afternoon and then go round the houses in the town; at each house they are given one or two loaves and from these they supply the needs of travellers. The householders are used to this practice and make provision for the extra loaves, in order to assist the darwíshes in their distribution of food. There is a Turkmen sultan in the town of Lár, who sent us a hospitality gift,[24] but we did not visit or see him.

We went on to the town of Khunjubál,[25] the residence of the Shaykh Abú Dulaf, whom we had come to visit. We lodged in his hermitage and he treated me kindly and sent me food and fruit by one of his sons. From there we journeyed to the town of Qays, which is also called Síráf.[26] The people of Síráf are Persians of noble stock, and amongst them there is a tribe of Arabs, who dive for pearls. The pearl fisheries are situated between Síráf and Bahrayn in a calm bay like a wide river. During the months of April and May a large number of boats come to this place with divers and merchants from Fárs, Bahrayn and Qathíf. Before diving the diver puts on his face a sort of tortoiseshell mask and a tortoiseshell clip on his nose, then he ties a rope round his waist and dives. They differ in their endurance under water, some of them being able to stay under for an hour or two hours or less.[27] When he reaches the bottom of the sea he finds the shells there stuck in the sand between small stones, and pulls then out by hand or cuts them loose with a knife which he has for the purpose, and puts them in a leather bag slung round his neck. When his breath becomes restricted he pulls the rope, and the man holding the rope on the shore feels the movement and pulls him up into the boat. The bag is taken from him and the shells are opened. Inside them are found pieces of flesh which are cut out with a knife, and when they come into contact with the air solidify and turn into pearls. These are then collected, large and small together; the sultan takes his fifth and the remainder are bought by the merchants who are there in the boats. Most of them are the creditors of the divers, and they take the pearls in quittance of their debt or so much of it as is their due.

From Síráf we travelled to the town of Bahrayn, a fine large town with orchards, trees and streams. Water is easy to get at there; all one has to do is to scoop the ground with one's hands.[28] It is very hot and sandy, and the sand often encroaches on some of its settlements. From Bahrayn we went to the town of al-Quthayf [Qathíf], a fine large town inhabited by Arab tribes who are out-and-out Shi'ites and openly proclaim it, fearing nobody. Next we journeyed to the town of Hajar, which is now called al-Hasá.[29] It has become the subject of a proverb "Carrying dates to Hajar," because there are more palms there than in any other district, and they even feed their beasts with the dates. We travelled thence to the town of Yamáma,[30] in company with the governor of which I went on to Mecca to perform the pilgrimage. This was in the year 1332, the same year that al-Malik an-Násir, the sultan of Egypt, made his last pilgrimage. He made munificent gifts to the inhabitants of the twin shrines [Mecca and Madína] and to the devotees living there, and on the same journey he put to death by poisoning the amír Ahmad, who, it is said, was his own son, and his principal amír Bektimur the cup-bearer, on being warned that they were plotting to assassinate him and seize the throne.

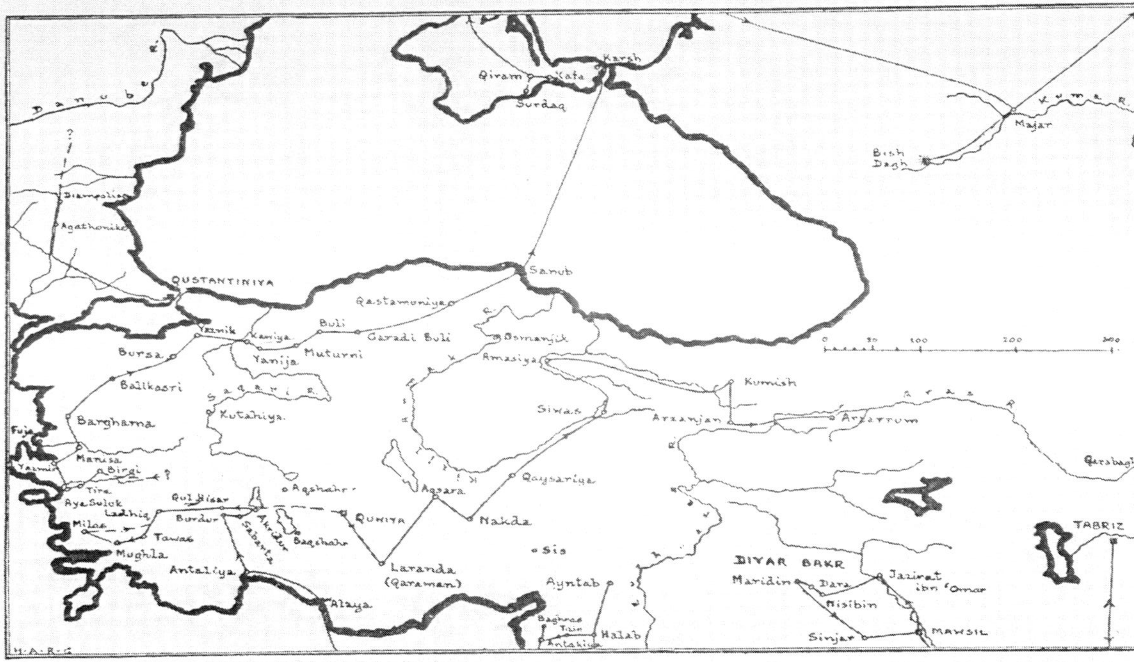

SKETCH MAP OF ANATOLIA TO ILLUSTRATE IBN BATTŪTA'S TRAVELS

[face p. 122

CHAPTER IV

AFTER the pilgrimage I went to Judda, intending to take ship to Yemen and India, but that plan fell through and I could get no one to join me. I stayed at Judda about forty days. There was a ship there going to Qusayr [Kosair], and I went on board to see what state it was in, but I was not satisfied. This was an act of providence, for the ship sailed and foundered in the open sea, and very few escaped. Afterwards I took ship for Aydháb, but we were driven to a roadstead called Ra's Dawá'ir [p. 107], from which we made our way with some Bejás through the desert to Aydháb. Thence we travelled to Edfu and down the Nile to Cairo, where I stayed for a few days, then set out for Syria and passed for the second time through Gaza, Hebron, Jerusalem, Ramlah, Acre, Tripoli, and Jabala to Ládhiqíya.

At Ládhiqíya we embarked on a large galley belonging to the Genoese, the master of which was called Martalmín, and set out for the country of the Turks known as *Bilád ar-Rúm* [Anatolia], because it was in ancient times their land.[1] Later on it was conquered by the Muslims, but there are still large numbers of Christians there under the government of the Turkmen Muslims. We were ten nights at sea, and the Christian treated us kindly and took no passage money from us. On the tenth day we reached 'Aláyá, where the province begins. This country is one of the best in the world; in it God has united the good features dispersed throughout other lands. Its people are the most comely of men, the cleanest in their dress, the most exquisite in their food, and the kindliest folk in creation. Wherever we stopped in this land, whether at a hospice or a private house, our neighbours both men and women (these do not veil themselves) came to ask after us. When we left them they bade us farewell as though they were our relatives and our own folk, and you would see the women weeping. They bake bread only once a week, and the men used to bring us gifts of warm bread on the day it was baked, along with delicious viands, saying "The women have sent this to you and beg your prayers." All the inhabitants are orthodox Sunnís; there are no sectarians or heretics amongst them, but they eat hashísh [Indian hemp], and think no harm of it.

The city of 'Aláyá is a large town on the seacoast.[2] It is inhabited by Turkmens, and is visited by the merchants of Cairo, Alexandria, and Syria. The district is well-wooded, and wood is exported from there to Alexandria and Damietta, whence it is carried to the other cities of Egypt. There is a magnificent and formidable citadel, built by Sultan 'Alá ad-Dín, at the upper end of the town. The qádí of the town rode out with me to meet the king of 'Aláyá, who is Yúsuf Bek, son of Qaramán, *bek* meaning king in their language. He lives at a distance of ten miles from the city. We found him sitting by himself on the top of a hillock by the shore, with the amírs and wazírs below him, and the troops on his right and left. He has his hair dyed black. I saluted him and answered his questions regarding my visit to his town, and after my withdrawal he sent me a present of money.

From 'Aláyá I went to Antáliya [Adalia], a most beautiful city.[3] It covers an immense area, and though of vast bulk is one of the most attractive towns to be seen anywhere, besides being exceedingly populous and well laid out. Each section of the inhabitants lives in a separate quarter. The Christian merchants live in a quarter of the town known as the Míná [the Port], and are surrounded by a wall, the gates of which are shut upon them from without at night and during the Friday service.[4] The Greeks, who were its former inhabitants, live by themselves in another quarter, the Jews in another, and the king and his court and mamlúks in another, each of these quarters being walled off likewise. The rest of the Muslims live in the main city. Round the whole town and all the quarters mentioned there is another great wall. The town contains many orchards and produces fine fruits, including an admirable kind of apricot, called by them Qamar ad-Dín, which has a sweet almond in its kernel. This fruit is dried and exported to Egypt, where it is regarded as a great luxury.

We stayed here at the college mosque of the town, the principal of which was Shaykh Shiháb ad-Dín al-Hamawí. Now in all the lands inhabited by the Turkmens in Anatolia, in every district, town, and village, there are to be found members of the organization known as the *Akhíya* or Young Brotherhood. Nowhere in the world will you find men so eager to welcome strangers, so prompt to serve food and to satisfy the wants of others, and so ready to suppress injustice and to kill [tyrannical] agents of police and the miscreants who join with them. A Young Brother, or *akhí* in their language, is one who is chosen by all the members of his trade [guild], or by other young unmarried men, or those who live in ascetic retreat, to be their leader. This organization is known also as the *Futúwa*, or Order of Youth. The leader builds a hospice and furnishes it with rugs, lamps, and other necessary appliances. The members of his community work during the day to gain their livelihood, and bring him what they have earned in the late afternoon. With this they buy fruit, food, and the other things which the hospice requires for their use. If a traveller comes to the town that day they lodge him in their hospice; these provisions serve for his entertainment as their guest, and he stays with them until he goes away. If there are no travellers they themselves assemble to partake of the food, and having eaten it they sing and dance. On the morrow they return to their occupations and bring their earnings to their leader in the late afternoon. The members are called *fityán* (youths), and their leader, as we have said, is the *akhí*.[6]

The day after our arrival at Antáliya one of these youths came to Shaykh Shiháb ad-Dín al-Hamawí and spoke to him in Turkish, which I did not understand at that time. He was wearing old clothes and had a felt bonnet on his head. The shaykh said to me "Do you know what he is saying?" "No" said I "I do not know." He answered "He is inviting you and your company to eat a meal with him." I was astonished but I said "Very well," and when the man had gone I said to the shaykh "He is a poor man, and is not able to entertain us, and we do not like to be a burden on him." The shaykh burst out laughing and said "He is one of the shaykhs of the Young Brotherhood. He is a cobbler, and a man of generous disposition. His companions, about two hundred men belonging to different trades, have made him their leader and have built a hospice to entertain their guests. All that they earn by day they spend at night."

After I had prayed the sunset prayer the same man came back for us and took us to the hospice. We found [ourselves in] a fine building, carpeted with beautiful Turkish rugs and lit by a large number of chandeliers of 'Iráqí glass. A number of young men stood in rows in the hall, wearing long mantles and boots, and each had a knife about two cubits long attached to a girdle around his waist. On their heads were white woollen bonnets, and attached to the peak of these bonnets was a piece of stuff a cubit long and two fingers in breadth. When they took their seats, every man removed his bonnet and set it down in front of him, and kept on his head another ornamental bonnet of silk or other material. In the centre of their hall was a sort of platform placed there for visitors. When we took our places, they served up a great banquet followed by fruits and sweetmeats, after which they began to sing and to dance. We were filled with admiration and were greatly astonished at their openhandedness and generosity. We took leave of them at the close of the night and left them in their hospice.

The sultan of Antáliya, Khidr Bek, son of Yúnus Bek, was ill when we reached the town, but we visited him on his sick-bed. He spoke to us very kindly, and when we took leave of him, sent us a gift of money.

We travelled on to the town of Burdúr [Buldur], a small place with many orchards and streams, and a strong fortress on a hilltop. We put up as the guests of the preacher there. The brotherhood held a meeting and wished us to stay with them, but he would not hear of it, so they prepared a banquet for us in a garden belonging to one of them and conducted us to the place. It was marvellous to see the joy and gladness with which they received us, though they were ignorant of our language and we of theirs, and there was no one to interpret between us. We stayed with them one day and then took our leave.

From Burdúr we went on to Sabarta [Isparta], and then to Akrídúr [Egirdir], a great and populous town with fine bazaars. There is a lake with sweet water here on which boats go in two days to Aqshahr and Baqshshr and other towns and villages.[6] The sultan of Akrídúr is one of the principal rulers in this country.

He is a man of upright conduct and attends the afternoon prayer at the cathedral mosque every day. While we were there his son died and after his burial the sultan and the students went out to his grave for three days. I went out with them the second day and the sultan, seeing me walking, sent me a horse with his apologies. On reaching the madrasa I sent back the horse, but he returned it saying " I gave it as a gift, not as a loan." He sent me also a robe and some money.

We left there for the town of Qul Hisár [" Lake Fortress "], a small town completely surrounded by reed-grown water.[7] The only way to it is by a sort of bridge between the rushes and the water, admitting only one horseman at a time. The town, which is on a hill in the midst of the lake, is impregnable. The sultan, who is the brother of the sultan of Akrídúr, was absent when we arrived, but after we had stayed there some days he came back and treated us kindly, supplying us with horses and provisions. He sent some horsemen to escort us to the town of Ládhiq [Denizli], as the country was infested by a troop of brigands called Jarmiyán [Kermian] who possess a town called Kútáhiya. Ládhiq is a most important town, with seven cathedral mosques. In it are manufactured matchless cotton fabrics with gold embroidered edges, which have a very long life on account of the excellence of the cotton and of the spinning. Most of the workers are Greek women, for there are many Greeks here, who are subject to the Muslims and pay a poll tax to the sultan. The distinctive mark of the Greeks is their tall peaked hats, red or white; their women wear capacious turbans. As we entered the town we passed through a bazaar. Some men got down from their booths and took our horses' bridles, then some others objected to their action and the altercation went on so long

INDIAN HAREM SCENE

A GROUP OF DARWISHES DANCING

that some of them drew knives. We of course did not know what they were saying and were afraid of them, thinking they were those brigands and that this was their town. At length God sent us a man who knew Arabic, and he explained that they were members of two branches of the "Young Brotherhood," each of whom wanted us to lodge with them. We were amazed at their generosity. It was decided finally that they should cast lots, and that we should lodge first with the winner. This being done the prior of the first hospice, Brother Sinán, conducted us to the bath and himself looked after me; afterwards they served up a great banquet with sweetmeats and many fruits. Some verses of the Koran were then read and after that they began to chant their litany and to dance. The next day we had an audience of the sultan, who is one of the principal rulers in Anatolia, and on our return were met by Brother Túmán, the prior of the other hospice, who entertained us even better than their friends had done, and sprinkled us with rose water when we came out of the bath.

We stayed at Ládhiq for some time, in view of the dangers of the road; then, as a caravan was ready to set out, we travelled with them for a day and part of the next night and reached the castle of Tawás [Davas]. We spent the night outside it and next morning, on coming to the gate, we were interrogated from the top of the wall. The commander then came out with his troops, and after they had explored the neighbourhood for fear of the robbers, their animals were driven out. This is their constant practice. From there we went on to Mughla and thence to Mílás, one of the finest and most important towns in the country. We lodged in a convent of one of the Young Brotherhood, who outdid by far all that our previous hosts had done in the way of generosity, hospitality, taking us to the bath, and other praiseworthy acts. The sultan of Mílás is an excellent ruler, and keeps company with theologians. He gave us gifts and supplied us with horses and provisions.

After receiving the sultan's gift we left for the city of Qúniya [Konia]. It is a large town with fine buildings, and has many streams and fruit-gardens. The streets are exceedingly broad, and the bazaars admirably planned, with each craft in a bazaar of its own. It is said that this city was built by Alexander. It is now in the territories of Sultan Badr ad-Dín ibn Qaramán, whom we shall mention presently, but it has sometimes been captured by the king of 'Iráq, as it lies close to his territories in this country. We stayed there at the hospice of the qádí, who is called Ibn Qalam Sháh, and is a member of the *Futúwa*. His hospice is very large indeed, and he has a great many disciples. They trace their affiliation to the *Futúwa* back to the Caliph 'Alí, and the distinctive garment of the order in their case is the trousers,[8] just as the Súfís wear the patched robe. This qádí showed us even greater consideration and hospitality than our former benefactors, and sent his son with us in his place to the bath.

In this town is the mausoleum of the pious shaykh Jalál ad-Dín [ar-Rúmí], known as *Mawláná* [" Our Master "]. He was held in high esteem, and there is a brotherhood in Anatolia who claim spiritual affiliation with him and are called after him the *Jalálíya*.[9] The story goes that Jalál ad-Dín was in early life a theologian and a professor. One day a sweetmeat seller came into the college-mosque with a tray of sweetmeats on his head, and having given him a piece went out again. The shaykh left his lesson to follow him and disappeared for some years. Then he came back, but with a disordered mind, speaking nothing but Persian verses which no one could understand. His disciples followed him and wrote down his productions, which they collected into a book called *The Mathnawí*. This book is greatly revered by the people of this country; they meditate on it, teach it, and read it in their religious houses on Thursday nights. From Qúniya we travelled to Láranda [Karaman], the capital of the sultan of Qaramán. I met this sultan outside the town as he was coming back from hunting, and on my dismounting to him, he dismounted also. It is the custom of the kings of this country to dismount if a visitor dismounts to them. This action on his part pleases them and they show him greater honour; if on the other hand he greets them while on horseback they are displeased and the visitor forfeits their goodwill in consequence. This happened to me once with one of these kings. After I had greeted the sultan we rode back to the town together, and he showed me the greatest hospitality.

We then entered the territories of the king of 'Iráq, visiting Aqsara [Akserai], where they make sheep's wool carpets which are exported as far as India, China, and the lands of the Turks, and journeyed thence through Nakda [Nigda] to Qaysáríya, which is one of the largest towns in the country. In this town resides one of the Viceroy's khátúns, who is related to the king of 'Iráq, and like all the sultan's relatives has the title of *Aghá*, which means Great. We visited her and she treated us courteously, ordering a meal to be served for us, and when we withdrew sent us a horse with saddle and bridle and a sum of money. At all these towns we lodged in a convent belonging to the Young Brotherhood. It is the custom in this country that in towns that are not the residence of a sultan one of the Young Brothers acts as governor, exercising the same authority and appearing in public with the same retinue as a king. We travelled on to Síwás, the largest town in the country and residence of the king of 'Iráq's viceroy, 'Alá ad-Dín Artaná. We were met near the town by a party belonging to the "Young Brother" Ahmad, and a little later by a party of the "Young Brother" Chelebi, who invited us to stay with them, but we were already pledged to the former. Our hosts showed the utmost joy on our arrival at their convent, and treated us with the most perfect hospitality. We visited the amír 'Alá ad-Dín Artaná who, speaking in excellent Arabic, asked me about the countries I had visited and their sovereigns, and afterwards sent us gifts. When we left Síwás he wrote to his lieutenants in the towns to give us hospitality and to supply us with provisions. We journeyed thence to Amásiya, a large and beautiful town with broad streets, Kumish [Gümüsh Khanah], a populous town which is visited by merchants from 'Iráq and Syria and has silver mines, Arzanján, where Armenians form the greater part of the population, and Arz ar-Rúm. This is a vast town but is mostly in ruins as the result of a civil war between two Turkmen tribes. We lodged there at the convent of the "Young Brother" Túmán, who was said to be more than a hundred and thirty years old. I saw him going about on foot supported by a staff, with his faculties unimpaired and assiduous in praying at the stated times. All these towns belong to the king of 'Iráq.

We went on to the town of Birgí[10] where we had been told there was a distinguished professor called Muhyí ad-Dín. On reaching the madrasa we found him just arriving, mounted on a lively mule and wearing ample garments with gold embroidery, with his slaves and servants on either side of him and preceded by the students. He gave us a kindly welcome and invited me to visit him after the sunset prayer. I found him in a reception hall in his garden, which had a stream of water flowing through a white marble basin with a rim of enamelled tiles. He was occupying a raised seat covered with embroidered cloths, having a number of his students and slaves standing on either side of him, and when I saw him I took him for a king. He rose to greet me and made me sit next him on the dais, after which we were served with food and returned to the madrasa. The sultan of Birgí was then at his summer quarters on a mountain close by and on receiving news of me from the professor sent for me. When I arrived with the professor he sent his two sons to ask how we were, and sent me a tent of the kind they call *Khargáh*. It consists of wooden laths put together like a dome and covered with pieces of felt; the upper part is opened to admit the light and air and can be closed when required. Next day the sultan sent for us and asked me about the countries I had visited, then after food had been served we retired. This went on for several days, the sultan inviting us daily to join him at his meal, and one afternoon visiting us himself, on account of the respect which the Turks show for theologians. At length we both became weary of staying on this mountain, so the professor sent a message to the sultan that I wished to continue my journey, and received a reply that we should accompany the sultan to his palace in the city on the following day. Next day he sent an excellent horse and descended with us to the city. On reaching the palace we climbed a long flight of stairs with him and came to a fine audience hall with a basin of water in the centre and a bronze lion at each corner of it spouting water from its mouth. Round the hall were daises covered with carpets, on one of which was the sultan's cushion. When we reached this place, the sultan removed his cushion and sat down beside us on the carpets. The Koran-readers, who always attend the sultan's audiences, sat below the dais. After syrup and biscuits had been served I spoke thanking the sultan warmly and praising the professor, which pleased the sultan a great deal.

As we were sitting there, he said to me "Have you ever seen a stone that has fallen from the sky?" I replied "No, nor ever heard of one." "Well," he said, "a stone fell from the sky outside this town," and thereupon called for it to be brought. A great black stone was brought, very hard and with a glitter in it, I reckon its weight was about a hundredweight. The sultan sent for stone breakers, and four of them came and struck it all together four times over with iron hammers, but made no impression on it. I was amazed, and he ordered it to be taken back to its place. We stayed altogether fourteen days with this sultan. Every night he sent us food, fruit, sweetmeats and candles, and gave me in addition a hundred pieces of gold, a thousand dirhems, a complete set of garments and a Greek slave called Michael, as well as sending a robe and a gift of money to each of my companions. All this we owed to the professor Muhyí ad-Dín—may God reward him with good!

We went on through the town of Tíra, which is in the territories of this sultan, to Ayá Sulúq [Ephesus], a large and ancient town venerated by the Greeks. It possesses a large church built of finely hewn stones each measuring ten or more cubits in length. The cathedral mosque, which was formerly a church greatly venerated by the Greeks, is one of the most beautiful in the world. I bought a Greek slave girl here for forty dinars. Thence we went to Yazmír [Smyrna], a large town on the coast, mostly in ruins. The governor 'Omar, a son of the sultan of Aydín, came to the convent to visit me and sent me a large hospitality-gift. Afterwards he gave me a young Greek slave named Nicolas. He was a generous and pious prince and constantly engaged in war with the Christians. He had galleys, with which he used to make raids on the environs of Constantinople the Great, taking prisoners and booty and after spending it all in largesse he would make another raid. Eventually the Greeks, under the pressure of his attacks, appealed to the Pope, who ordered the Christians of Genoa and France to make an attack on him. They did so, and the Pope sent an army from Rome, which captured the port and the city in a night attack. The amír 'Omar went down from the citadel and fought them, but he died a martyr's death together with a number of his troops. The Christians established themselves in the city, but could not capture the citadel on account of its strength.[11]

We travelled thence to Maghnísíya [Magnesia, now Manisa] where we prayed the Festival Prayer [of the Pilgrimage] in the company of Sultan Sarúkhán. Here my slave, on taking my horses to water along with a slave belonging to one of my companions, attempted to escape. The sultan sent in pursuit of them, but as everyone was occupied with the festival, they were not found. They made for a town on the coast named Fúja belonging to the infidels,[12] who send a gift to the sultan every year, in return for which he is content to leave them alone because of the strength of their city. Next day at noon some Turks brought them back with the horses. The fugitives had passed them the evening before, and becoming suspicious, they had questioned them until they confessed their design of escaping. We went on next to Barghama which is in ruins but has a strong fortress on the summit of a hill. Here we hired a guide and travelled among high and rugged mountains to the town of Balíkasrí. The sultan, whose name is Dumúr Khán, is a worthless person. It was his father who built this town, and during the son's reign it attracted a vast population of knaves, for "Like king, like people." I visited him and he sent me a silk robe. In this town I bought a Greek slave girl called Marguerite.

We journeyed next to Bursá [Brusa], a great city with fine bazaars and broad streets, surrounded by orchards and running springs. Outside it are two thermal establishments, one for men and the other for women, to which patients come from the most distant parts. They lodge there for three days at a hospice which was built by one of the Turkmen kings. In this town I met the pious Shaykh 'Abdulláh the Egyptian, a traveller, who went all round the world, except that he never visited China, Ceylon, the West, or Spain or the Negrolands, so that in visiting those countries I have surpassed him. The sultan of Bursá is Orkhán Bek, son of 'Othmán Chúk. He is the greatest of the Turkmen kings and the richest in wealth, lands, and military forces, and possesses nearly a hundred fortresses which he is continually visiting for inspection and putting to rights. He fights with the infidels and besieges them. It was his father who captured Bursá from the Greeks, and it is said that he besieged Yazník [Nicæa] for about twenty years, but died before it was taken. His son Orkhán besieged it twelve years before capturing it, and it was there that I saw him.[13] Yazník lies in a lake and can be reached only by one road like a bridge admitting only a single horseman at a time. It is in ruins and uninhabited except for a few men in the Sultan's service. It is defended by four walls with a moat between each pair, and is entered over wooden drawbridges. Inside there are orchards and houses and fields, and drinking water is obtained from wells. I stayed in this town forty days owing to the illness of one of my horses, but growing impatient at the delay I left it and went on with three of my companions and a slave girl and two slave boys. We had no one with us who could speak Turkish well enough to interpret for us, for the interpreter we had left us at Yazník. After leaving this town we crossed a great river called Saqarí [Sangarius] by a ferry. This consisted of four beams bound together with ropes, on which the passengers are placed, together with their saddles and baggage; it is pulled across by men on the further bank, and the horses swim behind. The same night we reached Káwiya [Gheiva] and lodged with one of the Brotherhood. As he neither understood Arabic nor we Turkish, he sent for a theologian, who spoke to us in Persian, and not understanding us when we spoke Arabic, excused himself to the brother saying *Íshán 'arabí kuhná migúyand waman 'arabí naw midánam*, which means "These men speak ancient Arabic and I know only modern Arabic." He said this only to shield himself from disgrace, for they thought he knew Arabic, when in reality he did not know it. But this turned out to be of service to us, for the brother, thinking that things were really as he had said, showed us the greatest consideration saying "These men must be honourably treated, since they speak the ancient Arabic tongue, which was the tongue of the Prophet and his Companions." I did not understand just then what the theologian had said, but the sound of his words stuck in my memory and when I learned the Persian language, I found out their meaning.

We spent that night at the hospice, and the Brother sent a guide with us to Yanija [Tarakli], which is a fine large town. We started to look for the akhí's hospice, and found one of those crazy darwíshes, so I said to him "Is this the akhí's hospice?" He replied *na'am* ["Yes"], and I felt so pleased at having found someone who knew Arabic. But when I tested him further the cat was out of the bag, for *na'am* was the only word of Arabic he knew. We put up at the hospice, and one of the students brought food to us. The akhí himself was away, but we became very friendly with this student. Though he knew no Arabic, he was very kind to us, and spoke to the governor of the town, who gave me one of his mounted men to take us to Kaynúk [Kevnik]. Kaynúk is a small town in the territiries of Sultan Orkhán Bek, inhabited by infidel [Christian] Greeks under Muslim protection. There is only one household of Muslims in the place, and that belongs to the governors of the Greeks, so we put up at the house of an old infidel woman. This was in the season of snow and rain. She treated us well,[14] and we spent that night in her house. Now this town has no trees or vineyards; the only thing cultivated there is saffron, and the old woman brought us a great quantity of it, thinking that we were merchants and would buy it from her.

When we mounted our horses in the morning, the horseman whom the member of the Brotherhood had sent with us from Kaynúk came to us and provided us with another horseman to guide us to the town of Muturní. The road was obliterated by a heavy fall of snow the previous night, so our guide went on ahead of us and we followed his tracks. About midday we came to a village of Turkmens, who brought us food, of which we ate. The horseman spoke to them and one of them went on with us. He led us over difficult and mountainous country, and a river channel which we crossed more than thirty times. When we got clear of this the guide asked us for some money, but we said "When we reach the town we shall give you plenty." He was not satisfied or else did not understand, for he took a bow belonging to one of our party and went off a little way, then returned and gave the bow back. I then gave him a little money and he took it and decamped, leaving us with no idea which way to go and with no road visible to us. About sunset we came to a hill on which we could make out the track by a quantity of stones on it. I was afraid that both I and my companions might perish, as I expected more snow to fall and the place was uninhabited; if we dismounted we were doomed and if we went on we did not know the road. I had a good horse however, so I said to myself "If I reach safety perhaps I may contrive to save my companions," and commending them to God, I set off. At length in the late evening I came to some houses and said "O God, grant they may be inhabited." I found that they were inhabited, and God of his goodness led me to a religious house belonging to some darwíshes. When they heard me speaking at the door, one of them came out; he was a man whom I knew, and I advised him to go out with the darwíshes to deliver my companions. They did so and set out with me, and so we all reached the convent in safety, praise be to God Most High for our safety! Each darwísh brought us what food he could and our distress was removed.

We set out next morning and reached Muturní [Mudurlu], where we fell in with a pilgrim who knew Arabic. We besought him to travel with us to Qastamúniya, which is ten days' journey from there; I gave him an Egyptian robe of mine and some money for current expenses, which he left with his family, and assigned him a mount, promising him a good reward. He turned out to be a wealthy man, but of base character. We used to give him money for our expenses, and he would take the bread that was left over and buy spices, herbs and salt with it, and appropriate the money for these. I was told too that he used to steal part of the money that we gave him for our expenses. We put up with him because of our difficulties in not knowing Turkish, but things went so far that we used to say to him in the evenings "Well, Hajjí, how much have you stolen today?"

He would reply "So much" and we would laugh and make the best of it. We came next to the town of Búlí, where we stayed at a convent of the Young Brotherhood. What an excellent body of men these are, how nobleminded, how unselfish and full of compassion for the stranger, how kindly and affectionate they are to him, how warm their welcome to him! A stranger coming to them is made to feel as though he were meeting the dearest of his own folk. Next morning we travelled on to Garadí Búlí, a large and fine town situated on a plain, with spacious streets and bazaars, but one of the coldest towns in the world. It is composed of several different quarters, each inhabited by different communities, none of which mixes with any of the others. The sultan, who is one of the less important rulers in this country, is a fine-looking and upright man, but not liberal. He came to visit us at the religious house and stayed for an hour, asking me about my travels, and afterwards sent me a saddled horse and a robe.

We went on through a small town named Burlú[15] to Qastamúniya, a very large and fine town, in which goods are plentiful, and prices cheaper than I have ever seen elsewhere. We stayed in the convent of a very deaf shaykh and I saw an astonishing thing in connection with him. One of his students used to write with his finger in the air or on the ground and he would understand and reply. Sometimes long stories were told him in this way. We remained here about forty days. The sultan of Qastamúniya is the illustrious Sulaymán Pádsháh, a man over seventy years of age with a fine face and long beard, a stately and venerable figure. I visited him in his reception hall and he made me sit beside him and asked me about my travels. He then commanded me to be lodged near him, and gave me on the same day a fine white horse and a robe, besides assigning me money for my expenses and forage. Later on he gave me an assignation of wheat and barley from a village half a day's journey from the town, but I could not find anyone to buy it because of the cheapness of provisions, so I gave it to the pilgrim who was in our company. It is a custom of this sultan's to take his seat in the audience chamber every afternoon; food is served and the doors are opened and no one, whether townsman or nomad, stranger or traveller, is prevented from partaking.

From Qastamúniya we travelled to Sanúb [Sinope], a populous town combining strength with beauty. It is surrounded by sea except on the east, where there is only one gate which no one is allowed to enter without permission from the governor, Ibrahim Bek, who is a son of Sulaymán Pádsháh. Outside the town there are eleven villages inhabited by Greek infidels. The cathedral mosque at Sanúb is a most beautiful building, constructed by Sultan Parwánah. He was succeeded by his son Ghází Chelebí, at whose death the town was seized by Sultan Sulaymán. Ghází Chelebí was a brave and audacious man, with a peculiar capacity for swimming under water. He used to sail out with his war vessels to fight the Greeks, and when the fleets met and everyone was occupied with the fighting he would dive under the water carrying an iron tool with which he pierced the enemy's ships, and they knew nothing about it until all at once they sank.

We stayed at Sanúb about forty days waiting for the weather to became favourable for sailing to the town of Qiram.[16] Then we hired a vessel belonging to the Greeks and waited another eleven days for a favourable wind. At length we set sail, but after travelling for three nights, we were beset in mid-sea by a terrible tempest. The storm raged with unparalleled fury, then the wind changed and drove us back nearly to Sanúb. The weather cleared and we set out again, and after another tempest like the former, we at length saw the hills on the land. We made for a harbour called Karsh [Kerch], intending to enter it, but some people on the hill made signs to us not to enter, and fearing that there were enemy vessels in the port, we turned back along the coast. As we approached the land I said to the master of the ship "I want to descend here," so he put me ashore. The place was in the Qipchaq desert which is green and verdant, but flat and treeless. There is no firewood so they make fires of dung, and you will see even the highest of them picking it up and putting it in the skirts of their garments. The only method of travelling in this desert is in waggons; it extends for six months' journey, of which three are in the territories of Sultan Muhammad Ūzbeg.[17] The day after our arrival one of the merchants in our company hired some waggons from the Qipchaqs who inhabit this desert, and who are Christians, and we came to Kafá, a large town extending along the sea-coast, inhabited by Christians, mostly Genoese, whose governor is called Damdír [Demetrio].[18]

We stayed at Kafá in the mosque of the Muslims. An hour after our arrival we heard bells ringing on all sides. As I had never heard bells before,[19] I was alarmed and bade my companions ascend the minaret and read the Koran and issue the call to prayer. They did so, when suddenly a man entered wearing armour and weapons and greeted us. He told us that he was the qádí of the Muslims there, and said "When I heard the reading and the call to prayer, I feared for your safety and came as you see." Then he went away, but no evil befel us. The next day the governor came to us and entertained us to a meal, then we went round the city and found it provided with fine bazaars. All the inhabitants are infidels. We went down to the port and saw a magnificent harbour with about two hundred vessels in it, ships of war and trading vessels, small and large, for it is one of the most notable harbours in the world.

We hired a waggon and travelled to the town of Qiram, which forms part of the territories of Sultan Úzbeg Khán and has a governor called Tuluktumúr. On hearing of our arrival the governor sent the imám to me with a horse; he himself was ill, but we visited him and he treated us honourably and gave us gifts. He was on the point of setting out for the town of Sará, the capital of the Khán, so I prepared to travel along with him and hired waggons for that purpose. These waggons have four large wheels and are drawn by two or more horses, or by oxen or camels, according to their weight. The driver rides on one of the horses and carries a whip or wooden goad. On the waggon is put a light tent made of wooden laths bound with strips of hide and covered with felt or blanket-cloth, and it has grilled windows so that the person inside can see without being seen. One can do anything one likes inside, sleep, eat, read or write, during the march. The waggons conveying the baggage and provisions are covered with a similar tent which is locked.

We set out with the amír Tuluktumúr and his brother and two sons. At every halt the Turks loose their horses, oxen and camels, and drive them out to pasture at liberty, night or day, without shepherds or guardians. This is due to the severity of their laws against theft. Any person found in possession of a stolen horse is obliged to restore it with nine others; if he cannot do this, his sons are taken instead, and if he has no sons he is slaughtered like a sheep. They do not eat bread nor any solid food, but prepare a soup with a kind of millet, and any meat they may have is cut into small pieces and cooked in this soup.

Everyone is given his share in a plate with curdled milk, and they drink it, afterwards drinking curdled mare's milk, which they call *qumizz*. They have also a fermented drink prepared from the same grain, which they call *búza* [beer] and regard as lawful to drink. It is white in colour; I tasted it once and found it bitter, so I left it alone. They regard the eating of sweetmeats as a disgrace. One day during Ramadán I presented Sultan Úzbeg with a plate of sweetmeats which one of my companions had made, but he did no more than touch them with his finger and then place it in his mouth.

Eighteen stations after leaving Qiram we came to a great expanse of water which took us a whole day to ford.[20] The crossing becomes very muddy and difficult when many beasts and waggons have crossed, so the amír, thinking of my comfort, sent me on ahead with one of his suite and wrote a letter for me to the governor of Azáq urging him to treat me honourably. We crossed a second sheet of water, which required half a day to ford, and on the third day from there, reached Azáq [Azov], which is on the sea coast. It is a wellbuilt town, visited by the Genoese and other merchants. The governor, on receiving the amír Tuluktumúr's letter, came out to meet me, along with the qádí and the students, and sent out food. After greeting him, we dismounted and ate, then went on to the town, outside which we camped. Two days later the amír arrived, and was met with great ceremony. A banquet was prepared for him in a specially prepared tent of coloured silk, and when he dismounted pieces of silk were laid down for him to walk on. Out of his generosity he made me precede him, in order that the governor should see the high esteem in which he held me, and made me sit on a great chair which had been placed for him, himself sitting beside me, while his two sons and his brother and

PILGRIMS CLIMBING TO ADAM'S FOOT

From an eighteenth century print

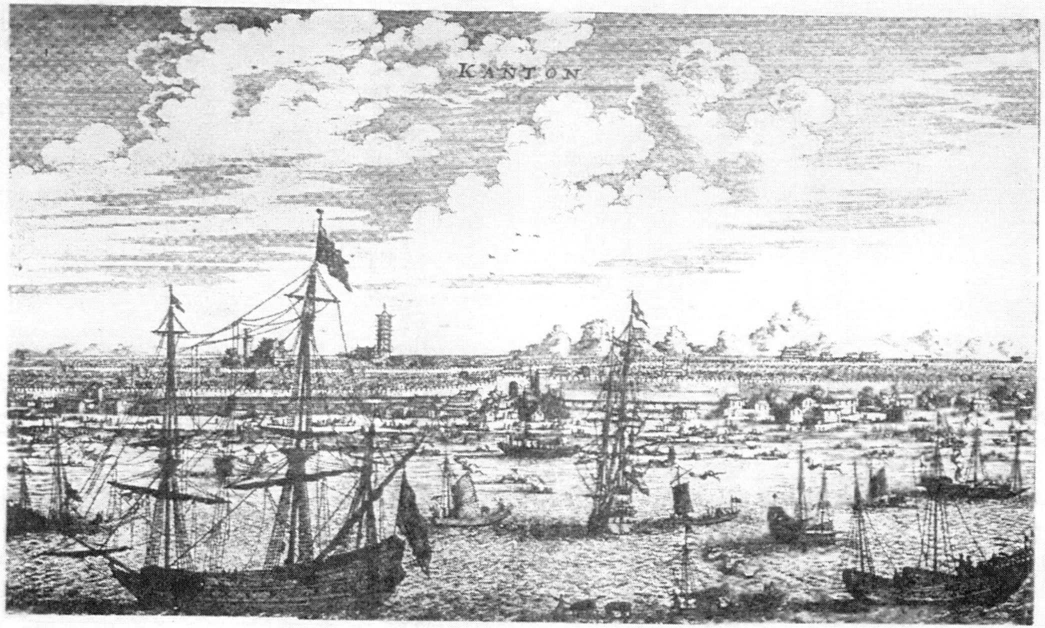

CANTON IN THE SEVENTEENTH CENTURY

nephews remained standing respectfully. After the banquet was over a robe was presented to the amír and to each member of his family and to me, then the amír and his brother were presented with ten horses, his two sons with six, and I too with one.

The horses in this country are very numerous and the price of them is negligible. A good one costs about a dinar of our money. The livelihood of the people depends on them, and they are as numerous as sheep in our country, or even more so. A single Turk will possess thousands of horses. They are exported to India in droves of six thousand or so, each merchant possessing one or two hundred of them or less or more. For each fifty they hire a keeper, who looks after their pasturage. He rides on one of them, carrying a long stick with a rope attached to it, and when he wishes to catch any horse he gets opposite it on the horse which he is riding, throws the rope over its neck and draws it towards him, mounts it and sets the other free to pasture. On reaching Sind the horses are fed with forage, because the vegetation of Sind will not take the place of barley, and the greater part of them die or are stolen. The owners pay a duty of seven silver dinars on entering Sind and a further duty at Multán. Formerly they were taxed a quarter of the value of their imports, but Sultan Muhammad abolished this tax and ordered that Muslim merchants should pay the legal tithe[21] and infidel merchants a tenth. Nevertheless the merchants make a handsome profit, for the least that a horse fetches is a hundred dinars (that is twenty-five dinars in Moroccan money) and it often sells for twice or three times that amount. A good horse sells for five hundred or more. The Indians do not buy them as racehorses, for in battle they wear coats of mail and cover their horses with armour; what they prize in a horse is its strength and length of pace. Their racehorses are brought from Yemen, 'Omán and Fárs, and they cost from a thousand to four thousand dinars each.

From Azáq I went on to Májar, travelling behind the amír Tuluktumúr. It is one of the finest of the Turkish cities, and is situated on a great river.[22] In the bazaar of this city I met a Jew, who greeted me in Arabic and told me that he had come from Spain. He said that he had come overland, through Constantinople the Great, Anatolia and the land of the Circassians [Transcaucasia], and that the journey had taken four months. The travelling merchants, who know about these matters, assured me of the truth of his statement.

A remarkable thing which I saw in this country was the respect shown to women by the Turks, for they hold a more dignified position than the men. The first time that I saw a princess was when, on leaving Qiram, I saw the wife of the amír in her waggon. The entire waggon was covered with rich blue woollen cloth, and the windows and doors of the tent were open. With the princess were four maidens, exquisitely beautiful and richly dressed, and behind her were a number of waggons with maidens belonging to her suite. When she came near the amír's camp she alighted with about thirty of the maidens who carried her train. On her garments there were loops, of which each maiden took one, and lifted her train clear of the ground on all sides, and she walked in this stately manner. When she reached the amír he rose before her and greeted her and sat her beside him, with the maidens standing round her. Skins of *qumizz* were brought and she, pouring some into a cup, knelt before him and gave it to him, afterwards pouring out a cup for his brother. Then the amír poured out a cup for her and food was brought in and she ate with him. He then gave her a robe and she withdrew. I saw also the wives of the merchants and commonalty. One of them will sit in a waggon which is being drawn by horses, attended by three or four maidens to carry her train, and on her head she wears a conical headdress incrusted with pearls and surmounted by peacock feathers. The windows of the tent are open and her face is visible, for the Turkish women do not veil themselves. Sometimes a woman will be accompanied by her husband and anyone seeing him would take him for one of her servants; he has no garment other than a sheep's wool cloak and a high cap to match.

We then prepared for the journey to the sultan's camp, which was four days' march from Májar in a place called Bíshdagh, which means "Five mountains."[23] In these mountains there is a hot spring in which the Turks bathe, claiming that it prevents illness. We arrived at the camp on the first day of Ramadán and found that it was moving to the neighbourhood from which we had just come, so we returned thither. I set up my tent on a hill there, fixing a standard in the ground in front of it, and drew up the horses and waggons behind. Thereupon the *mahalla* approached (the name they give to it is the *ordu*) and we saw a vast town on the move with all its inhabitants, containing mosques and bazaars, the smoke from the kitchens rising in the air (for they cook while on the march), and horse-drawn waggons transporting them. On reaching the encampment they took the tents off the waggons and set them upon the ground, for they were very light, and they did the same with the mosques and shops. The sultan's khátúns passed by us, each separately with her own retinue. The fourth of them, as she passed, saw the tent on top of the hill with the standard in front of it, which is the mark of a new arrival, and sent pages and maidens to greet me and convey her salutations, herself halting to wait for them. I sent her a gift by one of my companions and the chamberlain of the amír Tuluktumúr. She accepted it as a blessing and gave orders that I should be taken under her protection, then went on. Afterwards the sultan arrived and camped with his *mahalla* separately.

The illustrious Sultan Muhammad Úzbeg Khán is the ruler of a vast kingdom and a most powerful sovereign, victor over the enemies of God, the people of Constantinople the Great, and diligent in warring against them. He is one of the seven mighty kings of the world, to wit: our master the Commander of the Faithful, may God strengthen his might and magnify his victory! [the sultan of Morocco], the sultan of Egypt and Syria, the sultan of the Two 'Iráqs, this Sultan Úzbeg, the sultan of Turkistán and the lands beyond the Oxus, the sultan of India, and the sultan of China. The day after my arrival I visited him in the afternoon at a ceremonial audience; a great banquet was prepared and we broke our fast in his presence. These Turks do not follow the custom of assigning a lodging to visitors and giving them money for their expenses, but they send him sheep and horses for slaughtering and skins of *qumizz*, which is their form of benefaction. Every Friday, after the midday prayer, the sultan holds an audience in a pavilion called the Golden Pavilion, which is richly decorated. In the centre there is a wooden throne covered with silver-gilt plates, the legs being of pure silver set with jewels at the top. The sultan sits on the throne, having on his right the khátún Taytughlí with the khátún Kebek on her right, and on his left the khátún Bayalún with the khátún Urdujá on her left. Below the throne stand the sultan's sons, the elder on the right and the younger on the left, and his daughter sits in front of him. He rises to meet each khátún as she arrives and takes her by the hand until she mounts to the throne. All this takes place in view of the whole people, without any screening.

On the morrow of my interview with the sultan I visited the principal khátún Taytughlí, who is the queen and the mother of the sultan's two sons. She was sitting in the midst of ten aged women, who appeared to be servants of hers, and had in front of her about fifty young maidens with gold and silver salvers filled with cherries which they were cleaning. The khátún also had a golden tray filled with cherries in front of her and was cleaning them. She ordered *qumizz* to be brought and with her own hand poured out a cupful and gave it to me, which is the highest of honours in their estimation. I had never drunk *qumizz* before, but there was nothing for me but to accept it. I tasted it, but found it disagreeable and passed it on to one of my companions. The following day we visited the second khátún Kebek and found her sitting on a divan reading the holy Koran. She also served me with *qumizz*. The third khátún Bayalún is the daughter of the Emperor of Constantinople the Great.[24] On visiting her we found her sitting on a throne set with jewels, with about a hundred maidens, Greek, Turkish and Nubian, standing or sitting in front of her. Behind her were eunuchs and in front of her Greek chamberlains. She asked how we were and about our journey and the distance of our native lands, and wept, in pity and compassion, wiping her face with a handkerchief that lay before her. She ordered food to be served and we ate in her presence, and when we desired to leave she said "Do not sever relations with us, but come often to us and inform us of your needs." She showed great kindness to us and after we had gone sent us food, a great quantity of bread, butter, sheep, money, a magnificent robe and thirteen horses, three good ones and ten of the ordinary sort. It was with this khátún that I made my journey to Constantinople the Great, as we shall relate hereafter. The fourth khátún is one of the best, most amiable and sympathetic of princesses. We visited her and she showed us a kindness and generosity that cannot be surpassed. By the sultan's daughter however we were treated with a generosity and kindness that no other khátún showed us; she loaded us with surpassing favours, may God reward her!

I had heard of the city of Bulghár[25] and desired to visit it, in order to see for myself what they tell of the extreme shortness of the night there and also the shortness of the day in the opposite season. It was ten nights' journey from the sultan's camp, so I requested that he would give me a guide to take me to it, and he did so. We reached it in the month of Ramadán, and when we had breakfasted after the sunset prayer we had just sufficient time for the night prayers before dawn. I stayed there three days. I had intended to visit the Land of Darkness,[26] which is reached from Bulghár after a journey of forty days, but I renounced the project in view of the difficulty of the journey and the small profit to be got out of it. The only way of reaching it is to travel on sledges drawn by dogs, for the desert being covered with ice, neither man nor beast can walk on it without slipping, whereas the dogs have claws that grip the ice. The journey is made only by rich merchants who have a hundred sledges or thereabouts, loaded with food, drink, and firewood, for there are neither trees, stones nor habitation in it. The guide in this country is the dog which has made the journey many times, and the value of one of these reaches a thousand dinars. The sledge is tied to its neck and three other dogs are yoked with it; it is the leader, the other dogs following it with the sledges, and where it stops they stop. Its owner never beats or chides it, and when food is made the dogs are served first before the men; otherwise the [leading] dog is angered and escapes, leaving its owner to perish. When the travellers have completed forty stages they alight at the Darkness. Each one of them leaves the goods he has brought there and they return to their usual camping-ground. Next day they go back to seek their goods, and find opposite them skins of sable, minever, and ermine. If the merchant is satisfied with the exchange he takes them, but if not he leaves them. The inhabitants then add more skins, but sometimes they take away their goods and leave the merchant's. This is their method of commerce. Those who go there do not know whom they are trading with or whether they be jinn or men, for they never see anyone.

I returned from Bulghár with the amír whom the sultan had sent to accompany me, and found the *mahalla* at Bíshdagh on the 28th of Ramadán. When the ceremonies of the Festival [at the close of the month of fasting] were over we set out with the sultan and the *mahalla* and came to the town of Hájj Tarkhán [Astrakhan]. It is one of the finest of cities, with great bazaars, and is built on the river Itil [Volga], which is one of the great rivers of the world. In the winter it freezes over and the people travel on it in sledges; sometimes caravans cross it towards the end of winter and are drowned. On reaching this town the khátún Bayalún requested the sultan to permit her to visit her father, the king of the Greeks, that she might give birth to her child at her home and return again to him. He gave her permission and then I too asked him to allow me to go in her company to see Constantinople the Great. He demurred, fearing for my safety, but I said, "I shall go under your patronage and protection and I shall have nothing to fear from anyone." Thereupon he gave me permission and we bade him farewell. He presented me with 1,500 dinars, a robe, and a large number of horses, and each khátún gave me ingots of silver. The sultan's daughter gave me more than they did, along with a robe and a horse, so I found myself in possession of a considerable quantity of horses, garments, and furs of sable and minever.

We set out on the tenth of Shawwál in the company of the khátún Bayalún and under her protection. The sultan escorted her one stage, then returned, he and the queen and the heir to the throne; the other khátúns accompanied her for a second stage and then returned. The amír Baydara with five thousand troops travelled with her, and her own troops numbered about five hundred horsemen, two hundred of whom were her attendant slaves and Greeks, and the remainder Turks. She had with her also about two hundred maidens, most of whom were Greeks, and about four hundred carts and about two thousand draught and riding horses, as well as three hundred oxen and two hundred camels. She had also ten Greek youths and the same number of Indians, whose leader-in-chief was called Sunbul the Indian; the leader of the Greeks was a man of conspicuous bravery called Michael, but the Turks gave him the name of Lu'lu' [Pearl]. She left most of her maidens and her baggage at the sultan's camp, since she had set out only to pay a visit. We made for Ukak,[27] a medium-sized town, with fine buildings, plentifully supplied with natural products, and extremely cold. A day's march from this town are the mountains of the Russians. These are Christians, red-haired and blue-eyed, with ugly faces and treacherous. In their country are silver mines and thence are brought the ingots of silver with which selling and buying is done in this land. The weight of each of these ingots is five ounces.

After ten nights' travelling from this town we arrived at the town of Surdáq, which is on the sea coast of the Qipchaq desert, and possesses one of the biggest and finest of harbours.[28] Outside it there are orchards and springs, and it is inhabited by Turks and a number of Greeks under their dominion. These Greeks are artisans and most of their houses are made of wood. This town was formerly a big one, but most of it was laid in ruins as the result of a quarrel which broke out between the Greeks and the Turks. At first the Greeks had the upper hand, but the Turks on receiving assistance from their fellow-countrymen killed the Greeks remorselessly and expelled most of them. Some of them still remain there as subjects of the Turks. At every halting place in this land the khátún received hospitality-gifts of horses, sheep, cattle, millet, *qumizz*, and the milk of cows and sheep. In these countries travelling is done in the forenoon and in the evening. Every governor escorted the khátún with his troops right to the frontier of his territories, to show her honour, not through fear for her safety, for these lands are quite safe. We came next to the town known by the name of Bábá Saltúq,[29] who, they say, was an ecstatic mystic, though stories are told of actions by him which are condemned by the law. This is the last town in Turkish territory. From here to the beginning of Greek territory it is a journey of eighteen days through uninhabited desert, for eight days of which there is no water, so a stock of water is laid in and carried in large and small skins on the waggons. As it was in the cold weather that we passed through we did not need much water, and everything went well with us, praise be to God!

At the end of this march we reached the fortress of Mahtúlí, at the frontier of the territories of the Greeks.[30] The Greeks had heard that this khátún was returning to her country, and there came to this fortress to meet her the Greek Kifálí[31] Nicolas, with a large army and a large hospitality-gift, accompanied by the princesses and nurses from the palace of her father, the king of Constantinople. From Mahtúlí to Constantinople is a journey of twenty-two days, sixteen to the canal, and six thence to Constantinople. From this fortress one travels on horses and mules only, and the waggons are left behind there on account of the rough ground and the mountains. Kifálí had brought many mules, six of which the khátún sent to me. She also commended to the care of the governor of the fortress those of my companions and of my slaves whom I had left behind with the waggons and baggage, and he assigned them a house. The commander Baydara returned with his troops, and none travelled on with the khátún but her own people. She left her mosque behind at the fort and the practice of calling to prayer was abolished. As part of her hospitality-gifts she was given intoxicating liquors, which she drank, and swine, and I was told by one of her suite that she ate them. No one remained with her who prayed except one Turk, who used to pray with us. Sentiments formerly hidden were revealed because of our entry into the land of the infidels, but the khátún charged the amír Kifálí to treat us honourably, and on one occasion he beat one of his guards because he had laughed at our prayer.

Thereafter we reached the fortress of Maslama ibn 'Abd al-Malik, which is at the foot of a mountain beside a swift-running river called Istafílí. Nothing is left of this fortress except its ruins, but outside it is a large village. Thence we journeyed for two days and reached the canal, on the bank of which there is a large village. We found a rising tide on the canal and waited till the ebb set in before fording it, its breadth being about two miles. We then went four miles through sand and reached the second canal, and forded it, its breadth being about three miles. Then we went about two miles through stones and sand

and reached the third canal when the tide had begun to rise, so we had some trouble to ford it, its breadth being one mile. The breadth of the entire canal therefore, counting both water channels and dry stretches, is twelve miles. In the rainy season it is filled entirely with water and cannot be forded except in boats. On the bank of this third canal is the town of Faníka, small but beautiful and strongly fortified. Its churches and houses are beautiful; it is traversed by streams and surrounded by orchards, and in it grapes, pears, apples and quinces are preserved from one year to the next. We stayed in this town three nights, the khátún being lodged in one of her father's castles there.

Then her brother, whose name was Kifálí Qarás, arrived with five thousand horsemen, fully accoutred in armour. When they prepared to meet the princess, her brother, dressed in white, rode a grey horse, having over his head a parasol ornamented with jewels. On his right hand he had five princes and the same number on his left hand, all dressed in white also, and with parasols embroidered in gold over their heads. In front of him were a hundred foot soldiers and a hundred horsemen, who wore long coats of mail over themselves and their horses, each one of them leading a saddled and armoured horse carrying the arms of a horseman, consisting of a jewelled helmet, a breastplate, a bow, and a sword, and each man had in his hand a lance with a pennant at its head. Most of these lances were covered with plaques of gold and silver. These led horses are the riding horses of the sultan's son. His horsemen were divided into squadrons, two hundred horsemen in each squadron. Over them was a commander, who had in front of him ten of the horsemen, fully accoutred in armour, each leading a horse, and behind him ten coloured standards, carried by ten of the horsemen, and ten kettledrums slung over the shoulders of ten of the horsemen, with whom were six others sounding trumpets and bugles and fifes. The khátún rode out with her guards, maidens, slave boys and servants, these numbering about five hundred, all wearing silken garments, embroidered with gold and encrusted with precious stones. She herself was wearing a garment of gold brocade, encrusted with jewels, with a crown set with precious stones on her head, and her horse was covered with a saddle-cloth of silk embroidered in gold. On its legs were bracelets of gold and round its neck necklaces set with precious stones, and her saddle frame was covered with gold ornamented with jewels. Their meeting took place in a flat piece of ground about a mile distant from the town. Her brother dismounted to her, because he was younger than her, and kissed her stirrup and she kissed his head. The commanders and princes also dismounted and they all kissed her stirrup, after which she set out with her brother.

On the next day we reached a large city on the sea-coast, whose name I have forgotten, well furnished with streams and trees, and encamped in its outskirts. The heir to the throne, the brother of the khátún, arrived with a great array and a strong army of ten thousand mailed horsemen. He wore a crown on his head, and had at his right hand about twenty princes and a similar number on his left. His horsemen were arranged exactly as his brother's, but with greater pomp and larger numbers. His sister met him in a dress similar to the one she wore on the former occasion, and both dismounted together. A silken tent was brought and they both went into it, so I do not know how they greeted each other. We encamped at a distance of ten miles from Constantinople, and on the following day the population, men, women and children, came out riding or on foot, in their richest apparel. At dawn the drums, trumpets and fifes were sounded; the troops mounted, and the Emperor with his wife, the mother of this khátún, came out, accompanied by the high officials of state and the courtiers. Over the king's head there was a canopy, carried by a number of horsemen and men on foot, who had in their hands long staves, each surmounted by something resembling a ball of leather, with which they hoisted the canopy. In the centre of this canopy was a sort of pavilion which was supported by horsemen on staves. When the Emperor approached, the troops became entangled with one another and there was much dust. I was unable to make my way amongst them, so I kept with the khátún's baggage and party, fearing for my life. I was told that when the princess approached her parents she dismounted and kissed the ground before them, and then kissed the two hoofs of their horses, the principal members of her party doing the same.

Our entry into Constantinople the Great was made about noon or a little later, and they rang their bells until the very skies shook with the mingling of their sounds. When we reached the first gate of the king's palace we found there about a hundred men, with an officer on a platform, and I heard them saying *Sarakinu*, *Sarakinu*, which means Muslims. They would not let us enter, and when those who were with the khátún said that we belonged to their party, they answered "They cannot enter except by permission," so we stayed at the gate. One of the khátún's party sent a messenger to tell her of this while she was still with her father. She told him about us and he gave orders that we should enter, and assigned us a house near the khátún's house. He wrote also on our behalf an order that we should not be obstructed wheresoever we went in the city, and this order was proclaimed in the bazaars. We stayed indoors three days, receiving from the khátún gifts of flour, bread, sheep, chickens, butter, fruit, fish, money and beds, and on the fourth day we had audience of the sultan.

The Emperor of Constantinople is called Takfúr, son of the Emperor Jirjís [George].[32] His father, the Emperor George, was still alive, but had become an ascetic and monk, devoting himself to religious exercises in the churches, and had resigned the sovereignty to his son. We shall speak of him later. On the fourth day after our arrival in Constantinople, the khátún sent the slave Sunbul the Indian to me, and he took my hand and led me into the palace. We passed through four gateways, each of which had archways in which were footsoldiers with their weapons, their officer being on a carpeted platform. When we reached the fifth gateway the slave Sunbul left me, and going inside returned with four Greek youths, who searched me to see that I had no knife on my person. The officer said to me: "This is a custom of theirs; every person who enters the king's presence, be he noble or private citizen, foreigner or native, must be searched." The same practice is observed also in India. After they had searched me the man in charge of the gate rose and took me by the hand and opened the gate. Four of the men surrounded me, two of them holding my sleeves and two behind me, and brought me into a large hall, the walls of which were of mosaic work, in which there were pictures of creatures, both animate and inanimate. In the centre there was a stream of water, with trees on either side of it, and men were standing to right and left, silent, not one of them speaking. In the midst of the hall three men were standing, to whom those four men delivered me. These took hold of my garments as the others had done, and on a signal from another man led me forward.[33] One of them was a Jew, and he said to me in Arabic "Do not be afraid; this is their custom that they use with one who enters. I am the interpreter, and I come from Syria." So I asked him how I should salute the Emperor and he told me to say *As-salám alaykum*. After this I reached a great pavilion, where the Emperor was seated on his throne, with his wife, the mother of the khátún, before him. At the foot of the throne were the khátún and her brothers, to the right of it six men and to the left of it four, and behind it four, every one of them armed. The Emperor signed to me, before I had saluted and reached him, to sit down for a moment, in order that my apprehension might be calmed. After doing so I approached him and saluted him, and he signed to me to sit down, but I did not do so. He questioned me about Jerusalem, the Sacred Rock, the Church of the Holy Sepulchre, the cradle of Jesus, and Bethlehem, and about the city of Abraham [Hebron], then about Damascus, Cairo, 'Iráq, and Anatolia, and I answered all his questions about these, the Jew interpreting between us. He was pleased with my replies and said to his sons "Treat this man with honour and ensure his safety." Then he bestowed upon me a robe of honour and assigned me a horse with saddle and bridle, and an umbrella of the kind which the king has carried above his head, that being a sign of protection. I requested him to designate someone to ride in the city with me every day, that I might see its marvellous and rare sights and tell of them in my own country, and he appointed a man as I had asked. They have a custom that anyone who wears the king's robe of honour and rides his horse is paraded round with trumpets, fifes and drums, so that the people may see him. They do this mostly with the Turks who come from the territories of Sultan Ūzbeg, so that the people may not molest them, and I was paraded in this fashion through the bazaars.

The city is enormous in size, and in two parts

separated by a great river [the Golden Horn], in which there is a rising and ebbing tide. In former times there was a stone bridge over it, but it fell into ruins and the crossing is now made in boats. The part of the city on the eastern bank of the river is called Istambúl, and contains the residence of the Emperor, the nobles and the rest of the population. Its bazaars and streets are spacious and paved with flagstones; each bazaar has gates which are closed upon it at night, and the majority of the artisans and sellers in them are women. The city lies at the foot of a hill which projects about nine miles into the sea, its breadth being the same or greater. On the top of the hill there is a small citadel and the Emperor's palace. Round this hill runs the city-wall, which is very strong and cannot be taken by assault from the sea front. Within its circuit there are about thirteen inhabited villages. The principal church is in the midst of this part of the city. The second part, on the western bank of the river, is called Galata, and is reserved to the Frankish Christians who dwell there. They are of different kinds, including Genoese, Venetians, Romans and people of France; they are subject to the authority of the king of Constantinople, who sets over them one of their own number of whom they approve, and him they call the *Comes*. They are bound to pay a tax every year to the king of Constantinople, but often they revolt against him and he makes war on them until the Pope makes peace between them. They are all men of commerce and their harbour is one of the largest in the world; I saw there about a hundred galleys and other large ships, and the small ships were too many to be counted. The bazaars in this part of the town are good but filthy, and a small and very dirty river runs through them. Their churches too are filthy and mean.

Of the great church I can only describe the exterior,

for I did not see its interior. It is called by them Ayá Súfiyá [St. Sophia], and the story goes that it was built by Asaph, the son of Berechiah, who was Solomon's cousin. It is one of the greatest churches of the Greeks, and is encircled by a wall so that it looks as if it were a town. It has thirteen gates and a sacred enclosure, which is about a mile long and closed by a great gate. No one is prevented from entering this enclosure, and indeed I went into it with the king's father; it resembles an audience-hall paved with marble, and is traversed by a stream which issues from the church. Outside the gate of this hall are platforms and shops, mostly of wood, where their judges and the recorders of their bureaux sit. At the gate of the church there are porticoes where the keepers sit who sweep its paths, light its lamps and close its gates. They allow none to enter it until he prostrates himself to the huge cross there, which they claim to be a relic of the wood upon which the pseudo-Jesus was crucified.[34] This is over the gate of the church, set in a golden case whose height is about ten cubits, across which a similar golden case is placed to form a cross. This gate is covered with plaques of silver and gold and its two rings are of pure gold. I was told that the number of monks and priests in this church runs into thousands, and that some of them are descendants of the apostles, and that inside it is another church exclusively for women, containing more than a thousand virgins and a still greater number of aged women who devote themselves to religious practices. It is the custom of the king, the nobles and the rest of the people to come every morning to visit this church. The Pope comes to visit it once a year. When he is four days' journey from the town the king goes out to meet him, and dismounts before him and when he enters the city walks on foot in front of him. During his stay in

Constantinople the king comes to salute him every morning and evening.

A monastery is the Christian equivalent of a religious house or convent among the Muslims, and there are a great many such monasteries at Constantinople. Among them is the monastery which King George built outside Istambúl and opposite Galata, and two monasteries outside the principal church, to the right as one enters it. These two monasteries are inside a garden traversed by a stream of water; one of them is for men and the other for women. In each there is a church and they are surrounded by the cells of men and women who have devoted themselves to religious exercises. Each monastery possesses pious endowments for the clothing and maintenance of the devotees. Inside every monastery there is a small convent designed for the ascetic retreat of the king who built it, for most of these kings, on reaching the age of sixty or seventy, build a monastery and put on garments of hair, investing their sons with the sovereignty and occupying themselves with religious exercises for the rest of their lives. They display great magnificence in building these monasteries, and construct them of marble and mosaic-work. I entered a monastery with the Greek whom the king had given me as a guide. Inside it was a church containing about five hundred virgins wearing hair-garments; their heads were shaved and covered with felt bonnets. They were exceedingly beautiful and showed the traces of their austerities. A youth sitting on a pulpit was reading the gospel to them in the most beautiful voice I have ever heard; round him were eight other youths on pulpits with their priest, and when the first youth had finished reading another began. The Greek said to me "These girls are kings' daughters who have given themselves to the service of this church, and likewise the boys who are reading [are kings' sons]." I entered with him also into churches in which there were the daughters of ministers, governors, and the principal men of the city, and others where there were aged women and widows, and others where there were monks, each church containing a hundred men or so. Most of the population of the city are monks, ascetics, and priests, and its churches are not to be counted for multitude.[35] The inhabitants of the city, soldiers and civilians, small and great, carry over their heads huge parasols, both in winter and summer, and the women wear large turbans.

I was out one day with my Greek guide, when we met the former king George who had become a monk. He was walking on foot, wearing haircloth garments and a bonnet of felt, and he had a long white beard and a fine face, which bore traces of his austerities. Behind and before him was a body of monks, and he had a staff in his hand and a rosary on his neck. When the Greek saw him he dismounted and said to me "Dismount, for this is the king's father." When my guide saluted him the king asked him about me, then stopped and sent for me. He took my hand and said to the Greek (who knew the Arabic tongue) "Say to this Saracen (meaning Muslim) 'I clasp the hand which has entered Jerusalem and the foot which has walked within the Dome of the Rock and the great church of the Holy Sepulchre and Bethlehem,'" and he laid his hand upon my feet and passed it over his face. I was astonished at their good opinion of one who, though not of their religion, had entered these places. Then he took my hand and as I walked with him asked me about Jerusalem and the Christians who were there, and questioned me at length. I entered with him the sacred enclosure of the church which we have described above. When he approached the principal gate, a party of priests and monks came out to salute him, for he is one of their chief men in monasticism, and on seeing them he let go my hand. I said to him "I should like to enter the church with you." Then he said to the interpreter, "Say to him 'He who enters it must needs prostrate himself before the great cross, for this is a rule which the ancients laid down and which cannot be contravened.'" So I left him and he entered alone and I did not see him again. After leaving the king I entered the bazaar of the scribes, where I was noticed by the judge, who sent one of his assistants to ask the Greek about me. On learning that I was a Muslim scholar he sent for me and I went up to him. He was an old man with a fine face and hair, wearing the black garments of a monk, and had about ten scribes in front of him writing. He rose to meet me, his companions rising also, and said "You are the king's guest and we are bound to honour you." He then asked me about Jerusalem, Syria, and Egypt, and spoke with me for a long time. A great crowd gathered round him, and he said "You must come to my house that I may entertain you." After that I went away, but I did not see him again.

When it became clear to the Turks who were in the khátún's company that she professed her father's religion and wished to stay with him, they asked her for leave to return to their country. She made them rich presents and sent them an amír called Sarúja with five hundred horsemen to escort them to their country. She sent for me, and gave me three hundred of their gold dinars, called *barbara*, which are not good money,[36] and a thousand Venetian silver pieces, together with some robes and pieces of cloth and two horses, which were a gift from her father, and commended me to Sarúja. I bade her farewell and left, having spent a month and six days in their town. On reaching the frontier, where we had left our party and waggons we picked them up and returned through the desert. Sarúja came with us to Bábá Saltúq, where he stayed as a guest for three days, and then went back to his land. This was in the depths of winter and I used to wear three fur coats and two pairs of trousers, one lined, and on my feet I had woollen boots, with a pair of linen-lined boots on top of these and a pair of horse skin boots lined with bearskin on top of these again. I performed my ablutions with hot water close to the fire, but every drop of water froze on the instant. When I washed my face the water ran down my beard and froze, and when I shook it off it was a sort of snow that fell from it. Water dripping from the nose froze on the moustache. I was unable to mount my horse for the quantity of clothes I was wearing and my companions had to help me into the saddle.

On reaching Hájj Tarkhán [Astrakhan], where we had parted from Sultan Ūzbeg, we found that he had moved and was living in the capital of his kingdom. We travelled on the river Itil [Volga] and the neighbouring waters, which were frozen over, and used to break a piece of the ice whenever we needed water, and put it in a cauldron till it melted, when we used it for drinking and cooking. On the fourth day we reached the city of Sará, which is the capital of the sultan.[37] We visited him, and after we had answered his questions about our journey and the king of the Greeks and his city he gave orders for our maintenance and lodging. Sará is one of the finest of towns, of immense extent and crammed with inhabitants, with fine bazaars and wide streets. We rode out one day with one of the principal men of the town, intending to make a circuit of the place and find out its size. We were living at one end of it and we set out in the morning, and it was after midday when we reached the other. One day we walked across the breadth of the town, and the double journey, going and returning, took half a day, this too through a continuous line of houses, with no ruins and no orchards. It has thirteen cathedral and a large number of other mosques. The inhabitants belong to divers nations; among them are Mongols, who are the inhabitants and rulers of the country and are in part Muslims, As [Ossetes], who are Muslims, and Qipchaqs, Circassians, Russians, and Greeks, who are all Christians. Each group lives in a separate quarter with its own bazaars. Merchants and strangers from 'Iráq, Egypt, Syria, and elsewhere, live in a quarter surrounded by a wall, in order to protect their property.

CHAPTER V

FROM Sará I set out for Khwárizm, which is separated from the capital by a desert extending for forty days' march. It is impassable for horses on account of the scarcity of fodder and the waggons are drawn only by camels. Ten days after leaving Sará we reached Saráchúk, which means " Little Sará," a town on the bank of a great and swift-flowing river called Ulúsú [Ural],[1] which is crossed by a bridge of boats like the bridge at Baghdád. Here we hired camels to take the place of the horses that had drawn our waggon hitherto, and sold the horses at the rate of four silver dinars per head or less, on account of their exhaustion and the cheapness of horses in this town. From this point we made a rapid march for thirty days, halting only for two hours each day, one in the forenoon and one at sunset, to cook and drink millet broth. They have with them dried preserved meat which they put on top of this, and pour sour milk over the whole. Each person eats and sleeps in his waggon while it is on the move. Travellers make this journey with the utmost speed, because of the scarcity of herbage. The greater number of camels which cross the desert perish and the remainder are of no use until the following year, when they are fattened up again. Water is obtained from rain-pools or shallow wells at known points separated by two or three days' march.

After crossing this desert we reached Khwárizm, which is the largest, greatest, most beautiful and most important city of the Turks.[2] It shakes under the weight of its population, whose movements lend it the semblance of a billowy sea. One day as I was riding in the bazaar I became stuck in the crowd, unable to go either forward or backward. I did not know what to do and only with great difficulty made my way back. The city is in the dominions of Sultan Úzbeg, who is represented by a powerful amír called Qutlúdumúr. I have never seen anywhere in the world more excellent people than the Khwárizmians, or more generous or more friendly to strangers. They have a praiseworthy custom in regard to the prayer-services which I have not seen elsewhere. Each muezzin goes round the houses adjoining his mosque warning them to attend the service, and any person who absents himself from the communal prayers is beaten by the qádí in the presence of the people. In each mosque there is a whip hung up for this purpose. The culprit is fined in addition five dinars, which are spent on the purposes of the mosque or in charity. They say that this custom is one which they have had from ancient times. Outside the city flows the river Jayhún [Oxus], one of the four rivers of Paradise, which freezes over for five months in the cold season like the Itil [Volga]. In the summer it is navigable for ships as far as Tirmidh [Termez], the journey down stream taking ten days. On reaching Khwárizm I encamped in the outskirts, and the qádí, being informed of my arrival, came out to greet me with a company of his followers. When we met he said to me "This town is densely populated, and you will have difficulty in entering it in the daytime, so my assistant will come to conduct you in towards the end of the night." We followed this suggestion and were lodged in a new academy, in which no one was living as yet. After the Friday service I went with the qádí to his house, which was near the mosque, and was taken into a magnificent apartment. It was furnished with rich carpets and the walls were hung with cloth, and in it there were a number of niches each containing vessels of silver-gilt and 'Iráqi glass. This is a custom followed by the people of this country.

I went with the qádí also to visit the amír Qutlúdumúr and found him reclining on a silk carpet with his feet covered, as he was suffering from gout, a malady very common among the Turks. He questioned me about his sovereign, and the khátún Bayalún and her father and the city of Constantinople. Then tables were brought in with roasted fowls, cranes, young pigeons, bread baked with butter, biscuits, and sweetmeats, which were followed by other tables with fruit, pomegranates prepared for the table, some of them served in vessels of gold and silver with golden spoons, and others in vessels of glass with wooden spoons,[3] and wonderful melons. On our return to the academy, the amír sent us rice, flour, sheep, butter, spices and loads of wood. The use of charcoal is unknown in all these countries, as also in India and Persia. In China they make fires with stones which burn like charcoal, and when they are burned to ashes they knead these with water, dry them in the sun, and use them for cooking again until they are entirely consumed. One of the habits of the amír is this. Every day the qádí goes to his audience-hall with his jurisconsults and scribes and sits on a chair placed for him, opposite one of the principal amírs, who is attended by eight other great amírs and shaykhs of the Turks. The inhabitants bring up their cases for trial, and those which come under the sacred Law are decided by the qádí, and the others by these amírs. Their judgments are sound and equitable, because they are free from suspicion of partiality and do not accept bribes. One Friday, after the service, the qádí said to me "The amír gave instructions that you should be given five hundred dirhams and that for another five hundred dirhams a banquet should be prepared in your honour, to which the shaykhs, doctors and principal men were to be invited. I said to him 'You are preparing a banquet at which the guests will only eat one or two mouthfuls. If you were to give him all the money it would be more useful to him.' He said that he would do so and has ordered the full thousand to be given to you." I received the sum (which is equivalent to three hundred Moroccan dinars) in a purse borne by a page. The same day I had bought a black horse for thirty-five silver dinars and ridden it to the mosque, and it was out of that thousand and no other that I paid its price. Thereafter I became possessed of so many horses that I dare not mention their number lest some sceptic may accuse me of lying, and things continued to go better with me all the time until I reached India. I had many horses, but I preferred this black horse and picketed it in front of all the others. It remained with me for three years, and when it died my affairs took a turn for the worse.

On my journey to Khwárizm I had been accompanied by a merchant from Karbalá, a sharíf called 'Alí. I commissioned him to buy me some garments and other things, and he bought me a robe for ten dinars, but charged up only eight dinars against me and paid the other two out of his own pocket. I was in total ignorance of what he had done until it came to my ears in a roundabout way. Not only that, but he had lent me some money and when I received the amír's gift and repaid him what I owed, I wished to make him a present over and above in return for his kindnesses, but he refused it and refused also my suggestion to present it to a slave boy of his. He was the most open-handed 'Iráqi whom I have ever met. He decided to travel with me to India, but afterwards a party from his native town arrived at Khwárizm on their way to China, and fearing lest they should accuse him to his fellow-townsmen of going to India to beg, he set out with them. I heard later on, when I was in India, that when he reached Almaliq, which is on the frontiers of Turkistán and China,[4] he stayed there and sent a slave boy on with all his goods. The slave boy was a long time in returning and meanwhile a merchant from his native town arrived and put up with him in the same caravanseray. The sharíf asked him to lend him some money until his boy should arrive, but the merchant would not do so, and, not content with his vile conduct in failing to succour the sharíf, he tried to put up the price of his lodging in the caravanseray against him. The sharíf heard of this, and was so upset that he went into his room and cut his throat. He was found with a spark of life still in him; they suspected a slave whom he had of murdering him, but he said to them "Do not wrong him, it was I who did this to myself," and expired the same day—may God forgive him!

When I made ready to leave Khwárizm I hired camels and bought a camel-litter. The servants rode some of the horses and we put rugs on the rest because of the cold. We entered the desert which is between Khwárizm and Bukhárá, an eighteen days' journey through sands, with no settlements on the way except the small town of Kát,[5] which we reached after four days' march. We encamped outside it, by a lake which was frozen over and on which the boys were playing and sliding. The qádí came out to greet us, followed an hour later by the governor and his suite, who pressed us to stay and gave a banquet in our honour. In this desert there is a journey of six nights without water, after which we reached the town of Wabkana [Wafkend]. Thence we travelled for a whole day through a continuous series of orchards, streams, trees and buildings, and reached the city of Bukhárá. This city was formerly the capital of the lands beyond the Oxus. It was destroyed by the accursed Tinkíz [Chingiz] the Tatar, the ancestor of the kings of 'Iráq, and all but a few of its mosques, academies, and bazaars are now lying in ruins. Its inhabitants are looked down upon and their evidence [in legal cases] is not accepted in Khwárizm and elsewhere, because of their reputation for fanaticism, falsehood and denial of the truth. There is not one of its inhabitants today who possesses any theological learning or makes any attempt to acquire it.[6] We lodged at a hospice in a suburb of Bukhárá called Fath Ábád. The shaykh entertained me at his house and invited the principal men of the town. We spent a most delightful night there; the Koran-readers recited in pleasing voices, and the preacher delivered an address, and then they sang melodiously in Turkish and Persian.

From Bukhárá we set out for the camp of the pious Sultan Tarmashírín, and passed by Nakhshab [Qarshi], a small city surrounded by gardens and water channels. On the following afternoon we reached the sultan's camp. A merchant lent us a tent in which we spent the night, and next day, as the sultan was away hunting, I visited his representative, the amír Taqbugha, who lodged me near his mosque and gave me a Turkish tent of the kind we have already described. That night one of my slave girls gave birth to a child. I was told at first that it was a boy but afterwards I found out that it was a girl. She was born under a lucky star, and from that time on I experienced everything to give me joy and satisfaction. She died two months after my arrival in India, as will be related in the sequel.

The Sultan of Turkistán, Tarmashírín, is a powerful sovereign, possessing a large army and a vast kingdom, and upright in his government. His territories lie between four of the great kings of the world, the kings of China, India, and 'Iráq and King Üzbeg, all of whom send him gifts and show him honour.[7] His two brothers who preceded him were both infidels. One day, after I had prayed the dawn-prayer in the mosque, according to my custom, I was told that the sultan was present. When he rose from his prayer-carpet I went forward to salute him and he welcomed me in Turkish. As he returned on foot to his audience hall the people came forward to him with their complaints and he stopped to listen to each petitioner, small or great, male or female. Thereafter he sent for me, and I found him in a tent seated on a chair covered with gold-embroidered silk. The tent was lined with silken cloth of gold, and a crown, set with jewels and precious stones, was suspended over the sultan's head at a cubit's height. The principal amírs were sitting on chairs to right and left of him and in front of him were princes holding fly-whisks. He interrogated me about my journeys, his chancellor acting as interpreter. We used to attend the prayer-services with him (this was during a period of intense and perishing cold weather) and he never failed to attend the dawn and evening prayers with the congregation. One day when I was present at the afternoon prayer, one of his pages came in with a prayer-mat and spread it in the place where the sultan usually prayed, saying to the imám "Our master desires you to delay the prayer for a moment while he performs his ablutions." The imám said in Persian "Is prayer for God or Tarmashírín?" and ordered the muezzin to recite the second call. The sultan arrived when the service was half over, and made the remaining two prostrations at the end of the ranks, in the place where the shoes are left near the door of the mosque. He then performed the prostrations that he had missed, and went up laughing to the imám to shake his hand, and sitting down in his place said to me "When you return to your country tell how a Persian mendicant acted thus with the sultan of the Turks." This shaykh used to preach every Friday, exhorting the sultan to act righteously and forbidding him in the harshest terms to act corruptly and tyrannically, and the sultan would sit silent before him and weep. He would never accept gifts from the sultan nor eat at his table, nor wear the robes presented to him; he was a virtuous servant of God.

When I decided to continue my journey after a stay of fifty-four days with the sultan, he gave me seven hundred silver dinars and a sable coat worth a hundred dinars, which I had asked of him on account of the cold, as well as two horses and two camels. After taking leave of him I journeyed to Samarqand, which is one of the largest and most perfectly beautiful cities in the world. It is built on the bank of a river where the inhabitants promenade after the afternoon prayer. There were formerly great palaces along the bank, but most of them are in ruins, as also is much of the city itself, and it has no walls or gates. Outside the city is the grave of Qutham ibn al-'Abbás, who met a martyr's death at the conquest of Samarqand.[8] The inhabitants go out to visit it every Sunday and Thursday night and the Tatars also visit it, bringing large votive offerings of cattle, sheep and money, which are used for the maintenance of travellers and of the guardians of the hospice.

We set out from Samarqand and reached Tirmidh [Termez], a large town with fine buildings and bazaars and traversed by canals. It abounds in grapes and quinces of an exquisite flavour, as well as in flesh-meats and milk. The inhabitants wash their heads in the bath with milk instead of fuller's earth; the proprietor of every bath-house has large jars filled with milk, and each man as he enters takes a cupful to wash his head. It makes the hair fresh and glossy.

The Indians put oil of sesame on their heads and afterwards wash their hair with fuller's earth. This refreshes the body and makes the hair glossy and long, and that is the reason why the Indians and those who live in their country have long beards. The old town of Tirmidh was built on the bank of the Oxus, and when it was laid in ruins by Tinkíz [Chingiz] this new town was built two miles from the river. Before reaching the city I fell in with its governor 'Alá al-Mulk Khudáwand Zádah, who sent on an order for our entertainment as guests, and provisions were brought to us every day during our stay there.

We crossed the river Oxus into the land of Khurásán and after a day and a half's march through a sandy uninhabited waste reached Balkh. It is an utter ruin and uninhabited, but anyone seeing it would think it inhabited on account of the solidity of its construction. The accursed Tinkíz destroyed this city and demolished about a third of its mosque on account of a treasure which he was told lay under one of its columns. He pulled down a third of them and found nothing and left the rest as it was. After leaving Balkh we travelled for seven days through the mountains of Qúhistán, in which there are numerous inhabited villages with running streams and leafy trees, mostly fig-trees, and many hospices inhabited by devotees. Thereafter we reached the city of Herát, which is the largest inhabited city in Khurásán. There are four large cities in this province, two of them, Herát and Naysábúr [Níshápúr] inhabited, and two, Balkh and Merv, in ruins.

The sultan of Herát is the illustrious Husayn, son of the sultan Ghiyáth ad-Dín al-Ghúrí, a man of notorious bravery and victorious by the Divine Favour on two fields of battle.[9] A pious ascetic of great merit, called Nizám ad-Dín Mawlána, spent his youth at Herát. He was beloved by the people, who would come to hear his sermons and exhortations, and who made a compact with him to repress evildoing. The preacher Malik Warná, who was a cousin of the king's, was also a party to this compact. Whenever they learned of any evil action, even on the part of the king, they took means to repress it. It is said that they found out one day that an unlawful act was being committed in King Husayn's palace, and they assembled to put a stop to it. The king fortified himself against them within the palace, but they assembled to the number of six thousand men at the gate. In fear of them he sent for Nizám ad-Dín and the chief men of the town. He had been drinking wine and there and then inside his castle they applied to him the punishment prescribed by law and left him.[10] Later on Nizám ad-Dín was killed by a Turkish amír whom he had offended. After this had happened King Husayn sent his cousin Malik Warná, who had been associated with Nizám ad-Dín in his reforming activities, as ambassador to the king of Sijistán, and when he arrived there, ordered him to stay there in Sijistán and not to return to him. Malik Warná went on to India, where I met him as I was leaving Sind. He was an excellent man with a liking for authority, hunting, falcons, horses, slaves, servants, and rich and kingly robes. Now India is no place for a man of this character. In his case the king of India appointed him governor of a small town, and he was assassinated there by a man from Herát who was living in India. It is said that the king of India was the instigator of his assassin at the instance of King Husayn, and it was for this reason that King Husayn acknowledged the king of India as his suzerain after the death of Malik Warná.

From Herát we journeyed to the town of Jám, which is of middling size in a fertile district.[11] Most of the trees are mulberries, and there is a great deal of silk there. This town derives its name from the saint and ascetic Ahmad al-Jám, to whose descendants it now belongs (for it is independent of the sultan) and who possess great wealth. We went next to Tús, which is one of the largest cities in Khurásán, and thence to Mashhad ar-Ridá [Meshhed], which is also a large town with abundant fruit-trees, streams, and mills.[12] The noble mausoleum is surmounted by a great dome of elegant construction, the walls being decorated with coloured tiles. Opposite the tomb [of the Imám] is the tomb of Caliph Hárún ar-Rashíd, which is surmounted by a platform bearing chandeliers. When a Shí'ite enters to visit it he kicks the tomb of ar-Rashíd with his foot, and pronounces a blessing on ar-Ridá.

Thence we journeyed through Sarakhs to Záwa, the town of the pious shaykh Qutb ad-Dín Haydar,[13] who has given his name to the Haydarí congregation of darwíshes. These are the darwíshes who place iron rings in their hands and ears and other parts of their bodies. We travelled from there to Naysábúr, one of the four capitals of Khurásán. It is given the name of "Little Damascus" because of its beauty and the quantity of its fruit-trees, orchards and streams. They manufacture here garments of silk and velvet, which are exported to India. I stayed at the convent of the learned shaykh Qutb ad-Dín an-Naysábúrí, who showed me great hospitality, and I was witness to some astonishing miracles performed by him. I had bought in this town a young Turkish slave, and the shaykh, seeing him with me, said "This boy is no good to you. Sell him." I did as he said and sold him next day to a merchant, then bade the shaykh farewell and left. When I stopped at Bistám, one of my friends wrote to me from Naysábúr and told me that the slave had killed a Turkish boy and had been put to death for it. This is an evident miracle to the credit of the shaykh.

From Naysábúr I travelled to the town of Bisṭám,[14] and thence to Qundús and Baghlán,[15] which are villages inhabited by shaykhs and pious persons. At Qundús we encamped by a stream, where there was a hospice belonging to an Egyptian shaykh called Shír-i Siyáh, which means "The Black Lion." We were hospitably received by the governor of that country, a man from Mosul, who lives in a large garden there. We stayed outside this village about forty days to pasture our camels and horses, for there is excellent pasturage there and perfect security, owing to the strict measures of the amír, who enforces the Turkish laws regarding horse-stealing which we have already mentioned [p. 143]. After we had been staying there ten days we missed three of our horses, but they were restored to us by the Tatars a fortnight later, through fear of the application of these laws to themselves.

Another reason for our halt was fear of the snow, for on the road there is a mountain called Hindúkúsh, which means "Slayer of Indians," because the slave boys and girls who are brought from India die there in large numbers as a result of the extreme cold and the quantity of snow. The passage extends for a whole day's march.[16] We stayed until the warm weather had definitely set in, and crossed this mountain by a continuous march from before dawn to sunset. We kept spreading felt cloths in front of the camels for them to tread on so that they should not sink in the snow. On setting out from Baghlán we journeyed to a place called Andar [Andaráb]. In former times there was a town here whose traces have disappeared, and we halted at a large village where there is a hospice belonging to an excellent man named Muhammad al-Mahrawí. We stayed with him and he treated us with consideration. When we washed our hands after eating he would drink the water in which we had washed because of the high esteem in which he held us. He travelled with us until we climbed the mountain of Hindúkúsh mentioned above. On this mountain we found a warm stream spring, and washed our faces in it, with the result that the skin peeled off our faces and we suffered some pain.

We halted next at a place called Banj Hír [Panjshír], which means "Five Mountains," where there was once a fine and populous city built on a great river with blue water like the sea. This country was devastated by Tinkíz, the king of the Tatars, and has not been inhabited since. We came to a mountain called Pasháy, where there is the convent of the shaykh Atá Awliyá, which means "Father of the Saints." He is also called Sísad Sálah, which is the Persian for "three hundred years," because they say that he is three hundred and fifty years old. They have a very high opinion of him and come to visit him from the towns and villages, and sultans and princesses visit him too. He received us with honour and made us his guests. We encamped by a river near his convent and went to see him, and when I saluted him he embraced me. His skin is fresh and smoother than any I have seen; anyone seeing him would take him to be fifty years old. He told me that he grew new hair and teeth every hundred years. I had some doubts about him, however, and God knows how much truth there is in what he says.

We travelled thence to Parwán, where I met the amír Buruntayh. He treated me well and wrote to his representatives at Ghazna enjoining them to show me honour. We went on to the village of Charkh [Charikar], it being now summer, and from there to the town of Ghazna. This is the town of the famous warrior-sultan Mahmúd ibn Sabuktagín, one of the greatest of rulers, who made frequent raids into India and captured cities and fortresses there.[17] His grave is in this city and is surmounted by a hospice. The greater part of the town is in ruins and nothing but a fraction of it remains, though it was once a large city. It has an exceedingly cold climate, and the inhabitants move from it in the cold season to Qandahár, a large and prosperous town three nights' journey from Ghazna, but I did not visit it. We travelled on to Kábul, formerly a vast town, the site of which is now occupied by a village inhabited by a tribe of Persians called Afgháns. They hold mountains and defiles and possess considerable strength, and are mostly highwaymen. Their principal mountain is called Kúh Sulaymán. It is told that the prophet Sulaymán [Solomon] ascended this mountain and having looked out over India, which was then covered with darkness, returned without entering it.

From Kábul we rode to Karmásh, which is a fortress belonging to the Afgháns, lying between two hills where they intercept traffic on the road. During our passage we had an engagement with them. They were posted on the lower slope of the hill, but we shot arrows at them and they fled. Our party was travelling light and had about four thousand horses. I had camels, as a result of which I became separated from the caravan along with a party including a number of Afgháns. We jettisoned some of our provisions and abandoned the loads of the camels that were jaded, on the route, but next day our horses returned and picked them up. We rejoined the caravan in the late evening and passed the night at the station of Shashnaghár, which is the last inhabited place on the confines of the Turkish lands. From here we entered the great desert which extends for fifteen days and can be traversed only in one season of the year, after the rains have fallen in Sind and India, that is at the beginning of July.[18] In this desert blows the deadly samúm wind. A great caravan which preceded us lost many camels and horses, but our company arrived safely—praise be to God!—at Panj Áb [Indus] which is the river of Sind and means "The Five Rivers." These flow into the great river and irrigate those districts. We reached this river on the night that the new moon of Muharram of the year 734 [12th September 1333] rose upon us. From this point the intelligence officials wrote to India informing the king of our arrival and giving him all the details concerning us.

Here ends the narrative of this journey. Praise be to God, Lord of the worlds.

BOOK II

CHAPTER VI

When we reached this river called Panj Áb, which is the frontier of the territories of the sultan of India and Sind, the officials of the intelligence service came to us and sent a report about us to the governor of the city of Multán. From Sind to the city of Dihlí [Delhi], the sultan's capital, it is fifty days' march, but when the intelligence officers write to the sultan from Sind the letter reaches him in five days by the postal service. In India the postal service is of two kinds.[1] The mounted couriers travel on horses belonging to the sultan with relays every four miles. The service of couriers on foot is organized in the following manner. At every third of a mile there is an inhabited village, outside which there are three pavilions. In these sit men girded up ready to move off, each of whom has a rod a yard and a half long with brass bells at the top. When a courier leaves the town he takes the letter in the fingers of one hand and the rod with the bells in the other, and runs with all his might. The men in the pavilions, on hearing the sound of the bells, prepare to meet him, and when he reaches them one of them takes the letter in his hand and passes on, running with all his might and shaking his rod until he reaches the next station, and so the letter is passed on till it reaches its destination. This post is quicker than the mounted post. It is sometimes used to transport fruits from Khurásán which are highly valued in India; they are put on plates and carried with great speed to the sultan. In the same way they transport the principal criminals; they are each placed on a stretcher and the couriers run carrying the stretcher on their heads. The sultan's drinking water is brought to him by the same means, when he resides at Dawlat Ábád, from the river Kank (Ganges), to which the Hindus go on pilgrimage and which is at a distance of forty days' journey from there.

When the intelligence officials write to the sultan informing him of those who arrive in his country, he studies the report very minutely. They take the utmost care in this matter, telling him that a certain man has arrived of such-and-such an appearance and dress, and noting the number of his party, slaves and servants and beasts, his behaviour both in action and at rest, and all his doings, omitting no details. When the new arrival reaches the town of Multán, which is the capital of Sind, he stays there until an order is received from the sultan regarding his entry and the degree of hospitality to be extended to him. A man is honoured in that country according to what may be seen of his actions, conduct, and zeal, since no one knows anything of his family or lineage. The king of India, Sultan Muhammad Sháh, makes a practice of honouring strangers and distinguishing them by governorships or high dignities of State. The majority of his courtiers, palace officials, ministers of state, judges, and relatives by marriage are foreigners, and he has issued a decree that foreigners are to be given in his country the title of '*Aziz* [Honourable], so that this has become a proper name for them.

Every person proceeding to the court of this king must needs have a gift ready to present to him, in order to gain his favour. The sultan requites him for it by a gift many times its value. When his subjects grew accustomed to this practice, the merchants in Sind and India began to furnish each newcomer with thousands of dinars as a loan, and to supply him with whatever he might desire to offer as a gift or to use on his own behalf, such as riding animals, camels, and goods. They place both their money and their persons at his service, and stand before him like attendants. When he reaches the sultan, he receives a magnificent gift from him and pays off his debt to them. This trade of theirs is a flourishing one and brings in vast profits. On reaching Sind I followed this practice and bought horses, camels, white slaves and other goods from the merchants. I had already bought from an 'Iráqí merchant in Ghazna about thirty horses and a camel with a load of arrows, for this is one of the things presented to the sultan. This merchant went off to Khurásán and on returning to India received his money from me. He made an enormous profit through me and became one of the principal merchants. I met him many years later, at Aleppo, when the infidels had robbed me of everything I possessed, but he gave me no assistance.

After crossing the river of Sind called Panj Áb, our way led through a forest of reeds, in which I saw a rhinoceros for the first time. After two days' march we reached Janání, a large and fine town on the bank of the river of Sind. Its people are a people called the Sámira, whose ancestors established themselves there on the conquest of Sind in the time of al-Hajjáj [712 A.D.]. These people never eat with anyone, nor may anyone observe them while they are eating, and they never marry outside their clan.[2] From Janání we travelled to Síwasitán [Sehwan], a large town, outside which is a sandy desert, treeless except for acacias. Nothing is grown on the river here except pumpkins, and the food of the inhabitants consists of sorghum and peas, of which they make bread. There is a plentiful supply of fish and buffalo milk, and they eat also a kind of small lizard stuffed with curcuma. When I saw this small animal and them eating it, I took a loathing at it and would not eat it. We entered Síwasitán during the hottest period of the summer. The heat was intense, and my companions used to sit naked except for a cloth round the waist and another soaked with water on their shoulders; this dried in a very short time and they had to keep constantly wetting it again.[3]

In this town I met the distinguished doctor 'Alá al-Mulk of Khurásán, formerly qádí of Herát, who had come to join the king of India and had been appointed governor of the town and province of Láharí in Sind. I decided to travel thither with him. He had fifteen ships with which he sailed down the river, carrying his baggage. One of these was a ship called the *ahawrah*, resembling the tartan of our country, but broader and shorter. In the centre of it there was a wooden cabin reached by a staircase, and on top of this there was a place prepared for the governor to sit in. His suite sat in front of him and slaves stood to right and left, while the crew of about forty men rowed. Accompanying the *ahawrah* were four ships to right and left, two of which carried the governor's standards, kettledrums, trumpets and singers. First the drums and trumpets were sounded and then the musicians sang, and this continued alternately from early morning to the lunch hour. When this moment arrived, the ships closed up and gangways were placed from one to the other. The musicians then came from on board the governor's *ahawrah* and sang until he finished eating, when they had their meal and returned to their vessel. The journey continued thereafter as before until nightfall. The camp was then set up on the bank of the river, the governor disembarked, tables were set and most of the troops joined in the meal. After the last evening prayer sentries were posted for the night in reliefs. As each relief finished its tour of duty one of them cried in a loud voice "O lord King,[4] so many hours of the night are past." At dawn the trumpets and drums sounded and the dawn prayer was said, then food was brought and when the meal was finished they resumed their journey.

After five days' travelling we reached 'Alá al-Mulk's province, Láharí, a fine town on the coast where the river of Sind discharges itself into the ocean.[5] It possesses a large harbour, visited by men from Yemen, Fárs, and elsewhere. For this reason its contributions to the Treasury and its revenues are considerable; the governor told me that the revenue from this town amounted to sixty lakhs per annum. The governor receives a twentieth part of this, that being the footing on which the sultan commits the provinces to his governors. I rode out one day with 'Alá al-Mulk, and we came to a plain called Tárna, seven miles from Láharí, where I saw an innumerable quantity of stones in the shape of men and animals. Many of them were disfigured and their forms effaced, but there remained a head or a foot or something of the sort. Some of the stones also had the shape of grains of wheat, chickpeas, beans and lentils, and there were remains of a city wall and house walls. We saw too the ruins of a house with a chamber of hewn stones, in the midst of which there was a platform of hewn stones resembling a single block, surmounted by a human figure, except that its head was elongated and its mouth on the side of its face and its hands behind its back like a pinioned captive. The place had pools of stinking water and an inscription on one of its walls in Indian characters. 'Alá al-Mulk told me that the historians relate that in this place there was a great city whose inhabitants were so depraved that they were turned to stone, and that it is their king who is on the terrace in the house, which is still called "the king's palace." They add that the inscription gives the date of the destruction of the people of that city, which occurred about a thousand years ago.[6]

When I had spent five days in this city with 'Alá al-Mulk, he gave me a generous travelling provision and I left for the town of Bakár, a fine city intersected by a channel from the river of Sind.[7] In the middle of this canal there is a fine hospice at which travellers are entertained. Thereafter I travelled from Bakár to the large town of Ūja [Uch] which lies on the bank of the river and has fine bazaars and buildings. The governor there at the time was the excellent king, the Sharíf Jalál ad-Dín al-Kíjí, a gallant and generous man. We formed a strong affection for one another, and met later on at the capital, Delhi. When the sultan left for Dawlat Ábád and bade me remain in the capital, Jalál ad-Dín said to me "You will require a large sum for your expenses and the sultan will be away for a long time, so take my village and use its revenues until I return." I did so and gained about five thousand dinars—may God give him richest recompense! From Uja I travelled to Multán, the capital of Sind and residence of the principal amír.

On the road to Multán and ten miles distant from it is the river called Khusraw Ábád, a large river that cannot be crossed except by boat.[3] At this point the goods and baggage of all who pass are subjected to a rigorous examination. Their custom at the time of our arrival was to take a quarter of everything brought in by the merchants, and exact a duty of seven dinars for every horse. The idea of having my baggage searched was very disagreeable to me, for there was nothing valuable in it, though it seemed a great deal in the eyes of the people. By the grace of God there arrived on the scene one of the principal officers from the governor of Multán, who gave orders that I should not be subjected to examination or search. We spent that night on the bank of the river and next morning were visited by the postmaster, who is the person who keeps the sultan informed of affairs in that town and district and of all that happens in it and all who come to it. I was introduced to him and went in his company to visit the governor of Multán, Qutb al-Mulk.

When I entered his presence, he rose to greet me, shook my hand, and bade me sit beside him. I presented him with a white slave, a horse, and some raisins and almonds. These are among the greatest gifts that can be made to them, since they do not grow in their land and are imported from Khurásán. The governor sat on a large carpeted dais, with the army commanders on his right and left and armed men standing at his back. The troops are passed in review before him and a number of bows are kept there. When anyone comes desiring to be enrolled in the army as an archer, he is given one of the bows to draw. They differ in stiffness, and his pay is graduated according to the strength he shows in drawing them. Anyone desiring to be enrolled as a trooper sets off his horse at a canter or gallop and tries to hit a target set up there with his lance. There is a ring there too, suspended to a low wall; the candidate sets off his horse at a canter until he comes level with the ring, and if he lifts it off with his lance he is accounted by them a good horseman. For those wishing to be enrolled as mounted archers there is a ball placed on the ground, and their pay is proportioned to their accuracy in hitting it with an arrow while going at a canter or gallop.

Two months after we reached Multán one of the sultan's household officers and the chief of police arrived to arrange for the journey of the new arrivals [to Delhi]. They came to me together and asked me why I had come to India. I replied that I had come to enter the service of the *Khúnd Álam* ["Master of the World"], as the sultan is called in his dominions. He had given orders that no one coming from Khurásán should be allowed to enter India unless he came with the intention of staying there. When I had given my answer they called the qádí and notaries and drew up a document witnessing to my undertaking and those of my company who wished to remain in India, but some of them refused to engage themselves. We then prepared for the journey to the capital, which is forty days' march from Multán through a continuous stretch of inhabited country. The principal member of our party was Khudháwand Zádah, qádí of Tirmidh, who had come with his wife and children. The chamberlain made special arrangements for his journey and took twenty cooks with him from Multán, himself going ahead with them every night to prepare his meals, etc.

The first town we reached after leaving Multán was Abúhar [Abohar], which is the first town in India proper, and thence we entered a plain extending for a day's journey. On the borders of this plain are inaccessible mountains, inhabited by Hindu infidels; some of them are subjects [ryots] under Muslim rule, and live in villages governed by a Muslim headman appointed by the governor in whose fief the village lies. Others of them are rebels and warriors, who maintain themselves in the fastnesses of the mountains and make plundering raids. On this road we fell in with a raiding party, this being the first engagement I witnessed in India. The main party had left Abúhar in the early morning, but I had stayed there with a small party of my companions until midday and when we left, numbering in all twenty-two horsemen, partly Arabs and partly Persians and Turks, we were attacked on this plain by eighty infidels on foot with two horsemen. My companions were men of courage and ability and we fought stoutly with them, killing one of the horsemen and about twelve of the footsoldiers. I was hit by an arrow and my horse by another, but God preserved me from them, for there is no force in their arrows. One of our party had his horse wounded, but we gave him in exchange the horse we had captured from the infidel, and killed the wounded horse, which was eaten by the Turks of our party. We carried the heads of the slain to the castle of Abú Bak'har, which we reached about midnight, and suspended them from the wall.

Two days later we reached Ajúdahan [Pakpattan], a small town belonging to the pious Shaykh Faríd ad-Dín.[9] As I returned to the camp after visiting this personage, I saw the people hurrying out, and some of our party along with them. I asked them what was happening and they told me that one of the Hindu infidels had died, that a fire had been kindled to burn him, and his wife would burn herself along with him. After the burning my companions came back and told me that she had embraced the dead man until she herself was burned with him. Later on I used often to see a Hindu woman, richly dressed, riding on horseback, followed by both Muslims and infidels and preceded by drums and trumpets; she was accompanied by Brahmans, who are the chiefs of the Hindus. In the sultan's dominions they ask his permission to burn her, which he accords them. The burning of the wife after her husband's death is regarded by them as a commendable act, but is not compulsory; only when a widow burns herself her family acquire a certain prestige by it and gain a reputation for fidelity. A widow who does not burn herself dresses in coarse garments and lives with her own people in misery, despised for her lack of fidelity, but she is not forced to burn herself. Once in the town of Amjarí [Amjhera, near Dhar] I saw three women whose husbands had been killed in battle and who had agreed to burn themselves. Each one had a horse brought to her and mounted it, richly dressed and perfumed. In her right hand she held a coconut, with which she played, and in her left a mirror, in which she looked at her face. They were surrounded by Brahmans and their own relatives, and were preceded by drums, trumpets and bugles. Everyone of the infidels said to them "Take greetings from me to my father, or brother or mother, or friend" and they would say "Yes" and smile at them. I rode out with my companions to see the way in which the burning was carried out. After three miles we came to a dark place with much water and shady trees, amongst which there were four pavilions, each containing a stone idol. Between the pavilions there was a basin of water over which a dense shade was cast by trees so thickly set that the sun could not penetrate them. The place looked like a spot in hell—God preserve us from it! On reaching these pavilions they descended to the pool, plunged into it and divested themselves of their clothes and ornaments, which they distributed as alms. Each one was then given an unsewn garment of coarse cotton and tied part of it round her waist and part over her head and shoulders. The fires had been lit near this basin in a low lying spot, and oil of sesame poured over them, so that the flames were increased. There were about fifteen men there with faggots of thin wood and about ten others with heavy pieces of wood, and the drummers and trumpeters were standing by waiting for the woman's coming. The fire was screened off by a blanket held by some men, so that she should not be frightened by the sight of it. I saw one of them, on coming to the blanket, pull it violently out of the men's hands, saying to them with a smile

"Do you frighten me with the fire? I know that it is a fire, so let me alone." Thereupon she joined her hands above her head in salutation to the fire and cast herself into it. At the same moment the drums, trumpets and bugles were sounded, the men threw their firewood on her and the others put the heavy wood on top of her to prevent her moving, cries were raised and there was a loud clamour. When I saw this I had all but fallen off my horse, if my companions had not quickly brought water to me and laved my face, after which I withdrew.

The Indians have a similar practice of drowning themselves and many of them do so in the river Ganges, the river to which they go on pilgrimage, and into which the ashes of those who are burned are cast. They say that it is a river of Paradise. When one of them comes to drown himself he says to those present with him, "Do not think that I drown myself for any worldly reason or through penury; my purpose is solely to seek approach to Kusáy," Kusáy being the name of God in their language.[10] He then drowns himself, and when he is dead they take him out and burn him and cast his ashes into this river.

Let us return to our original topic. We set out from the town of Ajúdahan, and after four days' march reached Sarasatí [Sarsúti or Sirsa], a large town with quantities of rice of an excellent sort which is exported to the capital, Delhi. The town produces a large revenue; I was told how much it is, but have forgotten the figure. Thence we travelled to Hánsí, an exceedingly fine, well built and populous city, surrounded by a wall. Two days later we came to Mas'úd Ábád, which is ten miles from Delhi,[11] and there we spent three days. The sultan was away at the time in the district of the town of Qanawj, which is ten days' march from Delhi, but the queen-mother was in the capital, and also the sultan's wazír. He sent his officers to receive us, designating for each one of us a person of his own rank. Meanwhile he wrote to inform the sultan of our arrival, sending the letter by courier post, and received the sultan's reply during the three days that we spent at Mas'úd Ábád. Thereafter the qádís, doctors and shaykhs, and some of the amírs came out to meet us. The Indians call the amírs "kings," using the term "king" where the people of Diyár-Bakr, Egypt, and elsewhere say "amír." We then set out from Mas'úd Ábád and halted near a village called Pálam. On the next day we arrived at the city of Dihlí [Delhi], the metropolis of India, a vast and magnificent city, uniting beauty with strength. It is surrounded by a wall that has no equal in the world, and is the largest city in India, nay rather the largest city in the entire Muslim Orient.

. The city of Delhi is made up now of four neighbouring and contiguous towns. One of them is Delhi proper, the old city built by the infidels and captured in the year 1188. The second is called Sírí, known also as the Abode of the Caliphate; this was the town given by the sultan to Ghiyáth ad-Dín, the grandson of the 'Abbásid Caliph Mustansir, when he came to his court. The third is called Tughlaq Ábád, after its founder, the Sultan Tughlaq, the father of the sultan of India to whose court we came. The reason why he built it was that one day he said to a former sultan "O master of the world, it were fitting that a city should be built here." The sultan replied to him in jest "When you are sultan, build it." It came about by the decree of God that he became sultan, so he built it and called it by his own name. The fourth is called Jahán Panáh, and is set apart for the residence of the reigning sultan, Muhammad Sháh. He was the founder of it, and it was his intention to unite these four towns within a single wall, but after building part of it he gave up the reſt because of the expenṣe required for its conſtruction.[12]

The cathedral mosque occupies a large area; its walls, roof, and paving are all conſtructed of white ſtones, admirably squared and firmly cemented with lead. There is no wood in it at all. It has thirteen domes of ſtone, its pulpit also is made of ſtone, and it has four courts. In the centre of the mosque is an awe-inspiring column, and nobody knows of what metal it is conſtructed. One of their learned men told me that it is called *Haft Júsh*, which means "seven metals," and that it is conſtructed from these seven. A part of this column, of a finger's breadth, has been polished, and gives out a brilliant gleam. Iron makes no impression on it. It is thirty cubits high,[13] and we rolled a turban round it, and the portion which encircled it measured eight cubits. At the eaſtern gate there are two enormous idols of brass proſtrate on the ground and held by ſtones, and everyone entering or leaving the mosque treads on them. The site was formerly occupied by an idol temple, and was converted into a mosque on the conqueſt of the city. In the northern court is the minaret, which has no parallel in the lands of Islám. It is built of red ſtone, unlike the reſt of the edifice, ornamented with sculptures, and of great height. The ball on the top is of gliſtening white marble and its "apples" [small balls surmounting a minaret] are of pure gold. The passage is so wide that elephants could go up by it. A person in whom I have confidence told me that when it was built he saw an elephant climbing with ſtones to the top. The Sultan Qutb ad-Dín wished to build one in the weſtern court even larger, but was cut off by death when only a third of it had been completed. This minaret is one of the wonders of the world for size, and the width of its passage is such that three elephants could mount it abreast. The third of it built equals in height the whole of the other minaret we have mentioned in the northern court, though to one looking at it from below it does not seem so high because of its bulk.

Outside Delhi is a large reservoir named after the Sultan Lalmish, from which the inhabitants draw their drinking water. It is supplied by rain water, and is about two miles in length by half that breadth. In the centre there is a great pavilion built of squared stones, two stories high. When the reservoir is filled with water it can be reached only in boats, but when the water is low the people go into it. Inside it is a mosque, and at most times it is occupied by mendicants devoted to the service of God. When the water dries up at the sides of this reservoir, they sow sugar canes, cucumbers, green melons and pumpkins there. The melons and pumpkins are very sweet but of small size. Between Delhi and the Abode of the Caliphate is the private reservoir, which is larger than the other. Along its sides there are about forty pavilions, and round about it live the musicians.

Among the learned and pious inhabitants of Delhi is the devout and humble imám Kamál ad-Dín, called "The Cave Man" from the cave in which he lives outside the city. I had a slave-boy who ran away from me, and whom I found in the possession of a certain Turk. I proposed to take him back from him, but the shaykh said to me "This boy is no good to you. Don't take him." The Turk wished to come to an arrangement, so he paid me a hundred dinars and kept the boy. Six months later the boy killed his master and was taken before the sultan, who ordered him to he handed over to his master's sons, and they put him to death. When I saw this miracle on the part of the shaykh I attached myself to him, withdrawing from the world and giving all that I possessed to the poor and needy. I stayed with him for some time, and I used to see him fast for ten and twenty days on end and remain standing most of the night. I continued with him until the sultan sent for me and I became entangled in the world once again—may God give me a good ending!

This king is of all men the fondest of making gifts and of shedding blood. His gate is never without some poor man enriched or some living man executed, and stories are current amongst the people of his generosity and courage and of his cruelty and violence towards criminals. For all that, he is of all men the most humble and the readiest to show equity and justice. The ceremonies of religion are strictly complied with at his court, and he is severe in the matter of attendance at prayer and in punishing those who neglect it. He is one of those kings whose felicity is unimpaired and surpassing all ordinary experience, but his dominant quality is generosity. We shall relate some stories of this that are marvellous beyond anything ever heard before, and I call God and his Angels and His Prophets to witness that all that I tell of his extraordinary generosity is absolute truth. I know that some of the instances I shall relate will be unacceptable to the minds of many, and that they will regard them as quite impossible, but in a matter which I have seen with my own eyes and of which I know the accuracy and have had a large share, I cannot do otherwise than speak the truth.[14]

The sultan's palace at Delhi is called *Dár Sará*, and contains many doors. At the first door there are a number of guardians, and beside it trumpeters and flute-players. When any amír or person of note arrives, they sound their instruments and say " So-and-so has come, so-and-so has come." The same takes place also at the second and third doors. Outside the first door are platforms on which the executioners sit, for the custom amongst them is that when the sultan orders a man to be executed, the sentence is carried out at the door of the audience hall, and the body lies there over three nights. Between the first and second doors there is a large vestibule with platforms along both sides, on which sit those whose turn of duty it is to guard the doors. Between the second and third doors there is a large platform on which the principal naqíb [keeper of the register] sits; in front of him there is a gold mace, which he holds in his hand, and on his head he wears a jewelled tiara of gold, surmounted by peacock feathers. The second door leads to an extensive audience hall in which the people sit. At the third door there are platforms occupied by the scribes of the door. One of their customs is that none may pass through this door except those whom the sultan has prescribed, and for each person he prescribes a number of his staff to enter along with him. Whenever any person comes to this door the scribes write down "So-and-so came at the first hour" or the second, and so on, and the sultan receives a report of this after the evening prayer. Another of their customs is that anyone who absents himself from the palace for three days or more, with or without excuse, may not enter this door thereafter except by the sultan's permission. If he has an excuse of illness or otherwise he presents the sultan with a gift suitable to his rank. The third door opens into an immense audience hall called *Hazár Ustún*, which means "A thousand pillars." The pillars are of wood and support a wooden roof, admirably carved. The people sit under this, and it is in this hall that the sultan holds public audiences.

As a rule his audiences are held in the afternoon, though he often holds them early in the day. He sits cross-legged on a throne placed on a dais carpeted in white, with a large cushion behind him and two others as arm-rests on his right and left. When he takes his seat, the wazír stands in front of him, the secretaries behind the wazír, then the chamberlains and so on in order of precedence. As the sultan sits down the chamberlains and naqíbs say in their loudest voice *Bismillah.* At the sultan's head stands the "great king" Qabúla with a fly-whisk in his hand to drive off the flies. A hundred armour-bearers stand on the right and a like number on the left, carrying shields, swords, and bows. The other functionaries and notables stand along the hall to right and left. Then they bring in sixty horses with the royal harness, half of which are ranged on the right and half on the left, where the sultan can see them. Next fifty elephants are brought in, which are adorned with silken cloths, and have their tusks shod with iron for greater efficacy in killing criminals. On the neck of each elephant is its mahout, who carries a sort of iron axe with which he punishes it and directs it to do what is required of it. Each elephant has on its back a sort of large chest capable of holding twenty warriors or more or less, according to the size of the beast. These elephants are trained to make obeisance to the sultan and incline their heads, and when they do so the chamberlains cry in a loud voice *Bismillah.* They also are arranged half on the right and half on the left behind the persons standing. As each person enters who has an appointed place of standing on the right or left, he makes obeisance on reaching the station of the chamberlains, and the chamberlains say *Bismillah*, regulating the loudness of their utterance by the rank of the person concerned, who then retires to his appointed place, beyond which he never passes. If it is one of the infidel Hindus who makes obeisance, the chamberlains say to him "God guide thee."

If there should be anyone at the door who has come to offer the sultan a gift, the chamberlains enter the sultan's presence in order of precedence, make obeisance in three places, and inform the sultan of the person at the door. If he commands them to bring him in, they place the gift in the hands of men who stand with it in front of the sultan where he can see it. He then calls in the donor, who makes obeisance three times before reaching the sultan and makes another obeisance at the station of the chamberlains. The sultan then addresses him in person with the greatest courtesy and bids him welcome. If he is a person who is worthy of honour, the sultan takes him by the hand or embraces him, and asks for some part of his present. It is then placed before him, and if it consists in weapons or fabrics he turns it this way and that with his hand and expresses his approval, to set the donor at ease and encourage him. He gives him a robe of honour and assigns him a sum of money to wash his head, according to their custom in this case, proportioned to his merits.

When the sultan returns from a journey, the elephants are decorated, and on sixteen of them are placed sixteen parasols, some brocaded and some set with jewels. Wooden pavilions are built several stories high and covered with silk cloths, and in each story there are singing girls wearing magnificent dresses and ornaments, with dancing girls amongst them. In the centre of each pavilion is a large tank made of skins and filled with syrup-water, from which all the people, natives or strangers, may drink, receiving at the same time betel leaves and areca nuts. The space between the pavilions is carpeted with silk cloths, on which the sultan's horse treads. The walls of the street along which he passes from the gate of the city to the gate of the palace are hung with silk cloths. In front of him march footmen from his own slaves, several thousands in number, and behind come the mob and the soldiers. On one of his entries into the capital I saw three or four small catapults placed on elephants throwing gold and silver coins amongst the people from the moment when he entered the city until he reached the palace.

I shall now mention a few of his magnificent gifts and largesses. The merchant Shiháb ad-Dín of Kázarún, who was a friend of al-Kázarúní, the "king" of the merchants in India, was invited by the latter to join him and arrived with a valuable present for the sultan. On their way they were attacked by a considerable force of infidels, who killed the "king" of the merchants and carried off as booty his money and treasures and Shiháb ad-Dín's present. Shiháb ad-Dín himself escaped with his life, and the sultan, on hearing of this, gave orders that he should be given thirty thousand dinars and return to his own country. He refused to accept it, however, saying that he had come for the express purpose of seeing the sultan and kissing the ground before him. They wrote to the sultan to this effect and he, gratified with what Shiháb ad-Dín had said, commanded him to be brought to Delhi with every mark of honour. When Shiháb ad-Dín was introduced into the sultan's presence, the sultan made him a rich present, and some days later asked where he was. On hearing that he was ill, he commanded one of his courtiers to go instantly to the treasury and take a hundred thousand tangahs of gold (the tangah being worth two and a half Moroccan dinars) and carry them to him to set him at ease. He ordered him to buy with this money what Indian goods he pleased, and gave instructions that no one else should buy anything at all until Shiháb ad-Dín had made all his purchases. In addition he ordered three ships to be made ready for his journey with complete equipment and full pay and provisions for the crew. So Shiháb ad-Dín departed and disembarked in the island of Hormuz, where he built a great house. I saw this house later on, and I saw also Shiháb ad-Dín, having lost all that he had, soliciting a gift at Shíráz from its sultan, Abú Isháq. That is the way with riches amassed in these Indian lands; it is only rarely that anyone gets out of the country with them, and when he does leave it and reaches some other country, God sends upon him some calamity which annihilates all that he possesses. So it happened to Shiháb ad-Dín, for everything that he had was taken from him in the civil war between the king of Hormuz and his nephews, and he left the country stripped of all his wealth.

The doctor Shams ad-Dín, who was a philosopher and a born poet, wrote a laudatory ode to the sultan in Persian. The ode contained twenty-seven verses, and the sultan gave him a thousand silver dinars for each verse. This is more than has ever been related of former kings, for they used to give a thousand dirhams for each verse, which is only a tenth of the sultan's gift. Then too when the sultan heard the story of the learned and pious qádí Majd ad-Dín of Shíráz, whose history we have written in the first volume, he sent ten thousand silver dinars to him at Shíráz. Again, Burhán ad-Dín of Ságharj [near Samarqand] was a preacher and imám so liberal in spending what he possessed that he used often to contract debts in order to give to others. The sultan heard of him and sent him forty thousand dinars, with a request that he would come to Delhi. He accepted the gift and paid his debts with it, but went off to Cathay and refused to come to the sultan, saying "I shall not go to a sultan in whose presence scholars have to stand."

One of the Indian nobles claimed that the sultan had put his brother to death without cause, and cited him before the qádí. The sultan walked on foot and unarmed to the qádí's tribunal, saluted him and made obeisance, having previously commanded the qádí not to rise before him or move when he entered his court, and remained standing before him. The qádí gave judgment against the sultan, to the effect that he must give satisfaction to his adversary for the blood of his brother, and he did so. At another time a certain Muslim claimed that the sultan owed him a sum of money. They carried the matter before the qádí, who gave judgment against the sultan for the payment of the debt, and he paid it.

When a famine broke out in India and Sind, and prices became so high that a maund of wheat rose to six dinars, the sultan ordered that every person in Delhi should be given six months' provisions from the granary, at the rate of a pound and a half per person per day, small or great, freeman or slave. The doctors and qádís set about compiling registers of the population of each quarter and brought the people, each of whom received six months' provisions.

In spite of all we have said of his humility, justice, compassion for the needy, and extraordinary generosity, the sultan was far too ready to shed blood. He punished small faults and great, without respect of persons, whether men of learning, piety, or high station. Every day hundreds of people, chained, pinioned, and fettered, are brought to his hall, and those who are for execution are executed, those for torture tortured, and those for beating beaten. It is his custom that every day all persons who are in his prison are brought to the hall, except only on Fridays; this is a day of respite for them, on which they clean themselves and remain at ease—may God deliver us from misfortune! The sultan had a half-brother named Mas'úd Khán, whose mother was the daughter of Sultan 'Alá ad-Dín, and who was one of the most beautiful men I have ever seen on earth. He suspected him of wishing to revolt, and questioned him on the matter. Mas'úd confessed through fear of torture, for anyone who denies an accusation of this sort which the sultan formulates against him is put to the torture, and the people consider death a lighter affliction than torture. The sultan gave orders that he should be beheaded in the market place, and his body lay there for three days according to their custom.

One of the gravest charges against the sultan is that of compelling the inhabitants of Delhi to leave the town. The reason for this was that they used to write missives reviling and insulting him, seal them and inscribe them, "By the hand of the Master of the World, none but he may read this." They then threw them into the audience-hall at night, and when the sultan broke the seal he found them full of insults and abuse. He decided to lay Delhi in ruins, and having bought from all the inhabitants their houses and dwellings and paid them the price of them, he commanded them to move to Dawlat Ábád.[16] They refused, and his herald was sent to proclaim that no person should remain in the city after three nights. The majority complied with the order, but some of them hid in the houses. The sultan ordered a search to be made for any persons remaining in the town, and his slaves found two men in the streets, one a cripple and the other blind. They were brought before him and he gave orders that the cripple should be flung from a mangonel and the blind man dragged from Delhi to Dawlat Ábád, a distance of forty days' journey. He fell to pieces on the road and all of him that reached Dawlat Ábád was his leg. When the sultan did this, every person left the town, abandoning furniture and possessions, and the city remained utterly deserted. A person in whom I have confidence told me that the sultan mounted one night to the roof of his palace and looked out over Delhi, where there was neither fire nor smoke nor lamp, and said "Now my mind is tranquil and my wrath appeased." Afterwards he wrote to the inhabitants of the other cities commanding them to move to Delhi to repopulate it. The result was only to ruin their cities and leave Delhi still unpopulated, because of its immensity, for it is one of the greatest cities in the world. It was in this state that we found it on our arrival, empty and unpopulated, save for a few inhabitants.

Let us return now to that which concerns us, and relate how we arrived first at the capital and our fortunes until we left his service. We reached Delhi during the sultan's absence, and proceeded to the palace, where, after passing the first, second, and third doors, the principal naqíb introduced us into a spacious audience-hall. Here we found the wazír awaiting us. On passing through the third door the great hall called *Hazár Ustún*, where the sultan holds his public audiences, met our eyes. Thereupon the wazír made obeisance until his head nearly touched the ground, and we too made obeisance by inclining the body and touching the ground with our fingers, in the direction of the sultan's throne. When we had performed this ceremony the naqíbs cried in a loud voice *Bismillah*, and we all retired.

After visiting the palace of the sultan's mother and presenting her with a gift, we returned to the house which had been prepared for our occupation, and hospitality-gifts were sent to us. In the house I found everything that was required in the way of furniture, carpets, mats, vessels, and bed. The beds in India are light, and can be carried by a single man; every person when travelling has to transport his own bed, which his slave boy carries on his head. It consists of four conical legs with four crosspieces of wood on which braids of silk or cotton are woven. When one lies down on it, there is no need for anything to make it pliable, for it is pliable of itself. Along with the bed they brought two mattresses and pillows and a coverlet, all made of silk. Their custom is to put linen or cotton slips on the mattresses and coverlets, so that when they become dirty they wash the slips, while the bedding inside is kept clean. Next day we rode to the palace to salute the wazír, who gave me two purses, each containing a thousand silver dinars, saying "This is for washing your head," and in addition gave me a robe of fine goathair. A list was made of all my companions, servants, and slave boys, and they were divided into four categories; those in the first category each received two hundred dinars, in the second a hundred and fifty, the third a hundred, and the fourth sixty-five. There were about forty of them, and the total sum given to them was four thousand odd dinars. After that the sultan's hospitality-gift was fixed. This was composed of a thousand pounds of Indian flour, a thousand pounds of flesh-meat, and I cannot say how many pounds of sugar, ghee, and areca-nuts, with a thousand betel leaves. The Indian pound equals twenty of our Moroccan pounds and twenty-five Egyptian pounds. Later on the sultan commanded some villages to be assigned to me to the yearly revenue of five thousand dinars.

On the 4th of Shawwal [8th June 1334] the sultan returned to the castle of Tilbat, seven miles from the capital, and the wazír ordered us to go out to him. We set out, each man with his present of horses, camels, fruits, swords, etc., and assembled at the gate of the castle. The newcomers were introduced in order of precedence and were given robes of linen, embroidered in gold. When my turn came I entered and found the sultan seated on a chair. At first I took him to be one of the chamberlains. When I had twice made obeisance the "king" of the

Sultan's intimate courtiers said "*Bismillah*, Mawlánà Badr ad-Dín," for in India they used to call me Badr ad-Dín, and *Mawlánà* ["Our Master"] is a title given to all scholars. I approached the sultan, who took my hand and shook it, and continuing to hold it addressed me most affably in Persian, saying "Your arrival is blessed; be at ease, I shall be compassionate to you and give you such favours that your fellow-countrymen will hear of it and come to join you." Then he asked me where I came from and I answered him, and every time he said any encouraging word to me I kissed his hand, until I had kissed it seven times. All the new arrivals then assembled and a meal was served to them.

Afterwards the sultan used to summon us to eat in his presence and would enquire how we fared and address us most affably. He assigned us pensions, giving me twelve thousand dinars a year, and added two villages to the three he had already commanded for me. One day he sent the wazír and the governor of Sind to us to say, "The Master of the World says 'Whoever amongst you is capable of undertaking the function of wazír or secretary or commander or judge or professor or shaykh, I shall appoint to that office.'" Everyone was silent at first, for what they were wanting was to gain riches and return to their countries. After some of the others had spoken the wazír said to me in Arabic "What do *you* say?" I replied "Wazírships and secretaryships are not my business, but as to qádís and shaykhs, that is my occupation, and the occupation of my fathers before me." The sultan was pleased with what I had said, and I was summoned to the palace to do homage on appointment as qádí of the Málikite rite at Delhi.

It happens often that there is a long delay in the payment of the money gifts of the sultan (though they are always paid in the end) and I waited six months before receiving the twelve thousand dinars promised to me. They have a custom also of deducting a tenth from all sums given by the sultan. Now, as I have related, I had borrowed from the merchants for the expenses of my journey and my present to the sultan, as well as for my residence at Delhi. When they prepared to return to their country, they importuned me to pay my debts, so I wrote a long poem in praise of the sultan and presented it to him. He received it with pleasure, and I was congratulated by everyone. After waiting for some time I wrote a petition and transmitted it to the sultan, who ordered the wazír to pay my debts. The wazír delayed for some days, and meanwhile received orders to proceed to Dawlat Ábád. During this time the sultan had gone out hunting; the wazír set off, and I received nothing at all until some time later. When my creditors were ready to travel I said to them "When I go to the palace, claim your debt from me according to the custom in this country," for I knew that when the sultan learned of that he would pay them. Their custom is this; the creditor awaits the debtor at the door of the palace, and when the debtor is on the point of entering he says to him "O enemy of the sultan, by the head of the sultan you shall not enter until you have paid me." The debtor may not leave the place after that until he pays him or obtains a delay from him. They did this, and the sultan sent a chamberlain to ask the merchants the amount of the debt. They replied "Fifty-five thousand dinars." The sultan then sent the chamberlain to say to them "The Master of the World says to you 'The money is in my possession, and I shall give you justice; do not demand it of him.'" He then commanded two officers to sit in the Hall of the Thousand Columns to examine and verify the creditors' documents. They found them in order and informed the sultan, who laughed and said "I know he is a qádí and has seen to his business with them." He then commanded the treasurer to pay the sum, but the treasurer greedily demanded a bribe for doing so and would not write the order. I sent him two hundred tangahs, but he returned them. One of his servants told me from him that he wanted five hundred tangahs and I refused to pay it. The matter came to the ears of the sultan, who in great displeasure ordered payment to be suspended until the treasurer's conduct was investigated.

Later on, when the sultan went out to hunt, I went out along with him at once, as I had already prepared all that is required according to the habits of the Indians, and had hired bearers, grooms, valets, and runners. One day when the sultan was in his tent he enquired who were outside. Násir ad-Dín, one of his courtiers, said "So-and-so, the Moroccan, who is very upset." "Why so?" asked the sultan, and he replied "Because of his debt, since his creditors are pressing for payment. The Master of the World had commanded the wazír to pay it, but he left before doing so. Would not the Master of the World order the creditors to wait until the wazír returns or else give orders for their claims to be met?" The "king" Dawlat-Sháh, who was present, said "O Master of the World, every day this man talks to us in Arabic, and I do not know what he is saying. Do *you* know, Násir ad-Dín?" He said this so that Násir ad-Dín might repeat what he had said. Násir ad-Dín answered "He talks about the debt which he has contracted." The sultan said "When we return to the capital, go yourself to the treasury and give him this money." The treasurer was present and said "O Master of the World, he is very extravagant. I have seen him before in our own land, at the court of Sultan Tarmashírín." After this the sultan invited me to his meal, I being in total ignorance of what had taken place. As I went out Násir ad-Dín said "Thank the king Dawlat-Sháh," and Dawlat-Sháh said to me "Thank the treasurer." The day after our return, I went to the palace, and presented to the sultan two camels with richly embroidered saddles and harness, along with eleven plates of sweetmeats. He ordered the sweetmeats to be taken into his private apartments and on retiring to them sent for me. After we had eaten he asked me the names of the sweetmeats which he had particularly enjoyed, and thereafter we took betel and withdrew. A few moments later the treasurer came to me and said "Send your friends to receive the money," so I sent them, and on returning to my house after the sunset prayer found the money there in three sacks, containing the fifty-five thousand dinars which was the amount of my debt, together with the twelve thousand which the sultan had previously commanded to be paid to me, less one-tenth according to their custom.

On the 9th of first Jumádá [21st October 1341], the sultan left Delhi for Ma'bar [Coromandel] to fight with a rebel in that district. I was all prepared to accompany him, but was commanded with some others to remain in Delhi, and the chamberlain took written acknowledgments of the order from us as a proof that we had received it. The sultan also commanded that I should take charge of the mausoleum of Sultan Qutb ad-Dín. He then sent for us to bid us farewell, and asked me if I had any requests. I took out a piece of paper with six petitions, but he said to me "Speak with your tongue." Amongst other things I said "What shall I do about the mausoleum of Sultan Qutb ad-Dín? I have given appointments in connection with it to four hundred and sixty persons, and the income from its endowment does not cover their salaries and food." He said to the wazír "Fifty thousand" and then added "You must have an anticipatory crop." This means "Give him a hundred thousand maunds of wheat and rice to be expended during this year, until the crops produced by the endowments come in." I asked also that my house might be repaired. When I had been granted my requests, he said "There is another recommendation, and that is that you incur no debts and so avoid being pressed for payment, for you will not find anyone to bring me news of them. Regulate your expenses according to what I have given you, as God has said [in the Koran] *Keep not thy hand bound to thy neck, neither open it to fullest extent* and again *Eat and drink, and be not prodigal.*" I desired to kiss his foot, but he prevented me and held back my head with his hand, so I kissed that and retired.

I returned to the capital and busied myself with repairing my house; on this I spent four thousand dinars, of which I received from the treasury six hundred and paid the rest myself. I also built a mosque opposite my house, and occupied myself with the dispositions for the mausoleum of Sultan Qutb ad-Dín. The sultan had fixed the daily issue of food there at twelve maunds of flour and a like quantity of meat. I saw that this amount was too small, and that the produce which the sultan had put at my disposal was plentiful, and consequently I dispensed every day thirty-five maunds of flour and thirty-five of meat, together with proportionate quantities of sugar, candy, ghee and betel, not only to the salaried employees but also to visitors and travellers. The famine at that time was severe, but the population were relieved by this food, and the news of it spread far and wide. The "King" Sabíh, having gone to join the sultan at Dawlat Ábád, was asked by him for news of the doings of the people [in Delhi] and answered "If there were in Delhi two such men as so-and-so there would be no complaints of famine." The sultan was pleased at this and sent me a robe of honour from his own wardrobe.

On setting out for Ma'bar [Coromandel] an epidemic broke out in the sultan's army, so he returned and built a camp near the river Ganges. I left Delhi and joined him there, and remained with him through the campaign against the rebel governor of Oudh. He gave me some thoroughbred horses when distributing them to his courtiers and included me in the number of the latter. I was present with him at the battle and capture of the rebel, and returned with him to Delhi. Afterwards I fell into disfavour with him because I had visited the shaykh Shiháb ad-Dín in his cave outside Delhi.[16] He had thoughts of punishing me and gave orders that four of his slaves should remain constantly beside me in the audience-hall. When this action is taken with anyone, it rarely happens that he escapes. I fasted five days on end, reading the Koran from cover to cover each day, and tasting nothing but water. After five days I broke my fast and then continued to fast for another four days on end, and was set free after the shaykh's death, praise be to God.

Some time later I withdrew from the sultan's service and attached myself to the learned and pious imám Kamál ad-Dín "The Cave Man," as I have already related. The sultan was in Sind at the time, and at hearing of my retreat from the world summoned me. I entered his presence dressed as a mendicant, and he spoke to me very kindly, desiring me to return to his service. I refused and asked him for permission to travel to Mecca, which he granted. This was at the end of second Jumádá 742 [early December 1341].

Forty days later the sultan sent me saddled horses, slave girls and boys, robes and a sum of money, so I put on the robes and went to him. I had a tunic of blue cotton which I wore during my retreat, and as I put it off and dressed in the sultan's robes I upbraided myself. Ever after when I looked at that tunic I felt a light within me, and it remained in my possession until the infidels despoiled me of it on the sea. When I presented myself before the sultan, he showed me greater favour than before, and said to me "I have sent for you to go as my ambassador to the king of China, for I know your love of travel." He then provided me with everything I required and appointed certain other persons to accompany me, as I shall relate presently.

CHAPTER VII

THE king of China had sent valuable gifts to the sultan, including a hundred slaves of both sexes, five hundred pieces of velvet and silk cloth, musk, jewelled garments and weapons, with a request that the sultan would permit him to rebuild the idol-temple which is near the mountains called Qarájíl [Himalaya]. It is in a place known as Samhal, to which the Chinese go on pilgrimage; the Muslim army in India had captured it, laid it in ruins and sacked it.[1] The sultan, on receiving this gift, wrote to the king saying that the request could not be granted by Islamic law, as permission to build a temple in the territories of the Muslims was granted only to those who paid a poll-tax; to which he added "If thou wilt pay the *jizya* we shall empower thee to build it. And peace be on those who follow the True Guidance." He requited his present with an even richer one—a hundred thoroughbred horses, a hundred white slaves, a hundred Hindu dancing- and singing-girls, twelve hundred pieces of various kinds of cloth, gold and silver candelabra and basins, brocade robes, caps, quivers, swords, gloves embroidered with pearls, and fifteen eunuchs. As my fellow-ambassadors the sultan appointed the amír Zahír ad-Dín of Zanján, one of the most eminent men of learning, and the eunuch Káfúr, the cup-bearer, into whose keeping the present was entrusted. He sent the amír Muhammad of Herát with a thousand horsemen to escort us to the port of embarkation, and we were accompanied by the Chinese ambassadors, fifteen in number, along with their servants, about a hundred men in all.

We set out therefore in imposing force and formed a large camp. The sultan gave instructions that we were to be supplied with provisions while we were travelling through his dominions. Our journey began on the 17th of Safar 743 [22nd July 1342]. That was the day selected because they choose either the 2nd, 7th, 12th, 17th, 22nd, or 27th of the month as the day for setting out. On the first day's journey we halted at the post-station of Tilbat, seven miles from Delhi, and travelled thence through Bayána, a large and well-built town with a magnificent mosque, to Kúl [Koel, Aligarh], where we encamped in a wide plain outside the town.

On reaching Koel we heard that certain Hindu infidels had invested and surrounded the town of al-Jalálí.[2] Now this town lies at a distance of seven miles from Koel, so we made in that direction. Meanwhile the infidels were engaged in battle with its inhabitants and the latter were on the verge of destruction. The infidels knew nothing of our approach until we charged down upon them, though they numbered about a thousand cavalry and three thousand foot, and we killed them to the last man and took possession of their horses and their weapons. Of our party twenty-three horsemen and fifty-five foot-soldiers suffered martyrdom, amongst them the eunuch Káfúr, the cup-bearer, into whose hands the present had been entrusted. We informed the sultan by letter of his death and halted to await his reply. During that time the infidels used to swoop down from an inaccessible hill which is in those parts and raid the environs of al-Jalálí, and our party used to ride out every day with the commander of that district to assist him in driving them off.

On one of these occasions I rode out with several

of my friends and we went into a garden to take our siesta, for this was in the hot season. Then we heard some shouting, so we mounted our horses and overtook some infidels who had attacked one of the villages of al-Jalálí. When we pursued them they broke up into small parties; our troop in following them did the same, and I was isolated with five others. At this point we were attacked by a body of cavalry and foot-soldiers from a thicket thereabouts, and we fled from them because of their numbers. About ten of them pursued me, but afterwards all but three of them gave up the chase. There was no road at all before me and the ground there was very stony. My horse's forefeet got caught between the stones, so I dismounted, freed its foot and mounted again. It is customary for a man in India to carry two swords, one, called the stirrup-sword, attached to the saddle, and the other in his quiver. My stirrup-sword fell out of its scabbard, and as its ornaments were of gold I dismounted, picked it up, slung it on me and mounted, my pursuers chasing me all the while. After this I came to a deep nullah, so I dismounted and climbed down to the bottom of it, and that was the last I saw of them.

I came out of this into a valley amidst a patch of tangled wood, traversed by a road, so I walked along it, not knowing where it led to. At this juncture about forty of the infidels, carrying bows in their hands, came out upon me and surrounded me. I was afraid that they would all shoot at me at once if I fled from them, and I was wearing no armour, so I threw myself to the ground and surrendered, as they do not kill those who do that. They seized me and stripped me of everything that I was carrying except a tunic, shirt and trousers, then they took me into that patch of jungle, and finally brought me to the part of it where they stayed, near a tank of water situated amongst those trees. They gave me bread made of peas, and I ate some of it and drank some water. In their company there were two Muslims who spoke to me in Persian, and asked me all about myself. I told them part of my story, but concealed the fact that I had come from the Sultan. Then they said to me: "You are sure to be put to death either by these men or by others, but this man here (pointing to one of them) is their leader." So I spoke to him, using the two Muslims as interpreters, and tried to conciliate him. He gave me in charge of three of the band, one of them an old man, with whom was his son, and the third an evil black fellow. These three spoke to me and I understood from them that they had received orders to kill me. In the evening of the same day they carried me off to a cave, but God sent an ague upon the black, so he put his feet upon me, and the old man and his son went to sleep. In the morning they talked among themselves and made signs to me to accompany them down to the tank. I realized that they were going to kill me, so I spoke to the old man and tried to gain his favour, and he took pity on me. I cut off the sleeves of my shirt and gave them to him so that the other members of the band should not blame him on my account if I escaped.

About noon we heard voices near the tank and they thought that it was their comrades, so they made signs to me to go down with them, but when we went down we found some other people. The newcomers advised my guards to accompany them but they refused, and the three of them sat down in front of me, keeping me facing them, and laid on the ground a hempen rope which they had with them. I was watching them all the time and saying to myself: "It is with this rope that they will bind me when they kill me." I remained thus for a time, then three of their party, the party that had captured me, came up and spoke to them and I understood that they said to them: "Why have you not killed him?" The old man pointed to the black, as though he were excusing himself on the ground of his illness. One of these three was a pleasant-looking youth, and he said to me: "Do you wish me to set you at liberty?" I said "Yes," and he answered "Go." So I took the tunic which I was wearing and gave it to him and he gave me a worn double-woven cloak which he had, and showed me the way. I went off but I was afraid lest they should change their minds and overtake me, so I went into a reed thicket and hid there till sunset.

Then I made my way out and followed the road which the youth had shewn me. This led to a stream from which I drank. I went on till near midnight and came to a hill under which I slept. In the morning I continued along the road, and sometime before noon reached a high rocky hill on which there were sweet lote-trees and zizyphus bushes. I started to pull and eat the lotus berries so eagerly that the thorns left scars on my arms that remain there to this day. Coming down from that hill I entered a plain sown with cotton and containing castor-oil trees. Here there was a *bá'in*, which in their language means a very broad well with a stone casing and steps by which you go down to reach the water. Some of them have stone pavilions, arcades, and seats in the centre and on the sides, and the kings and nobles of the country vie with one another in constructing them along the highroads where there is no water. When I reached the *bá'in* I drank some water from it and I found on it some mustard shoots which had been dropped by their owner when he washed them. Some of these I ate and saved up the rest, then I lay down under a castor-oil tree. While I was there about forty mailed horsemen came to the *bá'in* to get water and some of them entered the sown fields, then they went away, and God sealed their eyes that they did not see me. After them came about fifty others carrying arms and they too went down into the *bá'in*. One of them came up to a tree opposite the one I was under, yet he did not discover me. At this point I made my way into the field of cotton and stayed there the rest of the day, while they stayed at the *bá'in* washing their clothes and whiling away the time. At night time their voices died away, so I knew that they had either passed on or fallen asleep. Thereupon I emerged and followed the track of the horses, for it was a moonlit night, continuing till I came to another *bá'in* with a dome over it. I went down to it, drank some water, ate some of the mustard shoots which I had, and went into the dome. I found it full of grasses collected by birds, so I went to sleep in it. Now and again I felt the movement of an animal amongst the grass; I suppose it was a snake, but I was too worn out to pay any attention to it.

The next morning I went along a broad road, which led to a ruined village. Then I took another road, but with the same result as before. Several days passed in this manner. One day I came to some tangled trees with a tank of water between them. The space under these trees was like a room, and at the sides of the tank were plants like dittany and others. I intended to stop there until God should send someone to bring me to inhabited country, but I recovered a little strength, so I arose and walked along a road on which I found the tracks of cattle. I found a bull carrying a packsaddle and a sickle, but after all this road led to the villages of the infidels. Then I followed up another road, and this brought me to a ruined village. There I saw two naked blacks, and in fear of them I remained under some trees there. At nightfall I entered the village and found a house in one of whose rooms there was something like a large jar of the sort they make to store grain in. At the bottom of it there was a hole large enough to admit a man, so I crept into it and found inside it a layer of chopped straw, and amongst this a stone on which I laid my head and went to sleep. On the top of the jar there was a bird which kept fluttering its wings most of the night—I suppose it was frightened, so we made a pair of frightened creatures. This went on for seven days from the day on which I was taken prisoner, which was a Saturday. On the seventh day I came to a village of the unbelievers which was inhabited and possessed a tank of water and plots of vegetables. I asked them for some food but they refused to give me any. However, in the neighbourhood of a well I found some radish leaves and ate them. I went into the village, and found a troop of infidels with sentries posted. The sentries challenged me but I did not answer them and sat down on the ground. One of them came over with a drawn sword and raised it to strike me, but I paid no attention to him, so utterly weary did I feel. Then he searched me but found nothing on me, so he took the shirt whose sleeves I had given to the old man who had had charge of me.

On the eighth day I was consumed with thirst and I had no water at all. I came to a ruined village but found no tank in it. They have a custom in those villages of making tanks in which the rain-water collects, and this supplies them with drinking water all the year round. Then I went along a road and this brought me to an uncased well over which was a rope of vegetable fibre, but there was no vessel on it to draw water with. I took a piece of cloth which I had on my head and tied it to the rope and sucked the water that soaked into it, but that did not slake my thirst. I tied on my shoe next and drew up water in it, but that did not satisfy me either, so I drew water with it a second time, but the rope broke and the shoe fell back into the well. I then tied on the other shoe and drank until my thirst was assuaged. After that I cut the shoe and tied its uppers on my foot with the rope off the well and bits of cloth which I found there. While I was tying this on and wondering what to do, a person appeared before me. I looked at him, and lo! it was a black-skinned man, carrying a jug and a staff in his hand, and a wallet on his shoulder. He gave me the Muslim greeting "Peace be upon you" and I replied "Upon you be peace and the mercy and blessings of God." Then he asked me in Persian who I was, and I answered "A man astray," and he said: "So am I." Thereupon he tied his jug to a rope which he had with him and drew up some water. I wished to drink but he saying "Have patience," opened his wallet and brought out a handful of black chick-peas fried with a little rice. After I had eaten some of this and drunk, he made his ablutions and prayed two prostrations and I did the same. Thereupon he asked me my name. I answered "Muhammad" and asked him his, to which he replied "Joyous Heart." I took this as a good omen and rejoiced at it. After this he said to me "In the name of God accompany me." I said "Yes," and walked on with him for a little, then I found my limbs giving way, and as I was unable to stand up I sat down. He said "What is the matter with you?" I answered "I was able to walk before meeting you, but now that I have met you I cannot." Whereupon he said "Glory be to God! Mount on my shoulders." I said to him "You are weak, and have not strength for that," but he replied "God will give me strength. You must do so." So I got up on his shoulders and he said to me "Say *God is sufficient for us and an excellent guardian.*" I repeated this over and over again, but I could not keep my eyes open, and regained consciousness only on feeling myself falling to the ground. Then I woke up, but found no trace of the man, and lo! I was in an inhabited village. I entered it and found it was a village of Hindu peasants with a Muslim governor. They informed him about me and he came to meet me. I asked him the name of this village and he replied "Táj Búra." The distance from there to Koel, where our party was, is two farsakhs. The governor provided a horse to take me to his house and gave me hot food, and I washed. Then he said to me: "I have here a garment and a turban which were left in my charge by a certain Arab from Egypt, one of the soldiers belonging to the corps at Koel." I said to him "Bring them; I shall wear them until I reach camp." When he brought them I found that they were two of my own garments which I had given to that very Arab when we came to Koel. I was extremely astonished at this, then I thought of the man who had carried me on his shoulders and I remembered what the saint Abú 'Abdalláh al-Murshidí had told me, as I have related in the first journey, when he said to me: "You will enter the land of India and meet there my brother Dilshád, who will deliver you from a misfortune which will befall you there." I remembered too how he had said, when I asked him his name, "Joyous Heart" which, translated into Persian, is *Dilshád*. So I knew that it was he whom the saint had foretold that I should meet, and that he too was one of the saints, but I enjoyed no more of his company than the short space which I have related.

The same night I wrote to my friends at Koel to inform them of my safety, and they came, bringing me a horse and clothes and rejoiced at my escape.

I found that the sultan's reply had reached them and that he had sent a eunuch named Sunbul, the keeper of the wardrobe, in place of the martyred Káfúr, with orders to pursue our journey. I found, too, that they had written to the sultan about me, and that they regarded the journey as ill-omened on account of what had happened to me and to Káfúr, and were wanting to go back. But when I saw that the sultan insisted upon the journey, I urged them on with great determination. They answered: "Do you not see what has befallen us at the very outset of this mission? The sultan will excuse you, so let us return to him, or stay here until his reply reaches us." But I said: "We cannot stay, and wherever we are his reply will overtake us."

We left Koel, therefore, and encamped at Burj Búra [Burjpur], where there is a fine hermitage in which lives a beautiful and virtuous shaykh called Muhammad the Naked, because he wears nothing but a cloth from his navel to the ground. Thence we travelled to the river known as *Áb-i Siyah* ["Black Water," Kalindi] and from there reached the city of Qinawj [Kanauj]. It is a large, well-built and strongly fortified city; prices there are cheap and sugar plentiful, and it is surrounded by a great wall. We spent three days here and during this time received the sultan's reply to the letter about me. It ran thus "If no trace is found of so-and-so [*i.e.* Ibn Battúta], let Wajíh al-Mulk, the qádí of Dawlat Ábád, go in his place." We came next to the small town of Mawrí, and thence reached Marh, a large town, inhabited chiefly by infidels under Muslim control.[3] It takes its name from the Málawa, a tribe of Hindus, of very powerful build and good-looking; their women especially are exceedingly beautiful and famous for the charms of their company. From Marh we travelled to 'Alábúr [Alapur], a small town inhabited like the former by infidels under Muslim control. A day's journey from there lived an infidel sultan, named Qatam, who was sultan of Janbíl[4] and was killed after besieging Guyályur [Gwalior]. The governor of 'Alábúr was the Abyssinian Badr, a slave of the sultan's, a man whose bravery passed into a proverb. He was continually making raids on the infidels alone and single handed, killing and taking captive, so that his fame spread far and wide and the infidels went in fear of him. He was tall and corpulent, and used to eat a whole sheep at a meal, and I was told that after eating he would drink about a pound and a half of ghee, following the custom of the Abyssinians in their own country. He had a son nearly as brave as himself. During a raid on a village belonging to some Hindus Badr's horse fell with him into a matamore and the villagers surrounded him and killed him.

We journeyed thereafter to Gályúr or Guyályur [Gwalior], a large town with an impregnable fortress isolated on the summit of a lofty hill. Over its gate is an elephant with its mahout carved in stone. The governor of this town was a man of upright character, and he treated me very honourably when I stayed with him on a previous occasion. One day I came before him as he was about to have an infidel cut in two. I said to him "By God I beseech you, do not do this, for I have never seen anyone put to death in my presence." He ordered the man to be put in prison so my intervention was the means of his escape. From Gályúr we went to Parwán, a small town belonging to the Muslims, but situated in the land of the infidels. There are many tigers there, and one of the inhabitants told me that a certain tiger used to enter the town by night, although the gates were shut, and used to seize people. It killed quite a number of the townsfolk in this way. They used to wonder how it made its way in. Here is an amazing thing; a man told me that it was not a tiger who did this but a human being, one of the magicians known as *Júgis* [Yogis], appearing in the shape of a tiger. When I heard this I refused to believe it, but a number of people said the same, so let us give at this point some account of these magicians.

The men of this class do some marvellous things. One of them will spend months without eating or drinking, and many of them have holes dug for them in the earth which are then built in on top of them, leaving only a space for air to enter. They stay in these for months, and I heard tell of one of them who remained thus for a year. The people say that they make up pills, one of which they take for a given number of days or months, and during that time they require no food or drink. They can tell what is happening at a distance. The sultan holds them in esteem and admits them to his company. Some eat nothing but vegetables, and others, the majority, eat no meat; it is obvious that they have so disciplined themselves in ascetic practices that they have no need of any of the goods or vanities of this world. There are amongst them some who merely look at a man and he falls dead on the spot. The common people say that if the breast of a man killed in this way is cut open, it is found to contain no heart, and they assert that his heart has been eaten. This is commonest in the case of women, and a woman who acts thus is called a *kaftár*. During the famine in Delhi they brought one of these women to me, saying that she had eaten the heart of a boy. I ordered them to take her to the sultan's lieutenant, who commanded that she should be put to the test. They filled four jars with water, tied them to her hands and feet and threw her into the river Jumna. As she did not sink she was known to be a *kaftár*; had she not floated she would not have been one. He ordered her then to be burned in the fire. Her ashes were collected by the men and women of the town, for they believe that anyone who fumigates himself with them is safe against a *kaftár's* enchantments during that year.

The sultan sent for me once when I was at Delhi, and on entering I found him in a private apartment with some of his intimates and two of these *júgís.* One of them squatted on the ground, then rose into the air above our heads, still sitting. I was so astonished and frightened that I fell to the floor in a faint. A potion was administered to me, and I revived and sat up. Meantime this man remained in his sitting posture. His companion then took a sandal from a bag he had with him, and beat it on the ground like one infuriated. The sandal rose in the air until it came above the neck of the sitting man and then began hitting him on the neck while he descended little by little until he sat down alongside us. Then the sultan said "If I did not fear for your reason I would have ordered them to do still stranger things than this you have seen." I took my leave, but was affected with palpitation and fell ill, until he ordered me to be given a draught which removed it all.

To return to our subject. We went from Parwan to Kajarrá,[5] where there is a large tank about a mile long having on its banks temples with idols, which have been made examples of [*i.e.* mutilated] by the Muslims. Thence we journeyed through Chandírí to the town of Dhihár [Dhar],[6] which is the chief city of Málwa, the largest province in that district. It is twenty-four days' journey from Delhi, and all along the road between them there are pillars, on which is engraved the number of miles from each pillar to the next. When the traveller desires to know now many miles he has gone that day and how far it is to his halting place or to the town he is making for, he reads the inscription on the pillars and so finds out. From Dhihár we travelled to Ujayn [Ujjain], a fine and populous town, and thence to Dawlat Ábád, the enormous city which rivals Delhi, the capital, in importance and in the spaciousness of its planning. It is divided into three sections; one is Dawlat Ábád proper, and is reserved for the sultan and his troops, the second is called Kataka, and the third is the citadel, which is unequalled for its strength and is called Duwaygir [Deogiri].[7]

At Dawlat Ábád resides the great khán Qutlú Khán, the sultan's tutor, who is governor of the town, and the sultan's representative there and in the lands of Sághar, Tiling [Telingāna], and their dependent territories. This province extends for three months' march, is well-populated, and wholly under his authority and that of his lieutenants. The fortress of Duwaygir mentioned above is a rock situated in a plain; the rock has been excavated and a castle built on its summit. It is reached by a ladder made of leather, which is taken up at night. In its dungeons are imprisoned those convicted of serious crime, and in these dungeons there are huge rats, bigger than cats—in fact, cats run away from them and cannot defend themselves against them, so they can be captured only by employing ruses. I saw them there and marvelled at them. The inhabitants of Dawlat Ábád belong to the tribe of Marhata [Marathas], whose women God has endowed with special beauty, particularly in their noses and eyebrows. The infidels of this town are merchants, dealing principally in jewels, and their wealth is enormous. In Dawlat Ábád there is an exceedingly fine and spacious bazaar for singers and singing-girls, containing numerous shops, each of which has a door leading to the house of its proprietor. The shop is beautified with carpets, and in the centre of it there is a sort of large cradle on which the singing-girl sits or reclines. She is adorned with all kinds of ornaments and her attendants swing her cradle. In the centre of the bazaar there is a large carpeted and decorated pavilion in which the chief musician sits every Thursday after the afternoon prayer, with his servants and slaves in front of him. The singing-girls come in relays and sing and dance before him till the sunset prayer, when they withdraw. In the same bazaar there are mosques for the prayer-services. One of the infidel rulers in India used, on passing through this bazaar, to alight at the pavilion and the singing-girls used to sing before him. One of the Muhammadan sultans used to do the same.

We continued on our way to Nadhurbár [Nandurbar], a small town inhabited by the Marhatas, who possess great skill in the arts and are physicians and astrologers. The nobles of the Marhatas are Brahmans and Katrís [Kshatriyas]. Their food consists of rice, vegetables, and oil of sesame, and they do not hold with giving pain to or slaughtering animals. They wash themselves thoroughly before eating and do not marry among their relatives, unless those who are cousins six times removed. Neither do they drink wine, for this in their eyes is the greatest of vices. The Muslims in India take the same view, and any Muslim who drinks it is punished with eighty stripes, and shut up in a matamore for three months, which is opened only at the hours of meals.

From this town we journeyed to Sághar [Songarh], which is a large town on a great river of the same name [Tapti]. Its inhabitants are upright, religious, and trustworthy, and people go there to participate in the blessing they bestow, and because the town is exempt from taxes and dues. Thereafter we travelled to the town of Kinbáya [Cambay],[8] which is situated on an arm of the sea resembling a river; it is navigable for ships and its waters ebb and flow. I myself saw the ships there lying on the mud at ebb-tide and floating on the water at high tide. This city is one of the finest there is in regard to the excellence of its construction and the architecture of its mosques. The reason is that the majority of its inhabitants are foreign merchants, who are always building fine mansions and magnificent mosques and vie with one another in doing so. We journeyed from this town to Káwá,[9] which is on a tidal bay also, and is in the territories of the infidel rája Jálansí, of whom we shall speak later. Thence we went to Qandahár, a large town belonging to the infidels and situated on a bay. The sultan of Qandahár is an infidel called Jálansí, who is under Muslim suzerainty and sends a gift to the king of India every year.[10] When we reached Qandahár he came out to welcome us and showed us the greatest honour, himself leaving his palace and installing us in it. The principal Muslims at his court came to visit us, such as the children of the Khwája Bohra. One of these is the shipowner Ibráhím, who possesses six vessels of his own.

At Qandahár we embarked on a ship belonging to this Ibráhím, called *al-Jágir*. On this ship we put seventy of the horses of the sultan's present, and the rest we put with the horses of our companions on a ship belonging to Ibráhím's brother, called *Manúrt*. Jálansí gave us a vessel on which we put the horses of Zahír ad-Dín and Sunbul and their party, and he equipped it for us with water, provisions and forage. He sent his son with us on a ship called *al-Uqayrí*, which resembles a galley, but is rather broader; it has sixty oars and is covered with a roof during battle in order to protect the rowers from arrows and stones. I myself went on board *al-Jágir*, which had a complement of fifty rowers and fifty Abyssinian men-at-arms. These latter are the guarantors of safety on the Indian Ocean; let there be but one of them on a ship and it will be avoided by the Indian pirates and idolaters. Two days later we called at the island of Bayram,[11] and on the following day reached the town of Qúqa [Gogo, in Kathiawar], a large town with important bazaars. We anchored four miles from shore on account of the low tide, but I went on shore in a small boat with some of my companions. The sultan of Qúqa is a heathen called Dunqúl, who used to profess submission to the king of India but was in reality a rebel. On setting sail from this town we arrived after three days at the island of Sandabúr [Goa],[12] on which there are thirty-six villages. It is surrounded by a gulf, the waters of which are sweet and agreeable at low tide but salt and bitter at high tide. In the centre of the island are two cities, an ancient one built by the infidels, and one built by the Muslims when they first captured the island. We passed by this island and anchored at a smaller one near the mainland. Next day we reached the town of Hinawr [Honavar, Onore], which is on a large inlet navigable for large ships. During the *pushkál*, which is the rainy season, this bay is so stormy that for four months it is impossible to sail on it except for fishing. The women of this town and all the coastal districts wear nothing but loose unsewn garments, one end of which they gird round their waists, and drape the rest over their head and shoulders. They are beautiful and virtuous, and each wears a gold ring in her nose. One peculiarity amongst them is that they all know the Koran by heart. I saw in the town thirteen schools for girls and twenty-three for boys, a thing which I have never seen elsewhere. Its inhabitants live by maritime commerce, and have no cultivated land. The ruler of Hinawr is Sultan Jalál ad-Dín, who is one of the best and most powerful sultans. He is under the suzerainty of an infidel sultan named Haryab, of whom we shall speak later. The people of Mulaybár [Malabar] pay a fixed sum annually to Sultan Jalál ad-Dín, through fear of his sea-power. His army is composed of about six thousand men, horse and foot. On another occasion I stayed for eleven months at his court without ever eating bread, for their sole food is rice. I lived also in the Maldive Islands, Ceylon, and on the Coromandel and Malabar coasts for three years eating nothing but rice, until I could not swallow it except by taking water with it. On this occasion we stayed with the sultan of Hinawr for three days; he supplied us with provisions, and we left him to continue our journey.

Three days later we reached the land of Mulaybár [Malabar], which is the pepper country. It extends for two months' journey along the coast from Sandabúr [Goa] to Kawlam [Quilon, in Travancore]. The road over the whole distance runs beneath the shade of trees, and at every half-mile there is a wooden shed with benches on which all travellers, whether Muslims or infidels, may sit. At each shed there is a well for drinking and an infidel who is in charge of it. If the traveller is an infidel he gives him water in vessels; if he is a Muslim he pours the water into his hands, continuing to do so until he signs to him to stop. It is the custom of the infidels in the Mulaybár lands that no Muslim may enter their houses or eat from their vessels; if he does so they break the vessels or give them to the Muslims. In places where there are no Muslim inhabitants they give him food on banana leaves. At all the halting-places on this road there are houses belonging to Muslims, at which Muslim travellers alight, and where they buy all that they need. Were it not for them no Muslim could travel by it.

On this road, which, as we have said, extends for a two months' march, there is not a foot of ground but is cultivated. Every man has his own orchard, with his house in the middle and a wooden palisade all round it. The road runs through the orchards, and when it comes to a palisade there are wooden steps to go up by and another flight of steps down into the next orchard. No one travels on a animal in that country, and only the sultan possesses horses. The principal vehicle of the inhabitants is a palanquin carried on the shoulders of slaves or hired porters; those who do not travel on palanquins go on foot, be they who they may. Baggage and merchandise is transported by hired carriers, and a single merchant may have a hundred such or thereabouts carrying his goods. I have never seen a safer road than this, for they put to death anyone who steals a single nut, and if any fruit falls no one picks it up but the owner. Indeed we sometimes met infidels during the night on this road, and when they saw us they stood aside to let us pass. Muslims are most highly honoured amongst them, except that, as we have said, they do not eat with them nor allow them into their houses. In the Mulaybár lands there are twelve infidel sultans, some of them strong with armies numbering fifty thousand men, and others weak with armies of three thousand. Yet there is no discord whatever between them, and the strong does not desire to seize the possessions of the weak. At the boundary of the territories of each ruler there is a wooden gateway, on which is engraved the name of the ruler whose territories begin at that point. This is called the "Gate of Security" of such-and-such a prince. If any Muslim or infidel criminal flees from the territories of one and reaches the Gate of Security of another, his life is safe, and the prince from whom he has fled cannot seize him, even though he be a powerful prince with a great army. The rulers in these lands transmit their sovereignty to their sisters' sons, to the exclusion of their own children. I have seen this practice nowhere else except among the veiled Massúfa, who will be mentioned later.

The first town in the land of Mulaybár that we entered was the town of Abú-Sarúr [Barcelore], a small place on a large inlet and abounding in coco-palms. Two days' journey brought us to Fákanúr [Bacanor, now Barkur],[13] a large town on an inlet; here there is a large quantity of sugar-canes, which are unexcelled in the rest of that country. The chief of the Muslim community at Fákanúr is called Básadaw. He possesses about thirty warships, commanded by a Muslim called Lúlá, who is an evildoer and a pirate and a robber of merchants. When we anchored, the sultan sent his son to us to stay on board the ship as a hostage. We went on shore to visit him and he treated us with the utmost hospitality for three nights, as a mark of respect for the sultan of India and also from a desire to make some profit by trading with the personnel of our vessels. It is a custom of theirs that every ship that passes by a town must needs anchor at it and give a present to the ruler. This they call the "right of *bandar*." If anyone omits to do this, they sail out in pursuit of him, bring him into the port by force, double the tax on him, and prevent him from proceeding on his journey for as long as they wish. Three days after leaving Fákanúr we reached Manjarúr [Mangalore], a large town on the inlet called ad-Dumb, which is the largest inlet in the land of Mulaybár. This is the town at which most of the merchants from Fárs and Yemen disembark, and pepper and ginger are exceedingly abundant there. The sultan of Manjarúr is one of the principal rulers in that land, and his name is Ráma Daw. There is a colony of about four thousand Muslims there, living in a suburb alongside the town. Conflicts frequently break out between them and the townspeople, but the sultan makes peace between them on account of his need of the merchants. We refused to land until the sultan sent his son, as the previous sultan had done. When he had done so, we went on shore and were treated with great consideration.

After staying at Manjarúr for three days, we set sail for the town of Hílí,[14] which we reached two days later. It is large and well-built, situated on a big inlet which is navigable for large vessels. This is the farthest town reached by ships from China; they enter only this port, the port of Kawlam, and Cálicút. The town of Hílí is venerated by both Muslims and infidels on account of its cathedral mosque, and seafarers make many votive offerings to it. This mosque contains a number of students, who receive stipends from its revenues, and it has a kitchen from which travellers and the Muslim poor are supplied with food. Thence we sailed to Jurfattan [Cannanore], Dahfattan, and Budfattan; the sultan of these towns is called Kuwayl, and is one of the most powerful sultans of Mulaybár. At Dahfattan there is a great *bá'in* and a cathedral mosque, which were built by Kuwayl's grandfather, who was converted to Islám. Most of the inhabitants of Budfattan are Brahmans, who are venerated by the infidels and who hate the Muslims; for this reason there are no Muslims living amongst them. From Budfattan we sailed to Fandarayná [Panderani], a large and fine town with orchards and bazaars. The Muslims occupy three quarters in it, each of which has a mosque. It is at this town that the Chinese vessels pass the winter. Thence we travelled to the city of Qáliqút [Calicut], which is one of the chief ports in Mulaybár and one of the largest harbours in the world. It is visited by men from China, Sumatra, Ceylon, the Maldives, Yemen and Fárs, and in it gather merchants from all quarters.[15]

The sultan of Cálicút is an infidel, known as "the Sámarí." He is an aged man and shaves his beard, as some of the Greeks do. In this town too lives the famous shipowner Mithqál, who possesses vast wealth and many ships for his trade with India, China, Yemen, and Fars. When we reached the city, the principal inhabitants and merchants and the sultan's representative came out to welcome us, with drums, trumpets, bugles and standards on their ships. We entered the harbour in great pomp, the like of which I have never seen in those lands, but it was a joy to be followed by distress. We stopped in the port of Cálicút, in which there were at the time thirteen Chinese vessels, and disembarked. Every one of us was lodged in a house and we stayed there three months as the guests of the infidel, awaiting the season of the voyage to China. On the Sea of China travelling is done in Chinese ships only, so we shall describe their arrangements.

The Chinese vessels are of three kinds; large ships called *chunks*, middle-sized ones called *zaws* [dhows], and small ones called *kakams*. The large ships have anything from twelve down to three sails, which are made of bamboo rods plaited like mats. They are never lowered, but turned according to the direction of the wind; at anchor they are left floating in the wind. A ship carries a complement of a thousand men, six hundred of whom are sailors and four hundred men-at-arms, including archers, men with shields and arbalists, who throw naphtha. Each large vessel is accompanied by three smaller ones, the "half," the "third," and the "quarter."[16] These vessels are built only in the towns of Zaytun and Sın-Kalán [Canton]. The vessel has four decks and contains rooms, cabins, and saloons for merchants; a cabin has chambers and a lavatory, and can be locked by its occupant, who takes along with him slave girls and wives. Often a man will live in his cabin unknown to any of the others on board until they meet on reaching some town. The sailors have their children living on board ship, and they cultivate green stuffs, vegetables and ginger in wooden tanks. The owner's factor on board ship is like a great amír. When he goes on shore he is preceded by archers and Abyssinians with javelins, swords, drums, trumpets and bugles. On reaching the house where he stays they stand their lances on both sides of the door, and continue thus during his stay. Some of the Chinese own large numbers of ships on which their factors are sent to foreign countries. There is no people in the world wealthier than the Chinese.

When the time came for the voyage to China, the sultan Sámarí equipped for us one of the thirteen junks in the port of Cálicút. The factor on the junk was called Sulaymán of Safad, in Syria [Palestine]. I had previously made his acquaintance, and I said to him "I want a cabin to myself because of the slave-girls, for it is my habit never to travel without them." He replied "The merchants from China have taken the cabins for the forward and return journey. My son-in-law has a cabin which I can give you, but it has no lavatory; perhaps you may be able to exchange it for another." So I told my companions to take on board all my effects, and the male and female slaves embarked on the junk. This was on a Thursday, and I stayed on shore in order to attend the Friday prayers and join them afterwards. The *king* Sunbul and Zahír ad-Dín also went on board with the present. On the Friday morning a slave boy of mine named Hilál came to me and said that the cabin we had taken on the junk was small and unsuitable. When I spoke of this to the captain he said "It cannot be helped, but if you like to transfer to the kakam there are cabins on it at your choice." I agreed to this and gave orders accordingly to my companions, who transferred the slave girls and effects to the kakam and were established in it before the hour of the Friday prayer. Now it is usual for this sea to become stormy every day in the late afternoon, and no one can embark then. The junks had already set sail, and none of them were left but the one which contained the present, another junk whose owner had decided to pass the winter at Fandarayná, and the kakam referred to. We spent the Friday night on shore, we unable to embark on it, and those on board unable to disembark and join us. I had nothing left with me but a carpet to sleep on. On the Saturday morning the junk and kakam were both at a distance from the port, and the junk which was to have made for Fandarayná was driven ashore and broken in pieces. Some of those who were on board were drowned and some escaped. That night the same fate met the junk which carried the sultan's present, and all on board were drowned. Next morning we found the bodies of Sunbul and Zahír ad-Dín, and having prayed over them buried them. I saw the infidel, the sultan of Cálicút, wearing a large white cloth round his waist and a small turban, bare-footed, with the parasol carried by a slave over his head and a fire lit in front of him on the beach; his police officers were beating the people to prevent them from plundering what the sea cast up. In all the lands of Mulaybár, except in this one land alone, it is the custom that whenever a ship is wrecked all that is taken from it belongs to the treasury. At Cálicút however it is retained by its owners and for that reason Cálicút has become a flourishing city and attracts large numbers of merchants. When those on the kakam saw what had happened to the junk they spread their sails and went off, with all my goods and slave-boys and slave-girls on board, leaving me alone on the beach with but one slave whom I had enfranchised. When he saw what had befallen me he deserted me, and I had nothing left with me at all except ten dinars and the carpet I had slept on.

As I was told that the kakam would have to put in at Kawlam, I decided to travel thither, it being a ten days' journey either by land or by the river,[17] if anyone prefers that route. I set out therefore by the river, and hired one of the Muslims to carry the carpet for me. Their custom is to disembark in the evening and pass the night in the village on its banks, returning to the boat in the morning. We did this too. There was no Muslim on the boat except the man I had hired, and he used to drink wine with the infidels when we went ashore and annoy me with his brawling, which made things all the worse for me. On the fifth day of our journey we came to Kunjá-Karí which is on the top of a hill there; it is inhabited by Jews, who have one of their own number as their governor, and pay a polltax to the sultan of Kawlam. All the trees along this river are cinnamon and brazil trees. They use them for firewood in those parts and we used to light fires with them to cook our food on this journey. On the tenth day we reached the city of Kawlam [Quilon], one of the finest towns in the Mulaybár lands.[18] It has fine bazaars, and its merchants are called Súlís. They are immensely wealthy; a single merchant will buy a vessel with all that is in it and load it with goods from his own house. There is a colony of Muslim merchants; the cathedral mosque is a magnificent building, constructed by the merchant Khwája Muhazzab. This city is the nearest of the Mulaybár towns to China and it is to it that most of the merchants [from China] come. Muslims are honoured and respected in it. The sultan of Kawlam is an infidel called the Tírawarí; he respects the Muslims and has severe laws against thieves and profligates. I stayed some time at Kawlam in a hospice, but heard no news of the kakam. During my stay the ambassadors from the king of China who had been with us arrived there also. They had embarked on one of the junks which was wrecked like the others. The Chinese merchants provided them with clothes and they returned to China, where I met them again later.

I intended at first to return from Kawlam to the sultan to tell him what had happened to the present, but afterwards I was afraid that he would find fault with what I had done and ask me why I had not stayed with the present. I determined therefore to return to Sultan Jamál ad-Dín of Hinawr and stay with him until I should obtain news of the kakam. So I went back to Cálicút and found there a vessel belonging to the sultan [of India], on which I embarked. It was then the end of the season for voyaging, and we used to sail only during the first half of the day, then anchor until the next day. We met four fighting vessels on our way and were afraid of them, but after all they did us no harm. On reaching Hinawr, I went to the sultan and saluted him; he assigned me a lodging, but without a servant, and asked me to recite the prayers with him. I spent most of my time in the mosque[19] and used to read the Koran through every day, and later twice a day.

Sultan Jamál ad-Dín had fitted out fifty-two vessels for an expedition to Sandabúr [Goa]. A quarrel had broken out there between the sultan and his son, and the latter had written to Jamál ad-Dín inviting him to seize the town and promising to accept Islám and marry his daughter. When the ships were made ready I thought of setting out with them to the Holy War, so I opened the Koran to take an augury, and found at the top of the page *In them is the name of God frequently mentioned, and verily God will aid those who aid Him.* I took this as a good omen, and when the sultan came for the afternoon prayer I said to him "I wish to join the expedition." "In that case" he replied "you will be their commander." I related to him the incident of my augury from the Koran, which so delighted him that he resolved to join the expedition himself, though previously he had not intended to do so. He embarked on one of the vessels, I being with him, on a Saturday, and we reached Sandabúr on the Monday evening. The inhabitants were prepared for the battle and had set up mangonels, which they discharged against the vessels when they advanced in the morning. Those on the ships jumped into the water, shields and swords in hand, and I jumped with them, and God granted the victory to the Muslims. We entered the city at the point of the sword and the greater part of the infidels fled into their sultan's palace, but when we threw fire into it they came out and we seized them. The sultan thereafter set them free and returned their wives and children to them. They numbered about ten thousand, and he assigned to them one of the suburbs of the city and himself occupied the palace, giving the neighbouring houses to his courtiers.

When I had stayed with him at Sandabúr for three months after the conquest of the town, I asked him for permission to travel and he made me promise to return to him. So I sailed to Hinawr and thence by Manjarúr and the other towns as before to Cálicút. I went on from there to ash-Sháliyát, a most beautiful town, in which the fabrics called by its name are manufactured.[20] After a long stay in this town I returned to Cálicút. Two slaves of mine who had been on the kakam arrived at Cálicút and told me that the ruler of Sumatra had taken my slave-girls, that my goods had been seized by various hands, and that my companions were scattered to China, Sumatra and Bengal. On hearing this I returned to Hinawr and Sandabúr, reaching it after an absence of five months, and stayed there two months.

CHAPTER VIII

The infidel sultan of Sandabúr, from whom we had captured the town, now advanced to recapture it. All the infidels fled to join him, and our troops who were quartered in the [outlying] villages, abandoned us. We were besieged by the infidels and reduced to great straits. When the situation became serious, I left the town during the siege and returned to Cálicút, where I decided to travel to Dhíbat al-Mahal [Maldive islands], about which I had heard a number of tales. Ten days after embarking at Cálicút we reached these islands, which are one of the wonders of the world and number about two thousand in all.[1] Each hundred or less of them form a circular cluster resembling a ring, this ring having one entrance like a gateway, and only through this entrance can ships reach the islands. When a vessel arrives at any one of them it must needs take one of the inhabitants to pilot it to the other islands. They are so close-set that on leaving one island the tops of the palms on another are visible. If a ship loses its course it is unable to enter and is carried by the wind to the Coromandel coast or Ceylon.

The inhabitants of the Maldives are all Muslims, pious and uprig t. The islands are divided into twelve districts, each under a governor whom they call the *Kardúi*. The district of Mahal, which has given its name to the whole archipelago, is the residence of their sultans. There is no agriculture at all on any of the islands, except that a cereal resembling millet is grown in one district and carried thence to Mahal.

The inhabitants live on a fish called *qulb-al-más*, which has red flesh and no grease and smells like mutton. On catching it they cut it in four, cook it lightly, then smoke it in palm leaf baskets.[2] When it is quite dry, they eat it. Some of these fish are exported to India, China, and Yemen. Most of the trees on those islands are coco-palms, which with the fish mentioned above provide food for the inhabitants. The coco-palm is an extraordinary tree; it bears twelve bunches a year, one in each month. Some are small, some large, some dry and some green, never changing. They make milk, oil, and honey from it, as we have already related [p. 115].

The people of the Maldive Islands are upright and pious, sound in belief and sincere in thought; their bodies are weak, they are unused to fighting, and their armour is prayer. Once when I ordered a thief's hand to be cut off, a number of those in the room fainted. The Indian pirates do not raid or molest them, as they have learned from experience that anyone who seizes anything from them speedily meets misfortune. In each island of theirs there are beautiful mosques, and most of their buildings are made of wood. They are very cleanly and avoid filth; most of them bathe twice a day to cleanse themselves, because of the extreme heat there and their profuse perspiration. They make plentiful use of perfumed oils, such as oil of sandal-wood. Their garments are simply aprons; one they tie round their waists in place of trousers, and on their backs they place other cloths resembling the pilgrim garments. Some wear a turban, others a small kerchief instead. When any of them meets the qádí or preacher, he removes his cloth from his shoulders, uncovering his back, and accompanies him thus to his house. All, high or low, are bare-footed; their lanes are kept swept and clean and are shaded by trees, so that to walk in them is like walking in an orchard. In spite of that every person entering a house must wash his feet with water from a jar kept in a chamber in the vestibule, and wipe them with a rough towel of palm matting which he finds there. The same practice is followed on entering a mosque.

From these islands there are exported the fish we have mentioned, coconuts, cloths, and cotton turbans, as well as brass utensils, of which they have a great many, cowrie shells, and *qanbar*. This is the hairy integument of the coconut, which they tan in pits on the shore, and afterwards beat out with bars; the women then spin it and it is made into cords for sewing [the planks of] ships together. These cords are exported to India, China, and Yemen, and are better than hemp. The Indian and Yemenite ships are sewn together with them, for the Indian Ocean is full of reefs, and if a ship is nailed with iron nails it breaks up on striking the rocks, whereas if it is sewn together with cords, it is given a certain resilience and does not fall to pieces. The inhabitants of these islands use cowrie shells as money. This is an animal which they gather in the sea and place in pits, where its flesh disappears, leaving its white shell. They are used for buying and selling at the rate of four hundred thousand shells for a gold dinar, but they often fall in value to twelve hundred thousand for a dinar. They sell them in exchange for rice to the people of Bengal, who also use them as money, as well as to the Yemenites, who use them instead of sand [as ballast] in their ships. These shells are used also by the negroes in their lands; I saw them being sold at Mállí and Gawgaw [see Ch. XIV.] at the rate of 1,150 for a gold dinar.

Their womenfolk do not cover their hands, not even their queen does so, and they comb their hair and gather it at one side. Most of them wear only an apron from their waists to the ground, the rest of their bodies being uncovered. When I held the qádíship there, I tried to put an end to this practice and ordered them to wear clothes, but I met with no success. No woman was admitted to my presence in a lawsuit unless her body was covered, but apart from that I was unable to effect anything. I had some slave-girls who wore garments like those worn at Delhi and who covered their heads, but it was more of a disfigurement than an ornament in their case, since they were not accustomed to it. A singular custom amongst them is to hire themselves out as servants in houses at a fixed wage of five dinars or less. their employer being responsible for their upkeep; they do not look upon this as dishonourable, and most of their girls do so. You will find ten or twenty of them in a rich man's house. Every utensil that a girl breaks is charged up against her. When she wishes to transfer from one house to another, her new employers give her the sum which she owes to her former employers; she pays this to the latter and remains so much in debt to her new employers. The chief occupation of these hired women is spinning *qanbar*. It is easy to get married in these islands on account of the smallness of the dowries and the pleasure of their women's society. When ships arrive, the crew marry wives, and when they are about to sail they divorce them. It is really a sort of temporary marriage. The women never leave their country.

It is a strange thing about these islands that their ruler is a woman, Khadíja. The sovereignty belonged to her grandfather, then to her father, and after his death to her brother Shiháb ad-Dín, who was a minor. When he was deposed and put to death some years later, none of the royal house remained but Khadíja and her two younger sisters, so they raised Khadíja to the throne. She was married to their preacher, Jamál ad-Dín, who became Wazír and the real holder of authority, but orders are issued in her name only. They write the orders on palm leaves with a curved iron instrument resembling a knife; they write nothing on paper but copies of the Koran and works on theology. When a stranger comes to the islands and visits the audience-hall custom demands that he take two pieces of cloth with him. He makes obeisance towards the Sultana and throws down one of these cloths, then to her Wazír, who is her husband Jamál ad-Dín, and throws down the other. Her army comprises about a thousand men, recruited from abroad, though some are natives. They come to the palace every day, make obeisance, and retire, and they are paid in rice monthly. At the end of each month they come to the palace, make obeisance, and say to the Wazír "Transmit our homage and make it known that we have come for our pay," whereupon orders are given for it to be issued to them. The qádí and the officials, whom they call wazírs, also present their homage daily at the palace and after the eunuchs have transmitted it they withdraw. The qádí is held in greater respect among the people than all the other functionaries; his orders are obeyed as implicitly as those of the ruler or even more so. He sits on a carpet in the palace, and enjoys the entire revenue of three islands, according to ancient custom. There is no prison in these islands; criminals are confined in wooden chambers intended for merchandise. Each of them is secured by a piece of wood, as is done amongst us [in Morocco] with Christian prisoners.

When I arrived at these islands I disembarked on one of them called Kannalús, a fine island containing many mosques, and I put up at the house of one of the pious persons there. On this island I met a man called Muhammad, belonging to Dhafár, who told me that if I entered the island of Mahal the Wazír would detain me there, because they had no qádí. Now my design was to sail from there to Ma'bar [Coromandel], Ceylon, and Bengal, and thence on to China. When I had spent a fortnight at Kannalús, I set sail again with my companions, and having visited on our way several other islands, at which we were received with honour and hospitably entertained, arrived on the tenth day at the island of Mahal, the seat of the Sultana and her husband, and anchored in its harbour. The custom of the country is that no one may go ashore without permission. When permission was given to us I wished to repair to one of the mosques, but the attendants on shore prevented me, saying that it was imperative that I should visit the Wazír. I had previously enjoined the captain of the ship to say, if he were asked about me, "I do not know him," fearing that I should be detained by them, and ignorant of the fact that some busybody had written to them telling them about me and that I had been qádí at Delhi. On reaching the palace we halted in some porticoes by the third gateway. The qádí 'Isá of Yemen came up and greeted me and I greeted the Wazír. The captain brought ten pieces of cloth and made obeisance towards the Sultana, throwing down one piece, then to the Wazír, throwing down another in the same way. When he had thrown them all down he was asked about me and answered "I do not know him." Afterwards they brought out betel and rose-water to us, this being their mark of honour, and lodged us in a house, where they sent us food, consisting of a large platter of rice surrounded by plates containing salted meat, chickens, ghee, and fish. Two days later the Wazír sent me a robe, with a hospitality-gift of food and a hundred thousand cowries for my expenses.

When ten days had passed a ship arrived from Ceylon bringing some darwíshes, Arabs and Persians, who recognized me and told the Wazír's attendants who I was. This made him still more delighted to have me, and at the beginning of Ramadán he sent for me to join in a banquet attended by the amírs and ministers. Later on I asked his permission to give a banquet to the darwíshes who had come from visiting the Foot [of Adam, in Ceylon]. He gave permission, and sent me five sheep, which are rarities among them because they are imported from Ma'bar, Mulaybár, and Maqdashaw, together with rice, chickens, ghee, and spices. I sent all this to the house of the wazír Sulaymán, who had it excellently cooked for me, and added to it besides sending carpets and brass utensils. I asked the Wazír's permission for some of the ministers to attend my banquet, and he said to me "And I shall come too." So I thanked him and on returning home to my house found him already there with the ministers and high officials. The Wazír sat in an elevated wooden pavilion, and all the amírs and ministers who came greeted him and threw down an unsewn cloth, so that there were collected about a hundred cloths, which were taken by the darwíshes. The food was then served, and when the guests had eaten, the Koran-readers chanted in beautiful voices. The darwíshes then began their ritual chants and dances. I had made ready a fire and they went into it, treading it with their feet, and some of them ate it as one eats sweetmeats, until it was extinguished. When the night came to an end, the Wazír withdrew and I went with him. As we passed by an orchard belonging to the treasury he said to me "This orchard is yours, and I shall build a house in it for you to live in." I thanked him and prayed for his happiness. Afterwards he sent me two slave-girls, some pieces of silk, and a casket of jewels.

The attitude of the Wazír afterwards became hostile to me for the following reason. The wazír

Sulaymán had sent to me proposing that I should marry his daughter, and I sent to the Wazír Jamál ad-Dín to ask his permission for my acceptance. The messenger returned to me and said "The proposal does not find favour with him, for he wishes to marry you to his own daughter when her period of widowhood comes to an end." But I for my part refused that, in fear of the ill luck attached to her, for she had already had two husbands who had died before consummating the marriage. Meanwhile I was seriously attacked by fever, for every person who comes to this island inevitably contracts fever. I determined therefore to leave it, sold some of the jewels for cowries, and hired a vessel to take me to Bengal. When I went to take leave of the Wazír, the qádí came out to me and said "The Wazír says 'If you wish to go, give us back what we have given you and go.'" I replied "I have bought cowries with some of the jewels, so do what you like with those." He came back to me and said "He says 'We gave you gold, not cowries.'" I said "I shall sell them and give you back the gold." So I went to the merchants, asking them to buy back the cowries from me, but the Wazír forbade them to do so, his purpose in all this being to prevent my leaving him. Afterwards he sent one of his courtiers to me to say "The Wazír says 'Stay with us, and you shall have what you will.'" So reasoning with myself that I was in their power and that if I did not stay of my own free will I should be kept by main force, and that it was better to stay of my own choice, I said to his messenger "Very well, I shall stay with him." When the messenger returned to him he was overjoyed, and summoned me. As I entered he rose and embraced me saying "We wish you to stay near us and you wish to go away from us!" I made my excuses, which he accepted, and said to him "If you wish me to stay I have some conditions to make." He replied "Granted. Name them." I said "I cannot walk on foot." (Now it is their custom that no one rides there except the Wazír, and when I had been given a horse and rode out on it, the population, men and boys, used to follow me in amazement. At length I complained to him, so he had the *dunqura* beaten and a public proclamation made that no one was to follow me. The *dunqura* is a sort of brass basin which is beaten with an iron rod and can be heard at a great distance; after beating it any proclamation which it is desired to make is publicly announced.) The Wazír said "If you wish to ride in a palanquin, do so; if not we have a horse and a mare—choose which of them you wish." So I chose the mare and it was brought to me on the spot, along with a robe. Then I said "What shall I do with the cowries I bought?" He replied "Send one of your companies to sell them for you in Bengal." I said "I shall, on condition that you too send someone to help him in the transaction." He agreed to that, so I sent off my companion Abú Muhammad and they sent a man named al-Hájj 'Alí.

Immediately after the Ramadán fast I made an agreement with the wazír Sulaymán to marry his daughter, so I sent to the Wazír Jamál ad-Dín requesting that the ceremony might be held in his presence at the palace. He gave his consent, and sent the customary betel and sandalwood. The guests arrived but the wazír Sulaymán delayed. He was sent for but still did not come, and on being summoned a second time excused himself on the ground of his daughter's illness. The Wazír then said to me privily "His daughter has refused, and she is her own mistress. The people have assembled, so what do you say to marrying the Sultana's mother-in-law?" (It was her daughter to whom the Wazír's son was married.) I said "Very well," so the qádí and notaries were summoned, and the profession of faith recited. The Wazír paid her dowry, and she was conducted to me a few days later. She was one of the best of women.

After this marriage the Wazír forced me to take the office of qádí. The reason for this was that I had reproached the qádí for his practice of taking a tenth of all estates when he divided them amongst the heirs, saying to him "You should have nothing but a fee agreed upon between you and the heirs." Besides he never did anything properly. When I was appointed, I strove my utmost to establish the prescriptions of the Sacred Law. There are no lawsuits there like those in our land. The first bad custom I changed was the practice of divorced wives of staying in the houses of their former husbands, for they all do so till they marry another husband. I soon put that to rights. About twenty-five men who had acted thus were brought before me; I had them beaten and paraded in the bazaars, and the women put away from them. Afterwards I gave strict injunctions that the prayers were to be observed, and ordered men to go swiftly to the streets and bazaars after the Friday service; anyone whom they found not having prayed I had beaten and paraded. I compelled the salaried prayer-leaders and muezzins to be assiduous in their duties and sent letters to all the islands to the same effect. I tried also to make the women wear clothes, but I could not manage that.

Meanwhile I had married three other wives, one the daughter of a wazír whom they held in high esteem and whose grandfather had been sultan, another the former wife of Shiháb ad-Dín. After these marriages the islanders came to fear me, because of their weakness, and they exerted themselves to turn the Wazír against me by slanders, until our relations became strained. Now it happened that a slave belonging to the sultan Shiháb ad-Dín was brought before me on a charge of adultery, and I had him beaten and put in prison. The Wazír sent some of his principal attendants to me to ask me to set him at liberty. I said to them "Are you going to intercede for a negro slave who has violated his master's honour, when you yourselves but yesterday deposed Shiháb ad-Dín and put him to death because he had entered the house of one of his slaves?" Thereupon I sent for the slave and had him beaten with bamboo rods, which give heavier blows than whips, and paraded through the island with a rope round his neck. When the Wazír heard of this he fell into a violent rage, assembled the ministers and army commanders and sent for me. I came to him, and though I usually made obeisance to him, I did not make obeisance but simply said *Salám 'alaykum*. Then I said to those present "Be my witnesses that I resign the office of qádí because of my inability to carry out its duties." The Wazír addressed me, whereupon I mounted [to the dais], sat down in a place facing him, and answered him in the most uncompromising manner. At this point the muezzin chanted the call to the sunset prayer and he went into his palace saying "They say that I am sultan, but I sent for this fellow to vent my wrath on him and he vented his wrath on me." The respect in which I was held amongst them was due solely to the sultan of India, for they were aware of the regard in which he held me, and even though they are far distant from him yet the fear of him is in their hearts.

When the Wazír entered his palace he sent for the former qádí who had been removed from office. This man had an arrogant tongue, and said to me "Our master asks you why you violated his dignity in the presence of witnesses, and did not make obeisance to him." I answered "I used to make obeisance to him only because I was on good terms with him, but when his attitude changed I gave that up. The greeting of Muslims is *Salám* and nothing more, and I said *Salám*." He sent him to me a second time to say "You are aiming only at leaving us; give back your wives' dowries and pay your debts and go, if you will." On hearing this I made obeisance to him, went to my house, and acquitted all the debts I had contracted. On learning that I had done so and was bent upon going, the Wazír repented of what he had said and withheld his permission for my departure. So I swore with the most solemn oaths that I had no alternative but to leave, and removed all my possessions to a mosque on the coast. I made a compact with two of the ministers that I should go to the land of Ma'bar [Coromandel], the king of which was the husband of my wife's sister, and fetch troops from there to bring the islands under his authority, and that I should be his representative in them. I arranged that the signal between us should be the hoisting of white flags on the ships; when they saw these they were to rise in revolt on the shore. I had never suggested this to myself until the Wazír became estranged from me. He was afraid of me and used to say "This man will without doubt seize the wazírate, either in my lifetime or after my death." He was constantly making enquiries about me and saying "I have heard that the king of India has sent him money to aid him to revolt against me." He feared my departure, lest I should fetch troops from Ma'bar, and sent to me asking me to stay until he could fit out a vessel for me, but I refused. The ministers and chief men came to me at the mosque and begged me to return. I said to them "If I had not sworn I should return." They suggested that I should go to one of the islands to avoid breaking my oath and then return, so I said "Very well," in order to satisfy them. When the night fixed for my departure came I went to take leave of the Wazír, and he embraced me and wept so copiously that his tears dropped on my feet. He passed the following night guarding the island in person, for fear that my relatives by marriage and my friends would rise in revolt against him.

I set sail and reached the island of the wazír 'Alí. Here my wife was attacked by severe pains and wished to go back, so I divorced her and left her there, sending word to that effect to the Wazír, because she was the mother of his son's wife. We continued to travel through the islands from one district to another and came to a tiny island in which there was but one house, occupied by a weaver. He had a wife and family, a few coco-palms and a small boat, with which he used to fish and to cross over to any of the islands he wished to visit. His island contained also a few banana trees, but we saw no land birds on it except two ravens, which came out to us on our arrival and circled above our vessel. And I swear I envied that man, and wished that the island had been mine, that I might have made it my retreat until the inevitable hour should befall me. We then came to the island of Mulúk where the ship belonging to the captain Ibráhím was lying. This was the ship in which I had decided to travel to Ma'bar. Ibráhím and his companions met me and showed me great hospitality. The Wazír had sent instructions that I was to receive in this island thirty dinars' worth of cowries, together with a quantity of coconut, honey, betel, areca-nuts, and fish every day. I stayed seventy days at Mulúk and married two wives there. The islanders were afraid that Ibráhím would plunder them at the moment of sailing, so they proposed to seize all the weapons on his ship and keep them until the day of his departure. A dispute arose over this, and we returned to Mahal but did not enter the harbour. I wrote to the Wazír to tell him what had occurred, whereupon he wrote to say that there was no cause for seizing the weapons. We returned to Mulúk and set sail from there in the middle of Rabí' II., 745 (22nd August 1344). Four months later the Wazír Jamál ad-Dín died—may God have mercy upon him.

We set sail without an experienced pilot on board, the distance between the island and Ma'bar being a three days' journey, and travelled for nine days, emerging on the ninth day at the island of Saylán [Ceylon]. We saw the mountain of Sarandíb there, rising into the heavens like a column of smoke.[3] When we came to the island, the sailors said "This port is not in the territory of the sultan whose country can safely be visited by merchants. It is in the territory of Sultan Ayrí Shakarwatí, who is an evil tyrant and keeps pirate vessels."[4] We were afraid to put into this harbour, but as a gale arose thereafter and we dreaded the sinking of the ship, I said to the captain "Put me ashore and I shall get you a safe-conduct from this sultan." He did as I asked and put me ashore, whereupon the infidels came to us and said "What are you?" I told them that I was the brother-in-law and friend of the sultan of Ma'bar, that I had come to visit him, and that the contents of the ship were a present for him. They went to their sultan and informed him of this. Thereupon he summoned me, and I visited him in the town of Battála [Puttelam], which is his capital. It is a small and pretty town, surrounded by a wooden wall with wooden towers. The whole of its coasts are covered with cinnamon trees brought down by torrents and heaped up like hills on the shore. They are taken without payment by the people of Ma'bar and Mulaybár, but in return for this they give presents of woven stuffs and similar articles to the sultan. It is a day and a night's journey from this island to the land of Ma'bar.

When I entered the presence of the infidel Sultan Ayrí Shakarwatí, he rose to meet me, seated me beside him, and spoke most kindly to me. He said "Your companions may land in safety and will be my guests until they sail, for the sultan of Ma'bar and I are friends." He then ordered me to be lodged and I stayed with him three days, enjoying great consideration which increased every day. He understood Persian and was delighted with the tales I told him of kings and countries. One day, after presenting me with some valuable pearls, he said "Do not be shy, but ask me for anything that you want." I replied "Since reaching this island I have had but one desire, to visit the blessed Foot of Adam." (They call Adam Bábá, and Eve they call Mámá.) "That is simple," he answered, "We shall send an escort with you to take you to it." "That is what I want," said I, then I added "And this ship that I came in can set out in safety for Ma'bar, and when I return you will send me in your own vessels." "Certainly" he replied. When I related this to the captain, however, he said to me "I shall not sail until you return, even if I wait a year on your account," so I told the sultan of this, and he said "He will remain as my guest until you come back."

The sultan then gave me a palanquin, which was carried by his slaves, and sent with me four Yogis, whose custom it is to make an annual pilgrimage to the Foot, three Brahmans,[6] ten other persons from his entourage, and fifteen men to carry provisions. Water is plentiful along that road. On the first day we encamped beside a river, which we crossed on a raft, made of bamboo canes. Thence we journeyed to Manár Mandalí [Minneri-Mandel], a fine town situated at the extremity of the sultan's territories. The inhabitants entertained us with a fine banquet, the chief dish at which was buffalo calves, which they hunt in a forest there and bring in alive. After passing the small town of Bandar Saláwát [Chilaw] our way lay through rugged country intersected with streams. In this part there are many elephants, but they do no harm to pilgrims and strangers, through the blessed favour of the Shaykh Abú 'Abdalláh, who was the first to open up this road for the pilgrimage to the Foot. These infidels used formerly to prevent Muslims from making this pilgrimage and would maltreat them, and neither eat nor trade with them, but since the adventure that happened to the Shaykh, as we have related above [p. 95], they honour the Muslims, allow them to enter their houses, eat with them, and have no suspicions regarding their dealings with their wives and children. To this day they continue to pay the greatest veneration to this Shaykh, and call him "the Great Shaykh."

After this we came to the town of Kunakár, which is the capital of the principal sultan in this land.[6] It lies in a narrow valley between two hills, near a great lake called the Lake of Rubies, because rubies are found in it. Outside the town is the mosque of Shaykh 'Othmán of Shíráz, known as the Sháwush; the sultan and inhabitants visit his tomb and venerate him. He was the guide to the Foot, and when his hand and foot were cut off, his sons and slaves took his place as guides. The reason for his mutilation was that he killed a cow. The Hindu infidels have a law that anyone who kills a cow is slaughtered in the same fashion or else put in its skin and burned. As Shaykh 'Othmán was so highly revered by them, they cut off his hand and foot instead, and assigned to him the revenues of one of the bazaars. The sultan of Kunakár is called the Kunar, and possesses a white elephant, the only white elephant I have seen in the whole world. He rides on it at festivals and puts great rubies on its forehead. The marvellous rubies called *bahramán* [carbuncles] are found only in this town. Some are taken from the lake and these are regarded by them as the most valuable, and some are obtained by digging. In the island of Ceylon rubies are found in all parts. The land is private property, and a man buys a parcel of it and digs for rubies. Some of them are red, some yellow [topazes], and some blue [sapphires]. Their custom is that all rubies of the value of a hundred *fanams* belong to the sultan, who pays their price and takes them; those of less value belong to the finders. A hundred *fanams* equal in value six gold dinars.

We went on from Kunakár and halted at a cave called after Ustá Mahmúd the Lúrí, a pious man who dug out this cave at the foot of a hill beside a small lake. Thence we travelled to the Lake of Monkeys. There are in these mountains vast numbers of monkeys. They are black and have long tails, and their males are bearded like men. Shaykh 'Othmán and his sons and others as well told me that these monkeys have a chief, whom they obey as if he were a king. He fastens on his head a fillet of leaves and leans upon a staff. On his right and his left are four monkeys carrying staves in their hands. When the chief monkey sits down the four monkeys stand behind him, and his female and young come and sit in front of him every day. The other monkeys come and sit at a distance from him, then one of the four monkeys addresses them and all the monkeys withdraw. After this each one brings a banana or a lemon or some such fruit, and the monkey chief with his young and the four monkeys eat. One of the Yogis told me that he had seen the four monkeys in the presence of their chief beating a monkey with sticks and after the beating pulling out its hair. We continued our journey to a place called "The Old Woman's Hut," which is the end of the inhabited part, and marched thence by a number of grottoes. In this place we saw the flying leech, which sits on trees and in the vegetation near water. When a man approaches it jumps out at him, and wheresoever it alights on his body the blood flows freely. The inhabitants keep a lemon in readiness for it; they squeeze this over it and it falls off them, then they scrape the place on which it alighted with a wooden knife which they have for the purpose.

The mountain of Sarandíb [Adam's Peak] is one of the highest in the world. We saw it from the sea when we were nine days' journey away, and when we climbed it we saw the clouds below us, shutting out our view of its base. On it there are many evergreen trees and flowers of various colours, including a red rose as big as the palm of a hand. There are two tracks on the mountain leading to the Foot, one called Bábá track and the other Mámá track, meaning Adam and Eve. The Mámá track is easy and is the route by which the pilgrims return, but anyone who goes by that way is not considered by them to have made the pilgrimage at all. The Bábá track is difficult and stiff climbing. Former generations cut a sort of stairway on the mountain, and fixed iron stanchions on it, to which they attached chains for climbers to hold on by.[7] There are ten such chains, two at the foot of the hill by the "threshold," seven successive chains farther on, and the tenth is the "Chain of the Profession of Faith," so called because when one reaches it and looks down to the foot of the hill, he is seized by apprehensions and recites the profession of faith for fear of falling. When you climb past this chain you find a rough track. From the tenth chain to the grotto of Khidr is seven miles;

this grotto lies in a wide plateau, and near by it is a spring full of fish, but no one catches them. Close to this there are two tanks cut in the rock on either side of the path. At the grotto of Khidr the pilgrims leave their belongings and ascend thence for two miles to the summit of the mountain where the Foot is.

The blessed Footprint, the Foot of our father Adam, is on a lofty black rock in a wide plateau. The blessed Foot sank into the rock far enough to leave its impression hollowed out. It is eleven spans long. In ancient days the Chinese came here and cut out of the rock the mark of the great toe and the adjoining parts. They put this in a temple at Zaytún, where it is visited by men from the farthest parts of the land. In the rock where the Foot is there are nine holes cut out, in which the infidel pilgrims place offerings of gold, precious stones, and jewels. You can see the darwíshes, after they reach the grotto of Khidr, racing one another to take what there is in these holes. We, for our part, found nothing in them but a few stones and a little gold, which we gave to the guide. It is customary for the pilgrims to stay at the grotto of Khidr for three days, visiting the Foot every morning and evening, and we followed this practice. When the three days were over we returned by the Mámá track, halting at a number of villages on the mountain. At the foot of the mountain there is an ancient tree whose leaves never fall, situated in a place that cannot be got at. I have never met anyone who has seen its leaves. I saw there a number of Yogis who never quit the base of the mountain waiting for its leaves to fall. They tell lying tales about it, one being that whosoever eats of it regains his youth, even if he be an old man, but that is false. Beneath the mountain is the great lake from which the rubies are taken; its water is a bright blue to the sight.

We travelled thence to Dínawar, a large town on the coast, inhabited by merchants. In this town there is an idol, known as Dínawar, in a vast temple,[8] in which there are about a thousand Brahmans and Yogis, and about five hundred women, daughters of the infidels, who sing and dance every night in front of the idol. The city and all its revenues form an endowment belonging to the idol, from which all who live in the temple and who visit it are supplied with food. The idol itself is of gold, about a man's height, and in the place of its eyes it has two great rubies, which, as I was told, shine at night like lamps. We went on to the town of Qálí [Point de Galle], a small place eighteen miles from Dínawar, and journeyed thence to the town of Kalanbú [Colombo], which is one of the finest and largest towns in Ceylon. In it resides the wazír and ruler of the sea Jálasti, who has with him about five hundred Abyssinians. Three days after leaving Kalanbú we reached Battála again and visited the sultan of whom we have spoken above. I found the captain Ibráhím awaiting me and we set sail for the land of Ma'bar.

CHAPTER IX

On our voyage to Ma'bar [Coromandel] a gale sprang up and our ship nearly filled with water. We had no experienced pilot on board. We narrowly escaped being wrecked on some rocks, and then came into some shallows where the ship ran aground. We were face-to-face with death, and those on board jettisoned all that they had, and bade farewell to one another. We cut down the mast and threw it overboard, and the sailors made a wooden raft. We were then about six miles from the shore. I set about climbing down to the raft, when my companions (for I had two slave girls and two of my companions with me) said to me "Are you going to go on the raft and leave us?" So I put their safety before my own and said "You two go and take with you the girl that I like." The other girl said "I am a good swimmer and I shall hold on to one of the raft ropes and swim with them." So both my companions and the one girl went on the raft, the other girl swimming. The sailors tied ropes to the raft and swam with their aid. I sent along with them all the things that I valued and the jewels and ambergris, and they reached the shore in safety because the wind was in their favour. I myself stayed on the ship. The captain made his way ashore on the rudder. The sailors set to work to make four rafts, but night fell before they were completed, and the ship filled with water. I climbed on the poop and stayed there until morning, when a party of infidels came out to us in a boat and we went ashore with them in the land of Ma'bar. We told them that we were friends of their sultan, under whose protection they live, and they wrote informing him of this. He was then two days' journey away, on an expedition. I too wrote to him telling him what had happened to me.

We stayed there three days, at the end of which an amír arrived from the sultan with a body of horse and foot, bringing a palanquin and ten horses. I and my companions, the captain, and one of the slave-girls rode, and the other was carried in the palanquin. We reached the fort of Harkátú,[1] where we spent the night, and where I left the slave-girls and some of my slaves and companions. On the following day we arrived at the camp of the sultan, who was Ghiyáth ad-Dín of Dámaghán.[2] He was married to the daughter of the late Sultan Jalál ad-Dín, and it was her sister that I had married in Delhi. It is a custom throughout the land of India that no person enters the sultan's presence without boots on. I had no boots with me so one of the infidels gave me a pair. There were a number of Muslims there and I was astonished to find an infidel show greater courtesy than they did. When I appeared before the sultan he bade me be seated and assigned to me three tents in his vicinity, sending me carpets and food. Later on I had an interview with him and put before him the project to send an army to the Maldive Islands. He resolved to do so, decided what vessels were to be sent, and designated a gift for the Sultana, together with robes and presents for the ministers and amírs. He charged me to draw up his contract of marriage with the Sultana's sister and ordered three vessels to be loaded with alms for the poor of the islands. Then he said to me "You will return in five days' time," but the admiral said to him "It is impossible to sail to the islands for three months yet." "Well then" he replied to me, "if that is the case, come to Fattan until we finish the present campaign and return to our capital Mutra [Madura], and the expedition will start from there."

The country through which we were to pass was an uninterrupted and impassable jungle of trees and reeds. The sultan gave orders that every man in the army, great and small alike, should carry a hatchet to cut it down, and when the camp was struck, he rode forward with his troops and they cut down those trees from morning to noon. Food was then brought, and the whole army ate in relays, afterwards returning to their tree-felling until the evening. All the infidels whom they found in the jungle were taken prisoner, and brought to the camp with their wives and children. Their practice is to fortify their camp with a wooden palisade, which has four gates. Outside the palisade there are platforms about three feet high on which they light a fire at night. By the fire there is posted a night guard of slaves and footsoldiers, each of whom carries a bundle of thin canes. If a party of infidels should attempt to attack the camp by night each sentry lights the bundle he has in his hand, so that the night becomes as bright as the day, and the horsemen ride out in pursuit of the infidels. In the morning the infidels whom our troops had captured the previous day were divided into four groups and impaled at the four gates of the camp. Their women and little children were butchered also and the women tied by their hair to the pales. Thereafter the camp was struck and they set to work cutting down another patch of jungle, and all those who were taken prisoner were treated in the same way. This [slaughtering of women and children] is a dastardly practice, which I have never known of any [other] king, and it was because of it that God brought him to a speedy end.

I left the camp and reached Fattan, which is a large

and fine city on the coast, with a wonderful harbour.[3] There is a great wooden pavilion in it, erected on enormous beams and reached by a covered wooden gallery. When an enemy attacks the place they tie all the vessels in port to this pavilion, which is manned by soldiers and archers, so that the enemy has no chance [of capturing them]. In this city there is a fine mosque, built of stone, and it has also large quantities of grapes and excellent pomegranates. I met here the pious shaykh Muhammad of Níshápúr, one of the crazy darwíshes who let their hair hang loose over their shoulders. He had with him a lion which he had tamed, and which used to eat and sit along with the darwíshes. Accompanying him were about thirty darwíshes, one of whom had a gazelle. Though the gazelle and the lion used to be together in the same place, the lion did not molest it. While I was staying at Fattan the sultan fell ill and came to the city. I went out to meet him and made him a present. When he had taken up his residence there he sent for the admiral and said to him "Take no business in hand except [to equip] the ships which are to make the expedition to the islands." He wished also to give me the value of my present, but I refused it. Afterwards I was sorry for this, because he died and I received nothing. He stayed a fortnight at Fattan and then set out for his capital, but I stayed there for another fortnight.

I then journeyed to his capital, the city of Mutra [Madura], a large town with wide streets. On my arrival I found it in the grip of a plague. Those who were attacked by it died on the second or third day, or at the most on the fourth. When I went out I saw none but sick and dead. The sultan on reaching Mutra had found his mother, wife, and son ill, and after staying in the town for three days, he went out to a river three miles away. I joined him there, and he ordered me to be lodged alongside the qádí. Exactly a fortnight later the sultan died and was succeeded by his nephew Násir ad-Dín. The new sultan gave orders that I should be furnished with all the ships that his uncle had appointed for the expedition to the islands. Later on, however, I fell ill of a fever which is mortal in those parts, and thought that my time had come. God inspired me to have recourse to the tamarind, which grows abundantly there, so I took about a pound of it, put it in water and drank it. It relaxed me for three days, and God healed me of my illness. I took a dislike to this town in consequence, and asked the sultan for permission to depart. He said to me "Why should you go? It is only a month until the season for the expedition to the islands. Stay until we give you all that the Master of the World [the late sultan] ordered for you." I refused however, and he wrote on my behalf to Fattan, that I might sail in any ship I wished.

I returned to Fattan, and found eight vessels sailing to Yemen, on one of which I embarked. We fell in with four warships which engaged us for a short time, but afterwards they retired and we went on to Kawlam [Quilon]. As I was still feeling the effects of my illness, I stayed there for three months, afterwards embarking on a vessel with the intention of making for Sultan Jamál ad-Dín of Hinawr. When we reached the small island between Hinawr and Fákanúr,[4] we were assailed by the infidels with twelve warships, who fought us vigorously and got the better of us. They seized all that I had kept in reserve for emergencies, together with the jewels and precious stones which the king of Ceylon gave me, my clothes and the travelling provisions I kept with me which had been given me by pious men and saints, leaving me with no covering but my trousers. They seized the possessions of every one on board, and put us ashore on the coast. I made my way back to Cálicút, and went into a mosque; one of the theologians sent me a robe, the qádí sent a turban, and a merchant another robe.

At Cálicút I learned of the marriage of the Sultána Khadíja [of the Maldive islands] with the wazír 'Abdalláh after the death of the wazír Jamál ad-Dín, and that my wife, whom I had left there pregnant, had given birth to a son. I thought therefore of making a journey to the islands, but remembering the hostility of the wazír 'Abdalláh towards me I [sought an omen from the Koran and] opened the volume at these words *The angels shall descend upon them saying "Fear not, neither be sad."* So I commended myself to God, and set sail. Ten days later I disembarked at Kannalús, where the governor received me with honour, made me his guest, and fitted out a boat for me. Some of the islanders went to the wazír 'Abdalláh and informed him of my arrival. He asked about me and who had come with me, and was told that the purpose of my visit was to fetch my son, who was about two years old.[6] His mother came to the wazír to lay a complaint against this, but he replied to her "I for my part will not hinder him from taking away his son." He pressed me to visit the island [of Mahal], and lodged me in a house facing the tower of his palace, that he might observe my movements. My son was brought to me, but I thought it better that he should stay with them so I gave him back to them. After a stay of five days, it appeared to me that the best plan was to hasten my departure, and I asked permission to leave. The wazír summoned me, and when I entered his presence he seated me at his side and asked how I fared. I ate a meal in his company and washed my hands in the same basin with him, a thing which he does with no one. Betel was brought in and I took my leave. He sent me robes and hundreds of thousands of cowries, and was most generous in his treatment of me.

I set out again, and we spent forty-three nights at sea, arriving eventually at the land of Bangála [Bengal]. This is a vast country, abounding in rice, and nowhere in the world have I seen any land where prices are lower than there; on the other hand it is a gloomy place, and the people of Khurásán call it "A hell full of good things." I have seen fat fowls sold there at the rate of eight for a single dirham, young pigeons at fifteen to the dirham, and a fat ram sold for two dirhams. I saw too a piece of fine cotton cloth, of excellent quality, thirty cubits long, sold for two dinars, and a beautiful slave-girl for a single gold dinar, that is, two and a half gold dinars in Moroccan money. The first city in Bengal that we entered was Sudkáwán, a large town on the coast of the great sea.[6] Close by it the river Ganges, to which the Hindus go on pilgrimage, and the river Jún[7] unite and discharge together into the sea. They have a large fleet on the river, with which they make war on the inhabitants of the land of Laknawtí.[8]

The sultan of Bengal is Sultan Fakhr ad-Dín, an excellent ruler with a partiality for strangers, especially darwíshes and súfís. The kingship of this land belonged to Sultan Násir ad-Dín, whose grandson was taken prisoner by the sultan of Delhi, and released by Sultan Muhammad when he became king, on condition of sharing his sovereignty with him. He broke his promise and Sultan Muhammad went to war with him, put him to death, and appointed a relative by marriage of his own as governor of that country. This man was put to death by the troops and the kingdom was seized by 'Alí-Sháh, who was then in Laknawtí. When Fakhr ad-Dín saw that the kingship had passed out of the hands of Násir ad-Dín's descendants (he was a client of theirs), he revolted in Sudkáwán and Bengal and made himself an independent ruler. A violent struggle took place between him and 'Alí-Sháh. During the season of winter and mud, Fakhr ad-Dín used to make expeditions up the river against the land of Laknawtí, because of his naval superiority, but when the rainless season returned, 'Alí-Sháh would make raids by land on Bengal, because of his superiority in land-forces. When I entered Sudkáwán I did not visit the sultan, nor did I meet him, as he is a rebel against the king of India, and I was afraid of the consequences which a visit to him might entail.

I set out from Sudkáwán for the mountains of Kámarú, a month's journey from there. This is a vast range of mountains extending to China and also to the land of Thubbat [Tibet], where the musk deer are. The inhabitants of this range resemble the Turks; they possess great endurance, and their value as slaves is many times greater than a slave of any other nationality.[9] They are famous for their magical practices. My purpose in travelling to these mountains was to meet a notable saint who lives there, namely, Shaykh Jalál ad-Dín of Tabríz. At a distance of two days' journey from his abode I was met by four of his disciples, who told me that the Shaykh had said to the darwíshes who were with him "The traveller from the West has come to you; go out to welcome him." He had no knowledge whatever about me, but this had been revealed to him. I went with them to the Shaykh and arrived at his hermitage, situated outside the cave. There is no cultivated land there, but the inhabitants of the country, both Muslim and infidel, come to visit him, bringing gifts and presents, and the darwíshes and travellers live on these offerings. The Shaykh however limits himself to a single cow, with whose milk he breaks his fast every ten days. It was by his labours that the people of these mountains became converted to Islám, and that was the reason for his settling amongst them. When I came into his presence he rose to greet me and embraced me. He asked me about my native land and my travels, and when I had given him an account of them he said to me "You are the traveller of the Arabs." Those of his disciples who were there said "And the non-Arabs too, O our master." "And of the non-Arabs too" he repeated, "so show him honour." They then took me to the hermitage and gave me hospitality for three days.

On the day when I visited the Shaykh I saw that he was wearing a wide mantle of goatshair. It took my fancy and I said to myself "I wish the Shaykh could have given it to me." When I visited him to bid him farewell, he went to the side of the cave, took off the mantle and placed it upon me, together with a skull-cap from his head, himself putting on a patched garment. The darwíshes told me that the Shaykh was not in the habit of wearing this mantle and had put it on only when I arrived, saying to them "This mantle will be asked for by the Moroccan, and it will be taken from him by an infidel sultan, who will give it to our brother Burhán ad-Dín of Ságharj, whose it is and for whom it was made." When they told me this I said to them "I have obtained the blessing of the Shaykh through his clothing me with his garments, and I for my part shall not enter the presence of any sultan, infidel or Muslim, wearing this mantle." With this I withdrew from the Shaykh's presence. Now it came about a long time afterwards that I visited China and eventually reached the city of Khansá [Hang-chow-fu]. My party were separated from me by the pressure of the crowd and I was wearing this mantle. I happened to be in a certain street when the wazír came by with a large suite. His eye fell upon me, and summoning me he clasped my hand, asked me about my arrival, and continued talking to me until I came to the sultan's palace with him. At this point I wished to take leave of him, but he would not hear of it and introduced me into the sultan's presence. The latter questioned me about the Muhammadan sultans and when I replied to his questions, he looked at the mantle and took a liking to it. The wazír said to me "Take it off," and I could not resist his order. So the sultan took it and ordered me to be given ten robes, a horse and harness, and a sum of money. The incident roused my anger, but afterwards I recalled the Shaykh's saying that an infidel sultan would seize it and I was deeply amazed at the fulfilment of the prediction. The following year I entered the palace of the king of China at Khán-Báliq [Peking], and sought out the convent of the Shaykh Burhán ad-Dín of Ságharj. I found him reading and wearing that identical mantle. I was astonished and took it in my hand to examine it. He said to me "Why examine it when you know it already?" "True" I replied, "it is the one that was taken from me by the sultan of Khansá." "This mantle" he went on "was made specially for me by my brother Jalál ad-Dín, who wrote to me saying 'The mantle will reach you by the hand of so-and-so.'" Then he brought out the letter and I read it, marvelling at the Shaykh's perfect foreknowledge. I told Burhán ad-Dín the beginning of the story, and he said to me "My brother Jalál ad-Dín can do much more than all this, he has the powers of creation at his disposal, but he has now passed to the mercy of God. I have been told" he added, "that he prayed the dawn-prayer every day at Mecca, and that he made the pilgrimage every year, for he used to disappear from sight on the days of 'Arafa and the festival, and no one knew where he went."

When I had bidden farewell to Shaykh Jalál ad-Dín

I journeyed to Habanq, an exceedingly large and beautiful city, traversed by the river which descends from the Kámarú mountains. This river is called the Blue River,[10] and is used by travellers to Bengal and Laknawtí. On its banks there are water wheels, orchards, and villages to right and to left, like the Nile in Egypt. Its people are infidels under Muslim rule, who are mulcted of half their crops and pay taxes over and above that. We travelled down the river for fifteen days between villages and orchards, just as if we were going through a bazaar. There are innumerable vessels on it and each vessel carries a drum; when two vessels meet, each of them beats its drum and they salute one another. Sultan Fakhr ad-Dín gave orders that no passage-money should be taken on this river from darwíshes, and that provisions were to be supplied to those of them who had none, and when a darwísh comes to a town he is given half a dinar. After fifteen days' sailing down the river, as we have related, we reached the city of Sunurkáwán,[11] where we found a junk on the point of sailing for the land of Jáwa [Sumatra], which is a journey of forty days from there, so we embarked on it.

CHAPTER X

FIFTEEN days after leaving Sunarkáwán we reached the country of the Barahnakár, whose mouths are like those of dogs.[1] This tribe is a rabble, professing neither the religion of the Hindus nor any other. They live in reed huts roofed with grasses on the seashore, and have abundant banana, areca, and betel trees. Their men are shaped like ourselves, except that their mouths are shaped like those of dogs; this is not the case with their womenfolk, however, who are endowed with surpassing beauty. Their men too go unclothed, not even hiding their nakedness, except occasionally for an ornamental pouch of reeds suspended from their waists. The women wear aprons of leaves of trees. With them reside a number of Muslims from Bengal and Sumatra, who occupy a separate quarter. The natives do all their trafficking with the merchants on the shore, and bring them water on elephants, because the water is at some distance from the coast and they will not let the merchants go to draw it for themselves, fearing for their women because they make advances to well-formed men. Elephants are numerous in their land, but no one may dispose of them except the sultan, from whom they are bought in exchange for woven stuffs.

Their sultan came to meet us, riding on an elephant, which carried a sort of packsaddle made of skins. He himself was dressed in goatskins with the hair to the outside; on his head there were three coloured bands of silk, and he had a reed javelin in his hand. Accompanying were about twenty of his relatives, mounted on elephants. We sent him a present of pepper, ginger, cinnamon, [cured] fish from the Maldive Islands, and some Bengali cloth. They do not wear the cloth themselves, but cover their elephants with it on feast days. This sultan exacts from every ship that puts in at his land a slave girl, a white slave, enough cloth to cover an elephant, and ornaments of gold, which his wife wears on her girdle and her toes. If anyone withholds this tribute, they put a spell on him which raises a storm on sea, so that he perishes or all but perishes.

Twenty-five days after leaving these people we reached the island of Jáwa [Sumatra],[2] from which the incense called *jáwí* takes its name. We saw the island when we were still half a day's journey from it. It is verdant and fertile; the commonest trees there are the coco-palm, areca, clove, Indian aloe, jack-tree,[3] mango, jamún,[4] sweet orange, and camphor cane. The commerce of its inhabitants is carried on with pieces of tin and native Chinese gold, unsmelted. The majority of the aromatic plants which grow there are found only in the districts occupied by the infidels; in the Muslim districts they are less plentiful. When we reached the harbour its people came out to us in small boats with coconuts, bananas, mangoes, and fish. Their custom is to present these to the merchants, who recompense them, each according to his means. The admiral's representative also came on board, and after interviewing the merchants who were with us gave us permission to land. So we went ashore to the port, a large village on the coast with a number of houses, called Sarhá.[5] It is four miles distant from the town. The admiral's representative having written to the sultan to inform him of my arrival, the latter ordered the amír Dawlasa to meet me, along with the qádí and other doctors of the law. They came out for that purpose, bringing one of the sultan's horses and some other horses as well. I and my companions mounted, and we rode in to the sultan's capital, the town of Sumutra, a large and beautiful city encompassed by a wooden wall with wooden towers.

The sultan of Jáwa, al-Malik az-Záhir, is a most illustrious and open-handed ruler, and a lover of theologians. He is constantly engaged in warring for the Faith [against the infidels] and in raiding expeditions, but is withal a humble-hearted man, who walks on foot to the Friday prayers. His subjects also take a pleasure in warring for the Faith and voluntarily accompany him on his expeditions. They have the upper hand over all the infidels in their vicinity, who pay them a poll-tax to secure peace.

As we went towards the palace we found near by it some spears stuck in the ground on both sides of the road. These are to indicate to the people to dismount; no one who is riding may go beyond them, so we dismounted there. On entering the audience-hall we found the sultan's lieutenant, who rose and greeted us with a handshake. We sat down with him and he wrote a note to the sultan informing him of our arrival, sealed it and gave it to a page, who brought the reply written on the back. After this a page brought a *buqsha*, that is, a linen bag. The lieutenant taking this led me by the hand into a small house, where he spends his hours of leisure during the day. He then brought out of the *buqsha* three aprons, one of pure silk, one of silk and cotton and the third of silk and linen, three garments like aprons which they call underclothing, three garments of different kinds called middleclothing, three woollen mantles, one of them being white, and three turbans. I put on one of the aprons in place of trousers, according to their custom, and one garment of each kind, and my companions took the rest of them. After food had been served we left the palace and rode in company with the lieutenant to a garden surrounded by a wooden wall. In the midst of the garden there was a house built of wood and carpeted with strips of cotton velvet, some dyed and others undyed. We sat down here along with the lieutenant. The amír Dawlasa then came bringing two slave girls and two men servants, and said to me "The sultan says to you that this present is in proportion to his means, not to those of Sultan Muhammad [of India]." The lieutenant left after this, and the amír Dawlasa remained with me.

The amír and I were acquainted with one another, as he had come as an envoy to the sultan at Delhi. I said to him "When can I see the sultan?" and he replied "It is the custom of our country that a newcomer waits three nights before saluting the sultan, that he may recover from the fatigue of his journey." We stayed for three days, food being sent to us thrice a day and fruits and rare sweetmeats every evening and morning. On the fourth day, which was a Friday, the amír Dawlasa came to me and said "You will salute the sultan [today] in the royal enclosure of the cathedral mosque after the service." After the prayer I went in to the sultan; he shook me by the hand and I saluted him, whereupon he bade me sit down upon his left and asked me about Sultan Muhammad and about my travels. He remained in the mosque until the afternoon prayers had been recited, after which he went into a chamber there, put off the garments he was wearing (these were robes of the kind worn by theologians, which he puts on when he comes to the mosque on Fridays), and dressed in his royal robes, which are mantles of silk and cotton. On leaving the mosque he found elephants and horses at the gate. Their custom is that if the sultan rides on an elephant his suite ride on horses, and *vice versa*. On this occasion he mounted an elephant, so we rode on horses, and went with him to the audience hall. We dismounted at the usual place [where the lances were] and the sultan rode on into the palace, where a ceremonial audience was held, the sultan remaining on his elephant opposite the pavilion where he sits [at receptions]. Male musicians came in and sang before him, after which they led in horses with silk caparisons, golden anklets, and halters of embroidered silk. These horses danced before him, a thing which astonished me, though I had seen the same performance at the court of the king of India.

My stay at his court in Sumutra lasted fifteen days, after which I asked his permission to continue my journey, since it was now the sailing season, and because it is not possible to travel to China at all times of the year. He fitted out a junk for us, provisioned us, and made us rich presents—may God reward him!—sending one of his courtiers with us to bring his hospitality gift to us on the junk. We sailed along the coast of his territories for twenty-one nights, and arrived at Mul-Jáwa, an infidel land, two months' ourney in length, and containing aromatic spices and the excellent aloes called *Qáqulí* and *Qamárí*. Qáqula and Qamára [after which these aloes are named] form part of the territories of this land.[6] In the territories of the sultan of Sumutra there is only incense, camphor, and a little cloves and Indian aloes, whereas the largest quantity of these is found in Mul-Jáwa.

On reaching the port of Qáqula, we found there a number of junks ready for making piratical raids, and also for dealing with any junks that might attempt to resist their exactions, for they impose a tribute on each junk [calling at that place]. We went ashore to Qáqula, which is a fine town with a wall of hewn stones, broad enough for three elephants to walk abreast on it. The first thing I saw outside the town was elephants bearing loads of Indian aloes, which they burn in their houses and which fetches the same price as firewood with us, or even less. That is when they are selling amongst themselves; to the merchants, on the other hand, they sell a load of it for a roll of cotton cloth, which is dearer in their land than silk. Elephants are very numerous there; they ride on them and use them to carry loads. Every person has his elephants picketed at his door, and every shop-keeper his elephant picketed near him, for riding on to his house and for carrying loads. The same is the case with all the people of China and Cathay [Northern China].

The sultan of Mul-Jáwa is an infidel; I saw him outside his palace sitting beside a pavilion on the bare ground. With him were the officers of state, and the troops were passing in review before him—foot-soldiers, for there are no horses there except those belonging to the sultan, and they have no beasts but elephants on which to ride and fight. He was told about me and summoned me, whereupon I came forward and said "Peace [*as-salám*] be upon those who follow the true religion."[7] They understood nothing but the word *as-salám*. The sultan then welcomed me and ordered a piece of cloth to be spread for me to sit upon. I said to the interpreter "How can I sit on the cloth when the sultan is sitting on the ground?" He replied "Such is his habit; he sits on the ground out of humility. You are a guest and have come from a great sultan, so he wishes to show you honour." Thereupon I sat down, and having asked me very briefly about the sultan [of India] he said to me "You shall stay with us as a guest for three days, and after that you may go."

While this sultan was sitting in audience, I saw a man with a knife in his hand resembling a book-binder's tool. He put this knife to his own neck, and delivered a long speech which I did not understand, then gripped it with both hands and cut his own throat. So sharp was the knife and so strong his grip that his head fell to the ground. I was amazed at his action. The sultan said to me "Does anyone do this in your country?" I replied "I have never seen such a thing." Then he laughed and said "These are our slaves, who kill themselves for love of us." He gave orders that the body should be carried away and burned, and the sultan's lieutenants, the officers of state, the troops, and the citizens went out to his cremation. The sultan assigned a large pension to his children, wife, and brothers, and they were held in high esteem because of this act. One of those present at this audience told me that the speech made by the man was a declaration of his affection for the sultan, and that he was slaying himself for love of him, as his father had slain himself for love of the sultan's father, and his grandfather for love of the sultan's grandfather. Thereafter I withdrew from the audience and he sent me a guest's portion for three days.

We continued our journey by sea and thirty-four days later came to the sluggish or motionless sea.[8] There is a reddish tinge in its waters, which, they say, is due to soil from a country in the vicinity. There are no winds or waves or movement at all in it, in spite of its wide extent. It is on account of this sea that each Chinese junk is accompanied by three vessels, as we have mentioned, which take it in tow and row it forwards. Besides this every junk has about twenty oars as big as masts, each of which is manned by a muster of thirty men or so, who stand in two ranks facing one another. Attached to the oars are two enormous ropes as thick as cables; one of the ranks pulls on the cable [at its side], then lets go, and the other rank pulls [on the cable at its side]. They chant in musical voices as they do this, most commonly saying *la'lá, la'lá*. We passed thirty-seven days on this sea, and the sailors were surprised at the facility of our crossing, for they [usually] spend forty to fifty days on it, and forty days is the shortest time required under the most favourable circumstances.

Thereafter we reached the land of Tawálisí, it being their king who is called by that name. It is a vast country and its king is a rival of the king of China. He possesses many junks, with which he makes war on the Chinese until they come to terms with him on certain conditions. The inhabitants of this land are idolaters; they are handsome men and closely resemble the Turks in figure. Their skin is most commonly of a reddish hue, and they are brave and warlike. Their women ride on horseback and are skilful archers, and fight exactly like men. We put in at one of their ports, at the town of Kaylúkarí, which is among their finest and largest cities. It was formerly the residence of the son of their king. When we anchored in the port their troops came down and the captain went ashore to them, taking with him a present for the prince. When he enquired of them about him, however, they told him that the prince's father had appointed him governor of another district and had made his daughter, whose name was Urdujá, governor of this city.[9]

The day following our arrival at the port of Kaylúkarí, this princess summoned the ship's captain and clerk, the merchants and pilots, the commander of the footsoldiers, and the commanders of the archers to a banquet which she had prepared for them, according to her custom. The captain wished me to go with them, but I declined, because, being infidels, it is not lawful to eat their food. When they came into her presence she asked them if there was any one else of their company who had not come. The captain replied "There is only one man left, a *bakhshí* (that is, a qáḍí, in their tongue), and he will not eat your food." Thereupon she said "Call him," so her guards came [to me] along with the captain's party and said "Comply with the princess's wish." I went to her then, and found her sitting in full state. On my saluting her she replied to me in Turkish, and asked me from what land I had come. I said to her "From the land of India." "From the pepper country?" she asked, and I replied "Yes." She questioned me about this land and events there, and when I had answered she said "I must positively make an expedition to it and take possession of it for myself, for the quantity of its riches and its troops attracts me." I replied "Do so." She ordered me to be given robes, two elephant loads of rice, two buffaloes, ten sheep, four pounds of syrup, and four *martabáns* (that is, large jars) filled with ginger, pepper, lemons, and mangoes, all of them salted, these being among the things prepared for sea vogayes.

The captain told that this princess has in her army women, female servants and slave-girls, who fight like men. She goes out in person with her troops, male and female, makes raids on her enemies, takes part in the fighting, and engages in single combat with picked warriors. He told me too that during a fierce engagement with certain of her enemies, many of her troops were killed and they were all but defeated, when she dashed forward and broke through the ranks until she reached the king against whom she was fighting, and dealt him a mortal blow with her lance. He fell dead and his army took to flight. She brought back his head on the point of a spear, and his relatives redeemed it from her for a large sum of money. When she returned to her father he gave her this town, which had formerly been in her brother's hands. The captain told me also that she is sought in marriage by various princes, but she says "I shall marry none but him who fights and overcomes me in single combat," and they avoid fighting with her for fear of the disgrace [that would attach to them] if she overcame them.

We then left the land of Tawālisī and after seventeen days at sea with a favouring wind, sailing with maximum speed and ease, reached the land of China.

CHAPTER XI

THE land of China is of vast extent, and abounding in produce, fruits, grain, gold and silver. In this respect there is no country in the world that can rival it. It is traversed by the river called the "Water of Life," which rises in some mountains, called the "Mountain of Apes," near the city of Khán-Báliq [Peking] and flows through the centre of China for the space of six months' journey, until finally it reaches Sín as-Sín [Canton].[1] It is bordered by villages, fields, fruit gardens, and bazaars, just like the Egyptian Nile, only that [the country through which runs] this river is even more richly cultivated and populous, and there are many waterwheels on it. In the land of China there is abundant sugar-cane, equal, nay superior, in quality to that of Egypt, as well as grapes and plums. I used to think that the 'Othmání plums of Damascus had no equal, until I saw the plums in China. It has wonderful melons too, like those of Khwárizm and Isfahán. All the fruits which we have in our country are to be found there, either much the same or of better quality. Wheat is very abundant in China, indeed better wheat I have never seen, and the same may be said of their lentils and chick-peas.

The Chinese pottery [porcelain] is manufactured only in the towns of Zaytún and Sín-kalán. It is made of the soil of some mountains in that district, which takes fire like charcoal, as we shall relate subsequently. They mix this with some stones which they have, burn the whole for three days, then pour water over it. This gives a kind of clay which they cause to ferment. The best quality of [porcelain is made from] clay that has fermented for a complete month, but no more, the poorer quality [from clay] that has fermented for ten days. The price of this porcelain there is the same as, or even less than, that of ordinary pottery in our country. It is exported to India and other countries, even reaching as far as our own lands in the West, and it is the finest of all makes of pottery.

The hens and cocks in China are very big indeed, bigger than geese in our country, and hens' eggs there are bigger than our goose eggs. On the other hand their geese are not at all large.[2] We bought a hen once and set about cooking it, but it was too big for one pot, so we put it in two. Cocks over there are about the size of ostriches; often a cock will shed its feathers and [nothing but] a great red body remains. The first time I saw a Chinese cock was in the city of Kawlam. I took it for an ostrich and was amazed at it, but its owner told me that in China there were some even bigger than that, and when I got to China I saw for myself the truth of what he had told me about them.

The Chinese themselves are infidels, who worship idols and burn their dead like the Hindus.[3] The king of China is a Tatar, one of the descendants of Tinkiz [Chingiz] Khán. In every Chinese city there is a quarter for Muslims in which they live by themselves, and in which they have mosques both for the Friday services and for other religious purposes. The Muslims are honoured and respected. The Chinese infidels eat the flesh of swine and dogs, and sell it in their markets. They are wealthy folk and well-to-do, but they make no display either in their food or their clothes. You will see one of their principal merchants, a man so rich that his wealth cannot be counted, wearing a coarse cotton tunic. But there is one thing that the Chinese take a pride in, that is, gold and silver plate. Every one of them carries a stick, on which they lean in walking, and which they call "the third leg." Silk is very plentiful among them, because the silk-worm attaches itself to fruits and feeds on them without requiring much care. For that reason it is so common to be worn by even the very poorest there. Were it not for the merchants it would have no value at all, for a single piece of cotton cloth is sold in their country for the price of many pieces of silk. It is customary amongst them for a merchant to cast what gold and silver he has into ingots, each weighing a hundredweight or more or less, and to put those ingots above the door of his house.

The Chinese use neither [gold] dinars nor [silver] dirhams in their commerce. All the gold and silver that comes into their country is cast by them into ingots, as we have described. Their buying and selling is carried on exclusively by means of pieces of paper, each of the size of the palm of the hand, and stamped with the sultan's seal. Twenty-five of these pieces of paper are called a *bálisht*, which takes the place of the dinar with us [as the unit of currency].[4] When these notes become torn by handling, one takes them to an office corresponding to our mint, and receives their equivalent in new notes on delivering up the old ones. This transaction is made without charge and involves no expense,[5] for those who have the duty of making the notes receive regular salaries from the sultan. Indeed the direction of that office is given to one of their principal amírs. If anyone goes to the bazaar with a silver dirham or a dinar, intending to buy something, no one will accept it from him or pay any attention to him until he changes if for *bálisht*, and with that he may buy what he will.

All the inhabitants of China and of Cathay[6] use in

place of charcoal a kind of lumpy earth found in their country. It resembles our fuller's earth, and its colour too is the colour of fuller's earth. Elephants [are used to] carry loads of it. They break it up into pieces about the size of pieces of charcoal with us, and set it on fire and it burns like charcoal, only giving out more heat than a charcoal fire. When it is reduced to cinders, they knead it with water, dry it, and use it again for cooking, and so on over and over again until it is entirely consumed. It is from this clay that they make the Chinese porcelain ware, after adding to it some other stones, as we have related.[7]

The Chinese are of all peoples the most skilful in the arts and possessed of the greatest mastery of them. This characteristic of theirs is well known, and has frequently been described at length in the works of various writers. In regard to portraiture there is none, whether Greek or any other, who can match them in precision, for in this art they show a marvellous talent. I myself saw an extraordinary example of this gift of theirs. I never returned to any of their cities after I had visited it a first time without finding my portrait and the portraits of my companions drawn on the walls and on sheets of paper exhibited in the bazaars. When I visited the sultan's city I passed with my companions through the painters' bazaar on my way to the sultan's palace. We were dressed after the 'Iráqí fashion. On returning from the palace in the evening, I passed through the same bazaar, and saw my portrait and those of my companions drawn on a sheet of paper which they had affixed to the wall. Each of us set to examining the other's portrait [and found that] the likeness was perfect in every respect. I was told that the sultan had ordered them to do this, and that they had come to the palace while we were there and had been observing us and drawing our portraits without our noticing it. This is a custom of theirs, I mean making portraits of all who pass through their country. In fact they have brought this to such perfection that if a stranger commits any offence that obliges him to flee from China, they send his portrait far and wide. A search is then made for him and wheresoever the [person bearing a] resemblance to that portrait is found he is arrested.

When a Muhammadan merchant enters any town in China, he is given the choice between staying with some specified merchant among the Muslims domiciled there, or going to a hostelry. If he chooses to stay with the merchant, his money is taken into custody and put under the charge of the resident merchant. The latter then pays from it all his expenses with honesty and charity. When the visitor wishes to depart, his money is examined, and if any of it is found to be missing, the resident merchant who was put in charge of it is obliged to make good the deficit. If the visitor chooses to go to the hostelry, his property is deposited under the charge of the keeper of the hostelry. The keeper buys for him whatever he desires and presents him with an account. If he desires to take a concubine, the keeper purchases a slave-girl for him and lodges him in an apartment opening out of the hostelry, and purveys for them both. Slave-girls fetch a low price; yet all the Chinese sell their sons and daughters, and consider it no disgrace. They are not compelled, however, to travel with those who buy them, nor on the other hand, are they hindered from going if they choose to do so. In the same way, if a stranger desires to marry, marry he may; but as for spending his money in debauchery, no, that he may not do. They say "We will not have it noised about amongst Muslims that their people waste their substance in our country, because it is a land of riotous living and [women of] surpassing beauty."

China is the safest and best regulated of countries for a traveller. A man may go by himself a nine months' journey, carrying with him large sums of money, without any fear on that account. The system by which they ensure his safety is as follows. At every post-station in their country they have a hostelry controlled by an officer, who is stationed there with a company of horsemen and footsoldiers. After sunset or later in the evening the officer visits the hostelry with his clerk, registers the names of all travellers staying there for the night, seals up the list, and locks them into the hostelry. After sunrise he returns with his clerk, calls each person by name, and writes a detailed description of them on the list. He then sends a man with them to conduct them to the next post-station and bring back a clearance certificate from the controller there to the effect that all these persons have arrived at that station. If the guide does not produce this document, he is held responsible for them. This is the practice at every station in their country from Sín as-Sín to Khán-Báliq. In these hostelries there is everything that the traveller requires in the way of provisions, especially fowls and geese. Sheep on the other hand, are scarce with them.

To return to the account of our journey. The first city which we reached after our sea voyage was the city of Zaytún. [Now although *zaytún* means " olives "] there are no olives in this city, nor indeed in all the lands of the Chinese nor in India; it is simply a name which has been given to the place.[8] Zaytún is an immense city. In it are woven the damask silk and satin fabrics which go by its name,[9] and which are superior to the fabrics of Khansá and Khán-Báliq. The port of Zaytún is one of the largest in the world, or perhaps the very largest. I saw in it about a hundred large junks; as for small junks, they could not be counted for multitude. It is formed by a large inlet of the sea which penetrates the land to the point where it unites with the great river. In this city, as in all Chinese towns, a man will have a fruit-garden and a field with his house set in the middle of it, just as in the town of Sijilmása in our own country.[10] For this reason their towns are extensive. The Muslims live in a town apart from the others.

On the day that I reached Zaytún I saw there the amír who had come to India as an envoy with the present [to the sultan], and who afterwards travelled with our party and was shipwrecked on the junk. He greeted me, and introduced me to the controller of the *douane* and saw that I was given good apartments [there].[11] I received visits from the qádí of the Muslims, the shaykh al-Islám, and the principal merchants. Amongst the latter was Sharaf ad-Dín of Tabríz, one of the merchants from whom I had borrowed at the time of my arrival in India, and the one who had treated me most fairly. He knew the Koran by heart and used to recite it constantly. These merchants, living as they do in a land of infidels, are overjoyed when a Muslim comes to them. They say "He has come from the land of Islám," and they make *him* the recipient of the tithes on their properties, so that he becomes as rich as themselves.[12] There was living at Zaytún, amongst other eminent shaykhs, Burhán ad-Dín of Kázarún, who has a hermitage outside the town, and it is to him that the merchants pay the sums they vow to Shaykh Abú Isháq of Kázarún [see p. 97].

When the controller of the *douane* learned my story he wrote to the Qán,[13] who is their Emperor, to inform him of my arrival on a mission from the king of India. I asked him to send with me someone to conduct me to the district of Sín [Sín as-Sín], which they call Sín-kalán,[14] so that I might see that district, which is in his province, in the interval before the arrival of the Qán's reply. He granted my request, and sent one of his officers to conduct me. I sailed up the river on a vessel resembling the war galleys in our country, except that in this the rowers plied their oars standing upright, their place being in the centre of the vessel,[15] while the passengers were at the forepart and the stern. They spread over the ship awnings made from a plant which grows in their country, resembling but different from flax, and finer than hemp [perhaps grass-cloth]. We sailed up this river for twenty-seven days.[16] Every day we used to tie up about noon by a village where we could buy what we needed and pray the noon prayers, then in the evenings we went ashore at another village and so on, until we reached the city of Sín-kalán or Sín as-Sín. Porcelain is manufactured there as well as at Zaytún, and hereabouts the river of the "Water of Life" flows into the sea, so they call the place "The Meeting of the Waters." Sín-kalán is a city of the first rank, in regard to size and the quality of its bazaars. One of the largest of these is the porcelain bazaar, from which porcelain is exported to all parts of China, to India, and to Yemen. In the centre of this city there is an enormous temple with nine portals;[17] inside each of which there is a portico with benches where the inmates of the temple sit. Between the second and third portals there is a place containing chambers, which are occupied by the blind and crippled. Each of the occupants receives subsistence and clothing from the endowment of the temple. There are similar establishments between all the portals. In the interior there is a hospital for the sick and a kitchen for cooking food, and it has a staff of doctors and servitors. I was told that aged persons who are incapacitated from gaining their livelihood receive subsistence and clothing at this temple, likewise orphans and destitute widows.

This temple was built by one of their kings, who moreover endowed it with [the revenues of] this city and the villages and fruit gardens belonging to it. The portrait of this king is painted in the temple we have described, and they worship it.

In one of the quarters of this city is the Muhammadan town, where the Muslims have their cathedral mosque, hospice and bazaar. They have also a qádí and a shaykh, for in every one of the cities of China there must always be a Shaykh al-Islám, to whom all matters concerning the Muslims are referred [*i.e.* who acts as intermediary between the government and the Muslim community], and a qádí to decide legal cases between them. My quarters were in the house of Awhad ad-Dín of Sinjár, one of their principal men, of excellent character and immensely wealthy. I stayed with him for fourteen days, during which gifts were poured upon me one after the other from the qádí and other Muslims. Every day they made a new entertainment, to which they came in beautifully-appointed boats, bringing musicians with them. Beyond the city of Sín-kalán there is no other city, either infidel or Muslim. It is sixty days' journey, so I was told, from there to the Rampart of Gog and Magog, the intervening territory being occupied by nomadic infidels, who eat men when they get hold of them.[18] On that account no one ever crosses their country or visits it, and I did not find in Sín-kalán anyone who had himself seen the Rampart or even seen anyone who had seen it.

A few days after my return to Zaytún, the Qán's order arrived with instructions to convey me to his capital with all honour and dignity, by water if I preferred, otherwise by land. I chose to sail up the river, so they made ready for me a fine vessel of the sort that is designed for the use of governors. The governor sent his staff with us, and he, and likewise the qádí and the Muslim merchants, sent us large quantities of provisions. We travelled as state-guests, eating our midday meal at one village, and our evening meal at another. After ten days' journey we reached Qanjanfú, a large and beautiful city set in a broad plain and surrounded by fruit-gardens,[19] which gave the place the look of the Ghúta at Damascus.[20] On our arrival, we were met outside the town by the qádí, the Shaykh al-Islám, and the merchants, with standards, drums, trumpets, and bugles, and musicians. They brought horses for us, so we rode in on horseback while they walked on foot before us. No one rode along with us but the qádí and the Shaykh al-Islám. The governor of the city with his staff also came out [to meet us], for the sultan's guest is held in very high honour by them, and so we entered the city. It has four walls; between the first and second live the sultan's slaves, who are some of them day-guards and others night-guards of the city; between the second and third are the quarters of the mounted troops and the general who governs the city; within the third wall live the Muslims (it was here that we lodged at the house of their shaykh), and within the fourth is the Chinese quarter, which is the largest of these four cities [in one]. The distance separating each gate in this city from the next is three or four miles, and every inhabitant, as we have said, has his own orchard, house, and grounds.

One day as I was staying at Qanjanfú, a very large vessel came in, belonging to one of their most respected doctors. I was asked if he might see me, and he was announced as "Mawláná [Our master *i.e.* The reverend] Qiwám ad-Dín of Ceuta." His name roused my interest, and when he came in and we fell to conversation after the usual greetings, it struck me that I knew him. I kept looking at him intently, and at last he said "I see you are looking at me as if you knew me." So I said to him "Where do you come from?" He replied "From Ceuta." "And I" said I "from Tangier." Whereupon he broke into fresh greetings to me, and wept until I wept in sympathy with him. I then said to him "Did you go to India?" He replied "Yes, I went to the capital, Delhi." Then when he told me that, I remembered him and said "Are you al-Bushrí?" and he replied "Yes." I remembered he had come to Delhi with his mother's brother, Abu-'l-Qásim of Murcia, as a beardless youth and a very clever student. I had spoken of him to the sultan of India, who gave him three thousand dinars and invited him to stay at his court, but he refused, as he was set on going to China, where he prospered exceedingly, and acquired enormous wealth. He told me that he had about fifty white slaves and as many slave-girls, and presented me with two of each, along with many other gifts. I met his brother in after years in the Negrolands—what a distance lies between them!

I stayed at Qanjanfú for fifteen days and then continued my journey. The land of China, in spite of all that is agreeable in it, did not attract me. On the contrary I was sorely grieved that heathendom had so strong a hold over it. Whenever I went out of my house I used to see any number of revolting things, and that distressed me so much that I used to keep indoors and go out only in case of necessity. When I met Muslims in China I always felt just as though I were meeting my own faith and kin. So great was the kindness of this doctor al-Bushrí that when I left Qanjanfú he accompanied me for four days, until I reached the town of Baywam Qutlú.[21] This is a small town, inhabited by Chinese, a proportion of them being troops, the rest common people. The Muslim community there consists of four houses only, the inhabitants of which are agents of my learned friend. We put up at the house of one of them, and stayed with him for three days, after which I bade the doctor adieu and set out again.

I sailed up the river with the usual routine, stopping for dinner at one village, and for supper at another. After seventeen days of this, we reached the city of Khansá [Hang-chow], which is the biggest city I have ever seen on the face of the earth.[22] It is so long that it takes three days to traverse in the ordinary routine of marches and halts. It is built after the Chinese fashion already described, each person, that is, having his own house and garden. It is divided into six cities, as we shall describe later. On our arrival a party came out to meet us, consisting of the qádí and the Shaykh al-Islám of the city, and the family of 'Othmán ibn Affán of Egypt, who are the principal Muslim residents there, accompanied by a white flag, drums, bugles, and trumpets. The governor of the city also came out [to meet us] with his escort, and so we entered the town.

Khansá consists of six cities, each with its own wall, and an outer wall surrounding the whole. In the first city are the quarters of the city guards and their commander; I was told by the qádí and others that they mustered twelve thousand men on the register of troops. We passed the first night after our entry in the house of their commander. On the second day we entered the second city through a gate called the Jews' Gate. In this city live the Jews, Christians, and sun-worshipping Turks, a large number in all; its governor is a Chinese and we passed the second night in his house. On the third day we entered the third city, and this is inhabited by the Muslims. Theirs is a fine city, and their bazaars are arranged just as they are in Islamic countries; they have mosques in it and muezzins—we heard them calling to the noon prayers as we entered. We stayed here in the mansion of the family of 'Othmán ibn 'Affán of Egypt. He was a wealthy merchant, who conceived a liking for this city and made his home in it, so that it came be be called 'Othmáníya after him, and he transmitted to his posterity the influence and respect which he enjoyed there. It was he who built the cathedral mosque of Khansá, and endowed it with large benefactions. The number of Muslims in this city is very large, and our stay with them lasted fifteen days. Every day and night we were the guests at a new entertainment, and they continuously provided the most sumptuous meats, and went out with us every day on pleasure rides into different quarters of the city.

One day they rode out with me and we entered the fourth city, which is the seat of government, and in which the chief governor Qurtay resides. When we entered the gate leading to it, my companions were separated from me, and I was found by the wazír, who conducted me to the palace of the chief governor Qurtay. It was on this occasion that he took from me the mantle which the saint Jalál ad-Dín of Shíráz had given me, as I have already related [p. 269]. No one resides in this city, which is the most beautiful of the six, except the sultan's slaves and servants. It is traversed by three streams, one of them being a canal taken off from the great river, which is used by small boats bringing provisions and coal to the town, and there are pleasure boats on it as well. The citadel[23] lies in the centre of this city. It is of enormous size, and the government house stands in the middle of it, surrounded by [the court of] the citadel on all sides. Within it there are arcades, in which sit workmen making rich garments and weapons. The amír Qurtay told me that there were sixteen hundred master-workmen there, each with three or four apprentices working under him. They are all without exception the slaves of the Qán; they have chains on their feet, and they live outside the fortress. They are permitted to go out to the bazaars in the city, but may not go beyond its gate. They are passed in review before the governor every day, a hundred at a time, and if any one of them is missing, his commander is held responsible for him. Their custom is that when one of them has served for ten years, he is freed from his chains and given the choice between staying in service, without chains, or going wherever he will within the Qán's dominions, but not outside them. When he reaches the age of fifty he is exempted from work and maintained [by the state]. In the same way anyone else who has attained this age or thereabouts is maintained.[24] Anyone who reaches the age of sixty is regarded by them as a child, and legal penalties cease to be applicable to him. Old men in China are greatly respected, and each one of them is called Atá, which means "Father."

The amír Qurtay is the principal amír in China.[25] He entertained us in his palace, and prepared a banquet (their name for it is *towa*),[26] which was attended by the principal men of the city. He had Muslim cooks brought, who slaughtered the animals [in accordance with Muslim ritual, so that the food should be ceremonially clean] and cooked the food. This amír, in spite of his exalted rank, presented the dishes to us with his own hand, and with his own hand carved the meat. We stayed with him as his guests for three days. He sent his son with us to the canal, where we went on board a ship resembling a fire-ship, and the amír's son went on another along with musicians and singers. They sang in Chinese, Arabic, and Persian. The amír's son was a great admirer of Persian melody, and when they sang a certain Persian poem he commanded them to repeat it over and over again, until I learned it from them by heart. It has a pleasant lilt, and goes like this:

Tá dil bimihnat dádim
dar bahr-i fikr uftádim
Chún dar namáz istádim
qaví bimihráb andarím.[27]

On this canal there was assembled a large crowd in ships with brightly-coloured sails and silk awnings, and their ships too were admirably painted. They began a mimic battle and bombarded each other with oranges and lemons.[28] We returned in the evening to the amír's palace, and spent the night there. The musicians were there, and sang all kinds of pleasing melodies.

That same night a certain juggler, one of the Qán's slaves, was there. The amír said to him "Show us some of your feats." So he took a wooden ball with holes in which there were long leather thongs, and threw it into the air. It rose right out of our sight, for we were sitting in the middle of the palace court, during the season of intense heat. When nothing, but a short piece of the cord remained in his hand, he ordered one of his apprentices to go up the rope, which he did until he too disappeared from our sight. The juggler called him three times without receiving any reply, so he took a knife in his hand, as if he were enraged, and climbed up the rope until he disappeared as well. The next thing was that he threw the boy's hand to the ground, and then threw down his foot, followed by his other hand, then his other foot, then his trunk, and finally his head. After that he came down himself puffing and blowing, with his clothes all smeared with blood, and kissed the ground in front of the amír, saying something to him in Chinese. The amír gave him some order, and thereupon he took the boy's limbs, placed them each touching the other, and gave him a kick, and up he rose as sound as ever. I was amazed and took palpitation of the heart, just as had happened to me when I saw something similar at the court of the king of India, so they administered some potion to me which removed my distress. The qádí Afkhar ad-Dín was sitting beside me, and he said to me: " By God, there was no climbing or coming down or cutting up of limbs at all; the whole thing is just hocus-pocus."

On the following day we entered the fifth and largest city, which is inhabited by the common folk. Its bazaars are good and contain very skilful artificers; it is there that the fabrics which take their name from this town are woven. We passed a night in this city as the guests of its governor, and on the morrow entered the sixth city through a gate called Boatmen's gate. This sixth city, which lies on the banks of the great river, is inhabited by seamen, fishermen, caulkers, and carpenters, along with archers and footsoldiers, all of them being slaves of the sultan. No other persons live [in this town] with them, and their numbers are very great. We spent a night there as the guests of its governor. The amír Qurtay equipped a vessel for us with all that was needed in the way of provisions, etc., and sent his suite with us to arrange for our hospitable reception [on the journey]. So we left this city, which is the last of the provinces of China [proper], and entered the land of Khitá [Cathay].

Cathay is the best cultivated country in the world. There is not a spot in the whole extent of it that is not brought under cultivation. The reason is that if any part is left uncultivated its inhabitants or their neighbours are assessed for the land-tax due thereon. Fruit-gardens, villages, and fields extend along both banks of this river without interruption from the city of Khansá to the city of Khán-Báliq [Peking], which is a space of sixty-four days' journey. There are no

Muslims to be found in these districts, except casual travellers, since the country is not suitable for [their] permanent residence, and there is no large city in it, only villages and wide spaces,[29] covered with corn, fruit-trees, and sugarcane. I have never seen anything in the world like it, except a space of four days' journey between Anbár and 'Ána [in 'Iráq; see p. 303]. We used to disembark every night and stay in the villages in order to receive our provisions as guests of the sultan.

Thus we completed our journey to the city of Khán-Báliq, also called Kháníqú,[30] the capital of the Qán—he being their emperor, whose dominion extends over the countries of China and Cathay. When we arrived there we moored at a distance of ten miles from the city, as is their custom, and a written report of our arrival was sent to the admirals, who gave us permission to enter the port of the city. Having done so, we disembarked and entered the town, which is one of the largest towns in the world. It is not laid out, however, after the Chinese fashion, with gardens inside the city, but is just like the cities in other countries with gardens outside the walls. The sultan's city lies in the centre, like a citadel, as we shall relate. I stayed with Shaykh Burhán ad-Dín of Ságharj—the same man to whom the king of India sent 40,000 dinars with an invitation to him [to come to India], and who took the money and paid his debts with them, but refused to go to the king and set out [instead] for China [see above p. 202]. The Qán set him at the head of all the Muslims who live in his territories, and gave him the title of *Sadr al-Jihán*. The word *qán* is a term applied by them to every person who exercises the sovereignty over [all] the provinces, just as every ruler of the country of Lúr is called *atábeg*.[31] His name is Páshái,[32] and there is no infidel on the face of the earth who owns an empire greater than his.

His palace lies in the centre of the [inner] city, which is appropriated to his residence. The greater part of it is constructed of carved wood, and it is excellently planned.

When we reached the capital Khán-Báliq, we found that the Qán was absent from it at that time, as he had gone out to fight his cousin Fírúz, who had rebelled against him in the district of Qaráqorum and Bish-Báligh in Cathay.[33] The distance between these places and the capital is a three months' journey through cultivated districts. After his departure the majority of his amírs threw off their allegiance to him and agreed to depose him because he had departed from the precepts of the *Yasáq*, that is, the precepts which were laid down by their ancestor Tinkíz [Chingiz] Khán, who laid waste the lands of Islám. They went over to his rebel nephew and wrote to the Qán to the effect that he should abdicate and retain the city of Khansá as an appanage. He refused to do so, fought them, and was defeated and killed.

It was a few days after our arrival at his capital that the news of this was received. The city was decorated; trumpets, bugles and drums were played, and games and entertainments held for the space of a month. Thereafter the slain Qán was brought, with about a hundred other slain, his cousins, relatives, and intimates. A great *ná'ús*, that is, a subterranean chamber, was dug for him and richly furnished. The Qán was laid in it with his weapons, and all the gold and silver plate from his palace was deposited in it with him. With him also were put four slavegirls and six of the principal mamlúks, who carried drinking vessels, then the door of the chamber was built up and the whole thing covered over with earth until it reached the size of a large mound. After that they brought four horses and drove then about the Qán's grave until they stopped [from exhaustion], then they set up a wooden erection over the grave and suspended the horses on it, having first driven a piece of wood through each horse from tail to mouth.[34] The abovementioned relatives of the Qán were also placed in subterranean chambers along with their weapons and house utensils, and they impaled over the tombs of the principal members, of whom there were ten, three horses each, and over the tombs of the rest one horse each.

This day was observed as a solemn holiday, and not one person was absent from the ceremony, men or women, Muslim or heathen. They were all dressed in mourning robes, which are white capes in the case of the infidels and [long] white garments in the case of the Muslims. The Qán's khátúns and courtiers lived in tents near his grave for forty days, some even more than that, up to a year; and a bazaar was established there to supply the food and other things which they required. Such practices as these are observed, so far as I can record, by no other people in these days. The heathen Indians and Chinese, on the other hand, burn their dead; other people do indeed bury the dead man, but they do not put anyone in with him. However, I have been told by trustworthy persons in the Negrolands that the heathen there, when their king died, used to make a *ná'ús* for him and put in with him some of his courtiers and servants, along with thirty of the sons and daughters of their principal families, first breaking their hands and feet, and they put in drinking vessels along with them.

When the Qán was slain, as we have related, and his nephew Fírúz obtained the sovereign power, he chose to make his capital at the city of Qaráqorum, on account of its proximity to the territories of his cousins, the kings of Turkistán and Transoxania.[35] Afterwards several of the amírs who were not present when the Qán was killed revolted against him and intercepted communications and the disorders grew to serious proportions.

CHAPTER XII

When the revolt broke out and the flames of disorder were kindled, Shaykh Burhán ad-Dín and others advised me to return to [Southern] China before the disturbances became chronic. They presented themselves with me to the representatives of Sultan Fírúz, who sent three of his suite to escort me and wrote orders for my treatment as a guest [on the journey]. We travelled down the river to Khansá, and thence to Qanjanfú and Zaytún, and on reaching the last I found the junks ready to sail for India. Amongst them was a junk belonging to al-Malik az-Záhir, the ruler of Jáwa [Sumatra], the crew of which were Muslims. His agent knew me and was delighted at my arrival. We sailed with fair winds for ten days, but as we approached the land of Tawálisí, the wind changed, the sky darkened, and it rained heavily. We passed ten days without seeing the sun, and then entered a sea which we did not know. The crew of the junk became alarmed and wished to return to China, but that was out of the question. We passed forty-two days not knowing in what sea we were.

On the forty-third day there was visible to us at early dawn a mountain, projecting from the sea at a distance of about twenty miles from us, and the wind was carrying us straight towards it. The sailors were puzzled and said "We are nowhere near land, and there is no record of a mountain in the sea. If the wind drives us on it we are lost." So all on board began to humble themselves and concentrate their thoughts on God, and renew their repentance. We implored

God in prayer and sought the mediation of his prophet [Muhammad]—on whom be the Blessing and Peace of God; the merchants vowed to distribute large sums in alms, and I wrote down their vows for them in a register with my own hand. The wind calmed a little, and later on when the sun rose we saw that the mountain had risen into the air, and that daylight was visible between it and the sea. We were amazed at this, and I saw the crew weeping, and taking farewell of one another. So I said "What is the matter with you?" They replied "What we thought was a mountain is the Rukh, and if it sees us it will make an end of us."[1] We were at that moment less than ten miles away from it. Just then God of His mercy sent us a favourable wind, which turned us in another direction, so that we did not see it and could not learn its true shape.

Two months after this we reached Jáwa and landed at [the town of] Sumutra. We found its sultan al-Malik az-Záhir just returned from a raid, with a large train of captives. He sent me two girls and two boys, and lodged me in the usual manner. I was present at the marriage of his son to the daughter of the sultan's brother. After two months' stay on this island I took a passage on a junk. The sultan on bidding me farewell, gave me a great deal of aloes-wood, camphor, cloves, and sandalwood. I left him and set sail, and after forty days reached Kawlam [Quilon]. Here I disembarked and put up in proximity to the qádí of the Muslims; this was in Ramadán [January 1347] and I attended the festival prayer in the cathedral mosque there. From Kawlam we went on to Cálicút, and stayed there for some days. I intended to return to Delhi, but on second thoughts I had some fears about doing so, so I re-embarked and twenty-eight days later I arrived at Dhafári (p. 113), that being in Muharram of the year [seven hundred and] fortyeight [end of April 1347].

Thereafter I took ship and arrived at Mascat, a small town in which there is a great abundance of the fish called *qulb al-más* (p. 242). Thence we sailed to the ports of Qurayyát, Shabba, Kalba,[2] and Qalhát, which has been mentioned before [p. 118]. All these towns form part of the province of Hormuz, though they are reckoned to be in the district of 'Omán. We sailed on to Hormuz, and after spending three nights there, travelled by land to Kawrástán, Lár, and Khunjubál—all of which have been mentioned before. (p. 120)—thence to Kárzí,[3] where we stayed for three nights, and so through a number of other towns and villages to the city of Shíráz. From Shíráz I travelled to Isfahán, and thence through Tustar [Shushtar] to Basra, where I visited the sacred tombs which are there, and so through Mash-had 'Alí [Najaf] and Hilla to Baghdád, which I reached in Shawwál of the year 48 [January 1348]. I met there a man from Morocco, who informed me of the disaster at Tarífa, and of the capture of al-Khadrá [Algeciras] by the Christians[4]—may God repair the breach that Islám has suffered thereby!

The sultan of Baghdád and of 'Iráq at the time of my arrival at the date mentioned was Shaykh Hasan,[5] the cousin of the late Sultan Abú Sa'íd by his father's sister. When Abú Sa'íd died, he took possession of his kingdom in 'Iráq, and married his widow Dilshád, the daughter of Dimashq Khwája, son of the amír Chúbán, just as Sultan Abú Sa'íd had done in marrying Shaykh Hasan's wife. Sultan Hasan was away from Baghdád at this time, on his way to fight Sultan Atábeg Afrásiyáb, the ruler of the country of Lúr.

After leaving Baghdád I travelled to the city of Anbár, then successively to Hít, Hadítha, and 'Ána.[6]

This district is one of the richest and most fertile in the world, and there are buildings all along the road between these points, so that one walks as it were through one [continuous] bazaar. We have already said that we have seen nothing to equal the country along the banks of the river of China, except this district. I came next to the town of Rahba, which is the finest town in 'Iráq, and the frontier town of Syria.[7] Thence we went on to as-Sukhna, a pretty town,[8] inhabited mainly by infidels, that is Christians. It is called as-Sukhna [" the hot town "] because of the heat of its water, and contains bathhouses for men and women. They draw their water by night and put it on the roofs to cool. Thereafter we journeyed to Tadmur [Palmyra], the city of the prophet Solomon, which was built for him by the jinn,[9] and thence to Damascus, which I thus revisited after twenty years' absence. I had left a wife of mine there pregnant, and I learned while I was in India that she had borne a male child, whereupon I sent to the boy's maternal grandfather, who belonged to Miknása [Mequinez] in Morocco, forty gold dinars in Indian money. When I arrived in Damascus on this occasion I had no thought but to enquire after my son. I went to the mosque, where by good fortune I found Núr ad-Dín as-Sąkháwí, the imám and principal [shaykh] of the Málikites. I greeted him but he did not recognize me, so I made myself known to him and asked him, about the boy. He replied " He is dead these twelve years." He told me that a scholar from Tangier was living in the Záhiriya academy, so I went to see him, to enquire after my father and relatives. I found him to be a venerable shaykh, and when I had greeted him and told him the name of my family he informed me that my father had died fifteen years before and that my mother was still alive. I remained at Damascus until the end of the year, though there was a great scarcity of provisions and bread rose to the price of seven ounces for a dirham *nuqra* [about 5d.]. Their ounce equals four Moroccan ounces.

On leaving Damascus I went to Aleppo, by way of Hims, Hamáh, Ma'arra, and Sarmín. It happened at this time that a certain darwísh, known as the Principal Shaykh, who lived on a hill outside the town of 'Ayntáb,[10] where he used to be visited by the people in search of the blessings he conveyed, having one disciple attendant on him but [otherwise] a solitary and unmarried, said in one of his discourses: "The Prophet—may God bless him and give him peace!—could not do without women, but I can do without them." Evidence to that effect was brought against him and proved before a qádí, and the case was referred to the commander-in-chief. The shaykh and his disciple, who had assented to his statement, were brought up [for examination]; the principal judges of the four rites decided on legal grounds that both should be punished by death, and they were duly executed.

Early in June we heard at Aleppo that the plague had broken out at Gaza, and that the number of deaths there reached over a thousand a day. On travelling to Hims I found that the plague had broken out there: about three hundred persons died of it on the day that I arrived. So I went on to Damascus, and arrived there on a Thursday. The inhabitants had then been fasting for three days; on the Friday they went out to the mosque of the Footprints, as we have related in the first book, and God eased them of the plague [p. 68]. The number of deaths among them reached a maximum of 2,400 a day. Thereafter I journeyed to 'Ajalún and thence to Jerusalem, where I found that the ravages of the plague had ceased. We revisited Hebron, and thence went to Gaza, the greater part of which we found deserted because of the number of those who died there of the plague. I was told by the qádí that the number of deaths there reached 1,100 a day. We continued our journey overland to Damietta, and on to Alexandria. Here we found that the plague was diminishing in intensity, though the number of deaths had previously reached a thousand and eighty a day. I then travelled to Cairo, where I was told that the number of deaths during the epidemic rose to twenty-one thousand a day.[11] From Cairo I travelled through the Sa'íd [Upper Egypt] to 'Aydháb, whence I took ship to Judda, and thence reached Mecca on 22nd Sha'bán of the year 49 [16th November 1348].

After the pilgrimage of this year [28th Feb.—2nd March 1349] I travelled with the Syrian caravan to Tayba [Madína], thence to Jerusalem, and back through Gaza to Cairo. Here we learned that through our master, the Commander of the Faithful, Abú 'Inán (may God strengthen him!), God had united the scattered forces of the House of Marín[12] and healed by his blessing the western lands when they had all but succumbed. [We were told that] he had poured out his bounty upon great and small, and overwhelmed the whole nation by the torrent of his favours, so that all hearts were filled with the desire of standing at his gate and with the hope of kissing his stirrup. Thereupon I decided to journey to his illustrious capital, moved also by the longing called forth within me by memories of my home, by yearning for my family and friends, and by love of my country, which surpasses in my eyes all other countries.

I took ship on a small trading-vessel belonging to a Tunisian in Safar of the year 50 [April-May 1349], and travelled to Jerba, where I disembarked. The vessel went on to Tunis, and was captured by the enemy.[13] From Jerba I went in a small boat to Qábis [Gabes], where I put up as the guest of the two illustrious brothers, Abú Marwán and Abu'l-Abbas, sons of Makkí, the governors of Jerba and Gabes. I attended with them the festival of the birthday of the Prophet [12th Rabi I.=31st May]. Thereafter I went by boat to Safáqus [Sfax] and continued by sea to Bulyána,[14] from which point I travelled on land in the company of the Arabs, and after some discomforts reached the city of Tunis, at the time when it was being besieged by the Arabs. I stayed at Tunis thirty-six days and then took ship with the Catalans. We reached the island of Sardániya [Sardinia], one of the islands belonging to the Christians, where there is a wonderful harbour, with great baulks of wood in a circle round it and an entrance like a gateway, which is opened only if they give permission.[15] In the island there are fortified towns; we went into one of them, and [saw] in it a large number of bazaars. I made a vow to God to fast for two successive months if He should deliver us from this island, because we found out that its inhabitants were proposing to pursue us when we left to take us captive. We then sailed away and ten days later reached the town of Tenes, then Mázúna, then Mustaghánim [Mostaganem], and so to Tilimsán [Tlemsen]. I went to al-'Ubbád and visited [the tomb of] Shaykh Abú Madín.[16] I left Tilimsán by the Nadrúma road, then took the Akhandaqán road, and spent the night at the hermitage of Shaykh Ibráhím. We set out from there and when we were near Azghanghán[17] we were attacked by fifty men on foot and two horsemen. I had with me the pilgrim Ibn Qarí'át of Tangier and his brother Muhammad, who afterwards perished as a martyr at sea. We resolved to make a fight for it and put up a flag, whereupon they made peace with us and we went with them, praise be to God. Thus we reached the town of Tázá, where I learned the news of my mother's death of the plague—may God Most High have mercy on her. Then I set out from Tázá and arrived at the royal city of Fez on Friday, at the end of the month of Sha'bán of the year 750 [13th November 1349].

I presented myself before our most noble master, the most generous imám, the Commander of the Faithful, al-Mutawakkil Abú 'Inán—may God enlarge his greatness and humble his enemies. His dignity made me forget the dignity of the sultan of 'Iráq, his beauty the beauty of the king of India, his fine qualities the noble character of the king of Yemen, his courage the courage of the king of the Turks, his clemency the clemency of the king of the Greeks, his devotion the devotion of the king of Turkistán, and his knowledge the knowledge of the king of Jáwa. I laid down the staff of travel in his glorious land, having assured myself after unbiassed consideration that it is the best of countries, for in it fruits are plentiful, and running water and nourishing food are never exhausted. Few indeed are the lands which unite all these advantages, and well spoken are the poet's words:

> Of all the lands the West by this token's the best:
> Here the full moon is spied and the sun speeds to rest.

The dirhams of the West are small, but their utility is great. When you compare its prices with the prices of Egypt and Syria, you will see the truth of my contention, and realize the superiority of the Maghrib. For I assure you that mutton in Egypt is sold at eighteen ounces for a dirham *nuqra*, which equals in value six dirhams of the Maghrib,[18] whereas in the Maghrib meat is sold, when prices are high, at eighteen ounces for two dirhams, that is a third of a *nuqra*. As for melted butter, it is usually not to be found in

Egypt at all. The kinds of things that the Egyptians eat along with their bread would not even be looked at in the Maghrib. They consist for the most part of lentils and chickpeas, which they cook in enormous cauldrons,[19] and on which they put oil of sesame; *basillá*, a kind of peas which they cook and eat with olive oil; gherkins, which they cook and mix with curdled milk; purslane[20] which they prepare in the same way; the buds of almond trees, which they cook and serve in curdled milk; and colocasia, which they cook. All these things are easily come by in the Maghrib, but God has enabled its inhabitants to dispense with them, by reason of the abundance of fleshmeats, melted butter, fresh butter, honey, and other products. As for green vegetables, they are the rarest of things in Egypt, and most of their fruit has to be brought from Syria. Grapes, when they are cheap, are sold amongst them at a dirham *nuqra* for three of their pounds, their pound being twelve ounces.

As for Syria, fruits are indeed plentiful there, but in the Maghrib they are cheaper. Grapes are sold there at the rate of one of their pounds for a dirham *nuqra* (their pound is three Maghribí pounds), and when their price is low, two pounds for a dirham *nuqra*. Pomegranates and quinces are sold at eight *fals* [coppers] apiece, which equals a dirham of our money. As for vegetables the quantity sold for a dirham *nuqra* is less than that sold for a small dirham in our country. Meat is sold there at the rate of one Syrian pound for two and a half dirhams *nuqra*. If you consider all this, it will be clear to you that the lands of the Maghrib are the cheapest in cost of living, the most abundant in good things, and blest with the greatest share of material comforts and advantages. Moreover, God has augmented the honour and excellence of the Maghrib by the imámate of our master, the Commander of the Faithful,[21] who has spread the shelter of security throughout its territories and made the sun of equity to rise within its borders, who has caused the clouds of beneficence to shed their rain upon its dwellers in country and town, who has purified it from evildoers, and established it in the ways alike of worldly prosperity and of religious observance.

CHAPTER XIII

After I had been privileged to observe this noble majesty and to share in the all-embracing bounty of his beneficence, I set out to visit the tomb of my mother. I arrived at my home town of Tangier and visited her, and went on to the town of Sabta [Ceuta], where I stayed for some months. While I was there I suffered from an illness for three months, but afterwards God restored me to health. I then proposed to take part in the *jihád* and the defence of the frontier, so I crossed the sea from Ceuta in a barque belonging to the people of Asílá [Arzila], and reached the land of Andalusia (may God Almighty guard her!) where the reward of the dweller is abundant and a recompense is laid up for the settler and visitor. This was after the death of the Christian tyrant Adfúnus [Alphonso XI.] and his ten-months' siege of the Jebel [Gibraltar], when he thought that he would capture all that the Muslims still retain of Andalusia; but God took him whence he did not reckon, and he, who of all men stood in the most mortal terror of the plague, died of it.[1] The first part of Andalusia that I saw was the Mount of Conquest [Gibraltar]. I walked round the mountain and saw the marvellous works executed on it by our master [the late Sultan of Morocco] Abu'l-Hasan and the armament with which he equipped it, together with the additions made thereto by our master [Abú 'Inán], may God strengthen him, and I should have liked to remain as one of its defenders to the end of my days.

Ibn Juzayy adds: "The Mount of Conquest is the citadel of Islám, an obstruction stuck in the throats of the idolaters. From it began the great conquest [of Spain by the Arabs], and at it disembarked Táriq ibn Ziyád, the freedman of Músá ibn Nusayr, when he crossed [the strait in 711]. Its name was linked with his, and it was called Jebel Táriq [The Mount of Táriq]. It is called also the Mount of Conquest, because the conquest began there. The remains of the wall built by Táriq and his army are still in existence; they are known as the Wall of the Arabs, and I myself have seen them during my stay there at the time of the siege of Algeciras (may God restore it [to Islám] !).

"Gibraltar was recaptured by our late master Abu'l-Hasan, who recovered it from the hands of the Christians after they had possessed it for over twenty years. He sent his son, the noble prince Abú Málik, to besiege it, aiding him with large sums of money and powerful armies. It was taken after a six months' siege in the year 733 [1333 A.D.]. At that time it was not in the present state. Our late master Abu'l-Hasan built in it the huge keep at the top of the fortress; before that it was a small tower, which was laid in ruins by the stones from the catapults, and he built the new one in its place. He built the arsenal there too (for there was no arsenal in the place before), as well as the great wall which surrounds the Red Mound, starting from the arsenal and extending to the tileyard. Later on our master, the Commander of the Faithful, Abú 'Inán (may God strengthen him) again took in hand its fortification and embellishment, and strengthened the wall of the extremity of the mount, which is the most formidable and useful of its walls. He also sent thither large quantities of munitions, foodstuffs, and provisions of all kinds, and thereby acquitted himself of his duty to God Most High with singleness of purpose and sincere devotion. His concern for the affairs of the Jebel reached such lengths that he gave orders for the construction of a model of it, on which he had represented models of its walls, towers, citadel, gates, arsenal, mosques, munition-stores, and corn-granaries, together with the shape of the Jebel itself and the adjacent Red Mound. This model was executed in the palace precincts; it was a marvellous likeness and a piece of fine craftsmanship. Any one who has seen the Jebel and then sees this copy will recognize its merit. This was due solely to his eagerness (may God strengthen him) to learn how matters stood there, and his anxiety to strengthen its defences and equipment. May God Most High grant victory to Islám in the Western Peninsula [Spain] at his hands, and bring to pass his hope of conquering the lands of the infidels and breaking the strength of the adorers of the cross."

To resume the narrative of our Shaykh. I went out of Gibraltar to the town of Ronda, one of the strongest and most beautifully situated fortresses of the Muslims. The qádí there was my cousin, the doctor Abu'l-Qásim Muhammad b. Yahyá Ibn Battúta. I stayed at Ronda for five days, then went on to the town of Marbala [Marbella]. The road between these two places is difficult and exceedingly rough. Marbala is a pretty little town in a fertile district. I found there a company of horsemen setting out for Málaqa, and intended to go in their company, but God by His grace preserved me, for they went on ahead of me and were captured on the way, as we shall relate. I set out after them, and when I had traversed the district of Marbala, and entered the district of Suhayl[2] I passed a dead horse lying in the ditch, and a little farther on a pannier of fish thrown on the ground. This aroused my suspicions. In front of me there was a watchtower, and I said to myself "If an enemy were to appear here, the man on the tower would give the alarm." So I went on to a house thereabouts, and at it I found a horse killed. While I was there I heard a shout behind me (for I had gone ahead of my party) and turning back to them, found the commander of the fort of Suhayl with them. He told me that four galleys belonging to the enemy had appeared there, and a number of the men on board had landed when the watchman was not in the tower. The horsemen who had just left Marbala, twelve in number, had encountered this raiding force. The Christians had killed one of them, one had escaped, and ten were taken prisoner. A fisherman was killed along with them, and it was he whose basket I had found lying on the road.

The officer advised me to spend the night with him in his quarters, so that he could escort me thence to Málaqa. I passed the night in the castle of the regiment of mounted frontiersmen called the Suhayl regiment. All this time the galleys of which we have spoken were lying close by. On the morrow he rode with me and we reached Málaqa, which is one of the largest and most beautiful towns of Andalusia. It unites the conveniences of both sea and land, and is abundantly supplied with foodstuffs and fruits. I saw grapes being sold in its bazaars at the rate of eight pounds for a small dirham, and its ruby-coloured Murcian pomegranates have no equal in the world. As for figs and almonds, they are exported from Málaqa and its outlying districts to the lands both of the East and the West. At Málaqa there is manufactured excellent gilded pottery, which is exported thence to the most distant lands. Its mosque covers a large area and has a reputation for sanctity; the court of the mosque is of unequalled beauty, and contains exceptionally tall orange trees.

On my arrival at Málaqa I found the qádí sitting in the great mosque, along with the doctors of the law and the principal inhabitants, all engaged in collecting money to ransom the prisoners of whom we have spoken. I said to him "Praise be to God, Who hath preserved me, and hath not made me one of them." I told him what had happened to me after they had gone, and he marvelled at it and sent me a hospitality-gift, as also did the preacher of the town.

From Málaqa I journeyed to the town of Ballash [Velez], a distance of twenty-four miles. Ballash is a fine town with a magnificent mosque; grapes, fruits, and figs are just as plentiful there as at Málaqa. We went on from there to al-Hamma [Alhama], which is a small town with a most elegant mosque in a fine situation. Near by, at a distance of a mile or so from the town, is the hot spring [from which the town derives its name],[3] on the bank of the river. There is a bathhouse here for men and another for women.

Thence I went to on the city of Gharnáta [Granada], the metropolis of Andalusia and the bride of its cities. Its environs have not their equal in any country in the world. They extend for the space of forty miles, and are traversed by the celebrated river of Shannîl [Xenil] and many other streams. Around it on every side are orchards, gardens, flowery meads, noble buildings, and vineyards. One of the most beautiful places there is '*Ayn ad-dama*' [the Fountain of Tears],[4] which is a hill covered with gardens and orchards and has no parallel in any other country. The king of Gharnáta at the time of my visit was Sultan Abu'l-Hajjáj Yúsuf. I did not meet him on account of an illness from which he was suffering,[5] but the noble, pious, and virtuous woman, his mother, sent me some gold dinars, of which I made good use.

I met at Gharnáta a number of its distinguished scholars and the principal Shaykh, who is also the superior of the Súfí orders. I spent some days with him in his hermitage outside Gharnáta. He showed me the greatest honour and went with me to visit the hospice, famed for its sanctity, known as the *Outpost of al-'Uqáb* [the Eagle]. Al-'Uqáb is a hill overlooking the environs of Gharnáta, about eight miles from the city and close by the ruined city of al-Bíra.[6] There is also at Gharnáta a company of Persian darwíshes, who have made their homes there because of its resemblance to their native lands. One is from Samarqand, another from Tabríz, a third from Qúniya [Konia], one from Khurásán, two from India, and so on.

On leaving Gharnáta I travelled back through al-Hamma, Ballash, and Málaqa, to the castle of Dhakwán, which is a fine fortress with abundant water, trees, and fruits.[7] From there I went to Ronda and on to Gibraltar, where I embarked on the ship by which I had crossed before, and which belonged to the people of Asílá [Arzila]. I arrived at Sabta [Ceuta] and went on to Asílá, where I stayed for some months. Thence I travelled to Salá [Sallee, by Rabát] and from there reached the city of Marrákush. It is one of the most beautiful of cities, spaciously built and extending over a wide area, with abundant supplies. It contains magnificent mosques, such as its principal mosque, known as the Mosque of the Kutubíyín [the Booksellers]. There is a marvellously tall minaret there; I climbed it and obtained a view of the whole town from it. The town is now largely in ruins, so that I could compare it only to Baghdád, though the bazaars in Baghdád are finer.[8] At Marrákush too there is a splendid college, distinguished by its fine site and solid construction; it was built by our master, the Commander of the Faithful, Abu'l-Hasan [the late sultan of Morocco].

CHAPTER XIV

From Marrákush I travelled with the suite of our master [the Sultan] to Fez, where I took leave of our master and set out for the Negrolands. I reached the town of Sijilmása, a very fine town, with quantities of excellent dates.[1] The city of Basra rivals it in abundance of dates, but the Sijilmása dates are better, and the kind called *Írár* has no equal in the world. I stayed there with the learned Abú Muhammad al-Bushrí, the man whose brother I met in the city of Qanjanfú in China. How strangely separated they are! He showed me the utmost honour.

At Sijilmása I bought camels and a four months' supply of forage for them. Thereupon I set out on the 1st Muharram of the year [seven hundred and] fifty-three [18th February 1352] with a caravan including, amongst others, a number of the merchants of Sijilmása. After twenty-five days we reached Taghází, an unattractive village, with the curious feature that its houses and mosques are built of blocks of salt, roofed with camel skins. There are no trees there, nothing but sand. In the sand is a salt mine; they dig for the salt, and find it in thick slabs, lying one on top of the other, as though they had been tool-squared and laid under the surface of the earth.[2] A camel will carry two of these slabs. No one lives at Taghází except the slaves of the Massúfa tribe, who dig for the salt; they subsist on dates imported from Dar'a[3] and Sijilmása, camels' flesh, and millet imported from the Negrolands. The negroes come up from their country and take away the salt from there.

At Íwálátan a load of salt brings eight to ten *mithqáls*; in the town of Málli it sells for twenty to thirty, and sometimes as much as forty. The negroes use salt as a medium of exchange, just as gold and silver is used [elsewhere]; they cut it up into pieces and buy and sell with it. The business done at Tagházá, for all its meanness, amounts to an enormous figure in terms of hundredweights of gold-dust.[4]

We passed ten days of discomfort there, because the water is brackish and the place is plagued with flies. Water supplies are laid in at Tagházá for the crossing of the desert which lies beyond it, which is a ten-nights' journey with no water on the way except on rare occasions. We indeed had the good fortune to find water in plenty, in pools left by the rain. One day we found a pool of sweet water between two rocky prominences. We quenched our thirst at it and then washed our clothes. Truffles are plentiful in this desert and it swarms with lice, so that people wear string necklaces containing mercury, which kills them. At that time we used to go ahead of the caravan, and when we found a place suitable for pasturage we would graze our beasts. We went on doing this until one of our party was lost in the desert; after that I neither went ahead nor lagged behind. We passed a caravan on the way and they told us that some of their party had become separated from them. We found one of them dead under a shrub, of the sort that grows in the sand, with his clothes on and a whip in his hand. The water was only about a mile away from him.

We came next to Tásarahlá, a place of subterranean water-beds, where the caravans halt.[5] They stay there three days to rest, mend their waterskins, fill them with water, and sew on them covers of sack-cloth as a precaution against the wind. From this point the *takshíf* is despatched. The *takshíf* is a name given to any man of the Massúfa tribe who is hired by the persons in the caravan to go ahead to Íwálátan, carrying letters from them to their friends there, so that they may take lodgings for them. These persons then come out a distance of four nights' journey to meet the caravan, and bring water with them. Anyone who has no friend in Íwálátan writes to some merchant well known for his worthy character, who then undertakes the same services for him. It often happens that the *takshíf* perishes in this desert, with the result that the people of Íwálátan know nothing about the caravan, and all or most of those who are with it perish. That desert is haunted by demons; if the *takshíf* be alone, they make sport of him and disorder his mind, so that he loses his way and perishes. For there is no visible road or track in these parts—nothing but sand blown hither and thither by the wind. You see hills of sand in one place, and afterwards you will see them moved to quite another place. The guide there is one who has made the journey frequently in both directions, and who is gifted with a quick intelligence. I remarked, as a strange thing, that the guide whom we had was blind in one eye, and diseased in the other, yet he had the best knowledge of the road of any man. We hired the *takshíf* on this journey for a hundred gold *mithqáls*; he was a man of the Massúfa. On the night of the seventh day [from Tásarahlá] we saw with joy the fires of the party who had come out to meet us.

Thus we reached the town of Íwálátan [Walata] after a journey from Sijilmása of two months to a day.[6] Íwálátan is the northernmost province of the negroes, and the sultan's representative there was one Farbá Husayn, *farbá* meaning deputy [in their language]. When we arrived there, the merchants deposited their goods in an open square, where the blacks undertook to guard them, and went to the *farbá*. He was sitting on a carpet under an archway, with his guards before him carrying lances and bows in their hands, and the headmen of the Massúfa behind him. The merchants remained standing in front of him while he spoke to them through an interpreter, although they were close to him, to show his contempt for them. It was then that I repented of having come to their country, because of their lack of manners and their contempt for the whites.

I went to visit Ibn Baddá, a worthy man of Salá [Sallee, Rabát], to whom I had written requesting him to hire a house for me, and who had done so. Later on the *mushrif* [inspector] of Íwálátan, whose name was Manshá Jú, invited all those who had come with the caravan to partake of his hospitality. At first I refused to attend, but my companions urged me very strongly, so I went with the rest. The repast was served—some pounded millet mixed with a little honey and milk, put in a half calabash shaped like a large bowl. The guests drank and retired. I said to them "Was it for this that the black invited us?" They answered "Yes; and it is in their opinion the highest form of hospitality." This convinced me that there was no good to be hoped for from these people, and I made up my mind to travel [back to Morocco at once] with the pilgrim caravan from Íwálátan. Afterwards, however, I thought it best to go to see the capital of their king [at Málli].

My stay at Íwálátan lasted about fifty days; and I was shown honour and entertained by its inhabitants. It is an excessively hot place, and boasts a few small date-palms, in the shade of which they sow water-melons. Its water comes from underground water-beds at that point, and there is plenty of mutton to be had. The garments of its inhabitants, most of whom belong to the Massúfa tribe, are of fine Egyptian fabrics. Their women are of surpassing beauty, and are shown more respect than the men. The state of affairs amongst these people is indeed extraordinary. Their men show no signs of jealousy whatever; no one claims descent from his father, but on the contrary from his mother's brother. A person's heirs are his sister's sons, not his own sons. This is a thing which I have seen nowhere in the world except among the Indians of Malabar. But those are heathens; *these* people are Muslims, punctilious in observing the hours of prayer, studying books of law, and memorizing the Koran. Yet their women show no bashfulness before men and do not veil themselves, though they are assiduous in attending the prayers. Any man who wishes to marry one of them may do so, but they do not travel with their husbands, and even if one desired to do so her family would not allow her to go.

The women there have "friends" and "companions" amongst the men outside their own families, and the men in the same way have "companions" amongst the women of other families. A man may go into his house and find his wife entertaining her "companion" but he takes no objection to it. One day at Íwálátan I went into the qádí's house, after asking his permission to enter, and found with him a young woman of remarkable beauty. When I saw her I was shocked and turned to go out, but she laughed at me, instead of being overcome by shame, and the qádí said to me "Why are you going out? She is my companion." I was amazed at their conduct, for he was a theologian and a pilgrim to boot. I was told that he had asked the sultan's permission to make the pilgrimage that year with his "companion" (whether this one or not I cannot say) but the sultan would not grant it.

When I decided to make the journey to Mállí, which is reached in twenty-four days from Íwálátan if the traveller pushes on rapidly, I hired a guide from the Massúfa (for there is no necessity to travel in a company on account of the safety of that road), and set out with three of my companions. On the way there are many trees, and these trees are of great age and girth; a whole caravan may shelter in the shade of one of them. There are trees which have neither branches nor leaves, yet the shade cast by their trunks is sufficient to shelter a man. Some of these trees are rotted in the interior and the rain-water collects in them, so that they serve as wells and the people drink of the water inside them.[7] In others there are bees and honey, which is collected by the people. I was surprised to find inside one tree, by which I passed, a man, a weaver, who had set up his loom in it and was actually weaving.

A traveller in this country carries no provisions, whether plain food or seasonings, and neither gold nor silver. He takes nothing but pieces of salt and glass ornaments, which the people call beads, and some aromatic goods. When he comes to a village the womenfolk of the blacks bring out millet, milk, chickens, pulped lotus fruit, rice, *fúni* (a grain resembling mustard seed, from which *kuskusú*[8] and gruel are made), and pounded haricot beans. The traveller buys what of these he wants, but their rice causes sickness to whites when it is eaten, and the *fúni* is preferable to it.

Ten days after leaving Iwálátan we came to the village of Zágharí, a large village,[9] inhabited by negro traders called *wanjaráta*,[10] along with whom live a community of whites of the 'Ibádite sect.[11] It is from this village that millet is carried to Iwálátan. After leaving Zágharí we came to the great river, that is the Nile, on which stands the town of Kársakhú.[12] The Nile flows from there down to Kábara, and thence to Zágha.[13] In both Kábara and Zágha there are sultans who owe allegiance to the king of Málli. The inhabitants of Zágha are of old standing in Islám; they show great devotion and zeal for study. Thence the Nile descends to Tumbuktú and Gawgaw [Gogo], both of which will be described later; then to the town of Múlí[14] in the land of the Límís,[15] which is the frontier province of [the kingdom of] Málli; thence to Yúfí, one of the largest towns of the negroes, whose ruler is one of the most considerable of the negro rulers.[16] It cannot be visited by any white man because they would kill him before he got there. From Yúfí the Nile descends to the land of the Núba [Nubians], who profess the Christian faith, and thence to Dunqula [Dongola], which is their chief town.[17] The sultan of Dunqula is called Ibn Kanz ad-Dín; he was converted to Islám in the days of [Sultan] al-Malik an-Násir [of Egypt].[18] Thence it descends to Janádil [the Cataracts], which is the end of the negro territories and the beginning of the province of Uswán [Aswan] in Upper Egypt.

I saw a crocodile in this part of the Nile, close to the bank; it looked just like a small boat. One day I went down to the river to satisfy a need, and lo, one of the blacks came and stood between me and the river. I was amazed at such lack of manners and decency on his part, and spoke of it to someone or other. He answered "His purpose in doing that was solely to protect you from the crocodile, by placing himself between you and it."

We set out thereafter from Karsakhú and came to the river of Sansara, which is about ten miles from Málli. It is their custom that no persons except those who have obtained permission are allowed to enter the city. I had already written to the white community [there] requesting them to hire a house for me, so when I arrived at this river, I crossed by the ferry without interference. Thus I reached the city of Málli, the capital of the king of the blacks.[19]

I stopped at the cemetery and went to the quarter occupied by the whites, where I asked for Muhammad ibn al-Faqíh. I found that he had hired a house for me and went there. His son-in-law brought me candles and food, and next day Ibn al-Faqíh himself came to visit me, with other prominent residents. I met the qádí of Mállí, 'Abd ar-Rahmán, who came to see me; he is a negro, a pilgrim, and a man of fine character. I met also the interpreter Dúghá, who is one of the principal men among the blacks.[20] All these persons sent me hospitality-gifts of food and treated me with the utmost generosity—may God reward them for their kindnesses! Ten days after our arrival we ate a gruel made of a root resembling colocasia, which is preferred by them to all other dishes. We all fell ill—there were six of us—and one of our number died. I for my part went to the morning prayer and fainted there. I asked a certain Egyptian for a loosening remedy and he gave me a thing called *baydar*, made of vegetable roots, which he mixed with aniseed and sugar, and stirred in water. I drank it off and vomited what I had eaten, together with a large quantity of bile. God preserved me from death but I was ill for two months.

The sultan of Mállí is Mansá Sulaymán, *mansá* meaning [in Mande] sultan, and Sulaymán being his proper name.[21] He is a miserly king, not a man from whom one might hope for a rich present. It happened that I spent these two months without seeing him, on account of my illness. Later on he held a banquet in commemoration of our master [the late sultan of Morocco] Abu'l-Hasan, to which the commanders, doctors, qádí and preacher were invited, and I went along with them. Reading-desks were brought in, and the Koran was read through, then they prayed for our master Abu'l-Hasan and also for Mansá Sulaymán. When the ceremony was over I went forward and saluted Mansá Sulaymán. The qádí, the preacher, and Ibn al-Faqíh told him who I was, and he answered them in their tongue. They said to me "The sultan says to you 'Give thanks to God,'" so I said "Praise be to God and thanks under all circumstances."[22]

When I withdrew the [sultan's] hospitality gift was sent to me. It was taken first to the qádí's house, and the qádí sent it on with his men to Ibn al-Faqíh's house. Ibn al-Faqíh came hurrying out of his house bare-footed, and entered my room saying "Stand up; here comes the sultan's stuff and gift to you." So I stood up thinking [since he had called it "stuff"] that it consisted of robes of honour and money, and lo! it was three cakes of bread, and a piece of beef fried in native oil, and a calabash of sour curds. When I saw this I burst out laughing, and thought it a most amazing thing that they could be so foolish and make so much of such a paltry matter.

For two months after this hospitality gift was sent to me I received nothing further from the sultan, and then followed the month of Ramadán. Meanwhile I used to go frequently to the palace where I would salute him and sit alongside the qádí and the preacher. I had a conversation with Dúghá the interpreter, and he said "Speak in his presence, and I shall express on your behalf what is necessary." When the sultan held an audience early in Ramadán, I rose and stood before him and said to him: "I have travelled through the countries of the world and have met their kings. Here have I been four months in your country, yet you have neither shown me hospitality, nor given me anything. What am I to say of you before [other] rulers?" The sultan replied "I have not seen you, and have not been told about you." The qádí and Ibn al-Faqíh rose and replied to him, saying "He has already saluted you, and you have sent him food." Thereupon he gave orders to set apart a house for my lodging and to pay me a daily sum for my expenses. Later on, on the night of the 27th Ramadán, he distributed a sum of money which they call the *Zakáh* [alms] between the qádí, the preachers, and the doctors.[23] He gave me a portion along with them of thirty-three and a third *mithqáls*, and on my departure from Mállí he bestowed on me a gift of a hundred gold *mithqáls*.

On certain days the sultan holds audiences in the palace yard, where there is a platform under a tree, with three steps; this they call the *pempi*.[24] It is carpeted with silk and has cushions placed on it. [Over it] is raised the umbrella, which is a sort of pavilion made of silk, surmounted by a bird in gold, about the size of a falcon. The sultan comes out of a door in a corner of the palace, carrying a bow in his hand and a quiver on his back. On his head he has a golden skull-cap, bound with a gold band which has narrow ends shaped like knives, more than a span in length. His usual dress is a velvety red tunic, made of the European fabrics called *mutanfas*. The sultan is preceded by his musicians, who carry gold and silver guimbris [two-stringed guitars], and behind him come three hundred armed slaves. He walks in a leisurely fashion, affecting a very slow movement, and even stops from time to time. On reaching the *pempi* he stops and looks round the assembly, then ascends it in the sedate manner of a preacher ascending a mosque-pulpit. As he takes his seat the drums, trumpets, and bugles are sounded. Three slaves go out at a run to summon the sovereign's deputy and the military commanders, who enter and sit down. Two saddled and bridled horses are brought, along with two goats, which they hold to serve as a protection against the evil eye. Dúghá stands at the gate and the rest of the people remain in the street, under the trees.

The negroes are of all people the most submissive to their king and the most abject in their behaviour before him. They swear by his name, saying *Mansá Sulaymán ki.*[26] If he summons any of them while he is holding an audience in his pavilion, the person summoned takes off his clothes and puts on worn garments, removes his turban and dons a dirty skull-cap, and enters with his garments and trousers raised knee-high. He goes forward in an attitude of humility and dejection, and knocks the ground hard with his elbows, then stands with bowed head and bent back listening to what he says. If anyone addresses the king and receives a reply from him, he uncovers his back and throws dust over his head and back, for all the world like a bather splashing himself with water. I used to wonder how it was they did not blind themselves. If the sultan delivers any remarks during his audience, those present take off their turbans and put them down, and listen in silence to what he says. Sometimes one of them stands up before him and recalls his deeds in the sultan's service, saying " I did so-and-so on such a day " or " I killed so-and-so on such a day." Those who have knowledge of this confirm his words, which they do by plucking the cord of the bow and releasing it [with a twang], just as an archer does when shooting an arrow. If the sultan says " Truly spoken " or thanks him, he removes his clothes and " dusts." That is their idea of good manners.

Ibn Juzayy adds: " I have been told that when the pilgrim Músá al-Wanjarátí [the Mandingo] came to our master Abu'l-Hasan as envoy from Mansá Sulaymán, one of his suite carried with him a basketful of dust when he entered the noble audience-hall, and the envoy ' dusted ' whenever our master spoke a gracious word to him, just as he would do in his own country."

I was at Málli during the two festivals of the sacrifice and the fast-breaking. On these days the sultan takes his seat on the *pempi* after the midafternoon prayer. The armour-bearers bring in magnificent arms—quivers of gold and silver, swords ornamented with gold and with golden scabbards, gold and silver lances, and crystal maces. At his head stand four amírs driving off the flies, having in their hands silver ornaments resembling saddle-stirrups. The commanders, qádí, and preacher sit in their usual places. The interpreter Dúghá comes with his four wives and his slave-girls, who are about a hundred in number. They are wearing beautiful robes, and on their heads they have gold and silver fillets, with gold and silver balls attached. A chair is placed for Dúghá to sit on. He plays on an instrument made of reeds, with some small calabashes at its lower end, and chants a poem in praise of the sultan, recalling his battles and deeds of valour. The women and girls sing along with him and play with bows. Accompanying them are about thirty youths, wearing red woollen tunics and white skull-caps; each of them has his drum slung from his shoulder and beats it. Afterwards come his boy pupils who play and turn wheels in the air, like the natives of Sind. They show a marvellous nimbleness and agility in these exercises and play most cleverly with swords. Dúghá also makes a fine play with the sword. Thereupon the sultan orders a gift to be presented to Dúghá and he is given a purse containing two hundred *mithqáls* of gold dust, and is informed of the contents of the purse before all the people. The commanders rise and twang their bows in thanks to the sultan. The next day each one of them gives Dúghá a gift, every man according to his rank. Every Friday after the '*asr* prayer, Dúghá carries out a similar ceremony to this that we have described.

On feast-days, after Dúghá has finished his display, the poets come in. Each of them is inside a figure resembling a thrush, made of feathers, and provided with a wooden head with a red beak, to look like a thrush's head. They stand in front of the sultan in this ridiculous make-up and recite their poems. I was told that their poetry is a kind of sermonizing in which they say to the sultan: "This *pempi* which you occupy was that whereon sat this king and that king, and such and such were this one's noble actions and such and such the other's. So do you too do good deeds whose memory will outlive you." After that, the chief of the poets mounts the steps of the *pempi* and lays his head on the sultan's lap, then climbs to the top of the *pempi* and lays his head first on the sultan's right shoulder and then on his left, speaking all the while in their tongue, and finally he comes down again. I was told that this practice is a very old custom amongst them, prior to the introduction of Islám, and that they have kept it up.[26]

The negroes disliked Mansá Sulaymán because of his avarice. His predecessor was Mansá Maghá, and before him reigned Mansá Músá, a generous and virtuous prince, who loved the whites and made gifts to them.[27] It was he who gave Abú Isháq as-Sáhilí[28] four thousand *mithqáls* in the course of a single day. I heard from a trustworthy source that he gave three thousand *mithqáls* on one day to Mudrik ibn Faqqús, by whose grandfather his own grandfather, Sáraq Játa, had been converted to Islám.

The negroes possess some admirable qualities. They are seldom unjust, and have a greater abhorrence of injustice than any other people. Their sultan shows no mercy to anyone who is guilty of the least act of it. There is complete security in their country. Neither traveller nor inhabitant in it has anything to fear from robbers or men of violence. They do not confiscate the property of any white man who dies in their country, even if it be uncounted wealth. On the contrary, they give it into the charge of some trustworthy person among the whites, until the rightful heir takes possession of it. They are careful to observe the hours of prayer, and assiduous in attending them in congregations, and in bringing up their children to them. On Fridays, if a man does not go early to the mosque, he cannot find a corner to pray in, on account of the crowd. It is a custom of theirs to send each man his boy [to the mosque] with his prayer-mat; the boy spreads it out for his master in a place befitting him [and remains on it] until he comes to the mosque. Their prayer-mats are made of the leaves of a tree resembling a date-palm, but without fruit.

Another of their good qualities is their habit of wearing clean white garments on Fridays. Even if a man has nothing but an old worn shirt, he washes it and cleans it, and wears it to the Friday service. Yet another is their zeal for learning the Koran by heart. They put their children in chains if they show any backwardness in memorizing it, and they are not set free until they have it by heart. I visited the qádí in his house on the day of the festival. His children were chained up, so I said to him "Will you not let them loose?" He replied "I shall not do so until they learn the Koran by heart." Among their bad qualities are the following. The women servants, slave-girls, and young girls go about in front of everyone naked, without a stitch of clothing on them. Women go into the sultan's presence naked and without coverings, and his daughters also go about naked. Then there is their custom of putting dust and ashes on their heads, as a mark of respect, and the grotesque ceremonies we have described when the poets recite their verses. Another reprehensible practice among many of them is the eating of carrion, dogs, and asses.

The date of my arrival at Mállí was 14th Jumáda I., [seven hundred and] fifty-three [28th June 1352] and of my departure from it 22nd Muharram of the year fifty-four [27th February 1353]. I was accompanied by a merchant called Abú Bakr ibn Ya'qúb. We took the Míma road. I had a camel which I was riding, because horses are expensive, and cost a hundred *mithqáls* each. We came to a wide channel which flows out of the Nile and can only be crossed in boats. The place is infested with mosquitoes, and no one can pass that way except by night. We reached the channel three or four hours after nightfall on a moonlit night. On reaching it I saw sixteen beasts with enormous bodies, and marvelled at them, taking them to be elephants, of which there are many in that country. Afterwards I saw that they had gone into the river, so I said to Abú Bakr "What kind of animals are these?" He replied "They are hippopotami which have come out to pasture ashore." They are bulkier than horses, have manes and tails, and their heads are like horses' heads, but their feet like elephants' feet. I saw these hippopotami again when we sailed down the Nile from Tumbuktú to Gawgaw. They were swimming in the water, and lifting their heads and blowing. The men in the boat were afraid of them and kept close to the bank in case the hippopotami should sink them.

They have a cunning method of catching these hippopotami. They use spears with a hole bored in them, through which strong cords are passed. The spear is thrown at one of the animals, and if it strikes its leg or neck it goes right through it. Then they pull on the rope until the beast is brought to the bank, kill it and eat its flesh. Along the bank there are quantities of hippopotamus bones.

We halted near this channel at a large village, which had as governor a negro, a pilgrim, and man of fine character, named Farbá Maghá. He was one of the negroes who made the pilgrimage in the company of Sultan Mansá Músá. Farbá Maghá told me that when Mansá Músá came to this channel, he had with him a qádí, a white man. This qádí attempted to make away with four thousand *mithqáls* and the sultan, on learning of it, was enraged at him and exiled him to the country of the heathen cannibals. He lived among them for four years, at the end of which the sultan sent him back to his own country. The reason why the heathens did not eat him was that he was white, for they say that the white is indigestible because he is not "ripe," whereas the black man is "ripe" in their opinion.

Sultan Mansá Sulaymán was visited by a party of these negro cannibals, including one of their amírs. They have a custom of wearing in their ears large pendants, each pendant having an opening of half a span. They wrap themselves in silk mantles, and in their country there is a gold mine. The sultan received them with honour, and gave them as his hospitality-gift a servant, a negress. They killed and ate her, and having smeared their faces and hands with her blood came to the sultan to thank him. I was informed that this is their regular custom whenever they visit his court. Someone told me about them that they say that the choicest parts of women's flesh are the palm of the hand and the breast.

We continued our journey from this village which is by the channel, and came to the town of Qurí Mansá.[29] At this point the camel which I was riding died. Its keeper informed me of its death, but when I went out to see it, I found that the blacks had already eaten it, according to their usual custom of eating carrion. I sent two lads whom I had hired for my service to buy me a camel at Zágharí, and waited at Qurí Mansá for six days till they returned with it.

I travelled next to the town of Míma and halted by some wells in its outskirts.[80] Thence we went on to Tumbuktú, which stands four miles from the river. Most of its inhabitants are of the Massúfa tribe, wearers of the face-veil. Its governor is called Farbá Músá. I was present with him one day when he had just appointed one of the Massúfa to be amír of a section. He assigned to him a robe, a turban, and trousers, all of them of dyed cloth, and bade him sit upon a shield, and the chiefs of his tribe raised him on their heads. In this town is the grave of the meritorious poet Abú Isháq as-Sáhilí, of Gharnáta [Granada], who is known in his own land as at-Tuwayjin [" Little Saucepan "].[31]

From Tumbuktú I sailed down the Nile on a small boat, hollowed out of a single piece of wood. We used to go ashore every night at the villages and buy whatever we needed in the way of meat and butter in exchange for salt, spices, and glass beads. I then came to a place the name of which I have forgotten, where there was an excellent governor, a pilgrim, called Farbá Sulaymán. He is famous for his courage and strength, and none ventures to pluck his bow. I have not seen anyone among the blacks taller or bulkier than him. At this town I was in need of some millet, so I visited him (it was on the Prophet's birthday) and saluted him. He took me by the hand, and led me into his audience hall. We were served with a drink of theirs called *daqnú*, which is water containing some pounded millet mixed with a little honey or milk. They drink this in place of water, because if they drink plain water it upsets them. If they have no millet they mix the water with honey or milk. Afterwards a green melon was brought in and we ate some of it.

A young boy, not yet full-grown, came in, and Farbá Sulaymán, calling him, said to me "Here is your hospitality-gift; keep an eye on him in case he escapes." So I took the boy and prepared to withdraw, but he said "Wait till the food comes." A slave-girl of his joined us; she was an Arab girl, of Damascus, and she spoke to me in Arabic. While this was going on we heard cries in his house, so he sent the girl to find out what had happened. She returned to him and told him that a daughter of his had just died. He said "I do not like crying, come, we shall walk to the river," meaning the Nile, on which he has some houses. A horse was brought, and he told me to ride, but I said "I shall not ride if you are walking," so we walked together. We came to his houses by the Nile, where food was served, and after we had eaten I took leave of him and withdrew. I met no one among the blacks more generous or upright than him. The boy whom he gave me is still with me.

I went on from there to Gawgaw [Gogo], which is a large city on the Nile, and one of the finest towns in the Negrolands.[32] It is also one of their biggest and best-provisioned towns, with rice in plenty, milk, and fish, and there is a species of cucumber there called *'indní* which has no equal. The buying and selling of its inhabitants is done with cowry-shells, and the same is the case at Mállí.[33] I stayed there about a month, and then set out in the direction of Tagaddá by land with a large caravan of merchants from Ghadámas. Their guide and leader was the pilgrim Wuchín, which means "wolf" in the language of the blacks. I had a riding-camel and a she-camel to carry my provisions, but when we had travelled the first stage, the she-camel could go no farther. So the pilgrim Wuchín took what was on it and distributed it amongst his party, each of whom undertook to carry a part of it. There was in the company a Maghrabin belonging to Tádalá, who refused to carry any of it at all, as the rest had done. My boy was thirsty one day, and I asked this man for water, but he would not give it.

We now entered the territory of the Bardáma, who are a tribe of Berbers. No caravan can travel [through their country] without a guarantee of their protection, and for this purpose a woman's guarantee is of more value than a man's. Their women are the most perfect in beauty and the most shapely in figure of all women, of a pure white colour and very stout; nowhere in the world have I seen any who equal them in stoutness.[34] I fell ill in this country on account of the extreme heat, and a surplus of bile. We pushed on rapidly with our journey until we reached Tagaddá. The houses at Tagaddá are built of red stone, and its water runs by the copper mines, so that both its colour and taste are affected. There are no grain crops there except a little wheat, which is consumed by merchants and strangers. The inhabitants of Tagaddá have no occupation except trade. They travel to Egypt every year, and import quantities of all the fine fabrics to be had there and of other Egyptian wares. They live in luxury and ease, and vie with one another in regard to the number of their slaves and serving-women. The people of Málli and Iwálátan do the same. They never sell the educated female slaves, or but rarely and at a high price.[35]

When I arrived at Tagaddá I wished to buy an educated female slave, but could not find one. After a while the qádí sent me one who belonged to a friend of his, and I bought her for twenty-five *mithqáls*. Later on her master repented [of having sold her] and wished to have the sale rescinded, so I said to him "If you can show me where to find another, I shall cancel it for you." He suggested a servant belonging to 'Alí Aghyúl, who was that very Maghrabin from Tádalá who had refused to carry any of my effects when my camel broke down, and to give my boy water when he was thirsty. So I bought her from him (she was better than the former one) and cancelled the sale with the first man. Afterwards this Maghrabin too repented of having sold the servant and wished to have the sale cancelled. He was very insistent about it but I refused, simply to pay him back for his vile conduct. He was like to go mad or die of grief, but afterwards I cancelled his bargain for him.

The copper mine is in the outskirts of Tagaddá. They dig the ore out of the ground, bring it to the town, and cast it in their houses. This work is done by their male and female slaves. When they obtain the red copper, they make it into bars a span and a half in length, some thin and others thick. The thick bars are sold at the rate of four hundred for a *mithqál* of gold, and the thin at the rate of six or seven hundred to the *mithqál*. They serve also as their medium of exchange; with the thin bars they buy meat and firewood, with the thick, slaves, male and female, millet, butter, and wheat. The copper is exported from Tagaddá to the town of Kúbar, in the regions of the heathens, to Zagháy,[36] and to the country of Barnú, which is forty days' journey from Tagaddá. The people of Barnú are Muslims, and have a king called Idrís, who never shows himself to his people nor talks to them, except from behind a curtain.[37] From this country come excellent slave-girls, eunuchs, and fabrics dyed with saffron. The copper from Tagaddá is carried also to Jawjawa, the country of the Muwartabún, and elsewhere.[38]

During my stay at Tagaddá I wished to meet the sultan, who is a Berber called Izár, and was then at a place a day's journey from the town. So I hired a guide, and set out thither. He was informed of my coming and came to see me, riding a horse without a saddle, as is their custom. In place of a saddle he had a gorgeous saddle-cloth, and he was wearing a cloak, trousers, and turban, all in blue. With him were his sister's sons, who are the heirs to his kingdom. We rose at his approach, and shook his hand, then he asked about me and my arrival, and was told my story. He had me lodged in one of the tents of the Yanátibún, who are like the *wusfán* in our country,[30] and he sent me a sheep roasted on a spit and a wooden bowl of cows' milk. Near us was the tent of his mother and his sister; they came to visit us and saluted us, and his mother used to send us milk after the time of evening-prayer, which is their milking time. They drink it at that time and again in early morning, but of cereal foods they neither eat nor know. I stayed with them six days, and every day received from the sultan two roasted rams, one in the morning and one in the evening. He also presented me with a she-camel and with ten *mithqáls* of gold, and I took leave of him and returned to Tagaddá.

After my return to Tagaddá, a messenger arrived with a command from our master bidding me proceed to his sublime capital. I kissed the order and conformed to its instructions. I bought two riding-camels for thirty-seven and a third *mithqáls* and prepared for the journey to Tawát. I took with me provisions for seventy days, for there is no corn to be had between Tagaddá and Tawát, only fleshmeat, milk, and butter, which are paid for with pieces of cloth.

I left Tagaddá on Thursday 11th Sha'bán of the year [seven hundred and] fifty-four [11th September 1353] with a large caravan which included six hundred women slaves. We came to Káhir, where there are abundant pasturages, and thence entered an uninhabited and waterless desert, extending for three days' march.[40] We journeyed next for fifteen days through a desert which, though uninhabited, contains water-points, and reached the place at which the Ghát road, leading to Egypt, and the Tawát road divide. Here there are subterranean water-beds which flow over iron; if a piece of white cloth is washed in this water it turns black.

Ten days after leaving this point we came to the country of Haggar, who are a tribe of Berbers; they wear face veils and are a rascally lot.[41] We encountered one of their chiefs, who held up the caravan until they paid him an indemnity of pieces of cloth and other goods. Our arrival in their country fell in the month of Ramadán, during which they make no raiding expeditions and do not molest caravans. Even their robbers, if they find goods on the road during Ramadán, do not touch them. This is the custom of all the Berbers along this route. We continued to travel through the country of Haggar for a month; it has few plants, is very stony, and the road through it is bad. On the festival of the Fast-breaking we reached the country of some Berbers, who wear the face-veils, like these others.

We came next to Búdá, one of the principal villages of Tawát. The soil there is all sand and saltmarsh; there are quantities of dates, but they are not good, though the local inhabitants prefer them to the dates of Sijilmása. There are no crops there, nor butter, nor olive oil; all these things have to be imported from the Maghrib. The food of its inhabitants consists of dates and locusts, for there are quantities of locusts in their country; they store them just like dates and use them as food. They go out to catch the locusts before sunrise, for at that hour they cannot fly on account of the cold.[42]

We stayed at Búdá for some days, and then joined a caravan and in the middle of Dhu'l-qa'da reached the city of Sijilmása. I set out thence on the second of Dhu'l-hijja [29th December], at a time of intense cold, and snow fell very heavily on the way. I have in my life seen bad roads and quantities of snow, at Bukhárá and Samarqand, in Khurásán, and the lands of the Turks, but never have I seen anything worse than the road of Umm Junayba. On the eve of the Festival we reached Dár at-Tama'. I stayed there during the day of the feast and then went on. So I arrived at the royal city of Fa's [Fez], the capital of our master the Commander of the Faithful (may God strengthen him), where I kissed his beneficent hand and was privileged to behold his gracious countenance. [Here] I settled down under the wing of his bounty after long journeying. May God Most High recompense him for the abundant favours and ample benefits which he has bestowed on me; may He prolong his days and spare him to the Muslims for many years to come.

Here ends the travel-narrative entitled *A Donation to those interested in the Curiosities of the Cities and Marvels of the Ways*. Its dictation was finished on 3rd Dhu'l-hijja 756 [9th December 1355]. Praise be to God, and peace to His creatures whom He hath chosen.

Ibn Juzayy adds: "Here ends the narrative which I have abridged from the dictation of the Shaykh Abú 'Abdalláh Muhammad ibn Battúta (may God ennoble him). It is plain to any man of intelligence that this shaykh is the traveller of the age: and if one were to say "the traveller *par excellence* of this our Muslim community" he would be guilty of no exaggeration.

NOTES

CHAPTER I

[1] Corresponding to 21 solar years and four months.

[2] Abú Táshifín I (reigned 1318-1348) of the Ziyánid dynasty of Tlemsen, whose authority reached at this time as far as Algiers (then a place of minor importance). About this same year (1325) Abú Táshifín opened a campaign against the sultan of Tunis.

[3] There were various methods in use for this purpose. One was to recite a special litany and await the issue in a dream; another, which was frequently practised by Ibn Battúta, was to take an augury from the Koran after some preliminary recitations.

[4] The fertile plain lying behind Algiers.

[5] Then the frontier district of the sultanate of Ifríqíya (Tunis); but on several occasions Bougie formed a separate principality, either alone or with Constantine.

[6] Tunisia and the eastern part of Algeria had been overrun in the middle of the eleventh century by nomad Arabs, despatched by the Fátimid Caliph of Egypt to punish a rebel governor, and only behind the walls of the cities were life and property secure.

[7] Under the Hafsid dynasty, which ruled Tunisia from 1228 until the advent of the "Barbary Corsairs" in the sixteenth century, Tunis was the chief cultural centre of Northwest Africa, and many Moorish families from Spain settled there. Abú Yahyá II reigned from 1318 to 1346, when Tunis was temporarily captured by the Marinid sultan of Morocco.

[8] The festival following the annual fast observed during the month of Ramadán, known as *'Íd al-Fitr* or *Bayrám* in the East. In 725 it fell on 9th September. A special plot of ground, called the *Musallá*, usually outside the walls, was set aside for the ceremonial prayers on festival days. It is customary to wear new garments on this occasion.

[9] The omission of the party to visit Qayrawán, the site of the most famous sanctuary in Northwest Africa, is explained by the disturbed state of the interior.

[10] The names of the four gates of Alexandria (West Gate, Sea Gate, Rosetta Gate, and Green Gate) were until recently preserved in the street names of the city. It is perhaps worth noting in this connection that Alexandria is apparently the only city in the East which has paid Ibn Battúta the tribute of naming a street after him.

[11] Ibn Battúta's estimate of three miles between the Pharos and the city is an evident exaggeration, though Idrísí also says that the lighthouse was three miles distant by land and one mile by sea. A later writer, al-Qalqashandí, puts the distance at a mile. The same author states that the Pharos was partially destroyed by the Greeks in the early part of the eighth century, and fell gradually into decay "until in the middle of the fourteenth century it had become a total ruin, only a fragment of it remaining."

[12] "Pompey's Pillar" is a red granite column from Assuan, which is supposed to have been erected in late Roman times on the site of the ancient temple of Serapis.

[13] *I.e.* brother by spiritual affiliation, as the term usually signifies in the language of the saints and mystics.

[14] The phrase seems to be used here as a polite manner of deprecating the preference shown by the shaykh to the traveller.

[15] A species of mullet from which the Italian caviare (*bottargo*) is obtained.

[16] Ibn Battúta is in error here; the city was destroyed by the Egyptian government after the Crusade of St. Louis in 1249-50, to prevent its recapture by the Franks.

[17] The rhetorical description in the text is an example (very much abridged) of the florid style of composition in balanced and rhymed sentences commonly found in such passages, and possibly intended to convey the emotions of admiration and astonishment. It is not all mere verbiage, however; the last sentence is confirmed by the Italian Frescobaldi, who visited Cairo in 1384, and remarks that a hundred thousand persons slept at night outside the city because of the shortage of houses. This too after the ravages of the two "Black Deaths" of 1348 and 1381.

[18] *Ar-Rawda*, now the island of Roda. The amenities of Roda are frequently mentioned in contemporary Arabic literature, and also in the *Arabian Nights*.

[19] Only the façade, entrance hall (with minaret), and some fragments of this magnificent hospital, built by Sultan Qalá'ún (1279-90), now remain. The sultan's mausoleum, now partially restored, is one of the most exquisite monuments of medieval Saracenic architecture and ornament. Part of the street still retains the name of "Between the two Castles," a name derived in all probability from the Fátimid palaces erected in this quarter in the tenth and eleventh centuries.

[20] The main Qaráfa lies to the south of modern Cairo, between Old Cairo and the Muqattam hills. In extent and in appearance it resembles a town, owing to the peculiar Egyptian custom here referred to of building chambers and houses over the tombs.

[21] On the night following the 14th Sha'bán (the eighth month of the Muslim year) special services are held in all mosques. The traditional reason is that "on this night the Lote-tree of Paradise, on the

leaves of which are inscribed the names of all living persons, is shaken, and the leaf of any mortal who is predestined to die during the ensuing year falls withering to the ground" (Michell, *Egyptian Calendar for the Koptic Year* 1617 (1900–1901 A.D.).

22 Al-Husayn, the younger son of the Caliph 'Alí, and grandson of the Prophet, was killed with most of his family at Karbalá in 'Iráq, while leading a revolt against the Umayyad Caliph of Damascus in 681. The death of the Prophet's grandson in this fashion caused a revulsion against the reigning house, and to this day the episode is commemorated by both Sunnis and Shi'ites on the 10th Muharram, the anniversary of the event. The mosque of *Sayyidna Husén* (to be carefully distinguished from the more famous college mosque of Sultan Hasan, not yet built) is an imposing edifice near the eastern boundary of the city.

23 So called in contrast to the "Sudanese Nile," *i.e.* the Niger.

24 This division is found in other Arabic geographers. The third branch is most probably either the Ibyár (Thermutiac) branch, which flows into Lake Burlus and out through the Sebennytic mouth, or the Tanaitic branch flowing into Lake Menzaleh.

25 This was the name given to the ancient Egyptian temples, round which, as round the Pyramids, many fantastic legends grew up. Their construction was popularly ascribed to Hermes "the Ancient," who was identified with Enoch. The temple of Ikhmím seems to have been the one antiquity which attracted Ibn Battúta's notice in Egypt, except the Pyramids.

26 It is noteworthy that our traveller says not a word of the temples of Luxor, although the tomb of Abu'l-Hajjáj (a famous saint who died here in 1244) is actually in the precincts of the temple of Ammon.

27 In the twelfth, thirteenth, and fourteenth centuries Aydháb was the terminal port of the Yemen and Indian trade, and a place of great importance. It was destroyed in 1422 by the sultan of Egypt, and its place taken by the rival port of Sawákin. Its ruins have been identified "on a flat and waterless mound" on the Red Sea coast, 12 miles to the north of Halayb, at 22.20 N., 36.32 E. (G. W. Murray, in *Geographical Journal* 68 (1926²), 235-40, where the longitude is given as 36° 9′ 32″, which does not agree with the map).

28 The Hudrubis were Arabs, not Bejas.

29 A hostelry (*funduq*, *khán*, or *karawánsarây*) is usually a square walled building enclosing a courtyard; beasts and baggage are lodged in the lower storey and travellers in chambers in the upper storey. If there is no upper storey all must lodge together.

30 Now a station on the Sinai Military railway, about thirty miles east by north of Qantara.

31 The *jinn* (genii) are a sub-celestial category of creatures akin to men, but created of fire, who are credited with superhuman powers. According to the Koran they were subjected to Solomon, and "made for him whatsoever he pleased, of lofty halls, and images, and dishes

like tanks, and great cooking-vessels." In a later passage Ibn Battúta refers to the legend that it was by the aid of the *jinn* that Solomon built Palmyra (*cf.* 1 Kings ix. 18).

[32] The mosque at Hebron is a Crusaders' church built on much older (probably pre-Roman) foundations, some of whose stones fully bear out Ibn Battúta's statement. The cave is now blocked up, but cenotaphs of the Patriarchs and their wives still stand in small chapels on either side of the nave. The (putative) tomb of Joseph is in a separate exterior chapel. The tomb of Lot lies several miles to the east.

[33] The reference is to the miraculous "night-journey" or "ascension" (*mi'ráj*) in which Muhammad was given a vision of heaven. Though living at the time in Mecca, he was, according to the tradition, first transported to "the farthest mosque" (*al-masjid al-aqsá*) in Jerusalem, and thence ascended on the celestial steed Buráq.

[34] The present walls were built by the Ottoman sultan Sulayman "the Magnificent" (1520-1566).

[35] The "royal" cubit measured about 26 inches.

[36] This railing was erected by the Franks during the Crusaders' occupation of Jerusalem.

[37] The mosque of the Ascension, on the brow of the Mount of Olives, on the farther side of the Valley of Jehoshaphat, not the Valley of Hinnom (Gehenna).

[38] This seems to be a confusion between Jerusalem and Bethlehem, where the crypt of the Church of the Nativity contains the shrine of the Manger as well as the shrine of the Birthplace.

[39] Ajalún, now Qal'at ar-Rabad, was a fortress in a conspicuous position on the eastern ridge of the Ghawr (the Jordan valley), 12 miles N.W. of Jerash.

[40] Ibn Battúta has obviously confused the details of three separate journeys in Syria—see below pp. 123 and 305.

[41] A village close to Zahla, formerly reputed to possess the tomb of Noah. Until the middle of the fourteenth century the floor of the Biqá' (Coele-Syria) was covered by a lake or marsh at this point, and there was a tradition that the Ark came to rest on the spur of Anjar on the opposite side to and S.E. of Zahla.

[42] Tripoli was recovered by Sultan Qalá'ún in 1289.

[43] A similar story is told of Muhammad the Daftardár during the Turko-Egyptian campaign in Kordofán in 1821. A complaint was preferred by a woman against a soldier, and the commander had the man cut open alive "on the woman agreeing to suffer the same fate if the milk was not found in the man's stomach" (*Journal of the African Soc.*, No. 98, Jan. 1926, p. 170).

[44] The "Ten" were the most prominent members of Muhammad's entourage, and are greatly revered by the orthodox; the Shi'ites on the other hand, regard them much as Judas Iscariot is regarded in the Christian tradition. Their especial hatred is reserved for 'Omar, who

was responsible for the election of the first Caliph and was himself the second, and whom they blame accordingly for the exclusion of 'Alí from the succession to which he was designated (as they aver, in defiance of all historical argument) by the Prophet.

[45] Several pages of the original are devoted to an elaborate description of Aleppo, consisting chiefly in quotations of ornate prose passages from Ibn Jubayr, and short extracts from eulogies of the city by famous poets.

[46] Tizín is situated 28 miles W. of Aleppo.

[47] In 1268. See his letter to Boemund describing the sack of the city, in Yule's *Marco Polo* (3rd ed., ed. Cordier), i. 24 note.

[48] The fortress of Pagræ, called by the Crusaders Gaston or Gastin, which defended the entry through the Baylan Pass, between Alexandretta and Antioch. It was recaptured by Saladin in 1188.

[49] Better known in Europe as the *Assassins*. They were sectaries of an offshoot of the Fátimid branch of the Shí'ites, founded in the eleventh century.

[50] Ibráhím ibn Adham, a famous ascetic and saint, originally from Balkh, who is said to have died during a naval expedition against the Greeks about 780. Little is known of his life, except that Syria was the principal centre of his religious activities, but he afterwards became the central figure in several cycles of Súfí legend, evidently derived from the legends of the Buddha.

[51] Son-in-law and cousin of the Prophet Muhammad, and the central figure in the doctrines of the Shí'ites.

[52] Here follows a lengthy extract from Ibn Jubayr in rhyming prose. In order that the reader may appreciate the rhetorical style employed in such passages, the first few sentences may be translated literally as follows: "As for Damascus, she is the Paradise of the Orient, and dawning-place of her resplendent light; the seal of the lands of Islám whose hospitality we have enjoyed, and bride of the cities which we have unveiled. She is adorned with flowers of sweet-scented plants, and appears amidst brocaded gardens; she has occupied an exalted position in the place of beauty, and is most richly bedecked in her bridal chair." Several pages of other quotations follow before the editor resumes the thread of Ibn Battúta's narrative.

[53] This is a popular tradition, intended to account for the fact that the Church of St. John was not converted into a mosque until seventy years after the Arab conquest of Damascus. The church was not demolished, but merely stripped of its Christian furnishings and refitted as a mosque. Ibn Battúta goes on to give a detailed description of the mosque as it existed in his day. This edifice was destroyed by fire during Tamerlane's occupation of Damascus in 1400, and has since been reconstructed more than once. The present building dates only from 1893, and preserves little trace of its former magnificence, except the three fine minarets.

54 The founder of the Umayyad dynasty of Caliphs, which reigned at Damascus from 660 to 749, and was supplanted by the 'Abbásid dynasty, who made their capital at Baghdád. The bazaar of the coppersmiths still occupies the same position, but is by no means " one of the finest in Damascus " at the present day.

55 This was originally a mechanical water-clock, which was still in working order when Ibn Jubayr visited Damascus in 1184 (see le Strange, *Palestine under the Moslems*, p. 250), but had fallen out of repair in the interval. Though the galleries have long since disappeared, the spouting fountain (a relic of Byzantine days) still exists.

56 As being contrary to the orthodox doctrine that no activity or quality in God is to be compared with the corresponding human activity or quality. The Hanbalite school, the most conservative of the four orthodox schools (see Introd., p. 23), disallowed the rationalizing interpretations of the other schools.

57 The wearing of silk is contrary to strict Muhammadan law.

58 On Ibn Taymíya, who died in 1328, see Introd., p. 38. His name is now held in great respect as the forerunner of the Wahhábí and other modern reform movements in Islam.

59 A Muhammadan fast is limited to the hours of daylight, but is absolute during that time, even water-drinking being prohibited.

60 It is probably this characteristic that has earned for Damascus the nickname of *al-matbakh*, " the kitchen."

61 Leaving his wife, or one of his wives, behind him, as he relates below (p. 304). This wife bore him a son, but the boy died in childhood.

62 'Aqabat as-Sawán, now 'Aqabat al-Hijázíya, a station on the Hijaz railway. On Prof. Alois Musil's map of the Northern Hijaz (1927) it is situated at 29.50 N., 35.48 E.

Dhát al-Hajj, a station at 29.05 N., 36.08 E.

Baldah is identified by Musil (*Northern Hejaz*, p. 329) with the valley of al-Bazwá, about fifty kilometres south of Dhát al-Hajj and near the station of al-Hazm at 28.41 N., 36.14 E.

63 " The halting-place of al-Ukhaydir (al-Akhzar) lies in a deep valley enclosed by high slopes, in places covered with lava. Ibn Battúta rightly compares this to a valley of hell " (Musil, *ib.* 329). Al-Akhzar, the name of which (" The little green place ") is obviously ironical, is situated at 28.08 N., 37.01 E.

64 The story of the impious tribe of Thamúd, who were annihilated for their disobedience, is frequently related in the Koran. It arose in all probability from the existence of these tombs, which belonged to an early South-Arabian trading community settled on the trade-route between the Yemen and the marts of Syria, and afterwards confused with the ancient North-Arabian tribe of Thamúd.

65 From al-Hijr (Madá'in Sálih) to al-'Elá is a distance of about

18 English miles. Al-Hijr is situated at 26.49 N., 37.56 E., al-'Elá at 26.36 N., 38.04 E.

[66] The battle at Badr in 633 A.D., in which the pagan Meccans were defeated by a much smaller force of Muslims, was the first important success of the new community, and one of the turning-points of Muhammad's career.

[67] According to the Arabic geographer Hamdání (pp. 184-5) the station of Juhfa was situated 103 (Arabic) miles from Rawhá', which was the second station from Madína and 47 miles distant from the city. An Arabic mile measured 1921 metres, as compared as 1609 in an English mile.

Khulays, described by the Arabic geographer Yáqút as a fortified enceinte between Mecca and Madína, seems to have taken the place of the older station of Qudayd, 24 miles from Juhfa and 23 from the next station of 'Usfán.

'Usfán and Marr (or Marr az-Zuhrán) still exist, the latter 23 miles from 'Usfán and 13 from Mecca.

[68] The descriptions of Mecca and the Pilgrimage which follow in the original are abridged from the work of Ibn Jubayr, and have been very fully annotated by Burton in his *Personal Narrative of a Pilgrimage to al-Madinqh and Meccah*. So many accounts of the Pilgrimage are now available in English in addition to this, that it is unnecessary to repeat all these details here.

CHAPTER II

[1] The pilgrim road from Baghdád and Najaf to Madína is known as the *Darb Zubayda*, after the wife of Caliph Hárún ar-Rashíd, who built reservoirs all along the route and provided endowments from her property for their upkeep. The route, consequently, has scarcely changed for twelve hundred years. According to Hamdání, the stations from Madína to Fayd were: Taraf (24 Arabic miles), Batn Nakhl (20 m.), 'Usayla (28 m.), Ma'din an-Naqira (26 m.), al-Hájir (28 m.), Samírá (23 m.), Túz (25 m.), Fayd (24 m.): total, 196 Arabic miles or 234 English miles. Ibn Battúta, evidently travelling by half-stages, takes six days to reach 'Usayla (I cannot find his Wádi'l-'Arús), then takes the alternative road through Naqira instead of Ma'din an-Naqira, rejoins the main route at Qárúra (between Ma'din an-Naqira and al-Hájir, and 12 miles from the latter), and thence follows it without variation. Al-Makhrúqa—the perforated hill—is shown on Musil's 1 : 1,000,000 map 27 English miles S.W. of Fayd, at 26.50 N., 41.36 E., and Fayd itself at 27.08 N., 41.53 E.

[2] Yáqút adds that a portion of the provisions and heavy baggage is given in remuneration to the parties in whose care they are left.

NOTES

[3] The various stages on the journey between Fayd and Kúfa, totalling 277 Arabic miles or 330 English miles, need not be detailed here. "Devil's Pass" is probably the pass marked *ash-She eb* on Musil's map, at 30.11 N., 43.42 E. Wáqisa is shown at 30.38 N., 43.51 E., Lawza lies 16 English miles N. by E. of Wáqisa, al-Masájid or al-Musayjid 56 m. S. by W. of Najaf, Manárat al-Qurún appears as Ummu Qurún, a sanctuary 30 m. S. by W. of Najaf. Qádisíya is fifteen miles due south of Najaf. The battle to which Ibn Battúta refers was fought in 637, five years after Muhammad's death, and resulted in the complete rout of the Persian army and the occupation of 'Iráq by the Arabs.

[4] The son-in-law of the Prophet, and fourth Caliph, assassinated in 661. His tomb is held in peculiar reverence by the Shi'ites, along with that of his son Husayn at Karbalá (see Ch. I, note 22). For the meaning of *qaysaríya* see note 29 below.

[5] The eve on the 27th Rajab is known as *Laylat al-Mi'ráj*, or Night of the Prophet's Ascension. See Ch. I, note 30.

[6] Ahmad ar-Rifá'í, died 1182 and buried at Umm 'Ubayda, was the nephew of Shaykh 'Abd al-Qádir al-Jílání, and founder of the Rifá'íya order of darwíshes, a sub-group of the Qádiríya order, and one of the principal orders in Egypt at the present day. The name of Ahmadí darwishes, which Ibn Battúta gives to the order, is now usually given to the sub-group founded by Shaykh Ahmad al-Badawí, who was a disciple of the convent of Umm 'Ubayda and died at Tanta in Egypt in 1276.

[7] The apparent shrinkage of Basra was due not entirely to decay, but to a gradual eastward shifting of the city: *cf.* note 10.

[8] The *nuqra* was an Egyptian silver coin worth about fivepence; see Chap. XII, note 18.

[9] Ibn Battúta's audience would all, of course, be familiar with the fact that it was at Basra that the rules of Arabic grammar were systematized in the second century after Muhammad, the "leader" referred to below being Sibawayh, the author of the first large systematic grammar of Arabic.

[10] Ubulla occupied the site of the present town of Basra, the medieval city of Basra lying on a canal to the west of the Shatt al-'Arab, and a mile or two east of the modern town of Zubair.

[11] Now Bandar Mashur, on Khor Musa, an inlet east of the delta.

[12] The petty Hazáraspid dynasty, founded in the mountains of Lúristán in the twelfth century, maintained itself throughout the Mongol period. Their capital Ídhaj, on the Dujayl river, is now called Málamír. The title *Atábeg* ("regent") was adopted by all the minor dynasties which established themselves after the break-up of the Saljuq empire in the twelfth century.

[13] The beauties of Rukn Ábád have been immortalized by the famous poet Háfiz of Shíráz, a younger contemporary of our traveller.

[14] Better known as Úljáytú (reigned 1305-1316), the eighth and penultimate of the line of Mongol Ílkháns of Persia (not to be confused with his contemporary Úljáytú, grandson of Qúbiláy Khán, Mongol Emperor of China, 1294-1307). As a child Úljáytú had been baptized into the Christian Church.

[15] Qarábágh was in the mountainous district N. of Tabriz, across the Aras river (see *Clavijo* in this series, Map II and p. 362). The Mongol sultans maintained the nomadic habit of migrating to the highlands in the summer.

[16] Ibn Battúta appears to have confused his first visit to Shíráz with his second, on his return journey in 1347. As related a few lines below, Shaykh Abú Isháq, of the house of Ínjú, did not obtain possession of Shíráz until after 1335, when his relative and predecessor Sharaf ad-Din Sháh Mahmúd Ínjú was put to death by the Mongols. In 1347 he was still at the height of his power, and in 1356 or 1357 he was captured and put to death by the rival house of the Muzaffarids.

[17] The great palace of the pre-Islamic Sásánid kings of Persia at Ctesiphon, the ruins of which are still to be seen a few miles below Baghdád.

[18] The author of the famous *Rose Garden* (*Gulistán*) and other poetical works, died in 1291.

[19] Zaydán is defined as a village between Arraján (now Bihbihan) and Dawraq (now Falláhíya), one day's march from the latter and less than three days from Arraján (Schwarz, *Iran*, IV, 384).

Huwayza is the modern Hawíza, seventy miles N. of Muhammarah.

Kúfa (a few miles north of Najaf) was, with Basra, one of the garrison cities founded by the Arabs in 638, on their conquest of 'Iráq. During the short reign of 'Alí (see note 4) it was the seat of the Caliphate.

[20] For the explanation of this title and the following ceremony see Introduction, p. 38.

[21] See Chap. I, note 22.

[22] Actually at this time (and until 1918) Baghdád was no more than a provincial town. Its high title was derived from the prestige it enjoyed as the seat of the Caliphate from 756 to 1258, when it was sacked and largely destroyed by the Mongols.

[23] In the baths at Damascus the bather receives anything from six to ten towels at successive stages.

[24] The last of the line of Mongol or Tatar Ílkháns of Persia.

[25] Dilshád was the daughter of Dimashq Kwájah, the son of Júbán (Chúbán) whom Abú Sa'íd had put to death.

[26] A *mahalla* was the mobile camp, consisting of the royal retinue and troops, which accompanied the sultan on his marches.

[27] Tabríz—the Tauris of Marco Polo and other western writers—was the capital of the Mongols in Persia. At this period it had taken

the place of Baghdád as the principal commercial centre in Western Asia, and was frequented by large numbers of European merchants.

[28] Between 836 and 883 Sámarrá was the seat of the Caliphs, and was adorned by them with many magnificent palaces and public buildings, of which vestiges still remain. The fort of Ma'shúq probably occupied the site of the palace of the same name (*al-ma'shúq* means "the Beloved") erected by the Caliph Mu'tamid (reigned 870-892).

[29] The word *qaysaríya* is defined variously as "a public place in which the market is held" or "a square building containing chambers, storerooms, and stalls for merchants." The name is evidently derived from the Latin or Greek, and was used orginally only by the Arabs of Syria and North Africa, but its origin is obscure. Of various theories which have been advanced the most probable is that it means a market building, privileged or authorized by the ruler (originally in these countries, of course, the Cæsar) in return for a certain fixed payment, but no corresponding term has been found in the Byzantine histories. It is now applied to the principal market of a town, and I have heard the term used in North Africa (Tlemsen) for the main shopping street. The provision of gates for bazaars was, and still is, quite common. (Dozy *s.v.*; le Strange, *Lands of the Eastern Caliphate*, p. 89).

[30] Sinjár is evidently misplaced. It is most probable that it was visited on the way back from Márídin to Mosul.

[31] Dárá, "the rampart of the Roman Empire," was built by Justinian as the frontier fortress over against the Persian territories.

[32] The fortress of Maridín was assigned in 1108 by the Saljuq ruler of Baghdád to Íl-Ghází "one of the most redoubtable of Muslim warriors against the Crusaders" (Lane-Poole), whose descendants, known as the Ortuqids of Máridín, retained possession of the city and its environs until after the death of Tamerlane. Al-Malik as-Sálih, the twelfth of the line, reigned from 1312 to 1363.

[33] The ritual "hastening to and fro" between the hillocks of Safá and Marwa, said to be in commemoration of Hagar's search for water for her son Ishmael, though usually performed on foot, is frequently carried out by pilgrims on donkeys or camels. It has been left for the present ruler of Najd, Sultan 'Abd al-'Azíz Ál-Sa'úd, to perform it in an automobile.

CHAPTER III[1]

[1] Ra's Dawá'ir, which is said to mean "The Cape of Whirlwinds (or Whirlpools)," is not mentioned in any work which I have consulted. It can hardly be other than the headland now called Ra's Raweiya

---

[1] The passages in this chapter dealing with the East Coast of Africa have been annotated by L. M. Devic, *Le Pays des Zendjs*, Paris, 1883.

(21° N.), and it is quite possible that Dawá'ir is in fact a wrong transcription of this name.

[2] Hali, properly "Haly (with consonantal y) of the Son of Ya'qúb," was a large town on the highroad from San'á to Mecca some thirty miles inland, and forty miles S.E. of Qunfuda, in a district sufficiently fertile to produce three crops a year. The port of Hali is a small sheltered anchorage in the district now called Asír, at 18.36 N., 41.19 E. At this time Hali was subordinate to the sultan of Yemen. (Hamdání 188; Redhouse, *History of the Resuliyy Dynasty* I, 307; III, 169; *Handbook of Arabia* 136, 144.)

[3] A place named Sarja is mentioned as a halt on the San'á-Mecca road, ten stations before Haly (Hamdání 188), but Ibn Battúta's port of call was Sharja, an anchorage in the neighbourhood of Luhayya (to be distinguished from Shárja in Trucial 'Omán). (Qalqashandí V, 14; Redhouse *op. cit.* III, 148).

[4] Zabíd was the winter residence of the sultan, Ta'izz being the summer capital. Zabíd lay fifteen (Arabic) miles from the coast, which is called in the Arabic authors Ghaláfiqa, and its port was al-Ahwáb (not al-Abwáb, as in the printed text). (Qalqashandí V, 9-10; Redhouse III, 149.)

[5] The *subút an-nakhl*, literally "Palm Saturdays," were a well-known feature of the social life of Zabíd. According to Redhouse "it was a local *Saturnalia*, and perhaps originated in the pagan times before the advent of Islam" (*op. cit.* III, 186, 197).

[6] Yemen, the Arabic name for Arabia Felix, consists of a high central table-land dropping abruptly to the coastal plain on the south and west. The mountains intercept the summer monsoon rains, and the country, being in consequence predominantly agricultural, has always enjoyed a greater measure of culture than the rest of the peninsula. San'á, the ancient and present capital, lies in the mountains in the interior; Ta'izz lies closer to the edge of the hills at a height of 4,000 feet. The Rasúlid dynasty, of which 'Alí (reigned 1321-63) was the fifth sovereign, made themselves independent of Egypt in 1229, and continued to govern Yemen until the middle of the fifteenth century.

[7] It was the practice of Muslim rulers to provide accommodation for ambassadors and visitors of quality and to supply them with provision or a daily sum of money in lieu thereof. Chardin, in his *Travels in Persia*, in the seventeenth century, relates that the Sháh had "above three hundred houses in Ispahan which are properly his own. . . . They are all large and fine, are almost always empty, and run to ruin for want of being kept up in sufficient repair. These they give to ambassadors and persons of consideration that come to Ispahan." Alternatively accommodation might be provided in some of the numerous religious establishments. See also *Clavijo*, p. 122.

[8] It was customary in Islamic lands for the sovereign to pray in

a part of the mosque railed off with a carved wooden screen, called the *maqsúra* or "enclosure." This practice was adopted partly as a measure against assassination.

[9] From *as-Sawáhil* ("The coast lands"), the name given by the Arabs to part of the coast of what is now Kenya and Tanganyika Territory, is derived the name of the Swahili language. *Zanj* is a word of unknown origin, employed in medieval times to denote the negroes of East Africa, and still preserved in the name of Zanzibar.

[10] This appears to mean, not that the island is two days' journey from the mainland (from which it is separated only by a narrow strait), but that the Sawáhil country began two days' journey to the southward.

[11] See note 15 to Chapter XIV.

[12] Instead of including them in the ordinary revenue and using them for the general expenses of government, as was more often done.

[13] Dhofár is backed by a high ridge which receives the summer monsoon rains, and is covered in consequence with tropical vegetation. The outlying population is not Arab, but of a Sudanic type.

[14] A small island in the Kuria-Muria group.

[15] According to Muhammadan law, no animal is lawful for food unless its throat has been cut before death.

[16] "Masira Island, the Sarapis of the unknown author of the *Periplus*, famous even in those days for its tortoises, and inhabited, then as now, by 'settlements of Fish Eaters, a villainous lot, who use the Arabian language and wear girdles of palm-leaves'" (Sir A. T. Wilson, *Geog. J.*, 69, 236-7, quoting from Schoff, *Periplus*).

[17] Súr and Qalhát owed their importance to their position at the southern end of 'Omán, just north of Ra's al-Hadd, the first point in Arabia reached by ships coming from India. Qalhát is Marco Polo's "Calatu . . . a noble city. . . . The haven is very large and good, and is frequented by numerous ships with goods from India." It also played an important part during the Portuguese period.

[18] 'Omán Proper lies inland, on the slopes of Jebel Akhdar.

[19] According to the local historians the succession of Azdite imams of 'Omán reigning at Nazwa was broken between 1154 and 1406, during which period a rival tribe, the Banú Nabhán, whose seat was at Makniyát in the Dháhira, became overlords of the country. From Ibn Battúta's account, however, it is clear that the Azdite imamate at Nazwa continued to exist, or was restored before 1332. (G. P. Badger, *Imams and Seiyids of Oman*, 37, 41; Wellsted, *Travels in Arabia*, I, 215.)

[20] The island of Ormuz, S.E. of Bandar Abbas. The island was captured by the Portuguese in 1512, and held by them until 1622, when it was recovered by the Persians with English aid.

[21] "They call these deadly pestiferous Storms *Bad Sammoun*, that is to say, the Winds of Poison. . . . It rises only between the 15th of

June and the 15th of August, which is the time of the excessive Heats near that Gulph. That Wind runs whistling through the Air, it appears red and inflam'd, and kills and blasts the People; it strikes in a manner, as if it stifled them, particularly in the Day time. Its surprizing Effects is not the Death it self, which it causes; what's most amazing is, that the Bodies of those who die by it, are, as it were, dissolved, but without losing their Figure and Contour; insomuch that one would only take them to be asleep; but if you take hold of any piece of them, the Part remains in your Hand" (Chardin, *Travels in Persia* (1927), 136).

22 This is taken by Schwarz (*Iran im Mittelalter*, III, 133) to be the same as Khawristán (otherwise called Sarvistán), about fifty miles S.E. of Shíráz. If so, the insertion of the town here is an error due to Ibn Battúta's faulty recollection of his route on the return journey from India in 1347 (see note 3 to Chap. XII), when he must have passed through Khawristán on his way to Shíráz. It is very unlikely, however, that an Arab should reproduce Khawristán as Kawrástán, unless the name was pronounced so locally.

23 Lár lies about 120 miles N.W. of Bandar Abbas.

24 The "hospitality gift" consisted of food or gifts in kind supplied to distinguished visitors (see note 7 above).

25 Khunjubál is probably a double name. The second part is mentioned by Yáqút as Fál, and described as a large village, verging on a town, at the southern extremity of the province of Fárs, near the seacoast. He adds that it lay on the route between Hormuz and Huzú (a fort on the mainland opposite Kísh island, now Qal'at al-'Ubayd). The first part of the name appears on our maps as Hunj or Hunju, 27.04 N., 54.02 E. (Schwarz, *Iran* III, 132; II, 80; *Z.D.M.G.*, 68, 533).

26 Ibn Battúta has fallen into a considerable error here. The ancient port of Síráf, once the entrepôt of the Persian Gulf, was situated near the present Tahiri. Qays or Kísh is an island some seventy miles further south, which in the twelfth century supplanted Síráf, and was itself supplanted by Hormuz about 1300, Hormuz in turn being supplanted by Bandar 'Abbás in the seventeenth century.

27 The more exact Chardin says: "The divers that fish for pearls are sometimes near half a quarter of an hour under water."

28 The underground waterbearing beds of eastern Arabia discharge into the sea at Bahrayn. During the Turkish occupation, the sailors used to dive into the sea and bring up fresh water in a leather sack for the use of the commander, and the Portuguese supplied themselves in the same way by pumps. There is a story that a camel once fell into a spring at al-Hasá, and was never seen again until it came up in the sea near Bahrayn.

29 A full description of the oasis of al-Hasá or Hajar (the former meaning *Pebbles* and the latter *Stones*), of which the chief town is now

called Hofúf, will be found in the *Geog. Journal*, 63 (1924), pp. 189-207. It appears from this article that at Hasá there is still a "considerable sprinkling of Shi'ahs, mostly descendants of Bahárina (Bahrayn Shi'ahs), who settled in the oasis long ago."

[30] Formerly the chief town of Najd, the sand-buried remains of which lie 58 miles S.E. of the present capital Riyád, at 24.07 N., 47.25 E. (see Philby, *Heart of Arabia*, II, 31-4).

CHAPTER IV[1]

[1] *Bilád ar-Rúm*, literally "the land of the Greeks," though used of the Byzantine territories generally, was naturally applied more specially to the frontier province of Anatolia. After some temporary conquests in earlier centuries, it had been finally overrun by the Saljúq Turks between 1071 and 1081. Down to the end of the thirteenth century, the whole peninsula, except those sections which were held by the Christians (Byzantium, Trebizond, and Armenia) or the ruler of 'Iráq, owed allegiance to the Saljúq sultan of Konia, but from a little before 1300 it was parcelled out between a score of local chiefs, whose territories were gradually absorbed into the Ottoman Empire.

[2] The port of 'Aláyá was constructed by one of the greatest of the Saljúq sultans of Rúm, 'Alá ad-Dín Kay-Qubád I (1219-37), and was renamed after him. To the Western merchants it was known as Candelor (from its Byzantine name *kalon oros*). Egypt, being notoriously deficient in wood, has always needed to import large quantities of it for the building of fleets, etc.

[3] Adáliya, known to the Western merchants as Satalia, was the most important trading station on the south coast of Anatolia, the Egyptian and Cypriote trade being the most active. The lemon is still called *Adáliya* in Egypt.

[4] The closing of the city gates and exclusion of Christians at night and during the hours of the Friday service was observed until quite recently in a number of places on the Mediterranean seaboard, such as Sfax, probably as a measure of precaution against surprise attacks.

[5] The history of the organizations called by the name of *Futúwa* is still obscure. They appear first in the twelfth century in several divergent forms, which can probably all be traced to the Súfís, or darwísh orders. The word *futúwa*, "manliness," had long been applied amongst the latter in a moral sense, defined as "to abstain from

---

[1] The section relating to Anatolia has been translated and annotated by Defrémery in *Nouvelles Annales des Voyages*, Dec. 1850–April 1851, and that relating to the Crimea and Qipchaq by the same in *Journal Asiatique*, July–Sept. 1850.

injury, to give without stint, and to make no complaint," and the patched robe, the mark of a Súfí, was called by them *libás al-futúwa*, "the garment of manliness." It was applied in a more aggressive sense among the guilds of "Warriors for the Faith," especially as the latter degenerated into robber bands, and it is in reference to the ceremony of admission into one such band at Baghdád in the middle of the twelfth century that trousers are first mentioned as the symbolic *libás al-futúwa* (Ibn al-Athír XI, 41). A few years later Ibn Jubayr found at Damascus an organization called the *Nubúya*, which was engaged in combating the fanatical Shí'ite sects in Syria. The members of this warrior guild, whose rule it was that no member should call for assistance in any misfortune that might befall him, elected suitable persons and similarly invested them with trousers on their admission.

In 1182 the Caliph an-Násir, having been invested with the *libás* or trousers by a Súfí shaykh, conceived the idea of organizing the *Futúwa* on the lines of an order of Chivalry (probably on the Frankish model), constituted himself sovereign of the order, and bestowed the *libás* as its insignia on the ruling princes and other personages of his time. The ceremony of installation included the solemn putting-on of the trousers and drinking from the "cup of manhood" (*ka's al-futúwa*), which contained not wine, but salt and water. The order took over from its Súfí progenitors a fictitious genealogy back to the Caliph 'Alí (see Chap. II, note 4), and continued to exist for some time after the reign of Násir in a languishing state. The Brotherhood which Ibn Battúta found in Konia, and which was distinguished from the other guilds in Anatolia by its special insignia of the trousers and its claim to spiritual descent from 'Alí, was probably a relic of the order founded by the romantic Caliph. The remaining Anatolian organizations seem to have been local trade-guilds with a very strong infusion of Sufism, oddly combined with a political tendency towards local self-government and the keeping in check of the tyranny of the Turkish sultans. (See generally Thorning, *Türkische Bibliothek*, Band XVI (Berlin, 1913), and Wacyf Boutros Ghali, *La Tradition Chevaleresque des Arabes* (Paris, 1919), pp. 1-33).

[6] This passage seems to mean that by taking boats across Egerdir-Gul and Kirili-Gul (the lake of Beyshahr, which Ibn Battúta apparently regarded as joined to Egerdir-Gul) Ákshahr and Beyshahr could be reached in two days. Defrémery thinks that this Áqshahr is not Akshahr, but the town of Oushar or Akshar, near Egerdir-Gul.

[7] Gul-Hisár, according to Defrémery, was a small fortress, afterwards destroyed, on the edge of the lake of Buldur; le Strange on the other hand places it on Sugud-Gul, west of Istanoz.

[8] See note 5 above.

[9] This is the well-known Mevlevi fraternity, or "dancing darwíshes," which was instituted by Jalál ad-Dín in memory of his master

Shamsí Tabríz (the sweetmeat-seller of Ibn Battúta's story). Jalál ad-Dín, who died at Konia in 1273, is generally held to be the greatest of the Persian mystical poets. (See R. A. Nicholson, *Selected Poems from the Diváni Shamsi Tabríz*, Introduction.)

[10] Birgí is the ancient Pyrgion, in the valley of the Cayster. There is an obvious gap in Ibn Battúta's narrative at this point, since he can hardly have crossed the entire breadth of Anatolia without touching some town or another, even if he went by the direct road from Sivas through the central plateau. It is more likely that he retraced his route to some extent towards Konia and thence through Egerdir.

[11] This refers to the capture of Smyrna in 1344 (many years *after* Ibn Battúta's visit) by a crusading force, with the assistance of the Knights of St. John.

[12] Fúja (Fuggia, the ancient Phocæa), which had been ceded by the Palælogi to the Genoese family of Zaccaria, was an important trading station, the Zaccaria family having sole control of the alum-mines there and of the mastic trade of Chios (which they had seized in 1304). It is not quite certain whether the Fúja of this period was Old Phocæa (Eski Foja) or New Phocæa (Yeni Foja).

[13] Ibn Battúta's account is one of the few firsthand accounts we possess of the early days of the Ottoman Empire. Brusa is said to have surrendered to the Turks in 1326, the year of 'Othmán's death, and Nicæa fell in 1329, but hostilities against both cities had begun very much earlier (see H. A. Gibbons, *Foundations of the Ottoman Empire*, 46-8). With regard to the name 'Othmán Chúk, given to 'Othmán, Prof. Kramers has suggested that it was derived not directly from the Arabic name 'Othmán, but from the fortress of Osmanjik on the Kizil Armak (*Z.D.M.G.*, 81, LXII f.).

[14] I prefer this, the reading of the best MS. to the reading "We treated her kindly," which is adopted in the text.

[15] Burlú is identified by Defrémery with Boyalu, S.W. of Kastamuni.

[16] More commonly called Solghát, now Stary-Krim, in the interior of the Crimea. At this time it was the residence of the Mongol governor of the Crimea, and later on the seat of an independent Khanate.

[17] The Khanate of Qipchaq or the Golden Horde was the western-most of the four great Mongol Khanates established in the thirteenth century, and was itself at this time divided into the Blue Horde and the White Horde. Though the latter held a titular suzerainty, the Blue Horde, whose appanage was on the Don and Volga, was actually the more powerful, and their territories extended from Kiev and the Caucasus to the Aral Sea and Khiva. Sultan Muhammad Úzbeg, who reigned from 1312 to 1340, was one of the greatest of the Khans of the Blue Horde.

[18] Caffa, now Feodosia, was rebuilt by the Genoese towards the end of the thirteenth century as their principal trading station on the northern coast of the Black Sea.

[19] Muslims hold the ringing of bells in the greatest abhorrence, and attribute to the Prophet the saying: "The angels will not enter any house wherein bells are rung."

[20] I take this to be the estuary of the Miuss river, west of Taganrog.

[21] The legal alms or "tithe" amounts to two and a half per cent.

[22] The ruins of Májar (now Burgomadzhary) lie on the Kuma river S.W. of Astrakhan, 110 kilometres N.E. of Georgiewsk, at 44.50 N., 44.27 E.

[23] Beshtaw, one of the foothills of the Caucasus, is a wooded hill rising to a height of nearly 1,400 metres, just north of Pyatigorsk, about 35 kilometres S.W. of Georgiewsk.

[24] There appears to be no record in the Byzantine historians of the marriage of a daughter of Andronicus III (who was thirty-five years of age in 1331) to a Khan of the Golden Horde, but there are at least two instances before this of bastard daughters of the Emperor being given in marriage to Tartar chiefs.

[25] Bulghár, the ruins of which lie on the left bank of the Volga just below the junction of the Kama, was the capital of the mediæval kingdom of Great Bulgaria, annexed by the Mongols in the thirteenth century. It possessed great commercial importance as the distributing centre for Russian and Siberian products. It is difficult to understand, however, how Ibn Battúta could have made the journey from Májar to Bulghár, some 800 miles, in ten days!

[26] This term apparently designates Northern Siberia; see Yule's *Marco Polo*[3], II, 484-6.

[27] It has been pointed out in a note to Yule's *Marco Polo* (II, 488) that this Ukak is not the well-known town of that name frequently mentioned by the mediæval writers, which was situated on the Volga about six miles below Saratov, but a small place mentioned in the portolans as Locachi or Locaq, on the Sea of Azof. The silver mines of which Ibn Battúta speaks are "certain mines of argentiferous lead-ore near the river Miuss (a river falling into the Sea of Azof, about 22 miles west of Taganrog). . . . It was these mines which furnished the ancient Russian *rubles* or ingots."

[28] Surdáq or Soldaia, now Sudak, in the Crimea, was until the rise of Caffa (see note 18) the principal trading port on the northern coast of the Euxine. It is not clear why the party should have made a detour through the Crimea; possibly Ibn Battúta has confused the details of the route, and visited Surdáq during his stay at Stary Krim.

[29] There seems to be no clue to the position of this sanctuary, but from Ibn Battúta's description it was somewhere between the Dniépr and the Crimea. It has been suggested that from this Bábá Saltúq (transported to Baba Dagh in Moldavia in 1389) arose the cult of Sari Saltik associated with the Bektashi order (see F. W. Hasluck, *Ann. Brit. Sch. Athens* XIX, 203-6; XX, 107, note 1).

[30] Ibn Battúta's route through Thrace to Constantinople is totally

unrecognizable from his account of it. Here, as again in China, the unfamiliarity of the names has led to strange perversions, especially when reproduced from memory after a lapse of twenty years. The frontier city of the Empire in 1331-2 (the date which must be assigned to this journey in spite of Ibn Battúta's chronology) was Diampolis, otherwise Kavúli (now Jamboli), for which " Mahtúlí " may perhaps pass. The " canal " is evidently a tidal river or estuary, and one naturally thinks of the Danube, though this involves a serious misplacing. But Fanfka is probably Agathonfkè, where the main road from Diampolis crossed the Tunja (Tontzos) river, at or near Kizil Agach. The " Fortress of Maslama ibn 'Abd al-Malik " belongs to the legendary accretions to the history of the Arab expedition against Constantinople in 716-7, of which Maslama was the commader-in-chief.

[31] *Kifálí* is a transliteration of the Greek *kephale*, head, chief.

[32] The Emperor at this time was Andronicus III, grandson of Andronicus II. The title *Takfúr* (from Armenian *tagavor* =" king ") was applied by the Muhammadan writers to the Emperor and the other Christian kings in Asia Minor, probably as a rhyming jingle with the title given to the Emperor of China, *Faghfúr* (for Bagh-púr, the Persian translation of the Chinese title " Son of Heaven "). There is some difficulty in explaining how Ibn Battúta came to call the retired Emperor Andronicus II (who had abdicated in 1328, become a monk, and died on February 13, 1332) by the name of George.

[33] The ceremonial here described is in accordance with the practice of the Byzantine court, afterwards adopted by the Ottoman sultans when they captured Constantinople.

[34] The Muslims believe that Jesus was not crucified but carried up to Heaven, and that a figure resembling him was crucified in his stead.

[35] The number of monks and churches in Constantinople seems to have struck most travellers at this time. Bertrandon de la Bloquière, who spent the winter of 1432-3 there, estimates the number of churches at 3,000, and implies that the greater number of the inhabitants lived in monasteries. See also *Clavijo*, p. 88.

[36] *Barbara* is a transcription of *hyperpyron*, the debased dinar of the Palæologues.

[37] There were two cities of " Sarray in the land of Tartarye," which were successively the capital of the Khans of the Golden Horde; Old Sarai, situated near the modern village of Selitrennoe, 74 miles above Astrakhan, and New Sarai, which embraced the modern town of Tsarev, 225 miles above Astrakhan. Sultan Muhammad Úzbeg moved the capital from Old Sarai to New Sarai about this period, most probably a few years before. Ibn Battúta's description agrees best with New Sarai, the ruins of which extend over a distance of more than forty miles, and cover an area of over twenty square miles. (See F. Balodis, in *Latvijas Universitates Rakſti* (*Acta Universitatis Latviensis*, XIII (Riga, 1926), pp. 3-82.)

NOTES

CHAPTER V[1]

[1] The ruins of Saráchúk or Saraijik lie a short distance from the shore of the Caspian Sea, near Guryev, at the mouth of the Ural river.

[2] The name Khwárizm was applied throughout the middle ages to the principal town for the time being of Khorezmia, the district now known as Khiva. At this time it was the town of Kunya Urgench.

[3] The glass vessels and wooden spoons were for the use of those whose religious susceptibilities debarred them from using the gold utensils, which are reprobated by strict Muhammadans.

[4] Almaliq or Almaligh rose suddenly into prominence at the beginning of the thirteenth century, and was ruined in the civil wars between the successors of Tarmashírín in the Jaghatáy Khanate (see note 7), whose capital it was. It was situated in the valley of the Ili river, some distance N.W. of the modern town of Kulja.

[5] Kát or Káth, a former capital of Khorezmia, stood near the modern town of Shaykh Abbas Wali.

[6] The force of this indictment lies in the fact that Bukhárá was formerly one of the principal centres of theological study in the Islamic world.

[7] "Turkistan and the lands beyond the Oxus," whose sultan has been included in a previous passage among the seven great sovereigns of the world, was one of the four Mongol Khanates into which the empire of Chingiz-Khán and his successors was divided. Its rulers were known as the Jaghatáy-Kháns, after Jaghatáy, the son of Chingiz-Khán to whom this country was assigned as an appanage. Ibn Battúta relates a curious story of the fate of Tarmashírín. His conversion to Islam roused the ill-will of the nobles, who charged him with violating the precepts of Chingiz-Khán, and in 1335 or 1336 rose in revolt. Tarmashírín fled across the Oxus, but was captured and reported to have been put to death. Later on a man arrived in India, claiming to be Tarmashírín, but though his claim is said to have been substantiated, the sultan, for political reasons, rejected it and had him expelled. He eventually found a refuge at Shíráz, where he was still living in honourable confinement when Ibn Battúta revisited the town in 1347.

[8] Now known as *Sháh-Zinda*. The mausoleum is still one of the principal edifices of Samarqand.

[9] From 1245 Herát was ruled by the local dynasty of the Karts, which under this king Husayn (commonly called Mu'izz ad-Dín, reigned 1331-70) became an important power in Khurásán. As he was still a child at the time of Ibn Battúta's visit the following anecdote

---

[1] This chapter has been annotated by Defrémery in *Nouvelles Annales des Voyages*, January-July 1848.

probably relates to a period some nine or ten years later. Husayn's son Ghiyáth ad-Dín Pír Sháh became a vassal of Tamerlane in 1381, and on his death in 1389 the dynasty was extinguished.

[10] The penalty prescribed by Islamic Law for wine-drinking is forty stripes.

[11] The town, which lies S.E. of Meshhed, is now known as Shaykh Jám. The province of Khurásán, which Ibn Battúta had now entered, was at this time still under the rule of the Mongol sultan of Persia and 'Iráq, at least nominally.

[12] The name of Mashhad means literally *Mausoleum of ar-Ridá*, ar-Ridá being the title by which the *Imáms* of the Shi'ites are known. The Imám buried here is the eighth of the line, 'Alí ibn Músá, who died in 818 A.D. Caliph Hárún ar-Rashíd died at Tús in 809 while leading an expedition to the frontiers of Khurásán.

[13] Now Turbat-i Haydari, south of Meshhed. The order in which these towns are mentioned seems to be thoroughly confused, and Sarakhs in particular should come either between Jám and Tús, or else on the return journey from Bistám.

[14] Bistám lies S.E. of Asterabad, at the S.E. angle of the Caspian Sea.

[15] Here again there is a gap in the narrative, since from the Caspian Ibn Battúta leaps across to northern Afghanistan, where Qundúz lies on the river of the same name, and Baghlán on the same river some way to the south. The eastern half of Afghanistan as far south as Ghazna was at this time subject to the Jaghatáy-Kháns.

[16] Ibn Battúta followed the route across the Kháwak Pass (13,000 feet high), N.E. of Kábul.

[17] Mahmúd of Ghazna, who reigned from 998 to 1030, paved the way for the establishment of Muhammadan rule in Northern India by his merciless raids into Sind, Panjab, and the neighbouring provinces.

[18] It is impossible to determine, on the basis of this description, the actual route by which Ibn Battúta entered India. The tale about the Afghan highwaymen indicates a regular road, and Shásnaghár has been identified with Hashtnagar, near Peshawar; these statements together would point to the Khyber Pass. On the other hand the mention of a desert extending for fifteen days, together with Ibn Battúta's visit to Ghazna (erroneously inserted before Kábul) indicates some more obscure route through the Sulayman mountains, leading out to the lower course of the Indus.

NOTES

CHAPTER VI[1]

[1] The postal service (*barid*) in Muhammadan countries, as in classical times, was purely an official organization for the rapid transmission of state business, and could not, of course, be utilized by private citizens.

[2] The customs of the Sámira so clearly indicate their Hindu origin that their identification with the Arab Sámira must be regarded as a fictitious genealogy dating from their conversion to Islam. It appears that these Sámira are the Rajput Sammás, who about this time made themselves masters of Lower Sind. Janání therefore lay probably halfway between Rohri and Sehwan.

[3] The summer heats in Sind fall in the months of June and July, and as Ibn Battúta reached the Indus in September there would appear to be a gap of some nine months in the narrative. It is more probable, however, that his chronology is slightly out, or else that the party experienced an unusual spell of heat.

[4] Ibn Battúta explains below that the title *king* was given in India to governors of provinces and other high officials.

[5] The ruins of Láharí ("Larrybunder") lie on the northern side of the Ráho channel, some 28 miles S.E. of Karachi, by which it was supplanted about 1800 owing to the shoaling of its entrance. The expression "on the coast" must not be taken too literally, as the shore is uninhabitable to a depth of several miles owing to the constant inundations during the S.W. monsoons.

[6] The ruins described by Ibn Battúta have not been identified with certainty. Haig suggested that they might be those of Mora-mari, eight miles N.E. of Láharí, and it has also been suggested (first by Cunningham) that they were the ruins of Daybul or Debal, a former port on the Indus 45 miles E.S.E. of Karachi, which was captured and burned by the Arabs on their invasion of Sind in 710-715.

[7] Bakhar (Bukkur in the *Indian Gazetteer*) is a fortified island in the Indus, lying between the towns of Sukkur and Rohri.

[8] This stream was the old channel of the Rawi, which at this time joined the united Jhelum and Chinab below Multan.

[9] Ajúdahan should have come before Abohar.

[10] *Kusáy* can hardly represent Krishna, as the French translation suggests; more probably it stands for *gusá'í*, "religious teacher" ("also name of deity"—Platt's Hindustani Dictionary).

[1] Ibn Battúta's travels in Sind are discussed by M. R. Haig in *Journal of the Royal Asiatic Society*, 1887, pp. 393-412. The entire travels in India and China (covering Chapters VI to XI) have been translated and annotated by H. von Mžik, *Die Reise der Arabers Ibn Batuta durch Indien und China*, Hamburg, 1911.

[11] The ruins of Mas'údábád lie a mile east of Najafgarh, and six miles W. by N. of Palem station.

[12] The ruins of mediæval Delhi lie some ten miles south of the present city, Delhi proper, Jahán Panáh, and Sírí in a continuous line N.E. from Mahrauli, Tughlaqábád four miles east of Delhi proper and two miles east of modern Tuglakabad. This group of towns never recovered from the loss inflicted on it by Sultan Muhammad, as related below by Ibn Battúta, and again suffered severely from Tímúr (Tamerlane) in 1398. New Delhi was the creation of the Mogul sultan Sháh Jahán (1627-58).

Some account of the early Muhammadan sultans of Delhi will be found in the Introduction, pp. 22-24.

[13] Here, as also in his description of the Kutub Minár and 'Alá'í Minár below, Ibn Battúta's figures are exaggerated. The iron pillar of Chandragupta, which was brought from Muttra and set up at Delhi by its Hindu founder in the eleventh century, is 16 inches in diameter and 23 feet in height. The Kutub Minár is 238 feet high, the unfinished portion of the 'Alá'í Minar (wrongly attributed by Ibn Battúta to Qutb ad-Dín) 70 feet high, and neither is so wide as he represents it to be.

[14] The character of Sultan Muhammad ibn Tughlaq portrayed in this passage is strictly historical; see Introduction, p. 23.

[15] Dawlatábád or Deogiri lies in the N.W. corner of the state of Hyderabad (Deccan). Sultan Muhammad decided to make it his capital, in view of its importance as a base for military operations in Southern India, and twice (or thrice) attempted to remove thither the whole population of Delhi. By the irony of fortune, however, it was captured during his lifetime by the founder of the Muhammadan Bahmání dynasty of the Deccan. See also Chap. VII, note 7.

[16] In a previous section, omitted in this edition, Ibn Battúta relates at length the history of Shaykh Shiháb ad-Dín. He had incurred the sultan's displeasure first by refusing to take office under him, and spent some years in an underground dwelling he dug for himself near Delhi, and which contained several rooms, store-rooms, an oven and a bath. On being summoned again to the court he openly branded Muhammad Sháh as a traitor, and when he refused to retract his statement, was executed.

CHAPTER VII

[1] Yule has suggested that this is Sambhal in Rohilkhand, some eighty miles east of Delhi (*Cathay*, IV, 18).

[2] Jalálí is a small place 11 miles S.E. of Aligarh. The fact that the country within a hundred miles of Delhi was in so disturbed a state throws a curious light on the nature of Sultan Muhammad's "empire."

NOTES

[3] Mawri is possibly Umri, near Bhind. Marh is not known, but evidently lay east of Gwalior.

[4] There is a village of Alapur a few miles S.E. of Gwalior. Janbíl is probably the same name as the river Chambal, and the infidel sultan the Rajah of Dholpur.

[5] Parwán is almost certainly Narwar in Gwalior state (Ibn Battúta here as elsewhere rendering a strange name by one more familiar, namely Parwán in Afghanistan), which was, according to the *Indian Gazetteer*, "once a flourishing place on a route between Delhi and the Deccan." Modern maps show also a place called Parwai, 25 miles N.E. of Narwar and 30 S. of Gwalior.

As regards Kajarrá, there can be no question that this is Khajuraho, 27 miles E. of Chhatarpur and 25 N.W. of Panna, in spite of the detour which it involves on the journey. The description given by Ibn Battúta is in complete agreement with the description of the site contained in Sir Alexander Cunningham's Reports (*Archæological Survey of India, Reports for* 1862-5, Vol. II, pp. 412-439).

[6] If, as is probable, this is Dhar in Malwa, it should come after Ujjain.

[7] The fortress of Deogiri is described as follows in the *Indian Gazetteer*: "The fortress is built upon a conical rock, scarped from a height of 150 feet from the base. The hill upon which it stands rises almost perpendicularly from the plain to a height of about 600 feet." It was first captured by the Muhammadans in 1294, and Sultan Muhammad ibn Tughlaq, recognizing its importance as a base for operations in Southern India, renamed it Dawlatabad, and conceived the idea of making it his capital. Even before his death, however, it had been seized by a rebel governor, and it remained independent of Delhi until the reign of Akbar.

[8] Cambay, at the head of the Gulf of Cambay, was at this time one of the principal seaports of India. Its decline was due to the silting-up of the Gulf, and the bore of its tides, and it is now used only by small craft.

[9] Káwá, a small place on the opposite side of the bay from Cambay.

[10] Qandahár is certainly an Arabicization of Gandhar or Gundhar, known to medieval seamen as Gandar, on the estuary of the small river Dhandar a short distance south of Kawa.

The name Jalansi probably represents the Rajput tribal name Jhalas, still preserved in the name of the district of Jhalawar or Gohelwar in Kathiawar.

[11] The small island of Perim or Piram, near the mouth of the Gulf of Cambay, which was a notorious pirate stronghold until shortly before this time, when it was captured by the Muhammadans and deserted.

[12] Sandabúr or Sindabúr was the name by which the island and bay of Goa were known to the early Muslim traders, and taken from them by the first European travellers. The older name Goa did not

come into general use until the sixteenth century. It was captured by the Muhammadans for the first time in 1312, and was subsequently taken and retaken more than once.

13 The sites of these medieval ports, many of which no longer exist, are discussed by Yule, *Cathay*, IV, 72-79.

14 The name of this kingdom, Ili or Eli, has left a trace in *Mount Delly*. The medieval port is probably now represented by the village of Nileshwar, a few miles north of the promontory.

15 Calicut, which Ibn Battúta has already ranked (p. 46), as one of the great seaports of the world, decayed rapidly after the establishment of the Portuguese trading stations in the sixteenth century. The title of its ruler, called by Ibn Battúta the Sámarí (which is an adaptation to Muslim ears of a foreign name, Sámarí being a word familiar to theologians as the legendary ancestor of the Samaritans), is the Malayalam word *Sámútiri* or *Sámúri* meaning "Sea-king," more familiar to European readers in its Portuguese form Zamorin.

16 The purpose of these was to tow the junk in calm weather, as Ibn Battúta explains below (p. 278).

17 Although a considerable part of the distance between Calicut and Quilon may be traversed by inland waterways, it does not seem possible to go the whole way by water. Ibn Battúta here, as again in the description of his travels in China, neglects the land stages.

18 Quilon, ranked by Ibn Battúta with Calicut, was from very early times the transhipment port for the Chinese trade. It is mentioned by the Arab and Persian sailors of the ninth century under the name of Kawlam-Malay, and fell into decay, like its rival Calicut, in the sixteenth century. Yule suggests that the title *Tírawarí* given by Ibn Battúta to its ruler may be the Tamil-Sanskrit compound *Tiru-pati* "Holy Lord" (*Cathay*, IV, 40).

19 "Always a sign that things were going badly with Ibn Battúta" (Yule).

20 Shálíyát, the Portuguese Chiliate or Chale, now Beypore, 6½ miles south of Calicut. The fabrics manufactured here were of various kinds, and the name *shali* is still used for a soft cotton fabric. It is possible that the name of this town is the origin of the French *châle*, and hence our *shawl*.

CHAPTER VIII

1 Although the Maldive Islands had long been known to sailors and travellers, and had become Islamized in the twelfth century, Ibn Battúta's narrative is the earliest descriptive account we possess of the islands and their inhabitants. Many of his names can still be traced on the map.

2 Maldive *kalu-bili-mas*, black bonito fish, from its black appearance after smoking.

NOTES

[3] The "mountain of Serendíb" is Adam's Peak. Serendíb is the old Arabic and Persian name of Ceylon (commonly derived from the Sanskrit *Simhala-dvipa*, Lion-dwelling-island), which was gradually replaced by the Pali form Sihalam=Saylan=Ceylon.

[4] The old Sinhalese kingdom of Ceylon was invaded about 1314 by the Pandyas, whose own kingdom at Madura in Ma'bar, which had existed since at least the third century B.C., was now in the hands of the Muhammadans. The leader of the invaders was Arya Chakravarti, but Ibn Battúta's patron was more probably a later general of the same name, who in 1371 erected forts at Colombo and elsewhere. The seat of the Pandyas was in the island of Jaffna.

[5] The hollow on the summit of Adam's Peak, venerated by the Muslims as the imprint of Adam's foot, was equally venerated by the Brahmans and the Buddhists, as the mark of Siva's and Buddha's foot respectively.

[6] Kunakár is certainly Kornegalle (Kurunagala), the residence of the old dynasty of Sinhalese kings at this period. The name Kunar is explained as Sanskrit *Kunwar*, "Prince."

[7] These chains are still in existence.

[8] Dínawar (which is properly the name of a medieval town in Kurdistan, to the N.E. of Kirmanshah) here stands for Dewandera, the site of a famous temple of Vishnu (destroyed by the Portuguese in 1587), near Dondra Head, the southermost point of Ceylon.

CHAPTER IX[1]

[1] Harkátú cannot be the modern town of Arcot, which lies too far north. As it was only a fort its location is very doubtful, though the name is probably connected with the district of Arcot (Tamil *aru-kadu*, six forests).

[2] Jalál ad-Dín, who had been appointed by Sultan Muhammad of Delhi to the post of military governor of Ma'bar (which had been occupied by the Muhammadans in 1311), made himself independent about 1338, and was murdered five years later. The throne was then occupied by a succession of generals, of whom Ghiyáth ad-Dín was the third.

[3] Of the many *-patans* and *-patams* of the Coromandel coast, it is difficult to determine exactly the original of this Fattan. The principal port of medieval Ma'bar was Kaveripattanam, at one of the mouths of the Kaveri, said to have been destroyed by an inundation about 1300. If this was Ibn Battúta's Fattan, its destruction must

---

[1] The sections dealing with Bengal, the Archipelago, and China have been annotated by Sir Henry Yule in *Cathay and the Way Thither*, new edition revised by H. Cordier, Vol. IV, Hakluyt Society, London, 1916.

be dated nearer 1350 (see *Marco Polo*, II, 335-6). Fattan may, however, have been Negapatam, which was an important harbour in after centuries. Yule's conjecture that the place must be farther south, in the neighbourhood of Ramnad, is unlikely if the name Harkátú has anything to do with Arcot (see note 1). At some time during his visit to Ma'bar, on the other hand, or else on his journey from Fattan to Kawlam, Ibn Battúta must have called at the small port of Kaylúkarí, 10 miles S. of Ramnad, which he afterwards transported to somewhere in the China Sea (see Chap. X, note 9). It is strange that Ibn Battúta does not mention the port of Káyal, Marco Polo's *Cail*, situated in the delta of the Tamraparni river, south of Tuticorin, which was a very important trading station at this time (see *Marco Polo*, II, 370-4).

[4] This is identified, following Yule, with the Pigeon Island, 25 miles south of Onore (Hinawr).

[5] This statement is impossible to reconcile with any chronology of Ibn Battúta's travels in the Far East. Judging by the course of the narrative, this second visit cannot have been made later than a year after his departure from the Maldive Islands.

[6] Sudkáwán is identified by some authorities with Satgaon (Satganw), a ruined town on the Hooghly lying N.W. of Hooghly town, which was the mercantile capital of Bengal from the days of Hindu rule until the foundation of Hooghly by the Portuguese. Yule, with more probability, identified it with Chittagong (Chatganw), which was a more convenient port than Satgaon, and is "on the shores of the Great Sea," as described by Ibn Battúta. There seems, however, to be some uncertainty whether Sultan Fakhr ad-Din had any connection with Chittagong (*cf. Book of Duarte Barbosa*, II, 139).

[7] Jún, which is Ibn Battúta's transcription for the Jumna, here obviously represents the Brahmaputra (*cf.* p. 52).

[8] Lakhnaoti (Lakshmanawati), the ancient name of the town of Gawr, long the capital of the Muhammadan governors of Bengal after its conquest in 1204, the ruins of which are situated near Maldah. The name was retained for one of the three districts of Bengal (see note 11), covering the area between the Ganges and the Brahmaputra.

[9] It has been fully established by Yule (*Cathay*, IV, 151-5), that the district visited by Ibn Battúta was Sylhet, where the tomb of *Shah Jelal* (=Shaykh Jalál ad-Dín) is still venerated. The name Kámrú, more correctly Kámrúb (for Kámarúpa), was applied to the district roughly corresponding to Assam, whose Indo-Chinese population (Khasis, etc.) present the usual Mongolian characteristics.

[10] The Blue River can only be the Meghna, and on the left bank of the Barak, one of its headwaters, there is still a *tillah*, or low hill, called Habang, a little to the south of Habiganj.

[11] Sonargaon (Sunarganw), 15 miles S.E. of Dacca, was one of the old Muhammadan capitals of Bengal, and gave its name to one of the three districts of Bengal, the third being Satganw.

NOTES

CHAPTER X[1]

[1] Barah Nakár, formerly identified, on account of the description given by Ibn Battúta of the natives, with the Andaman or Nicobar Islands, has been shown by Yule to have been more probably on the mainland of Arakan, in Burma, near the island of Negrais. But the text of Ibn Battúta appears to make Barah Nakár the name of the people rather than that of the country (*Cathay*, IV, 92; *Marco Polo*, II, 309-12).

[2] The name Jáwa was applied generally to the Malay Archipelago, Jáwa " the less " being the island of Sumatra, and Jáwa " the greater " or Jáwa proper the island now called Java. The introduction of Islam into Sumatra was effected gradually by traders and missionaries from Southern India during the thirteenth century. The beginnings of Muslim rule in the island date from the last decade of the same century, probably a few years before the foundation of the town of Sumatra. Al-Malik az-Záhir was a title borne by several of the Muslim rulers.

[3] On the jack-tree see Yule and Burnell, *Hobson-Jobson*.

[4] The jamún is a small fruit resembling an olive but sweet, as Ibn Battúta explains in an earlier passage. It is not the same as the jambú or rose-apple. See *Hobson-Jobson* under both entries.

[5] I suspect the word translated " houses " to refer to some kind of official establishments. In strict grammar the word *sarhá* may be taken to refer to the " houses " (as in the translation), but is more probably the name of the port.

[6] Mul-Jáwa has usually been taken to mean the island of Java, but Yule adduces several cogent reasons for identifying it with the Malay Peninsula. In accordance with this view the port and city of Qáqula are to be placed on the east coast of the Malay Peninsula, in the neighbourhood of Kelantan.

Qamára is almost certainly Khmer, the ancient name of Cambodia, on the opposite side of the gulf of Siam (*Cathay*, IV, 155).

[7] This somewhat aggressive phrase was the regular formula of greeting to non-Muslims (*cf.* p. 214), the words *as-Salám 'Alaykum* (" Peace be upon you ") being strictly applicable only to true believers, although, as we have seen, Ibn Battúta occasionally took the liberty of infringing this rule (p. 159).

[8] The " motionless sea," which in this passage Ibn Battúta calls by the Arabo-Persian name *al-bahr al-káhil*, is referred to by other

[1] Ibn Battúta's travels in the Indian Archipelago have been annotated also by E. Dulaurier, in *Journal Asiatique*, February-March, 1847, and by G. Ferrand, in *Textes arabes, etc., relatifs à l'Extrême-Orient*, t. II (Paris, 1914), pp. 436-455.

contemporary writers under varying names (*e.g.*, the pitchy sea, the sea of darkness) as lying in the extreme east. It seems therefore to correspond to our China Sea or some of the neighbouring waters. The following words in Ibn Battúta's narrative show that it was on the regular route.

[9] The problem of identifying the king Tawálisí and his city of Kaylúkarí is one that has exercised the ingenuity of all Ibn Battúta's commentators. Celebes, Tonkin, Cambodia, Cochin-China, the province of Kwan-si, the Philippine Islands, and the Sulu Archipelago have all been suggested. Yule accepts the last solution as more probable than any other, but only after confessing to " a faint suspicion . . . that Tawálisí is really to be looked for in that part of the atlas which contains the marine surveys of the late Captain Gulliver." The most surprising detail in the narrative is not the existence of the princess of amazonian characteristics, but her Turkish name (already given by Ibn Battúta as the name of Sultan Uzbeg-Khán's fourth queen, see above p. 148) and Turkish speech. Yule, followed by Dr. von Mžik, suggests that the details of her prowess may be derived from the story of Kaydú-Khán's valiant daughter Aijaruc, which Ibn Battúta may have heard from some of the ship's folk. Aijaruc is in fact a Turkish name, and it is quite probable that Ibn Battúta, whose memory for strange names was not of the best, confused it with the similar-sounding Urdujá. In the same way Kaylúkarí was really the name of a seaport in S.E. India (see Chap. IX, note 3), which Ibn Battúta has confused with the name of king " Tayálisí's " port (*Cathay*, IV, 157-60 ; *Marco Polo*, II, 465 ; G. Ferrand, *Textes relatifs à l'Extrême-Orient*, 431-3).

CHAPTER XI

[1] The description of this great river, traversing China from north to south and flowing into the sea at Canton, has sometimes been taken to prove that Ibn Battúta's journey to China, or at least in China, is a pure fiction. It must, however, be borne in mind that he knew no more of China than the fringe which he himself visited, supplemented by what he could gather from various (and doubtless not always reliable) informants, and in this passage he is merely reproducing the common view of his time. The " River of Life " is, in its first section, the Grand Canal, between Peking and the Yang-tsi. The merchants on the coast knew vaguely of the inland water system connecting Hang-chow and the Yang-tsi with the West River and Canton, probably by way of the Siang-kiang, and consequently regarded the estuary of the Pei-kiang as that of the entire system. There is greater difficulty in explaining Ibn Battúta's statements that Zaytún (Ts'wan-chow-fu) was linked by inland waterways with both Canton and Hang-chow, where presumably he was speaking from personal experience. As

we have seen above, however, in connection with his land journey between Cálicút and Quilon (Chap. VII, note 17), Ibn Battúta simply omits all reference to the land stages as secondary, or he may possibly have forgotten about them in the ten years that intervened between his visit to China and the dictation of his travels. It is not irrelevant to note that other writers, including even some Chinese sources, also speak of Zaytún as being on the same water system as Hang-chow (Khansá or Quinsay). (See in addition to Yule and von Mžik, R. Hartmann in *Der Islam*, IV, 434.)

[2] Friar Odoric of Pordenone also remarks, in connection with Fuchow, " Here be seen the biggest cocks in the world " ; but he says of the geese at Canton that they are " bigger and finer and cheaper than anywhere in the world " (*Cathay*, II, 181, 185).

[3] An earlier traveller (*Voyage du Marchand arabe Sulayman . . . en* 851, tr. G. Ferrand, p. 55) tells us that the Chinese buried their dead, as they do at the present day. Marco Polo, however, constantly refers to the practice of cremation, which must therefore have been a common custom in China at this period.

[4] The *bálisht* or *bálish*, originally an ingot of metal weighing about 4½ lbs., was the currency of the steppes at the beginning of the thirteenth century. The term was probably brought into China by the Mongols. On Chinese paper-money see *Marco Polo*, I, 423 *ff*.

[5] According to Marco Polo, the owner of used notes paid three per cent. on the value on receiving new pieces (I, 425).

[6] Cathay (*Khitáy*), a term employed first by the Muhammadans and from them by European travellers and missionaries from the thirteenth to the sixteenth centuries, denoted the northern part of China, in contrast to *Sín* or China proper in the south. The name was certainly derived from the Kitáy or Khitáy Turks, who founded a dynasty (the Liao) which reigned at Peking during the tenth and eleventh centuries. The name Sín or Chín (China) is, in all probability, to be derived similarly from the *Ts'in* dynasty (255-209 B.C.).

[7] In this passage Ibn Battúta obviously confuses coal and porcelain clay, possibly owing to a custom followed in China of powdering the coal and mixing it with clay to form " patent fuel " (see *Marco Polo*, I, 442-3).

[8] It is generally admitted that the city known to all Muhammadan and Christian travellers in the Middle Ages as Zaytún is Ts'wan-chow-fu (Chüan-chow-fu, 24.53 N., 118.33 E.). The arguments in favour of this identification, together with an examination of the claims of Chang-chow-fu (Amoy), will be found *in extenso* in *Marco Polo*, II, 237 *ff*.

[9] Yule adduces some strong arguments for the derivation of *satin* from *zaytúní* through medieval Italian *zettani* (*Cathay*, IV, 118).

[10] Sijilmása was in the neighbourhood of Tafilelt, in Southern Morocco; see below, Chap. XIV, note 1.

[11] I take the *díwán* mentioned in this passage to be, not the "Council" (whatever organization that may have been), but the institution commonly known by that name in North Africa and Egypt in all ports open to foreign commerce, from which originated the Italian *dogane* and French *douane*. It was at one and the same time custom-house, warehouse, lodging house and bourse for foreign merchants (for which reason Ibn Battúta is lodged in it), and its controller was one of the principal officers of the realm (see Mas Latrie, *Relations et Commerce de l'Afrique Septentrionale*, 335 *ff*.). A similar organization appears to be indicated in the Chinese ports. A few lines below Ibn Battúta says of Canton that it was "in the province" of the controller of the *díwán*, probably in the sense that the trading station there was also under his jurisdiction.

[12] The sense of this passage is quite clear. According to the Koran, the legal alms are to be given to "parents, kindred, orphans, the poor, and the wayfarer." The Muhammadan community at Zaytún was so wealthy that the only one of these five classes to which the alms were of any value was the last.

[13] The Arabic and Persian writers (like Marco Polo) conventionally use the term *Qán* or *Qa'án* for the "Great Khan" of the Mongols. It is not, however, as Yule considered, a different title from the ordinary Turkish title *Kháqán* (see Shiratori, *Memoirs of Research Dept. of the Toyo Bunko*, No. 1, Tokyo, 1926, pp. 19-26).

[14] Sín-kalán is an Arabicized form of the Persian Chín-kalán, for Sanscrit Mahácína=Great China, which is also the meaning of the Arabic name Sín as-Sín.

[15] The text is defective at this point, due either to the miswriting of a word, or to the omission of another word.

[16] Ibn Battúta's route "up the river" from Ts'wan-chow to Canton is, in the nature of things, uncertain. Yule thinks of a route up the Min from Foochow, and down the upper reaches of the Kan to the Pei-kiang *via* the Mei-ling Pass. It seems a peculiarly roundabout journey, when much more direct communication is offered by the Mei and the Tung, if these are navigable.

[17] This temple has not been identified with any certainty. Yule suggests that it is the *Temple of Glory and Filial Duty*, near the N.W. corner of the modern city.

[18] The site of the Rampart of Gog and Magog, the building of which is described in the Koran and attributed to Alexander the Great, was a standing problem to the Arabic geographers. It was generally regarded as lying at the north-eastern end of the habitable world, and was vaguely confused with the Great Wall of China. But Ibn Battúta could have had no idea that China was *within* the Wall, and his question appears to have been put at random, perhaps on hearing some chance reference to the Great Wall.

Marco Polo also speaks of a race of cannibals in the mountains between Fukien and Kiang-si or Che-kiang (II, 225; *cf.* H. Schmidt-thenner in *Zeitschrift der Ges. für Erdkunde zu Berlin*, 1927, p. 388).

[19] The identification of Qan-jan-fú is still uncertain. If Ibn Battúta is correct in placing it between Zaytún and Khansá, its position will depend on the route which he followed. Yule identified it with Kien-chang-fu on the Fu-ho in the province of Kiang-si, and the next station Baywam Qutlú with the Po-yang Sea. The objections to this identification are that (1) it involves a very roundabout journey to Hang-chow, and would indeed cut out Hang-chow altogether; (2) there is no evidence for the existence of a frequented trade-route (such as Ibn Battúta's route is represented to be) through Kien-chang-fu.

Since Ibn Battúta took 31 days for the journey to Hang-chow, while Marco Polo took 27, travelling in the reverse direction, there are very good grounds for assuming that their routes were substantially the same. In this case the most natural identification for Qan-jan-fú is Fuchow. In favour of this are: (1) the size of the city, with a governor of its own and a large garrison (which corresponds very well with Marco Polo's description); (2) the arrival of "a very large vessel" at the port, since Marco Polo expressly states that "From Zayton ships come this way right up to the city of Fuju by the river I have told you of, and 'tis in this way that the precious wares of India come hither." The name which Marco Polo gives to the district of Fuchow, Chonka or Concha (the proper name of the city being Chin-kiang), may possibly explain the transformation into Qan-jan-fú. On the other hand, Marco Polo allows only five days from Fuchow to Zaytún, which would suggest some place further up the Min river (on the navigability of the Min see *Marco Polo*, II, 234).

Dulaurier suggested that Qan-jan-fú may stand for Chin-kiang-fu at the junction of the Yang-tsi and the Grand Canal, in which case it should come between Khansá and Khán-báliq (Peking). Similar instances of misplacing are, as will have been noticed, not infrequent with Ibn Battúta, but Chin-kiang-fu scarcely seems large enough to fit his description. M. Ferrand takes Qan-jan-fú to be Marco Polo's Kenjanfu, the old capital of China, now Si-an-fu on the Wei river in Shen-si, which was called Khumdán by the Arabic geographers. This identification, however, hangs together with M. Ferrand's thesis that Ibn Battúta did not go to China at all. It is safest to assume either that Qan-jan-fú was a name used by the Muslim merchants for Fuchow (like Zaytún for Ts'wan-chow), or that Ibn Battúta has confused two similar-sounding names.

[20] The Ghúta is the name given to the wide plain covered with fruit-trees around Damascus.

[21] It would be a waste of time to search for anything corresponding to this name on a modern map of China, and its position can be determined only by reference to the other towns mentioned. It is quite

possible that it was not a place-name at all, but the name of some Turko-Tatar commander (? Bayán Qutlugh="Bayan the Lucky") which Ibn Battúta erroneously took to be the name of a town.

[22] It is agreed by all travellers, both Christian and Muslim, that what Marco Polo calls "the most noble city of Kinsay . . . beyond dispute the finest and noblest in the world" was indeed the largest city in the world in the fourteenth century. The admiration it aroused lent itself to exaggeration, and when even Marco Polo avers that "it hath an hundred miles of compass. And there are in it twelve thousand bridges of stone, for the most part so lofty that a great fleet could pass beneath them," it is not to be wondered at that in Ibn Battúta's account there are, in Yule's phrase, "several very questionable statements." The name Khansá is an Arabic modification (to accord with the name of a famous Arabic poetess), as Kinsay, Cansay, Cassay, etc., are European modifications, of the Chinese *King-sze* "Capital," Hang-chow having been the capital of the Sung synasty from 1127 to 1276.

[23] The word translated *citadel* means "inner city occupied by the ruler or governor." The viceroy's palace was not in the centre of Hang-chow, however, but at the southern end.

[24] In the *Chain of Histories* we are told that "On reaching the age of eighty a man is exempted from paying the poll-tax, and receives a grant from the imperial treasury. The Chinese say of this "We made him pay the tax when he was young; now that he is old we will give him a pension'" (Ferrand, *Voyage du marchand Sulayman*, p. 63).

[25] Qurtay appears to be a contraction of Qarátáy, a common Turkish title, but no governor of this name is mentioned in Chinese works, so far as is known. It is probable that it was the title given to the commander by the Turkish troops, like many other of the terms employed by Ibn Battúta in this section, which are not Chinese but Turkish or Persian. In the same way he gives as the name of the Emperor his Perso-Turkish title of "king"; see below, note 32.

[26] *Towa* or *tuwi* is a Turkish word meaning feast or festival.

[27] Yule, remarking that the "pretty cadence" is precisely that of

We won't go home till morning,

gives a "somewhat free" rendering:

My heart given up to emotions,
Was o'erwhelmed in waves like the ocean's;
But betaking me to my devotions,
My troubles were gone from me!

The last line of the poem, however, neither reads nor scans properly.

[28] Marco Polo also speaks at length of pleasure parties on the lake, but does not mention mimic battles (II, 205).

[29] This statement is justifiably challenged by Yule, who regards

it as " so contrary to fact, that one's doubts arise whether Ibn Battúta could have travelled beyond Hang-chau " (*Cathay*, IV, 137).

[30] Peking, called by the Mongols Khán-Báliq, " City of the Khán," the Cambalu and Cambuluc of Western writers. The name *Khániqú* has been explained as an adjective, "(City) of the Khán" (*Journal Asiatique*, May 1913, p. 701).

[31] See Chap. II, note 12.

[32] Probably a corruption of the Persian *pádsháh*, " king " (see note 25). The reigning Emperor was Togon Timur (reigned 1333-71).

[33] Qaráqorum, the first capital of the Mongols, the site of which is now occupied by the monastery of Erdeni-tso, lay above the right bank of the Orkhon river, about 200 miles W.S.W. of Urga and 20 miles S.E. of Karabalgasun, in Outer Mongolia.

Bíshbáliq was situated on or near the present Guchen, to the east of Urumtsi in Dzungaria.

[34] Ibn Battúta here gives an accurate account of the ceremonial observed at the burial of a Tatar chief, but it is obvious that it cannot have been the Emperor's burial which he witnessed, if indeed the narrative is at firsthand.

[35] As this Fírúz appears to be totally unknown, and as the seat of the Great Kháns was not removed to Qaráqorum until after the death of Togon Timur in 1371 (if the Chinese records are true), the existence of this passage in a book of which a copy written in 1356 is still extant is a problem better suited for investigation by the Psychic Society than by the matter-of-fact historian.

CHAPTER XII

[1] The rukh is sufficiently well known in Europe, thanks to Sindbad the Sailor, to need no explanation. Yule has written in connection with Marco Polo's account (II, 415-20) a long note discussing possible originals for this gigantic bird. One or two Arabic writers had already shown some scepticism on the subject, and Ibn Battúta, it will be noticed, is prudently non-committal. His narrative certainly suggests the part played by mirage or abnormal refraction in giving currency to this widespread story.

[2] Qurayyát (Quryát) still appears on our maps; Shabba and Kalba are not shown, at least under these names, but are probably still in existence, as there is an almost continuous belt of villages along the coast of 'Omán.

[3] Kárzí or Kárzín lay on the right bank of the Sakkán (Mund) river, a little above its eastward bend. Ibn Battúta's route lay up the valley of the river from this point to Shíráz. On the main road between Bassá (Fasá) and Shíráz was the town of Khawristán, which may possibly be Ibn Battúta's Kawrástán (see Chap. III, note 22).

NOTES

[4] In 1340 the Moorish Sultan Abu'l-Hasan led an army into Spain, which was totally defeated by Alphonso XI of Castile at the Rio Salado, near Tarifa, on 30th October of the same year. Alphonso followed up his victory by the capture of Algeciras in 1342, but died in 1350 while attempting to retake Gibraltar. The siege of Gibraltar on that occasion is referred to by Ibn Battúta in the following chapter.

[5] The relations between Shaykh Hasan and Sultan Abú Sa'íd have already been explained by Ibn Battúta (above, p. 100). This Shaykh Hasan "the Great," after an eight-years' struggle with his rival Shaykh Hasan "the Little," grandson of the Amír Chúbán, founded the Jalá'ir or Ilkání dynasty, which continued to rule in 'Iráq and Adharbayján until the early years of the fifteenth century.

[6] Hít and Ána still appear on our maps, on the Euphrates to the N.W. of Baghdad. Hadítha, now called Qal'at Habulia, was about 35 miles below Ána, and Anbár, formerly one of the principal cities of 'Iráq, some distance below Hít, at the head of the Ísá canal, the first of the great navigable canals uniting the Euphrates with the Tigris. The district of Hít was especially remarkable for its immense quantities of fruit and its dense population.

[7] Rahba lay some eighteen miles below the junction of the Khábúr river with the Euphrates and west of the river, on a loop canal.

[8] Sukhna is an important station on the routes between the Middle Euphrates and Palmyra, about 35 miles N.E. of the latter.

[9] See note 28 to Chap. I.

[10] A large town now in Turkey, 55 miles N. by E. of Aleppo.

[11] This plague was the famous "Black Death," which wrought indescribable havoc in the Muslim lands during this year, and is probably to be accounted a catastrophe no less overwhelming than the invasions of the Mongols and Tamerlane. Ibn Battúta's figures are not greatly exaggerated; indeed some estimates are much higher. The historian Ibn Khaldún, whose father was one of the victims at Tunis, speaks of it as "the devouring pestilence which ravaged the nations and carried off the men of this generation, which destroyed and effaced many of the fair fruits of civilization. . . . Cities and palaces were laid in ruins, roads and waymarks were obliterated. . . . It was as though the voice of creation itself had summoned the world to abasement and contraction, and the earth had hastened to obey."

[12] The Marínid dynasty of Morocco. See Introduction, p. 19.

[13] "The enemy" unquestionably means the Christians, but the phrase does not, in all probability, refer to any organized maritime warfare. The only Christian state which was not at this time on friendly terms with Tunis was Sicily, whose admiral Roger Doria had captured Jerba about 1289. In 1335 it, along with the other islands, was recovered by the Muslims, and some ineffectual attempts upon it were made in the succeeding decades by the Sicilians. It is more likely that the vessel fell into the hands of Christian pirates, whose

ravages in the Mediterranean during these centuries were (in Mas Latrie's view) even greater than those of the Barbary pirates (*Relations de l'Afrique septentrionale*, pp. 404-7).

[14] Bulyána does not appear in any medieval or modern works that I have been able to consult. I should hazard that the place meant is Nábeul, a small port 30 miles S.E. of Tunis, where, according to Idrísí, there was a fortress.

[15] The description of the harbour makes it certain that the port was Cagliari, which, as it belonged at this time to Aragon, was a natural port of call for Catalan vessels. It is described in the Rizzo Portolan as "bon porto fato per forza de palangade." The fear felt by Ibn Battúta for his safety is explained by the piratical activities of its inhabitants ("Les faubourgs de Cagliari servaient de repaire aux forbans": Mas Latrie, *ibid.*, 405).

[16] The village of al-'Ubbád, usually called Sídí Bú Madín after the sanctuary, lies a mile east of Tlemsen. The mosque, built in 1339, is the finest example of Moorish architecture in Algeria.

[17] The Azghanghán (Azgangan in Leo Africanus) were a Berber tribe settled near the coast between Melilla and the Mulúya river.

[18] This statement is confirmed by the geographer 'Omarí, who relates that the *mithqál* (=dinar) of gold contained 120 dirhams, equal to 60 full dirhams, and that three full dirhams were equal to one dirham of good money (*nuqra*) in Egypt and Syria. The word "dirham" used without qualification, he adds, means "small dirham." The large gold dinar of the Marínids weighed 87 grains, valued at 14.50 francs; the small gold dinar of the Almoravids 65 grains, valued at 10.93 francs. Ibn Battúta constantly refers to the Indian gold tangah, which contained 175 grains, as worth 2½ Moroccan dinars, a proportion which fits the small dinar much better than the large. The small dirham at 120 to the gold dinar of the Marínids had an absolute value of 12 centimes; if the Almoravid dinar is meant it would be worth nine centimes. The highest estimate of the value of the dirham *nuqra* of Egypt is in the neighbourhood of 75 centimes, and it is more usually put at between 50 and 60 centimes (Yule, *Cathay*, IV, 54 *ff.*; Massignon, *Le Maroc dans les premières années du XVIe siècle* (Alger, 1906), 101-2; al-'Omarí, *Masálik al-Absár*, tr. Demombynes (Paris, 1927), I, 173).

[19] The phrase is again a reminiscence of Solomon; see Chap. I, note 28.

[20] I take this to refer to the popular *mulúkhiya* (*Corchorus olitorius*) of Egypt.

[21] The *Imámate* in this sense is the Caliphate. Ibn Battúta means that the dignity of the West has been enhanced by the assumption of the Caliph's title *Commander of the Faithful* by the rulers of Morocco, and in particular by Abú 'Inán. For the same reason he gives him, a few lines back, the throne-title *al-Mutawakkil*, adopted by the sultan

in imitation of the Caliphs of Baghdad. There was no universal Caliphate at this time, the nominal Caliphs at Cairo not being recognized in the west. The sultans of Morocco have retained the title to the present day.

CHAPTER XIII

[1] For Alphonso XI and the siege of Gibraltar see Chap. XII, note 4. The unusually bitter tone of this chapter reflects the temper which animated both Moors and Spaniards during the reconquest of Andalusia, and for centuries afterwards.

[2] Suhayl, which is not mentioned in Idrísí, is described by Maqqarí (I, 103) as "a large district to the west of Malaqa containing numerous villages. Within it is the mountain of Suhayl, which is the only mountain in Andalus from which the constellation of Suhayl (Canopus) can be seen." From Ibn Battúta's account it is clear that it comprised the stretch of coast between Marbella and Malaga.

[3] Al-Hamma, *i.e.*, Hot Springs, or Thermæ, a place-name which occurs very frequently in all Arabic countries. A contemporary of Ibn Battúta describes the town as follows: "The castle of al-Hamma is situated on the summit of a mountain, and those who have travelled all over the world declare that there is no place on earth that can compare with it for solidity of construction and for the warmth of its water. Sick persons from all parts visit it and stay there until their diseases are relieved. In the spring the inhabitants of Almeria go there with their wives and families and spend large amounts on food and drink" (*Masálik al-Absár*).

[4] The locality "preserves to this day its Arabic name, corrupted into Dinamar or Adinamar. It is a pleasant and much frequented spot close to Granada" (Pascual de Gayangos, *History of the Muhammadan Dynasties in Spain*, I, 349).

[5] Sultan Abu'l-Hajjáj Yúsuf I, the seventh ruler of the Nasrid dynasty of Granada, reigned from 1333 to 1354. The nature of his malady does not appear to be mentioned by other writers. As Ibn Battúta did not visit him, it is probable that he did not see the interior of the Alhambra. It would have been interesting to have his opinion of its architectural features as compared with other contemporary palaces.

[6] The reading Bíra, which is found in one manuscript, is preferable to the reading Tíra, adopted in the printed text. No place of the name of Tíra seems to be mentioned in any Spanish Arabic work. Al-Bíra is the ancient Elvira, which was supplanted in the Moorish period by Granada, and lay fifteen miles to the west of the latter. The ruinous condition in which Ibn Battúta found it was possibly the result of the battle of Elvira, in which the Muslims defeated the Castilians in 1319. The town must have been rebuilt later on, since it is mentioned again

in the history of Ferdinand's final campaign against Granada, as having been captured by him in 1486 (Pascual de Gayangos, II, 350-1, 377; Maqqarí, II, 805; *al-'Omari* tr. Demombynes, p. 245).

[7] Dhakwán or Zakwán is mentioned by an early writer as a village to the west of Málaqa, and on its capture by Ferdinand in 1485 is described as a fortified town with a fairly large population (Ibn al-'Abbár, *Takmila*, 348; P. de Gayangos, II, 374; Maqqarí, II, 803).

[8] Marrákush was founded in 1077 as the capital of the Almoravid dynasty. It was, according to Idrísí, more than a mile long and about as much in breadth. The city wall, which still stands, is about seven miles in length. After its siege and capture by the Marínids and the transference of the capital to Fez, it fell into decay. The minaret of the Kutubíya mosque is still in existence, and is justly admired as one of the finest monuments of Moorish art.

CHAPTER XIV[1]

[1] Between the eighth and the sixteenth centuries Sijilmása was the principal trading station south of the Atlas mountains. The ruins of the ancient town lie on the Wádí Zíz, over a distance of five miles, in the neighbourhood of the modern Tafilelt.

[2] The saline of Tagháza lies to the N.W. of Taodeni. On account of its salt it formed an important outpost of the negro empires.

[3] The Wadi Dra, which drains the southern slopes of the Anti-Atlas.

The name Massúfa appears to have been given at this time to the Sanhája, who, with the Lamtúna, have been from time immemorial the principal stocks in the western Sahara. From Ibn Battúta's account the Massúfa occupied the entire central Sahara from Tagháza to Timbuktu, and eastwards as far as Air and the Hoggar.

[4] The phrase used in the text (which may be rendered *cantars encantared*) is taken from the Koran, where it means "untold wealth."

[5] Tásarahlá probably corresponds to Idrísí's well of Tísar, in the desert of Azawwad (Cooley, 14-15).

---

[1] Ibn Battúta's travels in the Sahara and Niger territories were first elucidated (on the basis of a very imperfect text) by W. D. Cooley, *The Negroland of the Arabs*, London, 1841. The full text was translated and annotated by de Slane in *Journal Asiatique*, March 1843. The material is very fully rehandled by M. Delafosse, *Haut-Sénégal-Niger*, Paris, 1912 (quoted in the following notes as *H.S.N.*; an abridged account of Ibn Battúta is contained in tome II, pp. 194-203), and by J. Marquart in the Introduction to *Die Benin-Sammlung . . . in Leiden*, Leiden, 1913.

[6] Íwálátan is the plural of Waláta, the place consisting, according to Leo Africanus, of three hamlets. Modern maps show two places called Walata; Ibn Battúta's Íwálátan is the southern one at 17.02 N., 6.44 W. It took the place of Ghána as the southern terminus of the trans-Saharan trade-route in the thirteenth century (see note 21 below), being built (according to Hartmann, *Mit. Sem. Or. Stud.*, XV^3, 162) on the site of the old Berber town of Audaghusht.

[7] The baobab tree (*Adansonia digitata*), which rapidly attains a very great girth, is frequently artificially hollowed for the storage of water, and thus enables settlements to be made in places where there are no wells. These trees were introduced for that purpose into the Eastern Sudan (Kordofan) from West Africa in the eighteenth century, but from Ibn Battúta's description it would appear that artificial hollowing was not yet practised there.

[8] Kuskusú (in French *couss-couss*), the ordinary cereal dish in N.W. Africa, is made by steaming coarsely-ground flour, and is served up with savoury or sweet condiments.

[9] Zágharí, identified by Delafosse with Dioura, has been shown by Lippert to be identical with the village called by Barth Ture-ssangha, S.S.E. of Ba-ssikunnu or Bacikounou (*Barth's Travels*, Engl. ed., 1857-8, V, 481; *Mit. Sem. Or. St.*, III^3, 198-9).

[10] Wangara (Wankore, Wakore) is one of the names given by the Peuls (Fulani) and Songhay to the people called the Soninke (called by the Portuguese Sarakole), and used by extension to mean both Soninke and Malinke, thus being equivalent to the modern use of the term Mande or Mandingo, which is properly the name of the Malinke. Both Malinke and Soninke belong to the same family, the latter to its northern group and the former to its central group (Delafosse, *H.S.N.*, I, 114-5, 122-7).

[11] The 'Ibádites are the remnant of an important puritanical sect of the first Islamic century, known as the *Khawárij* or Dissenters. The only existing communities are found in 'Omán, Zanzibar, and the M'zab district in southern Algeria, round Ghardaia. The latter are noted for their enterprise and success in trade, but hold (or are held) very much aloof from the orthodox Muslim population, and it is probable that the community mentioned in this passage was an outpost of M'zabite traders (see also *M.S.O.S.*, *loc. cit.*)

[12] Kársakhú is taken by Delafosse to be Kara-Sakho, *i.e.* market of Kara, "close to and facing the present locality of Kongokuru, on the left bank of the Niger some distance north of Kara."

[13] The Kábara of this passage is probably not the well-known port of that name near Timbuktu; Delafosse regards it as a name of Ja'faraba (Diafarabe).

Zágha or Zágháy, more correctly called Jáka or Jága (Diaga), after the ancient capital of the kingdom of Takrúr, was a large district on the N.W. branch of the Niger, half a day's journey north of Ja'faraba.

It was in Takrúr that Islam obtained its first foothold in the Sudan in the early part of the eleventh century (Marquart, *Benin-Sammlung*, Intr., 150-1, 154, 241).

[14] Múlí was in all probability the district later called Múrí, on the left bank of the Niger about Niamey, the opposite bank being occupied by the Qumburi (perhaps Ibn Battúta's Qanburnl).

[15] The *Límíyún* of Ibn Battúta are taken by Delafosse and Marquart to be the inhabitants of the Kebbe (Kiba) district. There is, however, a great deal to be said in favour of Cooley's view that the Límís are identical with the *Lamlam* mentioned by other Arabic geographers, and placed by the geographer Bakrí (who calls them *Damdam*) on the Niger below Gaogao. The latter word unquestionably means "Cannibals," and is not the name of a specific tribe. In the Fulbe language it became *nyam-nyam* (from Fulbe *nyám*=eat), which is variously reproduced as *nam-nam* and *yam-yam* in Arabic script. The term was current also on the east coast of Africa in both forms. Ibn Battúta (above, p. 112) heard at Kilwa that gold dust was brought to Sofála from "Yúfí in the country of the Límís" (see next note), which was distant a month's journey from there. For this trans-continental trade see note 33 below. The word Nyam-nyam finally became particularized as the name of a cannibal tribe in Belgian Congo. Meanwhile it had passed into Mediterranean folklore; F. W. Hasluck heard from an Albanian muleteer of "an entirely new kind of vampire called Niam-Niam soi, which he has seen. You know it because (1) it is excessively fond of liver and (2) has donkey's teeth and (3) large feet" (Cooley, 112 *ff.*; Hartmann in *M.S.O.S.*, XV[3], 172; Hasluck, *Letters on Religion and Folklore*, 9).

[16] Cooley's identification (p. 93) of Yúfí with Nupe, on the left bank of the Niger between Jebba and Lokoja, has been accepted by all later authorities.

[17] In thus linking the Niger on to the Nile (probably by way of the Bahr al-Ghazál) Ibn Battúta is at least professing the less erroneous of two wrong views commonly held before the discoveries of Mungo Park. Idrísí, followed by Leo Africanus and many early European geographers, imagined the Niger to flow west, and identified it with the Senegal river.

[18] The Christian kingdom of Nubia was invaded by the sultans of Egypt on several occasions between 1272 and 1323. These expeditions, which were productive of no advantage to Egypt, hastened the break-up of the Nubian kingdom, and early in the fourteenth century Dongola fell into the hands of the Arab tribe of Kanz or Kanz ad-Dawla, formerly the hereditary amírs of Aswán. It is the chief of this tribe whom Ibn Battúta calls by the name of Ibn Kanz ad-Dín, and who, though not himself a convert, may be reckoned quite fairly as the first Muslim king of Nubia (Marquart, 252-4).

[19] The name Mállí is the Fulani pronunciation of Mande or

Manding, and was strictly the name of the ruling tribe, not of the town. The site of the latter has long been a matter of controversy. Cooley (pp. 81-2) placed it near Segu, at a village called Binni "seven miles above Samee," and took the Sansara river to be a channel of the Niger. Delafosse (*H.S.N.*, II, 181) accepts the view that the site of Malli was "a place situated on the left bank of the Niger, S.W. of Niamina and S.S.W. of Moribugu, level with the villages of Konina and Kondu. . . . Malli lay therefore a little to the west of the present road from Niamina to Kulikoro." The name Sansara, given by Ibn Battúta to the stream ten miles north of Málli, was found by Barth to be still applied to the small tributary which joins the Niger just below Niamina. Marquart (105, 191) prefers Cooley's view, but puts Málli a little lower down the river, a day's march above Sille (Sele), and identifies it with Kúgha or Júga, the Quioquia of the Portuguese.

[Since the writing of this note and preparation of the map, I find that MM.Vidal and Gaillard claim to have definitely established that the name of Malli was Nyani, and that it was situated "near the present village of Nyani, on the left bank of the Sankarani, a little to the north of Balandugu and to the south of Jeliba (Diéliba), the other capital of the same empire," *i.e.* at 11.22 N., 8.18 W., about 150 miles S.W. of the position shown on the map. See Demombynes, trans. of al-'Omari's *Masalik al-Absar*, p. 52, note 2.]

[20] Delafosse remarks that "Dúghá is the name of a kind of vulture and also that of a demon among the Banmana and the Malinke, and is often given as a name to men."

[21] The following is a brief account of the early negro empires.

The earliest Sudanic empire was that of Ghána (which was really the title of its later Soninke rulers). This empire was founded about the fourth century, apparently by some white immigrants. The site of its capital seems to have changed more than once. From the ninth to the eleventh century the Soninke of Kumbi were masters of the Ghána empire, until its destruction by the Almoravids of Morocco in 1076. A number of small states were constituted on its ruins, and one of these, the Soninke dynasty of the Kannte, whose capital was at Sosso (to the west of Sansanding), recaptured Ghána in 1203 and restored the Soninke empire. To this was due also the foundation of Waláta, as the Muslim inhabitants of Ghána, refusing to live under infidel rule, established themselves at the water-point of Waláta or Bírú (see note 6). The conqueror, Sumanguru, was killed in battle in 1235 with the Malinke, whose king Sunjáta or Márí Játa annexed the Soninke empire, was converted to Islam (see p. 329), and established the new capital at Málli. He captured and destroyed Ghána in 1240, and died in 1255. After a succession of rulers, the next emperor of importance was Músá (Ibn Battúta's Mansá Músá), in whose reign (1307-32) the Málli empire reached its widest dimensions. Músá was the grandson of a sister of Sunjáta. The reign of his son and successor Mansá Maghán (1332-6) marks a brief retrogression, but under Músá's brother Sulaymán (1336-59), the Málli regained much of their power and prestige. With his death there set in a sharp decline, accentuated by civil wars. The Málli kingdom, however, still remained the most powerful of the Niger states until the rise of the Songhay kingdom (see note 32), and did not finally disappear until 1670.

22 The addition of "under all circumstances" is a gentle hint that things are not so well as they might be.

23 The eve of the 27th Ramadán is known as the *Laylat al-Qadr*, the "Night of Power" referred to in the Koran. It is believed that on this night the gates of Heaven are opened, and all prayers of the truly devout are favourably received.

24 *Bembe* in Mandingo means "platform." Al-'Omari describes the *bembe* as an ivory bench surmounted by an arch of tusks.

25 *I.e.* "The Emperor Sulayman has commanded," in Mandingo.

26 Delafosse remarks that this custom, like almost all those described by Ibn Battúta, has been retained down to the present day in most of the countries of the Sudan.

27 See note 21 above.

28 See note 31 below.

29 Qurí Mansá is placed by Delafosse near the present villages of Kokri and Massamana, N.E. of Sansanding, and not far from Ibn Battúta's former halting place at Kársakhú (see note 12).

30 Míma seems to have been one of the chief towns in the district which Ibn Battúta mentions above under the name of Zágha (see note 13). In later times the name was applied to the area above the lakes (and possibly including them), corresponding to part of modern Masina. According to Barth, the site of Míma is still in existence, though now deserted, a few miles west of Lere (*Travels*, Engl. ed., V, 487).

31 Timbuktu was annexed by Mansá Músá after the conquest of Gao in 1325. In 1333 the town was pillaged and burned in a raid by the Mossi from Yatenga (Upper Volta), but was rebuilt by Sulaymán shortly after his accession. The poet as-Sáhilí met Mansá Músá at Mecca during the Pilgrimage, and was persuaded by the sultan to accompany him back to the Sudan. He was the architect of the mosques at Gao and Timbuktu, and died at Timbuktu in 1346.

32 Gao or Gaogao (which is apparently a variant of the original name Kúgha) was an important trading station at the convergence not only of the salt route from the west and the trans-Saharan route from the north-east, but also the trans-continental trade-route. Early in the eleventh century it became the capital of the state of Songhay (Songhoy), on the conversion to Islam of the first Songhay dynasty, which is said to have been of Berber origin. The Songhay kingdom was annexed to Málli by Mansá Músá in 1325, but in 1335 the

dynasty was re-established (with the title of *sonni*), though it still remained in at least nominal subjection to Málli until the reign of Sonni 'Ali (1465-92), the last ruler of the original Berber line, who enlarged his kingdom chiefly at the expense of Málli. He was succeeded by his Soninke general Muhammad (1493-1529), the founder of the *askia* dynasty, who brought Songhay to the height of its power. The Songhay empire was broken up and the dynasty extinguished by the Moroccans, who captured Gao and Timbuktu in 1591.

[33] The existence of a cowry exchange in the Málli empire, alongside the salt exchange, is conclusive evidence of the commercial relations across the African continent referred to in note 14, as cowries are found in Africa only on the east coast between the Equator and Mozambique (*Grande Encyclopédie s.v.* Cauri). In Ibn Battúta's time, however, cowries were imported by merchants from the north (al-'Omari 75-76).

[34] The description of the Bardáma tribe, and particularly of their women, corresponds very closely with Barth's description of the Tagháma tribe to the south and S.W. of Air.

[35] Tagaddá or Takaddá was at this time the largest town in the Tuareg country. Its Berber sultan, who was nominally subject to the Emperor of Málli, is probably to be regarded as the ruling chief of the Massúfa (Sanhája). The problem of the site of Tagaddá is not yet cleared up. It is generally taken, on the basis of Barth's identification, to be Tegidda n'Tisemt, 97 miles W.N.W. of Agades. Barth added that although "nothing is known of the existence of copper hereabouts," a red salt is obtained from mines there. Gautier and Chudeau (*Missions au Sahara*, II, 257) also remark on the absence of copper in the Sahara except at Tamegroun in the Ougarta range (29.15 N., 1.40 W.), and state that all the copper used in Air and in Ahaggar comes from Europe. The absence of copper at Tegidda is confirmed by F. R. Rodd, who thinks that Ibn Battúta's Tagaddá must be looked for "at some considerable distance south of Agades" (*People of the Veil*, 452-6). The meaning of the word *Tegidda*, according to the latter, is "a small hollow where water collects," and the name is applied to a number of different places (*Cf. H.S.N.*, II, 193; Marquart, 98). The existence of copper mines at Tagaddá is, however, confirmed by al-'Omari on the authority of Mansá Músá (tr. Demombynes, I, 80-81).

[36] Kúbar is Gobir, the country north of the present Sokoto, and consequently bordering on Tagaddá to the south. Whether Zágháy stands here for the district S.W. of Timbuktu, or for the central areas round Kanem and Wadai, vaguely known as Zagháwa, is quite uncertain.

[37] Barnú here stands for Kanem, rather than Bornu in Nigeria. The empire of Kanem at this period extended across the central Sahara northwards to Fezzan and eastwards towards Dár Fúr, as well as into Northern Nigeria. This Idrís (1353-76, not to be confused with

the famous Mai Idrís of Bornu in the sixteenth century) was the son of one Ibráhím Nikále, who claimed to be of South Arabian descent and was sultan of Kanem from 1307-26. The concealment of the king was due to a belief in the magical qualities of his office (Barth, I, 638-9; Meek, *Northern Nigeria*, I, 254).

[38] Jawjawa, more often spelled Kawkaw or Kúkú, the Gaogao of Leo Africanus, is either Kúka on Lake Fitri in Wadai, S.E. of Kanem or else Kúka in Bornu (Marquart 95 *ff.*; Hartmann in *M.S.O.S.* XV[3], 176 *ff.*). I have not been able to trace the Muwartabún or Múrtabún.

[39] The corps of *wusfán* or "guards" at the court of the sultan of Morocco formed the nucleus of a standing army, as distinct from the tribal militia (*Masálik al-Absár*, tr. Demombynes, Index *s.v.*). Demombynes reads, with one MS., Inátiyún in place of Yanátibún (*ibid.* 210, n. 2).

[40] Káhir is a variant of the name Air, given to the sparsely populated hilly country lying to the south of In Azawa or Asiu, the well referred to below at the point where the routes leading to Twát and Egypt divide. It is strange that Ibn Battúta should apparently refer to Káhir as separated from the main ridge by a three days' march.

[41] Haggar or Hoggar, the Berber (Tuareg) tribes inhabiting the central Saharan massif, the ancient Atlas mountains, now called Ahaggar after its inhabitants.

[42] Búda lies at the northern end of the Twát valley at 28 N., 0.30 E An account of the district and its history is given by Gautier and Chudeau, *Missions au Sahara* (Paris, 1908), I, 250. According to the Arabic geographers, locusts were also eaten by the inhabitants of Marrákush.

I. INDEX OF GEOGRAPHICAL NAMES

INDEX

II. SELECT INDEX OF PERSONAL NAMES, ETC.*

* *Names compounded with Abú and Ibn are indexed under the letter of the following word* : e.g., *Ibn Battúta will be found under B.*

SELECT INDEX